Morgentaler v. Borowski

Morgentaler v. Borowski:

Abortion, the Charter,
and the Courts

F.L. Morton

M&S

Copyright © 1992 by F.L. Morton

Canadian Cataloguing in Publication Data

Morton, F.L. (Frederick Lee), 1949–
Morgentaler v. Borowski

Includes bibliographical references and index.
ISBN 0-7710-6513-2

1. Abortion – Law and legislation – Canada.   2. Trials (Abortion) –
Canada.   3. Morgentaler, Henry, 1923–   .   4. Borowski, Joseph.
I. Title.

KE8920.M77 1992   345.71′0285   C92-094043-9

Morgentaler v. Borowski: Abortion, the Charter, and the Courts is
published under licence in the U.S.A. by the University of Oklahoma
Press, Norman, Oklahoma, under the title *Pro-Choice vs. Pro-Life:
Abortion and the Courts in Canada.*

Cover Design: Randolph Rozema
Cover Photograph: Canapress Photo Service
Back Cover Photographs: Borowski, Canapress Photo Service;
Morgentaler, *The Globe & Mail* / Dennis Robertson

Typesetting by M&S
Printed and bound in Canada

McClelland & Stewart Inc.
The Canadian Publishers
481 University Avenue
Toronto, Ontario
M5G 2E9

CONTENTS

For my parents, and the memory of theirs

Preface

This is a book that tells three different stories. First and foremost it recounts the legal odysseys of Dr. Henry Morgentaler and Joe Borowski, Canada's pro-choice and pro-life crusaders whose private convictions made them public figures. Their respective campaigns of civil disobedience and constitutional challenges to Canada's abortion law spanned two decades, took each man to the Supreme Court of Canada twice, sent both to jail, and left in their wake a new abortion policy. The irony that Canada's premier abortion trials centred around two men was lessened somewhat when the final chapter of their stories was provided by two women, in the 1989 abortion-injunction trials of Barbara Dodd and Chantal Daigle.

Second, the book uses Canada's "abortion trilogy" – the *Morgentaler, Borowski,* and *Daigle* cases – as a vehicle to explore the judicial process in Canada. The reader follows the two protagonists from trial to appeal and on to the Supreme Court of Canada, in both criminal and civil proceedings. Along this journey, the reader navigates the structure of the Canadian legal system; learns some of the core concepts of that foreign language, legalese, and its new dialect, "rights talk"; and comes face to face with a varied cast of defence lawyers, crown prosecutors, judges, political leaders, and interest groups. Because the story is not restricted to courtrooms but meanders freely and widely across the Canadian political landscape, the reader is confronted with one of the most significant but least acknowledged facts of the judicial process: its constant interaction with the larger political process, influencing and being influenced in turn.

Finally, the book uses the abortion trilogy to tell the story of the Canadian Charter of Rights and Freedoms. The two are inextricably tied together. The Morgentaler and Borowski stories provide an unparalleled guided tour through "Charterland." To read the former is to begin to understand the latter. The Charter grafted a new regime of constitutional supremacy onto a 100-year-old Canadian tradition of legislative supremacy. The results have been tumultuous. Adopted in 1982, the Charter neatly divides the legal challenges of Morgentaler and Borowski into two equal parts. The different outcomes of the pre- and post-Charter chapters illustrate just how much the Charter has transformed Canadian politics.

I have chosen to use the language of "pro-life" and "pro-choice" to describe the partisan camps of the abortion issue. Of course each side objects to the positive connotations attached to these descriptions of their opponents, whom they see as "anti-choice" and "pro-abortion," respectively. My choice of terms is based on the fact that there are many people who are pro-choice but not pro-abortion, and many who are pro-life but not anti-choice. It also reflects my belief that respect for both privacy (freedom of choice) and individual human life is integral to a healthy liberal democracy. This is what makes abortion such a difficult issue and why both sides have attracted some very good people. As for the tension created between the usage of fetus or unborn child, I have chosen to use both terms interchangeably, precisely to preserve this tension.

History clearly shows that approval of Supreme Court decisions tends to vary according to one's political vantage point, and that what one generation hails as a wise decision often appears foolish and unjust to the next. In writing, as in teaching, it is important to bring a broader perspective to bear on the analysis of constitutional issues and decisions: to present the facts and counterfacts, the arguments and counterarguments; to push students and readers to think for themselves; and to accept – gladly – that many will reach different conclusions than those of the author or teacher. My objective has not been to say whether the Supreme Court made the right or the wrong choices in these cases, but simply to point out that the judges were indeed making choices. To understand this is to begin to understand the Charter and why it is much too important to be left only with lawyers.

This book was inspired by a book I read in my first political science course during my first year of university: Anthony Lewis's classic, *Gideon's Trumpet*.[1] Lewis told the story behind the U.S. Supreme Court's landmark 1961 decision *Gideon v. Wainright*, the case that created a constitutional right to publicly paid counsel for indigent defendants too poor to hire their own lawyers. Lewis did not limit his book to a legalistic parsing of constitutional doctrine, but uncovered the human drama and political dynamics that lie beneath the legal tip of landmark Supreme Court decisions. The focus of Lewis's book was the *Gideon* case, but it captured the larger mystique of the Warren Court era in American politics. Lewis brought constitutional law to life and first fired my interest in the subject I now teach.

Writing in 1985, Carl Baar observed that "the American style of judicial journalism [such as *Gideon's Trumpet*] has no counterpart in Canada. No Canadian writer has traced the long road of the lonely litigant as his or her dispute moves to inexorable triumph in the Supreme Court of Canada."[2] Cynics might retort that this was because, prior to the Charter, no individual ever won in the Supreme Court of Canada. Baar speculated, correctly I believe, that this trend in Canadian legal writing also reflected the English influence on Canadian legal culture and a corresponding bias against using litigation (as an alternative to legislation) to influence public policy.

Baar noted that with the advent of the Charter this seemed to be changing. The events of the next few years confirmed that indeed it was. The *Morgentaler* case, more than any other, illustrated how dramatic this change has been. It proved not only that litigating social change was no longer "un-Canadian," but that one could even win! Ten years after its adoption, we can now see that the Charter induced Canada's own version of a "bloodless revolution." The abortion trilogy contains almost everything an educated citizen need know about this Charter revolution. I decided that if ever there was a set of court decisions that cried out to be made into a book-length case study, this was it.

While the abortion trilogy represents only a thin slice of the Charter pie, it is a rich and revealing one. In the concluding chapter, I use these cases to draw some more general conclusions about "the politics of rights." I realize that not everyone will agree with these interpretations. This is only natural, and, as in the past, I will look forward to hearing from and replying to those who disagree. It is certainly my intention, however, that the accuracy, interest, and utility of the first twenty-three chapters stand independently of my more critical assessments of Charter politics set forth in the final chapter.

Acknowledgements

I follow in the footsteps of three previous authors who have treated various aspects of this subject – Alphonse de Valk,[3] Eleanor Wright Pelrine,[4] and Anne Collins.[5] This book would not have been possible without their prior work, and I have drawn heavily and freely from all three. My numerous debts are recorded in the footnotes. I want to acknowledge the assistance of my former students Shelley Kaupp and Christine Rideout, whose Master's thesis and Senior Honours thesis, respectively, helped to identify primary and secondary materials and started me thinking about many of the issues raised in these cases. Many of the persons who appear in this legal saga, including the two main protagonists, provided interviews and letters. Their assistance is indicated in the footnotes, and I thank them all. I acknowledge the helpful criticisms of the two anonymous reviewers, and also of Thomas Flanagan, who read an earlier draft. I would especially like to thank my friend, colleague, and frequent collaborator, Rainer Knopff, for his numerous suggestions that helped me to write and think more clearly. More experienced readers will recognize that Chapter 24 contains abridged versions of some of the arguments made in our recently published book, *Charter Politics*.[6] I also want to thank the Earhart Foundation, whose financial assistance provided a partial release from my teaching during 1989-90 to work on this project. Finally, I want to thank Michael Harrison, the acquisitions editor at McClelland & Stewart, for having confidence in this project when it was still just an idea and for supporting it through to completion. With so much help along the way, I happily accept responsibility for any remaining mistakes and shortcomings.

CHAPTER 1

The Story of
Two Unreasonable Men

It was the afternoon of January 21, 1973. The phone rang in Dr. Henry Morgentaler's east end Montreal clinic. That morning, like most weekday mornings, Morgentaler had performed six abortions. Under Canadian law, these abortions were illegal, each carrying a potential penalty of life imprisonment. At the time Morgentaler was already facing three criminal charges of illegal abortions.

On the other end of the line was Roy Lucas, one of the attorneys involved in the American case of *Roe v. Wade*. The United States Supreme Court, Lucas enthusiastically reported, had just struck down the abortion laws in forty-six of the fifty states.[1] The American court had ruled that any state-imposed restrictions on abortion during the first three months of pregnancy violated a woman's constitutional "right to privacy." In effect, Lucas explained excitedly, the American court had created a policy of abortion on demand for all fifty states.

For Henry Morgentaler, already one of the most outspoken advocates of abortion rights in Canada, *Roe v. Wade* was like a firebell in the night. It shook him out of the ennui induced by two and a half years of using procedural delays to avoid going to trial in his own abortion case. *Roe v. Wade* made him optimistic about the prospects for a similar change in Canada. The news seemed to signal that the tide of public opinion had finally changed and the time for action had come.

And act he did. Over the next eight months, Morgentaler conducted a campaign of civil disobedience unparalleled in Canadian history. He publicly claimed to have performed over 5,000 illegal abortions and even performed one on television – on Mother's Day! The result: a second arrest and ten more charges of illegal abortions.

Over the next three years, the Crown tried Henry Morgentaler three times, and three times juries acquitted him. Notwithstanding the judgment of his peers, Henry Morgentaler went to prison for ten months. In a decision unprecedented in any common-law country, the Quebec Court of Appeal overturned Morgentaler's first jury acquittal and substituted a verdict of guilty. Morgentaler's appeal to the Supreme Court of Canada was rejected. In the end it was politicians, not judges, who came to the aid of Henry Morgentaler. A new Attorney-General in Ottawa set aside Morgentaler's first conviction and ordered a new trial. A new government in Quebec – the rebellious and irreverent Parti Québécois – dropped all outstanding charges against him and announced that it would no longer enforce the abortion law in that province.

Despite Henry Morgentaler's successful crusade within Quebec, the Canadian abortion law did not change. Ten years after his first trial in Montreal, Morgentaler moved outside of Quebec and opened abortion clinics in Toronto and Winnipeg. This new round of civil disobedience was prompted in part by Canada's new Charter of Rights and Freedoms. Adopted in 1982, the Charter amended Canada's written constitution by adding a long list of individual and group rights, thereby offering the possibility of an American-style judicial activism by the Canadian Supreme Court. Morgentaler hoped that under the Charter, his original dream of a Canadian version of *Roe v. Wade* would be realized.

A second reason for Morgentaler's return to political battle was the recent success of his arch-rival and antagonist, Joe Borowski. Borowski, a rough-spoken ex-union activist and a former Manitoba NDP cabinet member, had emerged as Canada's premier pro-life crusader during the 1970s. In December, 1981, Borowski won a three-year legal battle to obtain the right to challenge Canada's abortion law. In a landmark decision that significantly broadened interest group access to the courts, the Supreme Court of Canada granted Borowski standing to challenge the constitutional validity of Canada's abortion law.

Borowski's victory deeply upset Henry Morgentaler, who recalled that the Supreme Court of Canada's rejection of his appeal in 1975 had sent him to prison. Even more appalling to Morgentaler was the prospect of Borowski winning the next stage of his legal crusade against abortion. Having been granted standing by the Supreme Court, Borowski and his lawyers returned to the Court of Queen's Bench in Regina, where they were assembling an impressive panel of medical experts to testify about human life before birth. Based on this medical evidence, Borowski argued that Canada's abortion law violated the right to life of the unborn and should be declared invalid. If Borowski won – and he was prepared to go all the way to the Supreme Court – access to abortion might be limited to life-threatening pregnancies. Ironically, Borowski's case was also strengthened by the adoption of the Canadian Charter of Rights and Freedoms in 1982. Like Morgentaler, Borowski was banking on the Supreme Court of Canada to exercise the new political power conferred on it by the Charter. For Morgentaler, Borowski's legal victory was "the last straw." If Borowski was going to use the Charter to advance the rights of the fetus, then someone needed to bring a case to advance the rights of women. Morgentaler decided to renew his campaign of civil disobedience, and, if necessary, to go all the way to the Supreme Court for a second time.

The legal odysseys of Henry Morgentaler and Joe Borowski, the champions of the opposing pro-choice and pro-life movements, brought to a climax a quarter-century of abortion politics in Canada. The juxtaposition of their two trials became a metaphor for a series of larger and older conflicts. Morgentaler versus Borowski became more than just the right to choose versus the right to life. Their trials irritated old wounds in the Canadian body politic: issues of West versus East, Protestant versus Catholic, English versus French, and Quebec versus Ottawa. Their personal rivalry conjured up the centuries-old Jewish-Christian conflict, a conflict that could be traced back to their common Polish homeland and agitated the politics of Europe long before the first European ever set foot in Canada. Both trials resonated with the ongoing battle between religion and modern science, between nature and technology. They also opened up one of the traditional debates of liberal democracy – the question of where the private ends and the public begins – and, with it, the new conflict between feminists and those supporting an older, traditional, family-centred view of society. As the stories of Morgentaler and Borowski spilled into the courtrooms, they evoked the challenge of civil disobedience to the rule of law, pitting judges against juries and legislators against judges. In the final analysis, the trials came to symbolize the new challenge posed by the Charter to Canadian democracy: parliamentary supremacy versus judicial supremacy.

Yet for all their differences, in one fundamental way, Morgentaler and Borowski were very much alike: they refused to compromise their principles and were willing to pay the price. Both conducted their lives according to the quotation from George Bernard Shaw that hung on the wall of Joe Borowski's cluttered office: "The reasonable man adapts himself to the world; the unreasonable man persists in trying to adapt the world to himself. Therefore all progress depends on the unreasonable man."[2] The story of these two unreasonable men begins with the 1969 abortion law reform, a compromise that neither was willing to accept.

CHAPTER 2

The 1969 Abortion Reform

In 1969 Canada amended its abortion law, culminating a decade of agitation for reform. Both the old law and the new one were directly influenced by Canada's British heritage. Prior to 1969, the Criminal Code of Canada made abortion a crime except to save the life of the mother. The origins of this policy could be traced back to the earliest centuries of the British common law.

Writing in the thirteenth century, the jurist Bracton recorded that under common law it was a crime to abort the fetus after it became "animated," that is, received its soul, something that was thought to occur between the eighth and twelfth week after conception. In the eighteenth century, in his celebrated *Commentaries on the Laws of England,* Sir William Blackstone observed that aborting the fetus was considered homicide upon "quickening," that is, when the mother becomes aware of the baby moving about inside her abdomen, an experience that usually occurs around twenty weeks. This internal movement of the baby was interpreted as a sign that it had "come to life."

The common law's prohibition against abortion was given a more restrictive statutory expression in 1803 when Parliament passed Lord Ellenborough's Act, which made abortion illegal both before and after quickening. This statutory criminalization was repeated in Britain's Offenses against the Persons Acts of 1861, and was subsequently carried forward into Canada's first Criminal Code in 1892. The latter, however, made it legal to perform an abortion to save the life of the mother and also reduced the penalty for self-induced abortions. This law remained relatively unchanged through various revisions of the Criminal Code until 1969. In England, and thus in Canada, the enforcement of the abortion law was further relaxed through judicial interpretation. In the 1937 case of *R. v. Bourne,* a British judge expanded the grounds for a legal abortion to include a pregnancy resulting from rape that would have made the innocent young victim a "physical or mental wreck."[1]

To summarize, prior to the 1960s British and Canadian law had always provided some protection for the fetus or unborn child, but the time varied from "animation" (eight-twelve weeks) to "quickening" (twenty weeks). In the nineteenth century, abortion was made a statutory crime, but this restriction was loosened by judicial interpretation. It should also be recalled that abortion was not a political issue in a predominantly rural, agricultural society, where large families – and thus children – were seen as a form of economic security.[2] Also, prior to the development of modern antisepsis at the end of the nineteenth century, the high probability of infection made abortion an extremely dangerous procedure for the woman. Finally, before the commercial availability of "the pill" in the 1960s, stricter sexual mores made unplanned teenage pregnancies less common. When they did occur, marriage at a young age was more socially and economically acceptable than today.[3]

Just as Canada's original abortion law was based on British precedent, so, too, was the movement during the 1960s to reform the law. British influence was still strong in Canadian society during the sixties, especially in legal circles. The Canadian Criminal Code, including its abortion provisions, was adapted from British criminal law in 1892 and tended to follow the latter. The Judicial Committee of the Privy Council had served as Canada's final court of appeal for constitutional questions until 1949, and British legal precedents were authoritatively cited in most fields of Canadian law. As recently as 1966, a president of the Canadian Bar Association could declare that "we tend to make a change in our law only after England has done so."[4] In the case of abortion, this proved to be prophetic.

In Britain the movement to decriminalize abortion was well under way in the early 1960s. The tone of the British debate had been set by an earlier (1957) parliamentary report on homosexuality and prostitution known as the Wolfenden Report. This report recommended that both homosexuality and prostitution be decriminalized, asserting that "there must remain a realm of private morality and immorality . . . which is not the law's business." While the report was not directly concerned with abortion, its underlying principle – that criminal law must not be used to enforce private morality – played a decisive role in the ensuing debate over abortion. When the Labour Party returned to power in 1966, an abortion reform bill was immediately introduced. A year later, Britain became the first major Western European nation to adopt what was in effect an "abortion on demand" policy. Abortion law reformers elsewhere, including Canada, hailed the new British law as a welcome breakthrough and urged their own lawmakers to follow suit.[5]

Political agitation to change Canada's abortion law was mounted by a diverse and what first appears an unlikely coalition. Two professional groups, the Canadian Medical Association and the Canadian Bar Association, spearheaded the effort. They received moral support from the United Church, the largest Protestant denomination in Canada, which began to support wider access to abortion in 1960. Surprisingly, women's groups played only a marginal role at this stage of the reform movement. Beginning in 1964, the National Council of Women of Canada submitted an annual brief (the same one for three years in a row) to Parliament, but otherwise this group did little to try to influence public opinion or the lawmakers in Ottawa. The Canadian feminist movement was still in its infancy, and lacked the self-confidence and political influence it subsequently developed. Last but not least, the abortion reformers received strategic support from the media, especially the Toronto *Globe and Mail*.[6] The members of these diverse groups who sought to change the abortion law were generally highly educated and enjoyed high socio-economic status. Abortion law reform in Canada, as in other Western societies, came from the top down.

The most influential demands for changing the abortion law came from the Canadian Medical Association, helped by the Canadian Bar Association. After three years of internal study and debate, in 1966 the annual national meetings of both associations adopted proposals calling for decriminalization of abortion in certain carefully defined circumstances. Their principal motivation appears to have been neither sexual equality nor social engineering but professional self-interest: to protect doctors against the legal uncertainties of the current law. Some doctors had already begun to perform abortions for patients with unwanted pregnancies under the pretence of alleged "medical reasons." However, advances in medical care had rendered this legal justification increasingly untenable, and the medical profession itself was becoming more divided over "abortions of convenience." To protect themselves, those Canadian doctors who had begun to perform abortions pushed for legislative reform that would legalize what they were already doing. The abortion law eventually adopted by Parliament in 1969 closely resembled the CMA's 1966 proposal.[7]

While the leaderships of the CMA and the CBA were well connected politically, they could hardly dictate this type of policy change to the government. Short-term success was unlikely without a sympathetic portrayal by the national media. Events are not "news" unless they are reported. Reporters, editors, and producers have the discretion to "make news" and to couch issues in either a positive or negative light. Normally, the policy recommendations of professional organizations are not front-page news, and politicians rarely feel pressed to respond to much else. It was thus the good fortune of the pro-reform forces to find not just a friend but a veritable ally in the Toronto *Globe and Mail*. Beginning in 1961, the *Globe and Mail* mounted an editorial crusade for abortion law reform. Abortion-related news was routinely accorded front-page coverage, while scores of editorials were used to cheer reformers, chide the timid, and castigate the opposition.[8]

Finally, the abortion reformers needed a political ally. While the forces that have pushed the abortion controversy to the political surface of Western societies are deeply rooted in our history, actual political change is achieved by individual men and women. The pro-reform forces needed an ally in Parliament, a person who shared their views on abortion and had the courage to speak out and to lead rather than follow. This ally could not be just an outspoken yet inconsequential backbencher; it had to be someone with clout – a cabinet member who commanded the respect of his or her peers and who was willing to try to lead public opinion rather than follow it. Both the timing and character of abortion reform in Canada depended on the emergence of such an individual. Although not apparent at the time, that individual arrived in April, 1967, when Prime Minister Lester Pearson appointed Pierre Elliott Trudeau as his new Justice Minister.

By the fall of 1967, the *Globe*'s persistent and partisan coverage had achieved its intended effect. It had nudged the abortion issue out of the backwaters of legal and medical journals and onto the centre of Canada's political agenda. On October 3, 1967, the House of Commons Standing Committee on Health and Welfare began hearings on

Morgentaler after testifying with regards to abortion reform legislation, with Dr. Harry Harley, MP (Liberal-Halton) and chairman of House of Commons Committee on Health, October 19, 1967. (*Courtesy Canapress Photo Service*)

abortion law reform. During the next five months, it held twenty-five meetings, received thirty-five briefs, and heard testimony from ninety-three witnesses.

The majority of submissions favoured change. They came from professional organizations such as the Canadian Medical Association and the Canadian Bar Association; many mainline churches, including United, Unitarian, Presbyterian, Anglican, and Jewish Reform; several women's groups, including the National Council of Women and the recently organized Association for the Modernization of Canadian Abortion Laws; and the Canadian Labour Congress. The reasons advanced were as varied as the groups. Putting an end to the "butchery of illegal abortions" was the most frequent argument. Most of the church groups favoured broadening the grounds for abortion to include threats to the health of the mother but stressed they were against abortions for social or economic reasons. When pressed by one committee member, the spokesman for the CMA conceded that their interest in reform was also "to end our life as lawbreakers."[9]

One of the most radical submissions received by the Committee came from Henry Morgentaler, then a little-known doctor and vice-president of the Humanist Fellowship of Montreal. While most pro-reform groups favoured only a slight expansion of the legal grounds for abortion (to include the health of the mother), Dr. Morgentaler urged a policy of abortion on demand during the first three months of pregnancy. While the other groups carefully justified their positions on utilitarian, lesser-of-two-evils arguments, Dr. Morgentaler boldly asserted that "unwanted pregnancies must be viewed as [biological] accidents. . . . [and that] it is a woman's inalienable right to have mastery of her own body."[10]

Opponents to change were less well organized and less numerous. A collection of hastily formed groups for the protection of the unborn stressed the traditional Judeo-Christian respect for the protection of innocent life. An effort was also made to demonstrate the humanity of the fetus or unborn child. The most sophisticated and sustained defence of the unborn against a more permissive abortion law came from the Canadian Catholic Conference. The Conference carefully explained that its opposition was not based just on moral beliefs unique to Catholics. Unlike divorce, which the Church condemned morally but was willing to allow for the rest of society, abortion was portrayed as a threat to the well-being of Canadian society as a whole. "We are much concerned," explained Bishop Remi de Roo of Victoria, "that a too-open health clause may result in widespread disrespect of, and assault on the life of the unborn child."[11]

The Catholic Conference's submission was too little, too late. It came at the Committee's last public hearing (March 5, 1968), only eight days before it issued its final report. In any case, the relevance of the Committee had been thrown into doubt midway through its hearings when, on December 21, 1967, Justice Minister Trudeau tabled in Parliament a seventy-two-page, 104-clause Omnibus Criminal Code Reform Bill. Strategically sandwiched in the middle of the Omnibus Bill was a provision broadening the legal grounds for abortion.

The Omnibus Reform Bill was front-page news across the country and focused Canadians' attention for the first time on their new Minister of Justice. Both the timing and the manner in which Trudeau dealt with the abortion issue disclosed the Machiavellian skill that would become his political trademark. By placing changes on abortion (and also homosexuality) in the midst of a bill touching such unrelated matters as drunken driving, firearms, lotteries, and harassing phone calls, the new Minister of Justice gained a tactical advantage. As he remarked to reporters at the time, "These amendments would have a better chance of passing if they were included in a bigger, diverse bill with its obvious advantages of psychological inertia."[12] Equally well calculated was the timing of the bill: it was introduced at the end of Canada's centennial year and only days before the Christmas holidays. The opposition was caught off guard and unprepared. Trudeau was able to hurry the bill through first reading the same day, only hours before Parliament adjourned for the holidays.[13]

Still more skilful was Trudeau's handling of the bill before the press and the public. The homosexuality and, by extension, the abortion provisions were justified in what turned out to be a rhetorical masterstroke. "The state," Trudeau quipped to reporters, "has no business in the bedrooms of the nation." This offhand, almost flippant remark would subsequently permeate the consciousness and political vocabulary of the entire society. It seemed to justify in a single sentence the new sexual freedom of the sixties, the ultimate rejoinder to any attempt by society to control the sexual behaviour of its citizens. Pierre Trudeau was obviously a man in tune with the spirit of the times. In retrospect, it is not surprising that this newcomer to Parliament and the Liberal Party would, within six months, be carried into the Prime Minister's office by a wave of political enthusiasm unparalleled in Canadian history.

In light of the government's decision to introduce a new abortion law before Parliament had even finished its hearings on the subject, the Standing Committee's final report was hardly a surprise. On March 13, 1968, the Committee recommended expanding the permissible grounds for abortion to include threats to the *health* of the mother. While this would result in narrower access than the socio-economic justification that had been adopted in Britain and recommended by Trudeau, it was clearly broader than a criterion of threat to the *life* of the mother.

Ten days later, Prime Minister Pearson released all cabinet members from their official responsibilities so that they could campaign for the Liberal Party leadership from which he was departing. The outcome of that contest, unsuspected at the time, was to guarantee the success of abortion reform. Elsewhere in Canada, Dr. Henry Morgentaler had recently performed his first abortion on the teenage daughter of a friend. In Manitoba, a radical labour union leader named Joe Borowski was waging a one-man crusade against the provincial Tory government's new sales tax.

In the summer of 1968 "Trudeaumania" carried the Liberals to a landslide electoral victory – 155 of 264 seats in Parliament – virtually guaranteeing that the former Justice Minister's Omnibus Criminal Code Reform Bill would now become law. Still, final enactment of the bill was not without its drama and significance. Parliamentary procedure requires that a bill be given three readings and approvals before it can become law, thus providing the opposition an opportunity to scrutinize and criticize government policy publicly. The Omnibus Bill had to be reintroduced after the 1968 elections. When second reading began on January 23, 1969, the Social Credit and, to a lesser extent, the Progressive Conservative members of Parliament took full advantage of this time-honoured practice of democracy.

The task of defending the Omnibus Reform Bill fell to the new Justice Minister of the Trudeau government, a highly touted and handsome young Toronto lawyer named John Turner. Turner basically followed the lead of his new boss, citing freely from the Wolfenden Report and stressing the necessity of separating sin and crime, private conscience and public order. The Liberal backbenchers were unusually quiet and somewhat uneasy during the abortion debate. The Prime Minister had never approved a free vote, yet party leaders claimed that no Liberals were being forced to vote against their conscience. In the end only three Liberal backbenchers spoke against the abortion provision, while nine spoke in support.[14]

Unlike the Liberals, the Progressive Conservatives suspended party discipline and allowed a free vote. Of the Conservatives who rose to speak on the bill, most were opposed, some simply out of the tradition of parliamentary opposition, but some for substantive reasons as well. The Conservative member from St. John's West, Walter Carter, challenged the government to consider the social consequences of the reforms.

> [A government] which relaxes . . . curbs on drugs, makes divorce easier, permits abortion and homosexuality, is in the process of remaking our society. The question we must ask is, in whose image and likeness?[15]

The response of the New Democratic Party contrasted sharply with that of the Conservatives. The New Democrats overwhelmingly supported the bill, including the abortion clause. The latter was actually criticized for not going far enough, as the New Democrats wanted abortion completely removed from the Criminal Code. The sanguine and modernistic perspective of the the New Democrats was captured by their spokesman, David Lewis (York South), who declared that "in our criminal law we ought to amend everything that is a relic of the past and not consistent with modern morality."[16]

The most cohesive and outspoken opposition to the abortion bill came from the fourteen remaining members of the Ralliement Créditiste in Parliament. All French, all Catholic, and all representing rural Quebec ridings, the Créditistes attacked the bill on many fronts – medical, legal, religious, and philosophical. Defending the right to life of the unborn, the Créditistes argued that the bill violated not just Catholic teaching but such secular norms as the Canadian Bill of Rights. They challenged the existence of legitimate medical reasons for abortion and asserted that the vagueness of the term "health" would lead to a policy of abortion on demand. The materialistic philosophy of contemporary capitalist society and its promoter, the mass media, were jointly condemned as sharing responsibility for the abortion bill.[17]

The vehemence of the Créditistes notwithstanding, Justice Minister Turner firmly guided the majoritarian machinery of Parliament toward final reading in April, 1969. Sensing the desperation of their position, the Créditistes refused to agree to the standard practice of a timetable for limiting debate. They then proceeded to mount a last-ditch filibuster by proposing almost fifty amendments to the abortion provision. Some were frivolous, some were serious. Among the latter were attempts to tighten up the meaning of the concept of a pregnancy that "would be likely to endanger [the] health" of the mother. The Créditistes charged that this wording was so vague as to allow untrammeled discretion to the therapeutic abortion committees. Such discretion, they predicted, would result in an "abortion on demand" policy. One by one these amendments were rejected by Justice Minister Turner and his obedient majority.[18]

Some of the most bitter attacks were directed not at the bill but at the Québécois members of Liberal caucus. Frustrated Créditistes characterized the proposed changes on abortion and homosexuality as British diseases, and intimated that the silence of the Quebec Liberals was a betrayal of French Quebec and its Catholic heritage. When the Liberal backbencher from Gatineau, Gaston Clermont, unexpectedly rose to propose a restrictive amendment to the abortion clause, the Créditistes sensed growing division behind the facade of Liberal unity. The

Free Vote to Eliminate Clause 18, May 9, 1969				
	For	Against	Absent	Total
Liberal	2	85	68	155
Progressive Conservative	25	7	40	72
New Democratic Party	1	15	6	22
Independent	0	0	1	1
Totals	36	107	111	264

Quebec Liberals, they taunted, "seem to be seated on six inches of Lepage's glue, and we do not hear a peep out of them." The government's firm refusal to allow a free vote led to accusations of "military dictatorship."[19]

The *Globe and Mail* had already sided with the Liberal leadership against a free vote. In March, 1969, Liberal Health Minister Allan MacEachen had proposed that his party not enforce party discipline on the abortion issue. Sensing mounting pressure within the Liberal caucus to allow a "free vote," the *Globe and Mail* moved to shore up the Grits' resolve to maintain party discipline. Catholic readers of its March 11 editorial were reminded of the *Globe*'s historical anti-Catholic bias.[20]

> In light of the opposition to reform from Quebec's Liberal caucus, one wonders if once again, the conscience of some Roman Catholic Canadians will be allowed to violate that of millions of other Canadians....
>
> It would be regrettable if a coherent and vociferous opposition to reform from Quebec MP's were to unleash old demons of anti-French-Canadian prejudice in English Canada. Exasperated English Canadians who strongly wish for a civilized abortion law might be tempted to blame a failure on the "priest-ridden Quebeckers."

In the end, Trudeau made one concession. On May 9, toward the end of the third reading, he allowed a free vote on a motion to eliminate completely clause 18, the abortion provision. In a classic display of political cowardice, sixty-eight of the 155 Liberal members of Parliament somehow managed to be absent from Parliament when the vote was taken. Only two Liberals voted for the motion. The Conservatives were no better. Of the seventy-two members, forty were absent. Indeed, in the vote that was to determine Canada's new abortion law, the "absents" outnumbered both the "ayes" and the "nays."[21] The motion was thus defeated, paving the way for adoption of the bill.

The May 9 vote effectively terminated the abortion debate in the House of Commons. On May 14 the entire bill was given final approval. The *Globe and Mail* hailed the May 14 vote as "a great day . . . [and] an important moment in Canadian history." Nor did it spare any praise for the man it regarded as the architect of reform: Pierre Elliott Trudeau. His original sponsorship of the legislation was characterized as "an act of courage . . . a public defence of personal liberty." While the *Globe* pointed out that the reforms did not go as far as they should, it concluded:[22]

> . . . it was the spirit of the bill that was important. It stepped boldly into a great many areas where legislators had never dared to step before. This is an essential spirit in our rapidly changing world. . . . The man to whom most of the honor must go is Mr. Trudeau.

The new law represented a political compromise. Abortions became more readily available, and there was now broader legal protection for doctors who performed them. Yet the reform stopped short of decriminalizing abortion. Section 251 of the Criminal Code still treated abortion as a serious crime punishable by a maximum sentence of life imprisonment for the abortionist and two years for the woman. The only legal abortions were those performed under the exculpatory or "excusing" provisions of subsection 4. Subsection 4 defined a "legal" abortion as one performed in an accredited hospital after approval by the hospital's therapeutic abortion committee (TAC). The TAC's approval hinged on three doctors finding that the pregnancy would be likely to endanger "the life or health" of the woman.

The new policy represented an accommodation that provided something for everyone. While the government used the rhetoric of reform, the new law basically legalized existing practice.[23] Doctors were now protected and maintained supervisory control over the abortion process. Reformers could be told that the law increased access to abortion services. Anti-abortion groups could be told that abortion was still illegal except in certain narrowly defined circumstances. And much to the relief of the Liberal caucus, the reform effectively shifted responsibility for administering and enforcing the new law to the provinces.[24]

No doubt Pierre Trudeau and his ministers hoped that their reform would prove to be a Solomon-like compromise, tidily disposing of the abortion issue. Under normal circumstances such optimism might have been justified. Compromise – the practice of giving half a loaf to both sides – is a venerable tactic of democratic politicians, who always have an eye on the next election. With issues such as this, the politician's objective is not so much to solve problems as to defuse them. While critics sometimes complain that in Canadian politics the art of compromise has been elevated to the status of a religious cult, most of the time political compromise is successful in that both sides are more or less content to get some of what they want. But this presupposes that the goods to be divided are indeed divisible. When the competing demands are material and financial, compromise usually works. But when the demands take on a moral character, when each side views its position as sanctioned by natural right and the opposition's as an immoral transgression of this right, compromise is challenged. Such was the fate of Canada's abortion reform law of 1969. The challenge from one side soon crystallized around the civil disobedience of Henry Morgentaler.

CHAPTER 3

Conscience versus Law: Morgentaler's Path to Civil Disobedience

Feminists had little influence on the 1969 reform, and they quickly took the lead in denouncing it. In the spring of 1970, the Vancouver Women's Caucus organized the "Abortion Caravan." Starting in Vancouver, they carried a coffin across the country to Parliament Hill, where they rallied 500 strong to protest the new law. Some of the protesters later chained themselves to the Visitors' Gallery of the House of Commons and disrupted proceedings by shouting "Free abortion on demand" and "Every child a wanted child."[1] That same year the Report of the Royal Commission on the Status of Women condemned the new abortion law as much too restrictive. Like their more radical counterparts in the Abortion Caravan, the authors of the Report based their criticism not just on pragmatic arguments but on the more absolutist grounds of the right of each woman to decide the abortion issue for herself.[2]

As the decade of the seventies opened, the focus for this argument and for much of the pro-choice movement quickly became Henry Morgentaler, the doctor from Montreal whose radical testimony before the 1967 Commons Committee on Health and Welfare had first captured national attention. Prior to this, Morgentaler was unknown outside of Montreal. By the end of the decade his name and face would be familiar to Canadians from coast to coast. People began to ask: Who is Henry Morgentaler? Where did he come from? What experiences and ideas had shaped the character of the man whose name was becoming synonymous with abortion in the Canadian consciousness?

Henry Morgentaler was born Jewish and poor in Poland in 1923. His parents were workers in the grey and crowded industrial centre of Lodz, 70 miles southeast of Warsaw. Both had rejected orthodox Judaism and were active in the Bund, the Jewish socialist labour movement. Henry's father helped found the Textile Workers' Union of which he became a leader. From his parents Morgentaler inherited the atheism and belief in reform and historical progress that were to mark his adult life.[3] His hostility toward religion was reinforced by his early experience with anti-Semitism. As a young boy he came to associate Polish Catholicism with anti-Jewish prejudice. He was bright and sensitive, although somewhat lonely and experienced the double isolation of being Jewish in Catholic Poland and a non-practising Jew in the still predominantly orthodox Jewish district of Lodz. He resented the long absences caused by his father's work for the Jewish Socialist Bund but developed a close and warm relationship with his younger brother, Mumek. At fifteen he fell in love with Chava Rosenfarb, and later he recalled it as one of the happiest years of his childhood.[4]

Whatever happiness Henry Morgentaler experienced as a youngster ended abruptly when the German armies overran Poland in 1939. His father, both a Jew and a socialist, was among the first to be arrested by the Nazi occupiers. On March 19, 1940, Henry's birthday, his father disappeared for the last time. Shortly afterwards, the Nazis forced all Jews into a designated Jewish ghetto. Jews were not permitted to leave the barbed wire-enclosed ghetto except by permission from the Nazi occupiers. For the next four years, the young Morgentaler experienced the poverty, hunger, filth, and fear of the Nazi holocaust in Poland. He was assigned to work in a steel mill and later in a paper bag factory. His older sister, Ghitel, was arrested, deported, and died at Treblinka.

In August, 1944, faced with the advancing Russian army, the Germans rounded up all remaining Jews in the Lodz ghetto and shipped them to the infamous Auschwitz-Birkenau concentration camp. There, at the dreaded "selection" of workers and non-workers, Morgentaler last saw his mother. He and his brother were shaved, stripped, showered, and numbered. Henry Morgentaler became 95077. Later they were transferred to Dachau. Life in the camps was a nightmarish struggle for survival. During the winter of 1945, Morgentaler caught bronchitis and was put in the infirmary, where for the first time in months he saw his reflection in a mirror. "I looked like death incarnate," he later recalled, "and started to cry."[5] Morgentaler was transferred yet again, this time to a camp for the sick and dying. It was there, close to death, he and his brother were liberated by the American army on April 29, 1945.

At the age of twenty-two, Henry Morgentaler emerged a survivor, young only in years. His experience of the Nazi Holocaust left permanent marks. It reinforced his atheism. "I wanted to believe in God," he recalled, "but I couldn't believe that a God could be so unmerciful." The experience also planted a strong distrust of government, the seeds of his future civil disobedience. The equation of the legal with the just was shattered in the political consciousness of the young Morgentaler.[6] But despite the horrors, Morgentaler was happy just to be alive and eager to get on with his life. Miraculously, he found his childhood sweetheart, Chava. He decided to study medicine and was accepted at a university, first in Germany, then in Belgium. After four years in Belgium, Morgentaler and Eva (English for Chava) emigrated to Canada in 1950.

Life in Montreal was hard at first. Morgentaler worked part-time while pursuing full-time studies at the University of Montreal. But the hard work led to success, first at medical school, and then in his new family practice in the east end of Montreal. By the end of his first decade in Canada, Morgentaler had achieved financial security and the respect of the Montreal medical community. Despite his outward signs of success, however, he found himself increasingly dissatisfied with life. In 1957 he entered psychoanalysis, and for the next four years, three times a week, he painfully explored the landscape of his inner self with the help of his therapist.

By his own confession, Morgentaler's psychoanalysis marked a major turning point in his life. Through analysis, he concluded that his childhood experiences of anti-Semitism and the Holocaust had caused him to fear competition, to be too passive and under-ambitious. Morgentaler began consciously to reorient his life. His new goals, he wrote, were "to feel vibrant, enjoying life, and to become a full person. To be open to experience – active and useful. . . . Active, as a sort of mover of history, doing something useful and important."[7] Morgentaler's new commitment to public action and social reform led to his involvement in the Montreal Humanist Fellowship. Its philosophy, based on the teachings of Bertrand Russell and Erich Fromm, was reflected in

Henry Morgentaler's new personal motto: "Nothing human is alien to me." In 1964, he became president of the Fellowship. During this same period, he became increasingly estranged from his wife.

Morgentaler's involvement with the humanist movement paralleled a growing interest in the new issues raised by the scientific control of human sexuality. At the middle of the twentieth century, new birth control techniques – oral contraception and vacuum abortion – offered the historically unique possibility of separating sexual intercourse from pregnancy and reproduction. Modern science once again offered the inviting prospect of extending men's and – most emphatically in this case – women's control over their own destiny. Pregnancy by rational choice rather than by biological accident, sexual intercourse for recreation rather than reproduction – these were powerful and appealing new possibilities. Opposed to this brave new world, however, were traditional morality, religion, and the Criminal Code of Canada.

In retrospect, not just Henry Morgentaler's future but the future of all of Canada was decisively influenced by this fateful coincidence of private and public, of Morgentaler's personal soul-searching and the emergence of abortion as a political issue. After four years of psychoanalysis, Morgentaler wrote: "I came to the conclusion that, under some circumstances, it is imperative to defy authority – necessary for my self-esteem, to prove my manhood in direct conflict."[8] Abortion seems to have provided the issue that the new Henry Morgentaler was looking for: science versus religion, technology versus nature, reason versus faith, individual conscience versus law, and – if he chose – Morgentaler versus the state.

A battle of epic proportions loomed, but the cause of science and humanistic self-determination needed foot-soldiers. Henry Morgentaler volunteered. He wrote articles for journals and letters to newspapers, appeared on radio and television talk shows, and in 1967 appeared before the parliamentary committee examining abortion reform. Within several years, the foot-soldier would become a general.

Henry Morgentaler's 1967 testimony before the Commons Committee on Health and Welfare served as a catalyst and a stepping-stone for his deepening involvement in the abortion controversy. Morgentaler had appeared before the Committee as the representative of the the the Humanist Associations of Montreal, Toronto, and Victoria. As the vice-president (and past president) of the Montreal Humanist Fellowship, Morgentaler used this appearance to help launch the Humanist Association of Canada in 1968. As its founder and first president, Morgentaler was able to use the new Association to publicize his ongoing campaign for abortion reform.

His growing media profile had a second important consequence. He found himself besieged with requests to perform abortions. This posed an agonizing dilemma. On the one hand, his passionate commitment to safe and accessible abortions demanded that he help the women who came to him for abortions. On the other hand was the criminal law of Canada. At first he was able to refer requests for abortion to several other doctors in Montreal who were willing to perform them. But as the number of requests escalated and his referral contacts disappeared, Morgentaler felt increasingly trapped between his conscience and the law.

> I was advocating abortion on request, agreeing with the right of women to safe, medical abortion, yet refusing to do it. My reason was obvious and understandable. Abortion was against the law. I could lose my license and my practice in medicine, which I had built up with a great deal of sacrifice and hard work. I could lose my reputation, my source of income for my family and myself. I could go to jail for five to ten years, even for life. To perform abortion at that time was risking everything I had achieved over the years.[9]

Morgentaler eventually chose conscience over law. In January, 1968, two months before the Commons Committee released its abortion reform report, Morgentaler performed his first abortion on the teenage daughter of a friend. The following year he sent a letter to all his patients announcing that he was discontinuing his general practice in order to specialize in family planning. Henceforth he would limit his practice to performing vasectomies, providing IUDs and oral contraceptives, and performing abortions.

Morgentaler set about his new project with the energy and enthusiasm of a man possessed. He scoured the medical journals for everything that had been written on abortion techniques but found little. As abortion was still illegal in the United States and only recently legalized in England, abortion techniques had not been a frequent subject of medical scholarship. Eventually Morgentaler found two articles by Dorothea Kerslake, an English doctor, describing the vacuum suction technique invented by the Chinese in the 1950s. He ordered a vacuum aspirator from England and soon began to perform abortions by following the directives in the Kerslake articles. "I trained myself by trial and error," he said later, not just learning but improving the vacuum suction technique.

In 1973 Morgentaler published a description of his abortion technique in the *Journal of the Canadian Medical Association.* Based on 5,641 abortions performed in his clinic, Morgentaler hoped his article would "dispel the myths about abortion" and "prove that abortions can be done safely in clinics."[10] Unlike the dilatation and curettage (D&C) technique then being used by others, Morgentaler's suction abortion required no surgeon, no general anesthetic, no hospital, and could be performed in five to fifteen minutes. Practising what he preached, Henry Morgentaler was also transforming his Champlain clinic – an ordinary residential bungalow with a neatly trimmed lawn and manicured flower beds – into what he envisioned as a prototype for all of Canada: a modern, free-standing abortion clinic.[11]

At the same time that he began secretly to break the law, Morgentaler continued to attack it in public. Shortly after the 1969 reform came into effect, he condemned it as "a liberalization on paper only, and ... a dismal failure. Under this law, 99 out of 100 women CANNOT get legal abortions and are driven in desperation to risk their lives at the hands of incompetent people. Why? Because the Canadian laws on abortion are unreasonably restrictive, unclear and unworkable."[12] In January, 1970, Morgentaler anonymously published an article in the American magazine, *The Humanist,* in which he described and defended his illegal abortions. "I consider my attitude as one of civil disobedience to a cruel and immoral law," he wrote.[13]

> I have not publicly declared that I am an abortionist, and am breaking the abortion laws, as is supposed to be done in classical cases of civil disobedience. Although I have toyed with the idea and might still do so if I think this would be useful. The reason is simply that I prefer to live for a cause than to be martyred for it; I prefer to be free and help people than be in the penitentiary and thereby deprive all those who can receive my help from possibly the only source of adequate help they have.[13]

Within five months of publishing these thoughts, Henry Morgentaler no longer had the leisure of "toying" with the idea of going public. On June 1, the police raided his Champlain clinic and arrested him. Morgentaler had been receiving a growing number of abortion referrals from his contacts in the United States. Evidently the boyfriend of a seventeen-year-old patient from Minneapolis had informed the

American FBI of a Canadian "abortion ring." The FBI had contacted the RCMP, who in turn informed the Montreal police. Morgentaler was charged with three counts of criminal abortions.

Long before his arrest, Morgentaler had already consulted one of Montreal's best-known criminal and corporate lawyers, Claude-Armand Sheppard. Co-founder and partner of a prestigious downtown law firm, Sheppard had been president of the Montreal Civil Liberties Union when Henry Morgentaler was on the board of directors. Sheppard had defended politically controversial defendants before, including members of the FLQ, and he agreed to help Henry Morgentaler when the time arrived.

Sheppard and one of his partners, Charles F. Flam, proved invaluable to Morgentaler at this stage. Morgentaler had somewhat naively assumed that with a few phone calls to well-placed friends in the Montreal establishment, the charges would be dropped and he could return to performing abortions. When this did not occur, his instinct was to attack – to proceed as quickly as possible to trial, challenging the law head on before a jury. It was here that Sheppard and Flam interceded and successfully counselled restraint and delay. Public opinion, they urged, was not yet ripe. Attitudes toward abortion were changing, but not enough . . . yet. Reluctantly, Morgentaler consented. With the green light from his client, Sheppard proceeded to tie the Quebec criminal justice system into knots. He peppered the courts with motion after motion on procedural questions. Each one that failed was immediately appealed. The case of *The Queen v. Morgentaler* ground to a halt, first for months, soon for years.

Morgentaler also benefited from a second and quite unrelated event shortly after his first arrest. In October, 1970, the FLQ crisis exploded across Quebec, absorbing all of the government's attention and energy for months to come. Under more normal circumstances, the influential Catholic elements in the Quebec Liberal government might have tried to make an example of a Jewish doctor who publicly flouted the abortion law in Catholic Quebec. But compared to the FLQ crisis, when two cells of the revolutionary Front de Libération du Québec kidnapped a British diplomat and abducted and later killed a Quebec cabinet minister, Henry Morgentaler was a small fish and could be safely ignored. This was the first but not the last time that the politics of Quebec nationalism would provide a timely boost to the fortunes of Henry Morgentaler.

Sheppard's strategy of procedural delay worked well, perhaps too well from Morgentaler's perspective. He was weary of waiting. He had begun to perform abortions again at his east end Montreal clinic, but after several thousand they had become routine. The challenge he sought was with the law of Canada, and he was impatient to get on with it. When the U.S. Supreme Court handed down its decision in *Roe v. Wade* in January of 1973, this provided the spark Morgentaler needed.

Roe v. Wade reinvigorated Morgentaler and other Canadian abortion-rights activists. For Morgentaler, the news confirmed the wisdom of Sheppard's strategy of delay. It seemed to signal that the tide of public opinion had finally changed, and the time for action had come.

In February, 1973, pro-choice reformers organized a cross-Canada rally on Parliament Hill with Morgentaler as the featured speaker. Renewing his attacks on the existing law, he cited the British and American reforms and urged Parliament to decriminalize abortion. In the following weeks, impatient with Parliament's apparent indifference, Morgentaler decided to go public for the first time with the true extent of his civil disobedience. In light of the still outstanding criminal charges against him, Morgentaler's lawyer, Charles Flam (Sheppard was out of town), strongly advised against it: "If you want to commit suicide, that is your privilege. If you want to gamble, why not try Las Vegas?" "This kind of gambling," Morgentaler is alleged to have responded, "gives *me* more of a thrill." [14]

On March 15, 1973, Morgentaler dramatically raised the ante of his challenge. At a rally on the University of Toronto campus, Morgentaler publicly announced that he had personally performed over 5,000 abortions in violation of section 251 of the Criminal Code. The following day he made the same shocking announcement at a Montreal news conference. While the Toronto papers somehow missed the story (the reporter for the *Globe and Mail* evidently left the Toronto rally early), it was front-page news in Montreal.

Morgentaler made sure that his civil disobedience would not be ignored by the authorities. The following month he sent letters to Claude Castonguay and Marc Lalonde, the provincial and federal health ministers, repeating his disclosure of having performed over 5,000 illegal abortions, requesting that his clinic be recognized as an authorized abortion clinic, and offering to share his acquired expertise with both governments to set up similar clinics across Canada. Copies were sent to Prime Minister Trudeau, Justice Minister Otto Lang, and the leaders of the three other parties in Parliament – Robert Stanfield (Tories), David Lewis (NDP), and Réal Caouette (Créditiste).

Not satisfied, Morgentaler further escalated his campaign of civil disobedience. With the help of his confidante and early abortion rights activist Eleanor Pelrine, he arranged for a crew from the CTV public affairs program *W5* to film him performing an illegal abortion at his Montreal clinic. The tape was shot on May 2 and was initially scheduled to be shown on Sunday, May 20. But when news of the controversial film leaked out, the *W5* producers worried that the government would seek an injunction to block the broadcast of a "crime" on television. To avoid this, they rescheduled the screening for the preceding Sunday.[15] Thus on May 13 – Mother's Day – CTV broadcast the abortion procedure from start to finish. Public reaction was predictably strong. Protests poured into the government and the press.

As if the government did not by this point have enough evidence, in July, 1973, Morgentaler sent the article describing his abortion procedure to the *Canadian Medical Association Journal*. The article began by declaring that it was based on "the author's experience resulting from 5641 ambulatory abortions done in his clinic with the vacuum suction technique under local anesthesia."[16] The fact that they were done in his clinic, not a hospital, automatically meant that all 5,641 abortions violated section 251 of the *Criminal Code*. As much as it might like, the Quebec government could no longer ignore Henry Morgentaler and the abortion issue.

On August 15, 1973, the inevitable finally happened. The Montreal police raided the Champlain clinic. Morgentaler, staff members, and patients were arrested and taken to the police station. Morgentaler spent two nights in jail and was eventually charged with ten illegal abortions. Combined with the three outstanding charges from the 1970 raid, Morgentaler now faced thirteen separate charges, each with a potential life sentence. In light of his incriminating public disclosures of the preceding months, the Crown would hardly have trouble establishing the facts to support its accusations. Yet despite the seriousness of his situation, Morgentaler felt vaguely relieved, even elated. The waiting was over. The confrontation he had been seeking was finally at hand. In his mind's eye, Henry Morgentaler thought he saw the tide of public opinion beginning to run in his direction, and he was there, ready to catch it.

CHAPTER 4

Rising Star in the West: The People's Politician

One thousand miles west of Montreal, Henry Morgentaler's future antagonist was also entering the political limelight for the first time. In 1969, the year after Morgentaler performed his first abortion, Joe Borowski was elected to the Manitoba legislature. Borowski's election as the NDP member from Churchill capped the stunning political ascent of a dirt-poor Polish farmboy from Saskatchewan.

Joe Borowski was born near Wishart, Saskatchewan, in 1932, the fourth of Joseph and Bernice Borowski's ten children. His parents had immigrated to Canada from Poland in 1930. His father came from an aristocratic family that owned an estate west of Bialystok, close to the Russian border. Bernice, however, came from a lower social class, and family disapproval and lack of support had driven the Borowskis to Canada in search of a new beginning. What they got was a quarter-section lease from the biggest landlord of the Prairies, the Canadian Pacific Railroad. It was poor, rocky soil, and one-third of every bushel went straight to their new landlord. Depression and drought made living hard. Only the oldest of their ten children finished high school. Borowski and the others dropped out as soon as they were old enough to work for wages. At the age of twelve Borowski left school to harvest the crop. At fourteen he left home altogether in search of "big money" in the mining, fishing, and lumber camps of the North.[1]

For the next twelve years of his life, the young Borowski worked his way across the North, from British Columbia to Quebec and back again. He put in time as a stevedore in Vancouver, dragline operator in Swift Current, and bull cook in bush camps from Kitimat to Fairbanks.[2] Borowski basically "dropped out" and hit the road a generation before it became fashionable. As he later explained to a reporter, "You'd work two weeks here, three weeks there, drifting from job to job. I was young and I wanted to see the country."[3] In 1952 he met and married Jean Zelinski, another nineteen-year-old from Saskatchewan. Together with Jean, he continued to work and live in the Yukon. "We had a good time, climbed mountains, fished in virgin lakes, shot grizzlies. No cares."[4]

Cares came with the arrival of their first child, Debra. They moved back to Wynyard, Saskatchewan, Jean's home town, and opened a restaurant. Soon they had a second daughter, Karen. The restaurant business was barely staying afloat financially, and Borowski missed mining. In 1958 he heard that they were hiring experienced miners at top dollar to open a nickel mine in Thompson, Manitoba, 700 miles north of Winnipeg. Borowski left Jean and his daughters in Saskatoon. Initially, Thompson was just another mining camp. But Borowski stayed on, and Thompson grew. Soon houses replaced tents, and then Jean and the girls along with other wives and children came to stay. Wages were good and there was plenty of work. The Borowskis' third daughter, Sandra, was born in 1960. In Joe's eyes, he and Jean and their fellow miners were building a new community and he liked the feeling: "Going up there seemed to me like a sort of historical event. We were in on the birth of something."[5]

International Nickel Company (INCO) owned the Thompson operation, but it had subcontracted out the initial phases of exploration and development to smaller firms. Borowski and most of the workers were initially employed by Patrick (Paddy) Harrison, a development contractor from Quebec. Once Harrison and his crews had completed the tough work of sinking shafts into the hardrock of northern Manitoba, INCO took over and everything began to change. Wages were cut, and productivity bonus pay was virtually abolished. The maximum monthly income for a miner fell from $1,500 to $600.[6] Joe Borowski had never liked big corporations. As a boy he watched the CPR take one-third of his father's annual crop. It had made a lasting impression. To Borowski, the CPR was "the biggest bunch of horsethieves in Canada."[7] Now, he saw INCO as no better – "callous, uncaring, heartless, cold-blooded."[8]

[T]he big joke in Thompson was that there were three shifts, one coming to Thompson, one working, and one leaving Thompson. The turnover was incredible and [INCO] couldn't care less. If somebody got hurt or killed, so what? And when I seen my brothers getting maimed and occasionally getting killed, not because it's dangerous – we know mining's dangerous – but because it just cost too much money to put in the safety features. . . .

Borowski became angry. INCO's callous treatment of the miners began to forge the new Joe Borowski – the political activist, the moralistic crusader, the champion of the little guy. In 1962 Borowski helped to kick out the Mine-Mill union and bring in the more militant United Steelworkers. He then helped to negotiate the new local's first contract and subsequently was elected vice-president. He discovered that the company had "forgotten" to add holiday pay on bonus income, a mistake that cost INCO $875,000. In 1964 he led his union in a successful strike against INCO. Before and after his election as vice-president, Borowski was a stickler for mine safety and a vocal critic of the company's mine safety record. At a coroner's inquest into a particularly gruesome accident, he jumped to his feet and accused INCO of murder.

Joe's constant agitation on behalf of his fellow workers made him a hero in their eyes but hardly endeared him to INCO management. In 1965, when he refused to go into a shaft he considered unsafe, the company seized the opportunity to fire Borowski for "insubordination."[9] Since there was nothing to do in Thompson except work the mines, INCO anticipated the imminent departure of the man who had been a constant thorn in their side. They underestimated the character of their adversary. By 1965, Thompson, Manitoba, was home for Joe Borowski. His family, his friends, and his life were all in Thompson. He was not going to let INCO run him off like a dog and decided to open a variety store in Thompson. For several years he had been making and selling nickel souvenirs and trinkets on the side. Now, he decided, he would do this full time.

Again, INCO sought to banish Borowski, this time by refusing to rent him any space for his would-be store. By 1965 Thompson had 8,000 residents but still no elected mayor or town council. INCO owned and ran everything, and the company was determined to prevent its ex-employee from opening a store – or his mouth. Once again they underestimated him. Within weeks, Borowski was on the steps of the legislature in Winnipeg, a one-man "sleep-in" protest against "INCO

DICTATORSHIP" and demanding self-government for the people of Thompson. Borowski caught the flu but the people caught the spirit of his protest. Within a year, Thompson had an independent town council and Borowski had his store.

The next year Borowski was back on the steps again. This time his target was political: the Conservative cabinet of Premier Duff Roblin had voted to give themselves a pay raise while refusing to enact a $1.25 minimum wage law. Borowski's message was as blunt as the crude, hand-lettered sign he held: "DUFF ROBLINHOOD IS NO DAMN GOOD (FOR MANITOBA)." The protest caught on, and others joined Borowski on the picket line. One supporter loaned Borowski a tent-trailer to protect him against the cool fall nights. One night – on orders from Tory Highways Minister Stewart McLean – the trailer was hauled away with Borowski inside. The last laugh, however, belonged to the eccentric nickel miner. Seven months later, under growing public criticism, the cabinet ministers cut their salary increase by half.

Despite his dim, can't-trust-the-bastards view of politicians, Joe's crusades were slowly drawing him into public life. "I realized I had to become involved because politics touches every facet of life of the guy who carries the lunch pail," he later explained.[10] His activism also transformed him from a Tory to an NDP supporter. Like many young westerners of his generation, he had been captivated by the charisma of John Diefenbaker and cast his first vote in 1958 for "Dief" and the victorious Tories. But his work for the Steelworkers in Tory-run Manitoba soon persuaded him that the Conservatives were no friends of the working man. "Hell," he later explained, "the Saskatchewan legislation was more generous than our contracts in Manitoba."[11] When the NDP established a constituency association in Thompson, Borowski was elected its first president.

In 1968 Borowski went to jail for refusing to collect a new provincial sales tax on purchases at his souvenir shop in Thompson. Borowski maintained the new Tory tax was illegal because the government had not told the people about it before it was elected in 1966. (By this standard, practically all taxes would be illegal!) While this argument was completely irrelevant to the legality of the tax, it hit a responsive political chord. His reputation as the champion of the little guy soared again. Borowski won even more public sympathy by actually paying the uncollected sales taxes out of his own pocket. The government said this would not do – that the tax had to be collected from the purchaser – and sent Borowski to jail three different times. Each time he was released, the Manitoba press trekked out to The Pas (site of the provincial penitentiary) to interview Borowski and beam his smiling and unrepentant mug into the homes and hearts of thousands of working-class Manitobans. The "crackpot" from Thompson was becoming a local media star.

In February of the next year (1969) a by-election was called for the northern riding of Churchill, where Thompson is located. Borowski ran and won. His by-election victory foreshadowed even larger changes in Manitoba politics. In June, Ed Schreyer led the NDP to a stunning upset victory over the Tories. The list of names in the NDP caucus "read like a petition for minority rights" – Poles, Jews, Ukrainians, Franco-Manitobans.[12] The perennial outsiders of Manitoba politics were now the insiders. And nobody had been more of an outsider than Joe Borowski.

The "honnerabel" new member from Churchill quickly gained a reputation for his malapropisms, poor spelling, and blunt language. Ed Schreyer, the new Premier, recognized the political charm of Borowski and appointed him as Minister of Highways. Borowski loved it. Everything was unfolding the way it should. Three years earlier, the Tory minister, Stewart McLean, had ordered Joe's tent-trailer unceremoniously towed away from the capital steps. Now it was his turn:

> Today, McLean is a judge on a magistrate court circuit in the sticks in Saskatchewan where I was born. And, here I am with McLean's car . . . his desk, his office, his job, and his secretary. And I'm enjoying all of them.[13]

Most politicians could not get away with that kind of public gloating. But Joe Borowski was no ordinary politician. He was, as one journalist described him, "the anti-politician in power. Just by being ordinary Joe, honest Joe, Joe the working stiff from the mine who used to carry a lunch pail, he has become a folk hero."[14]

Joe Borowski was at the height of his political career. With hindsight, however, one can now see that his anti-politics was destined to take him out of politics.

CHAPTER 5

Trial by Jury

The Morgentaler trial was clearly going to be a "political trial" in the fullest sense of that term. A political trial is a legal proceeding where the objective of one or both of the parties transcends the immediate verdict of guilt or innocence. The trial becomes a means to the much larger end of influencing public opinion and political mobilization. A government may try to politicize a trial by using the conviction and punishment of the accused to serve as an example that deters other "troublemakers." The trial and execution of Lount and Mathews, two of the leaders of the Rebellion of 1837 in Upper Canada, the similarly harsh treatment of Louis Riel, the Métis leader of the Red River and North-West rebellions, in 1885,[1] and the Duplessis government's numerous prosecutions of the Jehovah's Witnesses in Quebec during the 1940s[2] all were cases in which government sought to use the prosecution to demoralize and discourage the supporters and sympathizers of the accused.

For the accused, the objective of a political trial is to change government policy (or even the government itself) by arousing public opinion against it. This is most clear in cases of civil disobedience, such as Morgentaler's, where the facts of the charge are not contested. The accused seeks to dramatize publicly the injustice of a law by openly breaking it and then passively submitting to prosecution and punishment. Mahatma Gandhi's campaign of non-violent civil disobedience against British colonialism in India exemplified the successful use of political trials. Similarly, Martin Luther King (who was influenced by Gandhi) and the civil rights movement in the United States used civil disobedience successfully to challenge the regime of racial segregation during the 1950s and 1960s.

Henry Morgentaler hoped to emulate the victories of Gandhi and King in his challenge to the abortion law. It was not by accident, however, that his models of success were largely foreign to Canada. While Morgentaler was not the first Canadian to challenge government policy through litigation, his predecessors' track record was not encouraging. Indeed, as the examples of Lount and Mathews, Riel, and others indicated, in Canada there was more evidence of successful government efforts to use the courts to suppress social movements than vice versa. Indeed, at the very time of the Morgentaler trials, one of Canada's leading historians was writing that in Canada attempts to use the courts as an instrument for political change rarely succeeded and were generally regarded as illegitimate, not least because they smacked of Americanism.[3] The strong British influence, the higher value attached to law and order, the strong emphasis placed on separating law and politics, courts and legislatures, had all conspired against the successful use of political trials by dissidents and reformers. In his attempt to turn the tables and put the abortion law on trial, Henry Morgentaler was clearly swimming against the tide of Canadian political and judicial tradition.

On this otherwise dark historical horizon there was one bright spot of inspiration for Morgentaler: the 1937 acquittal of Dorothea Palmer from a charge of illegally distributing contraceptives contrary to section 207(c) of the Criminal Code.[4] Like Morgentaler, Palmer did not deny the facts of the case against her, but claimed she had acted for the public good. Her acquittal was one of the first public victories of the Canadian birth control movement and marked a turning point in the campaign to make contraception available in Canada.[5]

Dorothea Palmer worked as a "visiting nurse" for A.R. Kaufman, the Kitchener industrialist who was one of the first and most important leaders of the birth control movement in Canada.[6] Kaufman revolutionized the availability of contraception to married couples by abandoning the "clinic approach" and organizing a system of "visiting nurses" who went door-to-door. Calling on couples who had indicated to their doctors or ministers an interest in contraception, these nurses sold at cost (or, in some cases, gave for free) a kit containing contraceptive jelly and a nozzle and left forms with which to order future supplies by mail. Launched by Kaufman in 1933, within four years the Parents' Information Bureau (PIB) had nurses working from Newfoundland to Victoria and was averaging 20,000 "contacts" a year.

Kaufman and others had pursued their birth control activities for five years without police interference when Dorothea Palmer was arrested in the town of Eastview (now Vanier) on the Quebec-Ontario border. There is some dispute over whether Kaufman purposely provoked a "test case" in Eastview or whether the police, encouraged by local Catholic authorities, decided to crack down on the Bureau's operations. Whichever, once Palmer had been arrested and charged, Kaufman decided to use the case to challenge to section 207(c). He assigned his personal laywer, F.W. Wegenast, to defend Palmer.[7]

Wegenast was known primarily as a civil litigator, but he was a natural choice for the Palmer case. He was a member of both the PIB and the Eugenics Society of Canada and was also active in the Orange Lodge. His knowledge of and belief in the birth control movement, combined with his civil litigation skills, made Wegenast ideally suited to pull together the moral and scientific arguments against s.207(c). Wegenast's task was made easier when magistrate Lester Clayton, "a progressive and a Protestant," was assigned to the Palmer trial.[8]

Wegenast began by calling the twenty-one women visited by Palmer in Eastview, all of whom testified that they wanted the birth control information and had suffered from lack of it. Next he called a series of witnesses from the birth control movement – most of them women doctors – who testified as to the importance of contraception to women. Kaufman himself was called to testify as to the operation of the PIB. The birth control activists were followed by "a long roster of churchmen whose very presence indicated the extent to which birth control now had the support of progressive Protestants."[9] Wegenast concluded his defence by calling to the witness stand several well-known medical doctors from Toronto, who testified as to the safety and effectiveness of contraceptives.

This extravaganza lasted almost four months and received heavy press coverage. Even before a verdict was announced, Kaufman declared the trial a success because it had demonstrated such public support for his cause. In the end, Judge Clayton proved to be on the same wavelength as Wegenast, agreeing with all of Wegenast's arguments and acquitting Dorothea Palmer. The judge found that Palmer was just trying to help poor women who needed and wanted her services, services already available to the rich and the middle class. Besides, Palmer's activities would discourage "the breeding of large families" and thereby reduce the "burden on the taxpayer."[10] This evidence proved that Palmer was indeed "serving the public good," a defence that was explicitly allowed by section 207(c).

While the Palmer victory did not lead to a repeal of the anti-contraception law, it gave the fledgling birth control movement the public respect it previously lacked and effectively suspended the enforcement of s.207(c) in most of English Canada. Thirty-five years later, Henry Morgentaler was seeking the same results. The Palmer case also provided an example of the kind of judicial attitudes that Morgentaler's lawyers would need to win. Judge Clayton was not at all shy about his exercise of judicial discretion. "The Court is given the discretion to interpret wisely," he declared. "Here is an opportunity for the Courts of Law to keep abreast of the social development of the community and to break away from the criticism that the law is rigid and at times obsolete." Noting the "tremendous development of public opinion" on contraception in recent years, Judge Clayton concluded with an appeal to history: "Is Canada . . . still to be wandering in the intellectual and social wilderness on this vital subject?"[11] Henry Morgentaler could hardly have stated it better.

Morgentaler never doubted the political character of his trial. The government put him and his lawyers on notice that it, too, viewed the matter as political when it announced the decision to proceed by way of preferred indictments, an extraordinary procedure last used in the October, 1970, FLQ crisis. The symbolic connection with the FLQ was ominous for Morgentaler, and the preferred indictments also put him at a practical disadvantage.

The first judicial stage in the trial of an indictable offence is normally a preliminary inquiry. Conducted before a provincial court judge, the Crown must demonstrate that there is sufficient evidence to justify taking the case to full trial before the superior court. The preliminary inquiry protects and aids the accused in several important ways. It helps to protect individuals from police or government harassment based on false or inadequate evidence. The Crown must prove to the satisfaction of an independent and impartial judge that sufficient legal evidence exists to warrant continuing the prosecution. This process produces a second advantage for the accused: a preview of the Crown's evidence and legal strategy – a bit like being allowed to review the opposing team's play book before the game.

Under section 507 of the Criminal Code, an Attorney-General may proceed directly to trial by way of "preferred indictment" when he believes that the delay incurred by a preliminary inquiry would threaten the public good. Morgentaler's (really Sheppard's) persistent obstruction of the prosecution of the 1970 charges and his public flouting of the abortion law were cited as justifying the use of preferred indictments. That the indictments were personally signed by Jérôme Choquette, the Quebec Minister of Justice, confirmed the importance the Bourassa government attached to the trial. The not-so-implicit message was that Morgentaler and his lawyers had embarrassed the Quebec government for long enough.

Sheppard sought to quash the government's use of preferred indictments as unjustified and improper. The court's summary rejection of Sheppard's request suggested that the Quebec judiciary shared the government's impatience with Morgentaler and his perhaps overly clever lawyers. Trial date was set for October 18, 1973. The day of reckoning was at hand.

The trial began with the selection of the jury. The right of an accused to a trial by a jury of one's peers is one of the oldest and most important protections of individual liberty in the English common law tradition. It appears in Magna Carta as one of the important concessions wrung by the English nobles from King John on the fields of Runnymede in 1215. By placing the responsibility for determining the true facts of a case in the hands of twelve independent and impartial peers of the accused, trial by jury deprives unjust governments of one of their favourite means of persecuting innocent critics. On important occasions in English history, juries have even refused to enforce unjust laws.

Morgentaler had elected trial by a jury rather than by a judge alone. This was a strategic choice, based on the hunch that a jury would be more sympathetic than a judge. For an experienced criminal lawyer like Sheppard, the process of jury selection is one of the most important stages of the trial. The jury is the audience before whom the trial lawyer performs. But unlike other professional performers, lawyers are given the opportunity to help shape the composition and character of their audience. Despite the theory that the virtue of the jury is its unbiased and neutral character, in practice a skilled lawyer tries to choose jurors who, by outward appearances, are likely to be sympathetic toward the client.

Morgentaler and Sheppard had agreed that they wanted a French-speaking, working-class jury composed of the kind of people who had come to Morgentaler for abortions. Morgentaler was perfectly bilingual, and working-class Montrealers, they believed, would share his conviction that inexpensive, easily available abortions are the realistic and practical solution to the problem of unwanted pregnancies. The defence also hoped to select a jury that included women, on the hunch that they were more likely to sympathize with Morgentaler's efforts. Unfortunately for Morgentaler, the Crown attorney, Louis-Guy Robichaud, had the same hunch and peremptorily challenged every potential woman juror of child-bearing age. [12]

Initially the Crown also opposed Morgentaler's request to be tried in French before a French-speaking jury, but abandoned this position when it became obvious that it would cause a scandal in French-speaking Montreal. [13] In the end, Morgentaler faced a jury of eleven men and one woman. They were middle-aged, French-speaking, and predominantly Catholic. Would they fairly judge an immigrant Polish Jew, a highly educated and now wealthy doctor charged with performing abortions? There was still a latent strain of religious intolerance in Catholic working-class Quebec. Two decades earlier in the Jehovah's Witnesses trials, French juries routinely convicted while English juries acquitted. [14] Sceptics privately questioned Sheppard's strategy.

Morgentaler's public campaign of civil disobedience assured a packed courtroom. Partisans of both the pro-choice and pro-life camps were there in force. Many did not bother to conceal their mutual contempt, and the courtroom bristled with tension. The press was also abundantly represented, adding to the sense of political drama. As the trial began on October 18, 1973, everyone seemed to sense that it was not just Henry Morgentaler who was on trial but Canada's abortion law as well.

Presiding over the unfolding legal drama was James K. Hugessen, Associate Chief Justice of the Quebec Superior Court. While the assignment of Hugessen to the case was random, it was fortunate for Morgentaler. Though hardly a radical – he came from a wealthy, long-established Quebec family and his father was a senator – Hugessen had a reputation for intelligence, fairness and open-mindedness. He was also relatively young – only forty-two at the time of the trial. There was never any hint of favouritism for the accused or his cause, but at the same time there was never any sign of bias against Morgentaler. It is unlikely that such impartiality would have been displayed by all of the members of the Quebec Superior Court in the fall of 1973. Hugessen's strong sense of fairness and open-mindedness were to prove to be important factors in the success of Claude Sheppard's creative and unorthodox defence.

Louis-Guy Robichaud's assignment to the Morgentaler case as Crown attorney was initially by chance, the luck of the draw. However, Robichaud's personal involvement with the case seemed to increase with the growing political profile of the trial. Frustrated by Sheppard's unending delaying tactics, incensed by Morgentaler's brazen flouting of the law, and aware of the importance attached to the case by his political superiors, Louis-Guy Robichaud seemed to develop a personal vendetta against both Morgentaler and Sheppard. The dislike was mutual. Morgentaler began to refer to the Crown prosecutor as "Robichien." As a result, Robichaud's conduct of the prosecution at times became emotional and vindictive. His animated prosecution further heightened the courtroom drama, but it may have clouded his judgment to the detriment of his case.

The Crown's case seemed open and shut. There was never any question about the primary facts, since Morgentaler freely admitted performing the abortion of which he was accused. From the Crown's perspective, the basic legal issue was the question of non-compliance with section 251 of the Criminal Code – the fact that the abortion was not approved by a therapeutic abortion committee and not performed in an approved hospital.

Robichaud, however, allowed the prosecution to stray from the narrow issue of Morgentaler's non-compliance with section 251. He seemed determined also to discredit Morgentaler as a doctor and to prove the positive virtue of the existing abortion law. Both tactics backfired. The credibility of a star witness for the prosecution, Dr. Jacques DesRosiers, was destroyed when, on cross-examination, Sheppard forced him to admit that he had himself referred eight patients – including his own nurse – to the Morgentaler clinic. DesRosier's hypocrisy discredited the entire prosecution.

Robichaud also called a series of outspoken "pro-life" advocates to the witness stand, but their sweeping and dogmatic denunciations of abortion under any circumstances seemed out of touch with even the compromise policy envisioned by section 251. Particularly counterproductive was the testimony by Dr. Irene Ryan, a fiery anti-abortion crusader from New York. Like most Americans, she knew almost nothing about Canada and even less about Quebec. She quickly lost the sympathy of the all-Francophone jury.[15]

In contrast to the poorly managed prosecution, Sheppard masterfully orchestrated the defence. While tactically complex, Sheppard's defence strategy basically had only two stages. The first was to win the sympathy of jurors by focusing on the human side of the case before them. (He was aided in this to the extent that Robichaud and his witnesses alienated the jury.) The second and more difficult step was to persuade the judge and the jury that the law actually provided a justification for Morgentaler's otherwise illegal conduct.

Rather than flogging the jurors with abstract legal and medical issues, Sheppard drew their attention to the human tragedy before them. The woman on whom Morgentaler was charged with having performed the illegal abortion was Verona Parkinson, a twenty-six year-old black student from Sierra Leone. Sheppard portrayed her situation as desperate: single, poor, alone in a foreign country with an unwanted pregnancy. Fearing the reaction of both her family and her roommate and not wanting to give up her studies, she contacted several Montreal hospitals. To her dismay, she was told that an abortion would require three days' hospitalization at $140 a day – which she did not have – and that she could not be scheduled for three weeks. During this same time, she began to experience recurrent nausea and insomnia. Desperate to terminate her pregnancy before it progressed too far, Parkinson called the telephone number provided by an unnamed nurse. It was the Morgentaler clinic. To her relief, she was told that they could schedule her the following week, on August 15.

Against this background of personal tragedy and despair, Sheppard was successfully able to portray Morgentaler as a latter-day Good Samaritan rather than the criminal back-street abortionist described by the Crown. In Sheppard's version of the facts, the law was unreasonable, not Morgentaler. This was only half the battle, however, since it was still obvious that Morgentaler, by his own admission, had violated the law, however laudable his intentions. To acquit Morgentaler, Sheppard needed to find some doctrine or precedent that could make apparently illegal conduct legal – a tall order! But in keeping with his reputation as a courtroom genius, Sheppard proceeded to propose not one but two such legal justifications for Morgentaler's conduct: the "defence of necessity" and the "section 45" defence.

The defence of necessity is a long-recognized although rarely used legal defence that excuses otherwise criminal conduct if it is performed to avoid a more serious evil or crime. For example, a prisoner may legally escape from a burning jail to avoid certain death. While jail-breaking is itself a crime, it would be excused in these circumstances. Similarly, a driver who breaks the speed limit while rushing a heart-attack victim to the hospital could call on the defence of necessity. In both examples the conduct of the accused is technically illegal, but hardly morally blameworthy given the unusual circumstances.

The defence of necessity is one of the ingenious devices through which the British common law introduces flexibility and humanity into criminal law. It is a concession to contingency, intended to ensure that the letter of the law will be tempered by the spirit of the law and founded on an appreciation of the peculiar circumstances of the alleged crime. No case better illustrates the practical problem of reconciling what is legal with what is just than the celebrated case of *R. v. Dudley and Stephens*.[16]

Dudley and Stephens were British sailors who, along with Brooks, also a sailor, and Parker, a seventeen-year-old boy, were ship-wrecked 1,500 miles off the Cape of Good Hope in 1884. Adrift in a small boat, their food and water ran out after only four days. On the twentieth day, on the edge of starvation, Dudley and Stephens slit Parker's throat and ate his flesh in order to survive. They had chosen Parker, without his consent, because he was the youngest and had no family, and appeared to be the closest to death. Brooks refused to consent to or participate in the killing, but later fed on the blood and flesh of the boy. Four days later the three survivors were rescued and returned to England. There, Dudley and Stephens were arrested and charged with murder.[17]

At trial it was established that the two accused would have died before being rescued if they had not fed on the flesh and blood of the boy, that the boy would have died before them, and that on the day of the act there was no reasonable prospect of being rescued. The lawyer for Dudley and Stephens argued that under these circumstances, killing Parker was legally justified as a matter of necessity. This defence was rejected by Chief Justice Coleridge, who declared that to allow necessity as an excuse for killing an innocent person would result in the

> absolute divorce of law from morality. . . . A man has no right to declare temptation to be an excuse, though he might himself have yielded to it, nor allow compassion for the criminal to change or weaken in any manner the legal definition.

On December 9, 1884, Judge Coleridge found the accused guilty of murder and sentenced them to death. Less than a week later, the Queen, on the advice of the government, invoked the Crown prerogative of extending mercy and commuted the sentence to six months.

The case of *R. v. Dudley and Stephens* left an ambiguous legacy of judicial strictness offset by executive leniency. In what was to become an important precedent for Henry Morgentaler, this tension was resolved in favour of increased judicial prerogative in the 1938 case of *R. v. Bourne*. [18] Bourne was an early crusader for abortion law reform in Great Britain. In the case in question, he publicly acknowledged having performed an abortion on a fourteen-year-old girl who became pregnant after being raped by a group of soldiers. The abortion clearly violated the criminal law then in effect, which limited legal abortions to those performed to save the life of the mother. Bourne, however, invoked the defence of necessity, claiming that to allow the pregnancy to continue would have ruined the physical and mental health of the young girl.

Bourne found a sympathetic audience in the trial judge. Judge McNaghten told the jury that the abortion law "must be construed in a reasonable sense" to include cases when the continuation of the pregnancy would make the mother "a physical or mental wreck." Judge McNaghten accepted the testimony of Bourne and others that the continuation of the pregnancy could have done permanent damage to the young girl's pelvic bones and possibly left her an emotional wreck. While he cautioned the jurors that the defence of necessity could not justify all abortions, his final instructions left little doubt that in this case it did.

> You are the judges of the facts and it is for you to say what weight should be given to the testimony of the witnesses; but no doubt you will think it is only common sense that a girl who for nine months has to carry in her body the reminder of the dreadful scene and then go through the pangs of childbirth must suffer great mental anguish.

The jury duly acquitted Dr. Bourne, thereby significantly relaxing the abortion law in Britain. The Bourne case set the stage for abortion law reform in both Britain and Canada in the 1960s, and it also provided Sheppard with a very useful model.

Sheppard and Morgentaler skilfully shaped the facts of their own case to fit the contours of the defence of necessity. Under questioning by Sheppard, Morgentaler testified that on the morning Verona

Parkinson came to his clinic, he found her in a state of severe psycho-logical distress. He said that he feared if he did not perform the abortion Parkinson might "give up hope and go to a quack, that she would per-form the abortion herself, that she would commit suicide in a moment of despair. Therefore," he concluded, "it was absolutely necessary, in order to protect her life and her health, for me to perform this abor-tion."[19] All that remained for Sheppard was to explain to the jury that having committed a lesser evil (violating the bureaucratic details of section 251) to avoid a greater evil (the threat of death or permanent harm to Verona Parkinson), Henry Morgentaler was protected by the defence of necessity.

Sheppard's section 45 defence was different in detail but rested on the same facts. Section 45 of the Criminal Code, known as "the Good Samaritan defence," protects persons (not necessarily only doctors) who perform some form of emergency surgery in order to save the life or limb of an injured person.[20] The type of case envisioned by section 45 is illustrated by the person who performs an emergency tracheo-tomy on a choking person in a restaurant or emergency roadside sur-gery at the scene of an automobile accident in a remote area. Under nor-mal circumstances, non-consensual surgery could be prosecuted as criminal assault. Section 45 prevents this, provided that the surgery is reasonable given the circumstances and that it is performed with "rea-sonable care and skill."

Sheppard carefully poured the facts of Verona Parkinson's abortion into the section 45 mould. Witnesses were called to testify as to the high degree of medical care and skill of both Morgentaler and his clinic. Morgentaler himself testified that failure to perform the abortion when he did might have resulted in serious harm to the health or even the life of Verona Parkinson. The patient's own testimony, Sheppard emphasized, supported Morgentaler's. Like the roadside surgeon, Sheppard told the jury, Dr. Morgentaler was protected under section 45; he should not be punished for performing surgery that the patient both wanted and needed.

Crown attorney Robichaud protested vigorously that neither the defence of necessity nor section 45 was admissable, given the facts of the case. The availability of legal abortions at other Montreal hospitals, he argued, deprived Morgentaler of the element of emergency or necessity that was an essential ingredient of both defences. But Justice Hugessen found that both defences were at least plausible, and deemed the sufficiency of the emergency or necessity to be a question of fact,

54

thus leaving it to the decision of the jury. Toward the end of the trial, when the judge once again rejected his motion to exclude the section 45 defence, an angry and exasperated Robichaud called the ruling "absurd." The judge frowned, and Sheppard reportedly whispered to Morgentaler, "That's done it, he's finished himself."[21] By the time the trial ended, Morgentaler had come to share his attorney's optimism. In his diary for November 10, 1973, he wrote: "I expect an acquittal. . . . I do not expect a verdict of guilty. I think it's almost impossible under the circumstances."[22]

Justice Hugessen instructed the jury on Monday, November 12, 1973. He reviewed the charge and briefly summarized the necessary elements of both the defence of necessity and the section 45 defence. The jury deliberated twenty-four hours. Late on the afternoon of November 13, they returned to deliver their decision. A hushed courtroom waited for the jury foreman to announce the verdict: *"Non coupable!"* (Not guilty.)

Relief, then euphoria swept over Morgentaler and his numerous supporters. Bitter disappointment flashed across the tight-lipped faces of the pro-life contingent. Outside the courtroom, several women rushed up to Dr. Morgentaler and began kissing and hugging him, shouting, "A victory for women! A victory for women!" This prompted Crown prosecutor Robichaud to shout back, *"Une victoire pour la piastre!"* (A victory for the buck!) The angry Robichaud went on to describe the decision as *"une absurdité juridique . . .* a victory for the judge, not for the defence. He has legalized abortion on demand." The Crown, he said angrily, would appeal the decision.[23]

The next day a triumphant Morgentaler responded in an interview with a *Globe and Mail* reporter.

I've done about four or five [abortions] so far today. . . . Even if I lose the appeal the point will have been made. Public opinion will pressure the government to establish clinics so that women who want them can have abortions safely and with dignity instead of going to butchers. . . . It's been an open secret for years to the Montreal and Canadian medical communities that I practice abortion. I actually wanted a test case. . . . It's not just helping these people that interested me, but helping getting the law changed across Canada."[24]

Morgentaler's acquittal had a double significance. Most obviously, he was once again a free man, at least on this charge. For his family and close friends, this is what mattered. But for Morgentaler, his own acquittal was only a means to a more important goal: to make the restrictive provisions of Canada's abortion law unenforceable. The Crown had put Henry Morgentaler on trial. But in so doing, the government allowed him to put Canada's abortion law on trial. The law would be meaningless if every doctor who now performed abortions could claim the protection of section 45 or the defence of necessity.

The victory was remarkable in still another respect. It cut against the grain of a Canadian political tradition that attached a high value to "peace, order and good government" and had dealt harshly with civil disobedience in the past. Perhaps it was not by accident that it was a French, working-class jury that acquitted Henry Morgentaler. If there was one segment of Canadian society where the British constitutional tradition of "ordered liberty" was likely to have the shallowest roots, it was the east end of Montreal. Perhaps this was Sheppard's insight, drawn from years of experience defending other rebels against the status quo in Quebec.

Sheppard and Morgentaler were not as likely to find such an *indépendantiste* spirit at their next stop, the Quebec Court of Appeal. There were, of course, many Francophone members on the Court of Appeal, but they were drawn from a more elevated stratum of Québécois society that had long since made its peace with the British constitutionalism that animated English Canada.

CHAPTER 6

Trial by Judges

The euphoria of the November 13, 1973, acquittal was short-lived. On the morning of February 11, 1974, Morgentaler received an unexpected visit from the Quebec Department of Revenue. Two investigators informed Morgentaler that he owed more than $355,000 in unpaid back taxes. Armed with a search warrant, they searched the clinic, seizing accounting records, personal correspondence, and even Morgentaler's diary. Subsequently his bank account and other real assets in Quebec were frozen, and the city of Montreal even threatened to auction certain properties. Morgentaler publicly proclaimed his innocence and accused the Quebec government of deliberate persecution. [1]

That same month the Quebec Court of Appeal heard the Crown's appeal from the November 13 acquittal. The appeal is an integral and important part of the criminal justice process. First and foremost, it represents an important safeguard of individual liberty. If the appeal court finds that the trial judge has made an error of law, accidental or otherwise, it can reverse the conviction and order a new trial. To ensure this safeguard, Canadian law, like its British and American counterparts, guarantees the accused the right to at least one appeal hearing. What is unusual about Canadian criminal law is that it also gives the Crown the right to appeal jury acquittals – precisely what happened in the Morgentaler case. In the United States, the constitutional right against being tried twice for the same crime means that a jury acquittal is almost sacrosanct. Morgentaler's jury acquittal, in the U.S., would have meant the end of the case.[2] Not so in Canada.

Appeal hearings are not a spectator sport. They lack the colour and drama of trials: no witnesses, no jury, no courtroom antics by opposing lawyers. The purpose of an appeal hearing is limited to reviewing the decision of the trial court for alleged errors of law. The losing party at trial cannot appeal on the basis of an alleged factual error, and appeal courts are not permitted to overturn findings of fact. The appeal hearing is conducted on the basis of a complete, word-for-word transcript of the entire trial. (In the Morgentaler case, the "appeal book," as it is called, filled thirteen volumes and 1,588 pages) Prior to the appeal hearing, lawyers for both sides submit written arguments, called factums, presenting opposing positions on the disputed questions of law. At the hearing, the lawyer for each side presents an oral summary of his argument. The appeal judges can and do interrupt with questions, and in a complex or politically controversial case, oral argument can drone on for hours and even days. The typical appeal hearing is a dry and abstract affair, usually of little interest to either the public or the press.

The Morgentaler hearing before the Quebec Court of Appeal was no exception. There were no crowds of supporters and few reporters, just judges, lawyers, court officials, and two very interested "spectators" from the provincial Department of Revenue. Sheppard and Robichaud renewed their legal combat before the somber panel of five appeal judges.

Robichaud based the Crown appeal on the submission that the trial judge had made a fundamental error in law by failing to limit the defence for performing an abortion to the exculpatory provisions of section 251 of the Criminal Code. He argued that there was no evidence to support either the defence of necessity or the section 45 defence, and so neither should have been permissible. Justice Hugessen had misinterpreted the law on both points, Robichaud argued, and therefore had misinstructed the jury. He urged the Court of Appeal to reverse the acquittal.

Sheppard vehemently challenged Robichaud's arguments, maintaining that Justice Hugessen's rulings were completely correct. He seemed to sense, however, that his arguments were not having the same impact that they had at trial. Like most good trial lawyers, Sheppard was less comfortable in the somber, legalistic setting of an appeal court. "Technological law," he disdainfully called it, contrasted with the human and real-life ambience of the trial court.[3]

On April 26, 1974, Sheppard's sense of foreboding was realized. A unanimous Court of Appeal ruled that Judge Hugessen had indeed misinstructed the jury. While their reasons differed slightly, none of the five appeal court judges accepted the section 45 defence. Several stressed traditional rules of statutory interpretation in ruling that the only permissible statutory defence for performing an abortion is proof that it was performed in an accredited hospital after approval by a therapeutic abortion committee – that is, according to the new provisions of the 1969 reform. Traditional rules of statutory interpretation hold that more specific statutory language takes precedence over more general wording, and that a more recent provision overrides an older one. The exculpatory provisions of section 251 were both more specific and more recent than section 45. It would have been unnecessary and illogical for Parliament to enact the 1969 reform if section 45 already provided a general defence. It would be even more illogical for Parliament to have stipulated a set of narrowly defined conditions under which abortions could be legally performed and at the same time to have allowed abortionists to circumvent the new law by way of the much broader defence set out in section 45. The judges said they could not attribute such illogical or confused intentions to Parliament. Section 251 pre-empted section 45, so the latter was simply not a permissible defence for abortion under normal circumstances.

The question of the normalcy of the circumstances in Verona Parkinson's abortion was the focus of the judges' discussion of the defence of necessity. For this defence to be valid, the Court said, it is "not sufficient that the act be preferable or desirable, but necessary." The two essential ingredients of a successful use of the defence are "need" and "impossibility." Need refers to the seriousness of the threatening evil that the accused sought to avoid: the evil avoided must be worse than the evil committed. Impossibility denotes the imminent threat of the evil – usually an "emergency" – which precludes compliance with the law. While all the judges acknowledged at least the potential of serious harm to Verona Parkinson's health or life (i.e., some degree of "need"), none found any factual support for the element of "impossibility."

To the contrary, all five judges found that Morgentaler had made no effort whatsoever to comply with section 251. Verona Parkinson's initial telephone conversations with the Morgentaler clinic, during which she was told to bring $200, indicated Morgentaler's intention to perform an abortion without bothering to determine if there was indeed an "emergency." Morgentaler's examination of Parkinson on August 15 was criticized as cursory and showing no interest in complying with the law. Morgentaler testified that his examination indicated that Parkinson was six to eight weeks pregnant. Earlier he had testified that the twelfth week of pregnancy marked the limit of low-risk abortions. This left four to six weeks, by Morgentaler's own standards, for a safe and legal abortion at a certified hospital. Why, one of the judges asked, didn't Morgentaler avail himself of this time to avoid breaking the law? In fact, the record showed that Parkinson had a scheduled appointment at another Montreal hospital on August 28, only thirteen days after she came to the Morgentaler clinic.

Still more condemning was the fact that Morgentaler had performed five other abortions the morning of August 15 and thousands in the preceding several years. Was it plausible for Morgentaler to claim that there had been six emergencies the morning of August 15? When placed in the larger context of Morgentaler's repeated violations of section 251, the Court concluded that there was no emergency for Verona Parkinson on August 15, no evidence of "necessity," and therefore no possible defence.

In most cases like this, the appeal court simply orders a second trial based on its "correct" interpretation of the previously disputed legal question. This remedy was authorized by subsection 4(b)(ii) of section 613 of the Criminal Code and was a common occurrence. The Quebec Court of Appeal, however, went much further and entered a verdict of guilty. The judges based their decision on the obscure and seldom-used subsection 4(b)(i) of section 613 that authorized an appeal court to "enter a verdict of guilty with respect to the offence of which, in its opinion, the accused should have been found guilty, but for the error in law...."[4] The appeal judges reasoned that, stripped of the protection of the defence of necessity or the section 45 defence, Morgentaler could only be found guilty by a properly instructed jury. Accordingly, they declared him guilty and returned the case to the trial court for sentencing.

While the Quebec Court of Appeal had the legal authority to make this ruling, the decision was a political error. By departing from the normal remedy of simply ordering a new trial, the Court appeared to many to be unfairly singling out Morgentaler for special treatment. The highly unorthodox ruling lent credence to Morgentaler's claim that he was being persecuted by the Quebec government, and it cast suspicion on the impartiality of the judges. The Court of Appeal's reputation was further damaged when critics of the decision suggested that it was not by accident that Chief Justice Lucien Tremblay had excluded the Court's only two Protestant judges from the five-judge panel that heard the Morgentaler appeal.[5] Perhaps most importantly, the Quebec Court of Appeal's decision propelled the Morgentaler story back onto the front page of the nation's newspapers, toward the martyrdom he seemed to be seeking.

Morgentaler immediately appealed his conviction by the Quebec Court of Appeal. While there was no general right of appeal to the Supreme Court of Canada, Morgentaler's case fell into one of the two narrow exceptions – cases in which an appeal court overturns a jury acquittal.[6] But the wheels of justice turn slowly and it would be six months before the Supreme Court would hear his case. In the interim, Morgentaler was confronted with some bleak prospects. At first there was some confusion over sentencing and bail. Justice Hugessen was reluctant to sentence Morgentaler while his appeal to the Supreme Court was still pending. Presumably, he thought that it was incongruous for a man acquitted by a unanimous jury to be serving time in prison while his case was still before the courts. Jean-Guy Robichaud had no such doubts and petitioned the Court of Appeal to *order* Justice Hugessen to sentence Morgentaler. Not only did the Court of Appeal comply, it also ordered Morgentaler to be "detained" until bail could be set. On May 14, 1974, his son's birthday, Morgentaler entered Montreal's run-down Parthenais Detention Centre. Ten days passed before an exasperated Sheppard was able to arrange bail.[7] To comply with his bail conditions, Morgentaler had to agree to cease performing abortions. On May 30, he announced the closing of his clinic, his primary source of income.

A pre-sentence hearing was finally set for June 11, 1974. A long list of character witnesses appeared on Morgentaler's behalf. They testified as to the inadequacy of the current abortion law, the help that the accused's clinic had been to them and their patients, and the quality and care of Morgentaler's operations. Judges have considerable discretion in imposing sentences, and normally such positive character witnesses would help to obtain a lighter sentence. The potential for judicial leniency was probably negated, however, by Morgentaler's own long and defiant statement. Rather than repenting or trying to excuse his own lawlessness, Morgentaler accused his accusers:

> I am about to be sentenced for having helped Verona Parkinson to obtain a safe abortion in my clinic on August 15, 1973, after a jury of

my peers declared on November 13, 1973 that it was no crime at all, and declared me to be innocent.

I did help Verona Parkinson as I helped a few thousand women in distress to obtain medically safe abortions using the most modern methods of medicine in an atmosphere of caring and compassion and with concern for the preservation of dignity of all patients treated. . . .

Yet for this most natural and decent act, to help a person in distress, to offer help to a fellow human being when needed, I am now being threatened with life imprisonment. There is something awfully wrong here.

The abortion laws are unjust, unnecessarily restrictive and thereby cruel and dangerous to women, whom they expose to dangers of death and injury when denied access to safe abortions. I challenge this law as immoral and discredited and as an affront to the people of Canada. I believe it is my duty as a doctor to offer help to women desperately needing abortions in order to protect their very life and health. I believe that in the obvious conflict here, between the moral duty of a doctor to help protect the life and health of a patient and the law which states that he may not do so, justice and morality will prevail. I cannot believe that an immoral law will be upheld for long, and I still believe very strongly that what I did was not only morally right, but legal as well. If my view of the law turns out finally to have been incorrect, I will have to assume my responsibilities accordingly.

What is happening here today may be according to law as it now stands, but it is not justice. What I am asking for is justice – not only for me, but for the women in Canada.[8]

On July 25, 1974, Justice Hugessen announced his sentence. In explaining the sentence, the judge acknowledged many of the positive attributes of Henry Morgentaler – his good intentions, sincerity, the high quality of his medical care, moderate fees, and the courage of his convictions. But these virtues were then weighed against the negative side of the doctor's ledger, and the balance, concluded Justice Hugessen, indicated against leniency.

If the accused had truly wanted only to test the law or to demonstrate what he considers to be its absurdities, it would have been quite possible for him to do so without entering into the abortion business on a wholesale scale in the way that he has. By his massive and public flouting of the law, the accused has, in effect, forced the authorities to prosecute with more vigor and the courts to punish with more severity than would have been the case if he had simply initiated one test case for the pursuit of the ideals which he claims. . . .

The accused says he does not respect the present law. This is certainly his right, and perhaps his duty, in a democratic society, whose essence it is to allow every citizen to speak and fight his utmost against laws which he considers wrong or unjust. The law does not require respect; it demands obedience. It is one thing to say that a law is wrong, and bad, and should be done away with as soon as possible. It is quite another to openly break and defy that law, and thereby set at risk the entire fabric upon which our society is founded. The first course is that of the democrat, the second, that of the anarchist. . . .

Dr. Morgentaler, the sentence of the court is that you be incarcerated for a period of eighteen months in the common jail. Upon your release from prison you will be subject to the terms of a probation order for a period of three years, as a condition of which you shall refrain from using any means whatsoever to procure the miscarriage of a female person unless it be in an accredited or approved hospital.[9]

While eighteen months was light in view of the potential maximum sentence of life imprisonment, it seemed severe compared to sentences given to several other abortion "quacks" in recent years. Morgentaler was shocked by the sentence, as were the coterie of family and friends present. Apparently encouraged by the sentence, a triumphant Robichaud asked that Morgentaler be jailed immediately. Justice Hugessen curtly rejected the request.[10] There was little comfort in this for Henry Morgentaler. His clinic now closed, his real and personal assets frozen, his legal bills escalating, there was little left for him to do save await an uncertain outcome of his scheduled hearing before the Supreme Court of Canada.

CHAPTER 7

Fall from Power –
The Price of Conscience

In the West, things were not going so well for Joe Borowski either. Like Henry Morgentaler, Borowski was also learning the price of living according to conscience. Yesterday's folk hero had become today's fanatic. In 1973 he was defeated in his bid to retain his seat in the Manitoba legislature; earlier, he had resigned from the Schreyer cabinet. A year later he, too, would be headed for jail with Revenue Canada snapping at his heels. Like Morgentaler, Borowski's fall from political grace was the consequence of his very strong – but very different – convictions about abortion.

After Borowski's appointment to the Schreyer cabinet in 1969, his star initially continued to rise. The Premier was so pleased with his work as Minister of Transport that he appointed him Minister of Public Works as well. Together the two portfolios carried the largest budget in the cabinet. The reasons for Borowski's success were no secret: uncompromising honesty and a willingness to work fifteen-hour days. No public agencies are more rife with potential for corruption and kickbacks than highways and public works. As Borowski proudly told reporters at the time, he had received numerous offers of "a piece of the action" in return for advance information on highway construction, but he turned them all down. Even his harshest critics conceded that Borowski was "the most honest man in politics today."[1] At the end of

1969, the *Winnipeg Tribune* described Borowski as "a compelling and possibly powerful political force in this province."[2] In Borowski, the article continued, "the NDP government has itself a genuine instinctive hero figure, a creature the party has been without since the salad days of the late 1940s when Tommy Douglas led them out of the wilderness."

Such rectitude is popular with constituents, but it doesn't always sit well with other politicians, especially those in your own party with less altruistic agendas. While Borowski had an instinctive dislike of all politicians, he had come to office with a very idealized view of the New Democratic Party, "the party of the people." This illusion was soon shattered. "I used to think all these men who sat in the House were godlike creatures, orators," Borowski told a reporter in 1970. "And now I get into the Legislature and find jackasses and drunks."[3] NDP colleagues who came to Borowski for special favours for their constituents were usually shown the door.

Borowski's honesty was reinforced by a highly moralistic, albeit simplistic, approach to politics. As a local reporter noted at the time, "Joe has a clear-cut idea of how the world is divided, into little guys and bad guys. And he has it in for the bad guys – rich people, powerful people, large corporations and Conservatives – especially Conservatives."[4] This unbending sense of right and wrong had carried Borowski to power as the anti-politician of the sixties. In the 1970s it proved to be his undoing.

In 1970 his stubbornness almost brought down the entire NDP government. A critical vote on the NDP's new auto insurance bill was scheduled for the afternoon of August 5, 1970. The outcome was expected to be close, a matter of one or two votes either way. That morning the Minister of Transport was questioned by opposition MLAs about problems of corruption in his department. Borowski responded by turning the tables, blaming the Tory ministers who preceded him and suggesting that perhaps they should be suspended from the legislature pending further investigation. When furious Conservative MLAs demanded proof or a retraction, Borowski provided neither, adding that "if the Opposition doesn't like [my answer], the Opposition can go to hell."[5] Opposition leaders responded that Borowski either apologize or be expelled for breach of House rules. First the Premier, then the Attorney-General, and finally the entire caucus pleaded with Borowski to retract and apologize. Without his vote, the insurance bill might be defeated and the government would fall. Borowski refused and was expelled.

Outside, he angrily told reporters that it "was the bloody truth. I have a right to say it. If I can't tell the truth in the House, then I don't want to sit in that goddamn House."[6] This kind of behaviour still played well with the public – outside the legislature that day, someone had scrawled "Good work Joe" in lipstick on the windshield of a government car – but it was wearing down the patience of fellow NDP caucus members. Although he did not know it at the time, Joe Borowski's days in the House were numbered.

In six short months in 1971, Borowski's political career came to a crashing end. It began innocently. "I got involved [in the abortion issue] really by accident," he recalls.[7] In May, 1971, he received a telephone call from a local doctor, complaining that Borowski and the NDP were a bunch of "damn hypocrites" for paying for illegal abortions in the U.S. While Borowski thought abortion was morally wrong, he had never been involved with it as a political issue. But he sure didn't like being called a "damn hypocrite," so he decided to investigate. What he found was that the Mount Carmel Clinic in Winnipeg, jointly funded by government and the United Way, was arranging for abortions in American clinics for women who could not get them in Manitoba.[8] He took the matter to cabinet but ran up against a brick wall. It was a federal law, his colleagues smugly told him, and thus a federal problem.

Incensed by his colleagues' lack of concern, Borowski began to take matters into his own hands. In May, a "women's liberation" group came to the legislature on a Saturday morning to discuss broadening access to abortion with the Minister of Health. Borowski locked them out. Later he lamely explained that he did not know they had an appointment and thought they were a group of protesters. As Minister of Public Works, he thought he was defending the security of the legislative building.[9] No one believed him, and he was forced to apologize. His apology, however, got him into even deeper trouble. He accepted responsibility for the lockout and apologized, but then went on to say that he had not insulted the group because "it's impossible to insult any abortion group. . . . The sinister minority of which you are a part is made up of the same ultraliberals who say everything is relative and permissiveness is the new religion."[10]

Several months later Borowski sent a memo to all staff members in his ministry urging them not to contribute to the United Way because it gave money to the Mount Carmel Clinic. "We are being asked to be accomplices in this medieval act of barbarism," read the memo, by "forcing our doctors and nurses to commit murder ... so a handful of cheap, third-rate tramps (and also some good women) can escape the consequences of their actions."[11] The memo quickly turned up in the local press, provoking howls of protest. Surprisingly, Premier Schreyer still did not fire Borowski. They met, and Schreyer asked him to refrain from any further public crusades on abortion or any other of his sacred cows (which included pornography, adultery, and drugs). He gave Borowski a second chance. As it turned out, Borowski did not want it. On September 8, 1971, Borowski sent a letter resigning from the cabinet "on principle." What was the point in being in the cabinet if you could not speak out on what you thought was right and wrong? Schreyer accepted the resignation.[12]

Borowski continued to sit as an independent member of the legislature, but his effectiveness was gone. An MLA without a party is like a sailor without a ship. Borowski introduced a private member's bill that would have restricted abortion funding, but it was defeated. As the provincial elections of 1973 approached, Borowski decided not to seek re-election. Much of the local press had now turned on him, and both he and Jean were sick of the anger, the hatred, and the ugliness that had increasingly come into their lives. However, when he let his intentions be known, he was immediately prevailed upon by his new constituency – the local Winnipeg pro-life movement – to try to stay in the legislature. While he refused to stand for election in his old northern riding of Churchill, Borowski reluctantly agreed to run against an NDP candidate he personally disliked. The riding, however, was Point Douglas, just north of Portage Avenue, an NDP stronghold. "The joke was that the NDP could run a pig in North Winnipeg and still win," recalls Borowski.[13] On July 26, the inevitable occurred. Only three years after being described as "the most popular politician in Manitoba," Joe Borowski was soundly defeated. His career as an elected representative was over.

In retrospect, the immediate cause of Borowski's fall from power was his own moralistic and uncompromising approach to politics. This may work well for an "outsider." But the "anti-politician" as a cabinet minister was a paradox that could not last. On a larger scale, however, Borowski was also a victim of the changing nature of the Canadian

Left. Borowski himself sensed this. As he looked back and tried to explain why he resigned from the NDP cabinet, he reflected:

> The moral aspects of it really hurt me, because all my life I had been working and we talked as working people about better wages, better holidays, and safe working conditions – the things that unions fight for – that was really the sole purpose for existing. And the NDP was the political arm of the union and suddenly I find that we are not so much concerned with all these economic issues. We are now talking about things like abortion, prostitution, pornography, legalizing drugs – when I was in the trade union we never discussed that – and I don't remember working people saying, "These are the things we've got to bring about in this country."[14]

Did Borowski leave the NDP or did the NDP leave him? He thought the latter, and he was not alone. Thousands of other Canadians found their traditional political allegiances being challenged by the emerging abortion issue. Abortion seemed to cut across the old political cleavages of income, education, and class. Initially at least, support for the pro-choice side of the conflict tended to come from the better educated, more affluent, professional segments of society, hardly the traditional wellsprings of political reform. Conversely, working-class, immigrant Canadians, politically radical but socially very traditional, provided much of the initial pro-life support. Indeed, Morgentaler and Borowski themselves mirrored the shifting sociological bases of Canadian abortion politics. Rather than just being swept along by this sociological upheaval, however, they stepped forward to lead it. Soon both men became inseparable, indeed synonymous, with the opposing sides of the abortion debate.

Borowski's political defeat left him down but not out. He had been beaten before and come back. Never a quitter, he was determined to continue his battle. Even before leaving the Manitoba legislature, Borowski had spearheaded the formation of a new pro-life group, Alliance Against Abortion. Borowski started it in his living room in 1973 with seven friends who put up $1,000 each. According to Borowski, the group consisted of local community leaders who were "strongly committed [on abortion] but didn't want a public profile."[15] Allegedly it included an appeals court judge. The group "elected" Borowski as chair, and he served as their public spokesman. There were no meetings unless the chair called one. If they ran out of money, each member would ante up again.

Eventually the Alliance went public and received donations from thousands of supporters. But these were not tax-deductible donations, nor did they give the donors any right to vote on what the Alliance did. Borowski did not want to have to chair endless meetings canvassing the opinions of the membership. His union days had taught him that democracy and effectiveness rarely coincide. Nor did he want to be tied down by the "educational activities" restrictions that applied to tax-exempt charities. As far as he was concerned, there were plenty of other pro-life groups that were already trying to "educate the public" on the facts of abortion. Borowski wanted to work directly to stop abortions. Alliance Against Abortion was a group designed for "action not talk," with Borowski as its leader-martyr.

The martyrdom was supposed to be achieved through his one-man campaign of civil disobedience against the public funding of abortions by withholding his federal income taxes. He had successfully mobilized public opinion through tax protests before entering politics. Why shouldn't it work again? In 1975, a defiant Joe Borowski joined Henry Morgentaler as part of Canada's prison population.

CHAPTER 8

The Quiet Court in the Unquiet Country

During its first 100 years, the Supreme Court of Canada laboured more or less unnoticed in the wings of Canadian politics. Unlike its American counterpart, it rarely appeared on the centre stage of national politics. The low political profile of the Supreme Court had several causes. From its creation in 1875 until 1949, it worked in the shadows of the Judicial Committee of the Privy Council (JCPC), the final court of appeal for all questions of Canadian law. The Canadian Supreme Court was thus supreme in name only. It lacked the responsibility, influence, and prestige that normally accrue to a nation's final court of appeal.

The abolition of appeals to the JCPC in 1949 put an end to this vestige of British colonialism, but it did not solve the Court's problems. It continued to be viewed somewhat sceptically by provincial leaders, who were suspicious of the impartiality of a court whose judges were appointed by the federal cabinet without any provincial input. In the post-war era of "co-operative federalism," both provincial and federal leaders preferred to settle their disputes through political negotiation rather than constitutional litigation. The legalistic, inflexible, all-or-nothing procedures of the courts were seen as ill-suited to the requirements of governments' expanding public policy roles. First ministers' conferences, not the Supreme Court, became the preferred forum for settling federal-provincial differences. Economists, not lawyers, were the new managers of fiscal federalism. The Supreme Court's traditional and most important political function – that of the "neutral umpire" of the rules of Canadian federalism – appeared to be in permanent decline, eclipsed by the technocracy of the new welfare state.

Last but not least, the Supreme Court of Canada had not had the responsibility, and thus the power, of protecting constitutionally entrenched rights and liberties. The tradition of an "unwritten constitution," part of Canada's British parliamentary heritage, rejected the American approach of a written Bill of Rights enforced by judicial review. By contrast, the American Supreme Court's popularity and power were greatest in precisely this field. Through its leading role in eradicating the practice of racial segregation in the American South during the fifties and sixties, the "Warren Court" (named after its influential Chief Justice, Earl Warren) had achieved considerable moral authority. The Warren Court subsequently drew on this authority to extend its judicial activism into other areas, expanding the legal rights of criminal suspects and defendants, protecting freedom of speech and press, and more strictly enforcing the separation of church and state. The American Supreme Court's accomplishments won applause and admiration both at home and abroad. [1]

Partly in response to this American experience, Canada adopted its own Bill of Rights in 1960. Also known as the "Diefenbaker Bill of Rights" (it had long been a pet project of the Tory leader), it incorporated most of the legal rights and fundamental freedoms found in its American counterpart, with one important exception. The Canadian Bill of Rights was enacted as a federal statute and not as a constitutional amendment. This meant that it lacked the "higher law" status of a constitutionally entrenched bill of rights, and, partly as a result, was unclear about the Supreme Court's role as enforcer. If a statute conflicted with a provision of the Bill of Rights, should the Court declare it to be null and without effect (like the American Supreme Court)? Or would this be a violation of the tradition of parliamentary supremacy? The text of the Bill of Rights was ambiguous on this point, and for a decade the Canadian Supreme Court wrestled indecisively with this issue.

By the mid-seventies, a series of contradictory and confusing decisions indicated that the tradition of parliamentary supremacy, with its corollary of subordinate courts, had carried the day. As a result of its own sense of self-restraint and deference to Parliament, the Supreme Court had denied itself the opportunity to play a more influential role in Canadian politics through an activist interpretation of the 1960 Bill of

Rights. Canada's highest court seemed determined to follow the less intrusive role that characterized English courts rather than the more influential but controversial path of its American cousin. As the Quebec separatism issue heated up, one commentator dryly described Canada's Supreme Court as "the quiet court in an unquiet country."[2]

The morning of October 4, 1974, was *not* a typical day at the Supreme Court of Canada. Long before the doors opened, spectators began lining up to be assured of seating for the ten o'clock hearing. The Ottawa press corps were there in force. Television camera crews scurried about the lobby of the Supreme Court building seeking interviews with some of the high-powered lawyers and interest-group leaders assembled for the occasion: Henry Morgentaler's long-awaited hearing before the Supreme Court. When the appellant finally did arrive, the ensuing flurry and excitement might have led tourists to think that they were witnessing the arrival of the Prime Minister on Parliament Hill.

This sudden convergence of media attention on the Supreme Court, while unusual, was not unmerited. Morgentaler's much publicized five-year campaign of civil disobedience seemed to have reached its culmination. Before the highest court in the country, the Crown would once again try Henry Morgentaler for violating the abortion provisions of the Criminal Code. Simultaneously, Morgentaler would put on trial Canada's abortion law. The hearing was really two cases in one. It was further politicized by the Quebec Court of Appeal's controversial decision overturning Morgentaler's jury acquittal and declaring him guilty. To his supporters, the unprecedented use of this judicial power smacked of persecution. Even non-supporters were disturbed by the implications for the centuries-old right to be tried by a jury of one's peers.

In addition, the abortion controversy had become a more public and divisive issue in Canadian politics. It was no longer confined to the annual business meetings of the Canadian bar and medical associations. Canadian feminists, now more organized and powerful, fiercely embraced the abortion issue as their own and Morgentaler as their martyr-hero. Likewise, pro-life forces had learned from their defeat in 1969 and were better prepared.

Departing from its usual practice, the Supreme Court had granted intervener status to groups on both sides. Four different groups represented the pro-life position: Alliance for Life, La Fondation Pour la Vie, L'Association des Médecins du Quebec pour le Respect de la Vie, and Le Front Commun pour le Respect de la Vie. The pro-choice perspective was advanced by the Canadian Civil Liberties Association and the Foundation for Women in Crisis. The latter two groups were represented by two of English Canada's best known criminal lawyers – Edward Greenspan and Clayton Ruby, respectively.

Intervener status allowed these groups to present both oral and written legal arguments in support of their respective positions. This was only the second time in its history that the Supreme Court had allowed private "third party" intervention in a criminal case.[3] Their presence implied the existence of policy consequences beyond the narrow issue of the guilt or innocence of the appellant, thus underscoring the political dimension of the case.

It was appropriate that such a unique and controversial case would be heard by a Court led by an equally unique and controversial Chief Justice: Bora Laskin. In December of 1973, Prime Minister Trudeau had created a minor scandal by appointing Laskin as the new Chief Justice of Canada. For decades the appointment of the Chief Justice had been governed by the double convention of seniority and dualism. Dualism dictated alternating the appointment of the Chief Justice between Anglophones and Francophones. Seniority meant that the chief justiceship would be awarded to the judge, alternately French or English, with the most years of service on the Court. The purpose of the seniority principle was to depoliticize the selection process. Professional expertise and experience, not partisan political considerations, were supposed to govern the selection of the Chief Justice.

When Chief Justice Fauteux retired in December, 1973, convention dictated that the next Chief Justice should be the Anglophone member of the Court with the most seniority: Justice Ronald Martland. Instead, the predictably unpredictable Trudeau ignored convention and appointed Laskin, who had been on the Supreme Court only four years. Martland, who had served on the Court since 1958, and other more senior members of the Court were clearly offended by Trudeau's choice, and for several weeks there were persistent rumours that one or even several of the justices might resign in protest.

While the iconoclastic Prime Minister was not obliged to explain his choice of Laskin over Martland, his reasons were not difficult to divine. There were two major categories of political issues facing the Supreme Court in the early seventies: federalism and the 1960 Bill of Rights. Trudeau's position on both issues was no secret. He was simultaneously a centralist and a civil libertarian. Martland, an Albertan, had a judicial track record that was sympathetic to provincial rights and hostile toward the Bill of Rights. By contrast, Laskin had built an illustrious legal career as a strong defender of the section 91 powers of the national government. In the area of civil liberties, Laskin had distinguished himself as an activist by writing several stinging dissents, criticizing his colleagues for refusing to interpret the Bill of Rights more broadly.

Laskin's Bill of Rights decisions reflected his broader judicial philosophy. Unlike most of his colleagues, he did not believe there was an absolute wall of separation between law and politics, the work of judges and the work of legislators. In this respect Laskin departed from the British tradition in Canadian law and held a more American view of the role of judges. Before his appointment as Chief Justice, he had openly admired the American Supreme Court's greater willingness to consider explicitly the practical consequences of its decisions on public policy. "I do not shrink," he wrote, "from describing a court in the Anglo-American-Canadian tradition as a unit of government."[4]

In sum, Laskin shared much of Trudeau's political and constitutional vision, while Martland clearly did not. Not surprisingly, Laskin and Trudeau had also developed a personal friendship. The prescient Trudeau, looking toward the future, ignored tradition and convention and chose a Chief Justice who might serve as an ally in future constitutional battles.

For Henry Morgentaler, Laskin's appointment had to be viewed as positive. Laskin was a judicial non-conformist, a legal icebreaker. He was the first Jew ever appointed to the Supreme Court of Canada. First as a law professor and then as a judge, he had shown interest in and sympathy for minority rights. He had publicly criticized his fellow judges for being too wedded to legal precedent, too timid in assuming responsibility for the practical consequences of their decisions. The unusual step of allowing pro-choice and pro-life interest groups to intervene was almost certainly Laskin's initiative. In a sea of appellate-court conservatism, Bora Laskin stood out as a beacon of liberal activism, representing precisely the kind of jurisprudence that would be necessary for Morgentaler to win his appeal.

The "Laskin factor" further enriched the already potent chemistry of the Morgentaler hearing: a morally controversial and politically explosive issue; an equally controversial appellant; civil disobedience versus the rule of law; appeal court versus jury; unprecedented interest group participation; and as much media as a party leadership convention. For the first time in its 100-year history, the Supreme Court suddenly found itself at the centre of the nation's political life.

The legal-political drama boiled down to two questions. First, would the Supreme Court overturn the Quebec Court of Appeal decision and either free Morgentaler or order a new trial? Second, might the Court go still further and, following the lead of the American Supreme Court, actually declare the abortion law invalid under the 1960 Bill of Rights?

The narrower issue of the guilt or innocence of Henry Morgentaler turned on the same legal issues that had been argued at trial and on his first appeal: Was either the defence of necessity or the section 45 defence available to the accused? In addition, there was the new issue of whether the Quebec Court of Appeal erred in substituting a conviction where the jury had acquitted? For the third time in twelve months, Sheppard carefully laid out his now well-rehearsed arguments for the defence of necessity and the section 45 defence.

The broader issue of the validity of section 251 was new. The American Supreme Court's dramatic 1973 abortion decision had made a vivid impression on Morgentaler and other pro-choice activists in Canada. It had sparked Morgentaler's renewed campaign of civil disobedience in the spring of 1973. Why, Morgentaler and his lawyers had asked themselves, shouldn't the Supreme Court of Canada be given the opportunity to do the same? Charles Flam, Sheppard's assistant, relied on the Canadian Bill of Rights to advance nine different challenges to the validity of section 251 of the Criminal Code.[5] Like the American Bill of Rights, Flam urged the judges, the Canadian Bill of Rights contains an implicit "right to privacy" broad enough to include a woman's decision to terminate an unwanted pregnancy. He also argued that the differing availability of abortion services in the different regions of Canada violated the right to "equality before the law." The factum for the Canadian Civil Liberties Association supported this argument with a study that showed abortion services were much less available in certain rural areas of Canada than in the urban centres. "Unequal access," argued CCLA counsel Edward Greenspan, meant an unequal and thus invalid law.[6]

The drama started before oral argument even began. In the judges' chambers just prior to the hearing, Sheppard approached the Chief

Justice and brought to his attention a comment made by Justice Louis-Philippe de Grandpré prior to his appointment to the Court. Sheppard alleged that de Grandpré, while president of the Canadian Bar Association, had given a speech equating abortion with murder and thus implying that abortionists were murderers.[7] Sheppard suggested that these comments indicated an unacceptable bias against his client and asked that de Grandpré not be included in the panel of judges hearing the appeal.

Greenspan described what followed as one of the most tense moments he has ever witnessed in his many years as a trial lawyer. Laskin was silent for several moments, then calmly said "that judges could not be held accountable for what they said about issues before their appointment to the bench or in their role as law professors."[8] If they could, he noted wryly, he would have to eliminate himself from almost every federalism case that came before the Court. As far as he was concerned, Laskin told Sheppard, de Grandpré had cast off any prior prejudice he might have had against Morgentaler when he took the oath of office to render justice impartially.[9] With that, he suggested that they begin the hearing.

Greenspan was impressed with both Sheppard and Laskin: Sheppard for his courage to raise such an explosive issue; Laskin for the thoughtful and dignified manner in which he handled a challenge to the integrity of his Court.[10] Sheppard, however, was not at all satisfied. Inwardly, he was "surprised, to say the least," at Laskin's suggestion that the judicial oath had somehow cleansed de Grandpré's legal judgment from the influence of any personal attitudes toward abortion.[11] Sheppard indicated to the Chief Justice that he had a duty to his client to raise the issue via a formal motion when the hearing commenced. Moments later, with a stunned audience looking over his shoulder, Sheppard formally recused Justice de Grandpré.

Recusation is a seldom used procedure that allows the removal of a judge who is deemed to be incapable of impartially hearing a case. It was a high-risk tactic, and it seemed to backfire. After a thirty-minute conference, the Court returned to announce that there was no reason for Justice de Grandpré to withdraw. "Recuse one, and you effectively recuse them all," observed one experienced lawyer. "They won't take it kindly."[12]

Sheppard's luck never improved. Once again, he found judges less receptive to his creative but unorthodox legal arguments than the original jury of twelve laymen. He was peppered with sharp, almost hostile questions from the bench. Morgentaler, who beforehand was optimistic, became disillusioned. He had hoped the Canadian Supreme Court would be inspired by the example of its American counterpart and declare the Canadian abortion law invalid. As it turned out, the Canadian High Court never even considered this a serious possibility. After hearing the Bill of Rights arguments from Flam, Greenspan, and Ruby, the Court recessed briefly, then returned to inform Robichaud and the remaining interveners that their oral presentation was no longer required. Section 251, they announced, did not violate any provision of the Bill of Rights. [13]

At the end of the first week, Morgentaler returned to Montreal, bored and pessimistic. Others evidently had a similar reaction. On the following Monday, the courtroom was almost empty as both sides made their closing arguments. The Court, as usual, reserved judgment and adjourned.

As the few remaining spectators and press straggled out of the cavernous Supreme Court lobby, the uniformed official behind the reception desk sighed with relief. "Now the Court will get back to normal." [14] While he could certainly be excused for thinking so at the time, he was wrong. In many respects, the Court never really did get back to "normal." Eighteen months later it would again find itself in the spotlight of national politics, deciding the fate of the Trudeau government's controversial 1976 Anti-Inflation Act. [15] In succeeding years it found itself caught in the middle of an increasingly hostile federal-provincial crossfire over such issues as energy development and taxation, communications, and bilingualism. The average number of constitutional cases jumped from two or three a year to ten. And in 1981, the entire nation watched as the Court literally determined Canada's political future in the *Constitution Patriation Case*. The following year saw the adoption of a constitutionally entrenched Charter of Rights, and neither Canada nor its courts have been the same since. With the advantage of hindsight, the 1974 Morgentaler hearing can be seen as the beginning of the "new" Supreme Court of Canada.

CHAPTER 9

From Legal Defeat to
Political Victory

Following the Supreme Court hearing the months passed slowly for Henry Morgentaler. His clinic was closed in October, 1974. His bail agreement forbade him from performing abortions. He had run up $200,000 in legal fees, and the Quebec Department of Revenue was still holding many of his assets while demanding $350,000 in back taxes. Hard-pressed financially and with little to do but wait, Morgentaler found himself slipping into boredom and depression. He had hoped for a quick decision, but January and then February passed with no indication of a decision. Suddenly in late March, the word came down that the Supreme Court was about to release its decision. If he remained in Quebec and the decision went against him, Morgentaler would be arrested immediately. On the advice of his friends, Morgentaler reluctantly flew to Toronto to await the Court's announcement.[1]

On March 26, 1975, the Supreme Court rejected Henry Morgentaler's appeal by a 6–3 vote. The Quebec Court of Appeal's decision overturning the jury's acquittal and entering a finding of guilty was left intact. His avenues of appeal exhausted, Morgentaler now faced the eighteen months imprisonment to which Justice Hugessen had already sentenced him.

The six-man majority included Justices Dickson, Pigeon, Martland, Ritchie, Beetz, and de Grandpré. The majority's reasons for rejecting the appeal were implicit in the *obiter dicta* of Justice Dickson's opening paragraph.

> It seems to me to be of importance, at the outset, to indicate what the Court is called upon to decide in this appeal and, equally important, what it has not been called upon to decide. It has not been called upon to decide, or even to enter, the loud and continuous public debate on abortion. . . .

These six judges were determined to draw a strict line between law and politics, between Henry Morgentaler's guilt or innocence and the wisdom or folly of Canada's abortion law. The latter problem was Parliament's, not the Court's. Their message was clear: if you don't like the abortion law, lobby Parliament, not the courts.

In keeping with this judicial philosophy, the majority opinions did not even discuss the Bill of Rights challenges. As for the defence of necessity and section 45 defence, they reached the same conclusion as the Quebec Court of Appeal. The general protection afforded by section 45 was pre-empted by the more specific language of section 251, and there was simply no credible evidence to support the defence of necessity. As for the Court of Appeal's decision to reverse the jury acquittal and to declare Morgentaler guilty, Justice Pigeon allowed that it was "a major departure from the principles of English criminal law." This consideration, however, could not overcome "the clear literal meaning" of section 613(4)(b)(i) of the Criminal Code, which permitted such a ruling. While admonishing that this "is obviously a power to be used with great circumspection," Pigeon concluded that:

> it is hard to conceive of a case in which it could be used, if not here. There cannot be any doubt concerning the commission of the offence by the accused. He has admitted the fact and denied his guilt only on the basis of some defences which the Court of Appeal rightly held unavailable, one because it was unfounded in law, the other because there was no evidence to support it. [2]

Predictably, Chief Justice Laskin carried the banner for the dissenting judges. Joined by Justices Spence and Judson, Laskin argued that the appeal should be allowed and the jury's acquittal restored. Both the defence of necessity and the section 45 defence were at least plausible, Laskin argued, and the issue of the sufficiency of evidence was clearly for the jury to decide and not an appeal court. The new Chief Justice was particularly outspoken in his criticism of the Quebec Court of

Appeal. Emphasizing that the Crown could not provide a single precedent of a like case, Laskin declared that "the jury's verdict is not one that can be lightly interfered with by an appellate Court."

> It must be an unusual case, indeed, in which an appellate Court, which has not seen the witnesses, has not observed their demeanor and has not heard their evidence adduced before a jury, should essay to pass on its sufficiency, either as to a defence or in support of a charge, and thereupon to substitute its opinion for that of the jury and to enter a conviction rather than ordering a new trial, where the jury has acquitted.[3]

Laskin's caustic tone reflected his strong disapproval of what he saw as a serious erosion of the integrity of the age-old right to be tried by a jury of one's peers. While his spirited defence of the right to trial by jury failed to persuade a majority of his judicial colleagues, it would ultimately carry a parliamentary majority.

As for the Bill of Rights challenges to Canada's abortion policy, Laskin again distinguished himself from the majority by at least explaining why the Court had rejected them. In declining Flam's invitation to follow the American Supreme Court's 1973 *Roe v. Wade* decision, Laskin explained that there were fundamental differences between the two courts and their mandates. The American Supreme Court was charged with interpreting a Bill of Rights that was part of that nation's written constitution. The tradition of constitutional supremacy was well established, and the clear mandate of the American Court was to strike down any congressional or state legislation that violated the Bill of Rights.

The situation was quite different in Canada. Laskin emphasized "how foreign to our constitutional traditions, to our constitutional law and to our conceptions of judicial review was any interference by a court with the substantive content of legislation." This difference, Laskin explained, stemmed from the fact that the Canadian Bill of Rights was not constitutionally entrenched.

> It cannot be forgotten that it is a statutory instrument, illustrative of Parliament's primacy within the limits of its assigned legislative authority, and this is a relative consideration in determining how far the language of the Canadian Bill of Rights should be taken in assessing the quality of federal enactments which are challenged under s. 1(a).[4]

Laskin's careful explanation of the Court's self-restrained and mini-malist approach did nothing to help Henry Morgentaler in 1975. But Laskin's *obiter dicta* subsequently took on the character of a funeral oration for the 1960 Bill of Rights. Laskin had succinctly articulated what a growing number of civil libertarians, feminists, and social activists viewed as the chronic flaw of the Canadian Bill of Rights: its statutory rather than constitutional status. Frustrated by their inability to use Bill of Rights litigation as a vehicle for social reform, these would-be reformers began to call for a new, constitutionally entrenched bill of rights. Inadvertently or not, Laskin's dissent pro-vided powerful support for this critique. The difference between the outcome of *Roe v. Wade* and *Morgentaler v. the Queen,* it seemed, sim-ply reflected the difference in status between the American and the Canadian bills of rights. Seven years later this movement contributed to the adoption of the new Canadian Charter of Rights and Freedoms – setting the stage for Henry Morgentaler's second challenge to the abor-tion law.

While Morgentaler's legal odyssey began as a one-man show, by the time he reached the Supreme Court it had taken on the characteristics of a nation-wide political campaign. Its principal sponsor and co-ordi-nator was the recently formed Canadian Abortion Rights Action League (CARAL). On March 26 when Morgentaler stepped off the plane in Toronto, he was met by E.B. Ratcliffe, Cambridge industrialist and CARAL president. The news of the Supreme Court decision had broken while Morgentaler was en route from Montreal, and so Ratcliffe had the unpleasant task of informing him that his appeal had been rejected.[5]

Morgentaler was shocked by the news, but had little time to recover. CARAL, anticipating a Morgentaler victory in the Supreme Court, had planned a Toronto press conference to get maximum media coverage for their issue and their champion. The Supreme Court's decision had shattered their expectations for a media-rich victory celebration, but they had no choice but to go through with it. Grim-faced, Morgentaler, Ratcliffe, and a coterie of friends and supporters faced the press at the Westbury Hotel. Together they went through all the motions – the abor-tion law was woefully inadequate, the politicians were hypocrites, the Supreme Court had undermined the sacred right of trial by jury – but without much enthusiasm. The despair of defeat hung heavy in the

Morgentaler turns himself in at Montreal police station to begin serving his eighteen-month sentence after Supreme Court of Canada rejected his appeal, March 28, 1975. (*Courtesy Canapress Photo Service*)

room, and even the press seemed uncharacteristically reticent. The next day Morgentaler returned to Montreal and, after a final press conference in Sheppard's office, turned himself over to the Montreal police.[6]

After several days in the Parthenais holding centre, Morgentaler was transferred to Bordeaux Prison. Appalled at the prospect of spending the next eighteen months of his life in this "awfully dismal and depressing place," he wrote to a friend:

> What hit me first was the fact that we had to give up all our clothing and get into proper garb. Rags not worthy to be called clothing. It was the first time that the analogy to the concentration camp experience hit me with impact. I swallowed hard and vowed not to let it get me down.
>
> ... the building is old and decrepit and reminds you of a fortress. The cell is about ... 8 by 12 feet and in it are: a bed with a foam rubber mattress thin enough to feel the metal lattice underneath, a noncovered toilet bowl, a sink with cold water only, and a chair. No table, no mirror.[7]

Morgentaler's campaign against Canada's abortion policy had reached a low point, but also a turning point. Negative reaction to the Supreme Court's decision was widespread. In Parliament, a diverse group of MPs – John Diefenbaker, Gordon Fairweather, Ed Broadbent, Stanley Knowles, and Stewart Leggatt – all rose to denounce the decision. Citing Chief Justice Laskin's spirited defence of the right to trial by jury, they challenged Justice Minister Otto Lang to pardon Morgentaler and to amend the Criminal Code to protect jury acquittals. Lang, a practising Catholic and an acknowledged opponent of abortion, tried at first to dismiss the calls for reform as unnecessary. "I'll bet . . . ten to one that the same thing won't occur again within the next five years," he bantered with reporters outside Parliament. "This case was an exception."[8]

But the protests continued, reportedly even within Cabinet, and by July, 1975, Lang was singing a different tune. On July 3 he announced a proposed amendment to section 613 of the Criminal Code that would prevent appeal courts from replacing a jury acquittal with a verdict of guilty.[9] Two weeks later the amendment appeared as clause 75 of an omnibus amendment to the Criminal Code.[10] Henceforth, if an appeal court found that a jury's acquittal was caused by an error in law, the appeal judges could order a retrial but never again convict the accused by themselves. While Lang was unusually reticent about the genesis of the amendment, his silence did not fool anyone. The press immediately dubbed it "the Morgentaler amendment," and it was adopted without opposition several months later.

Lang, who had emerged as the strongest pro-life spokesman in the Trudeau cabinet, was also forced to retreat on another front. In October, 1974, on his own authority, he had issued a confidential memorandum to Canadian hospitals stating that the 1969 compromise on abortion was being threatened by the spiralling number of abortions performed under the new law. He declared that to combat this problem the law was to be applied "strictly; that social and economic considerations were not to be taken into account in determining whether a pregnancy could be legally terminated."[11]

Lang's memorandum was interpreted by the medical community as an attempt to intimidate hospital administrators and doctors, and it backfired. CMA president Dr. Bette Stephenson complained directly to the Prime Minister. In an open letter, she demanded that the government clarify the definition of health in section 251. Trudeau responded by defending the existing wording as permitting desirable flexibility, permitting requests for abortion to be dealt with on a case-by-case basis. Dissatisfied, Stephenson publicly demanded that Lang either clarify government policy or resign. Under pressure from cabinet not to further inflame the abortion issue, Lang backed down. "Health," he now said, "is a broad word that certainly includes mental and other factors."[12] One repercussion of the Lang-CMA confrontation was the government announcement in September, 1975, of a special commission to investigate and report on the operation of Canada's abortion law. A second was Lang's replacement as Attorney-General in January, 1976, by Ronald Basford, a known pragmatist on the abortion issue. Pro-choice forces applauded both decisions.

Morgentaler's fortunes were also on the rise within Quebec. Apparently encouraged by the Supreme Court's decision, the Bourassa government had decided to press ahead with the other outstanding charges against Morgentaler. To many, the decision to prosecute the additional charges smacked of harassment, and it was suggested that Quebec Justice Minister Jérôme Choquette seemed particularly eager to "make an example" of Morgentaler.[13] It quickly became evident that the Crown was looking for a deal with a "defeated" Morgentaler. In exchange for Morgentaler's pleading guilty to the five new charges of illegally performing abortions, the Crown would consent to the additional sentences being served concurrently with the eighteen months he was already doing. To Sheppard, the experienced criminal lawyer, it was a simple matter of arithmetic – less time in jail – and he recommended that Morgentaler co-operate. But Sheppard had forgotten that his client was more a crusader than a criminal. Morgentaler flatly refused the plea-bargaining offer. "How can I plead guilty now," exclaimed an angry Morgentaler, "when I have always contended in the past that I was not guilty of any criminal act?"[14]

This time his stubbornness served him well. The Crown, overconfident in the wake of its victory in the Supreme Court, never expected Morgentaler to refuse its plea-bargaining offer and was not prepared to proceed. It tried to stall for time but without success. Once again Morgentaler pleaded not guilty and chose to be tried in French and by a jury. The sense of *déjà vu* was unmistakable.

The trial began on May 26, 1975. Stripped of the section 45 defence by the Supreme Court decision, Morgentaler's fate rested wholly on Sheppard's ability to persuade the jury that the defence of necessity justified his aborting of Mary D'Abramo, a poor and unmarried seventeen-year-old patient. The trial seemed to go well for Morgentaler until the final day. Then, to the horror of both Sheppard and his client, the judge instructed the jury to ignore completely the defence of necessity, explaining that it could not apply to the facts in this case. The only question before them, the judge pointedly told the jury, was whether the defendant had violated section 251 of the Criminal Code. As Morgentaler himself recalled, it was as if the judge had "ordered them to convict me."[15]

Less than an hour later, their despair turned to joy. The jury's verdict: *Non-coupable!* Not guilty! The visibly stunned judge gave Morgentaler permission to address the jury.[16]

> You have struck a blow for the freedom of Canadian women and for Canadian justice. I hope this verdict will have repercussions that will be heard in Quebec City and in Ottawa.

After shaking the hands of the jurors, a vindicated and triumphant Morgentaler returned to prison. Shortly after the verdict was delivered, a reporter encountered one of the jurors and asked him how he and his fellow jurors could have so completely ignored the instructions of the judge. He replied curtly, *"Le juge, c'est pas le pape."*[17] ("The judge is not the Pope.")

While protests and calls for his pardon multiplied, Morgentaler was hardly out of the woods – or jail – yet. The day after this second jury acquittal, Quebec Justice Minister Jérôme Choquette not only appealed the decision but laid ten additional charges of illegal abortions. At the same time the Quebec Justice Department asked the Civil Law Board to review the functioning of the jury system. Their mandate: what to do about juries that refuse to follow the instructions of the judge. The Quebec Department of Revenue continued to freeze Morgentaler's assets but refused to take their claims against him to court. In September, the National Parole Board rejected Morgentaler's application for parole. In November, the Quebec College of Medicine began disciplinary proceedings that eventually stripped him of his medical licence for one year. In sum, while Quebec public opinion seemed to be on Morgentaler's side, Quebec officialdom was not. Now his fate was once again in the hands of the Quebec Court of Appeal, one of the most elite clubs of the Quebec political establishment.

This time, however, the Court of Appeal stayed its hand. On January 20, 1976, it rejected the Crown's appeal, declaring that the prosecution had failed to establish a question of law alone. Taking a page out of

Bora Laskin's vigorous dissent, the Court of Appeal declared that the sufficiency of evidence for the defence of necessity was a question of fact and for the jury alone to decide. The trial judge, they said, had erred in excluding the defence of necessity in his instructions to the jury.

This decision was a 180-degree reversal of the Court of Appeal's first *Morgentaler* decision, a decision upheld by the Supreme Court of Canada only nine months earlier. The facts in the D'Abramo abortion were not materially different from those in the Parkinson abortion. The Quebec Court of Appeal could easily have relied on the authority of the majority opinions of Justices Dickson and Pigeon to discard the jury acquittal and to order a new trial. Why had they followed Bora Laskin's dissent? There really was no legal explanation, only a political one: that judges are sensitive to the political environment as well as to legal precedent. Also relevant was the fact that not one of the Appeal Court judges in this decision had participated in the first Morgentaler appeal, suggesting that, in the final analysis, the rule of law still depends on the rule of actual men and women.

The Quebec Court of Appeal decision served as a catalyst for even better news for Morgentaler. Two days later, on January 22, the new federal Minister of Justice, Ron Basford, announced that he was setting aside Morgentaler's first conviction and ordering a retrial. Sheppard had requested a retrial on legal grounds. Since only the section 45 defence had been ruled unacceptable by the Supreme Court, Sheppard reasoned, the defence of necessity was still technically available. Shouldn't his client be entitled to a new trial based on that defence?

Basford's decision was permitted by a seldom-used section of the Criminal Code that allows a Minister of Justice to order a new trial if the circumstances merit it. Calling it the "one last safeguard in the whole judicial process," Basford noted that Morgentaler's circumstances were indeed unique: he had been twice acquitted by juries yet was still in prison because of an unprecedented appeal court conviction. Basford also pointed out that the case had resulted in an important amendment to the Criminal Code, strengthening the right to trial by jury and preventing a reoccurrence of what had happened to Morgentaler. Basford concluded:

While it is contrary to Canadian tradition that *Criminal Code* amendments should be applied retroactively, it seems to me in simple justice, in the largest sense of that expression, that the situation of the one man whose conviction and incarceration has led Parliament to consider an amendment . . . constitutes exceptional circumstances.[18]

If Basford sounded magnanimous in public, privately he remained sceptical about the wisdom of a retrial. After their last meeting, Basford's parting words to Sheppard were, "I hope, Mr. Sheppard, that you know what you're doing."[19]

Four days later, Morgentaler was released from prison. And his luck continued. In February, the Quebec government appealed its loss in the Court of Appeal to the Supreme Court of Canada. The latter, chastised by the storm of criticism provoked by its first *Morgentaler* decision, refused even to hear the appeal. The Supreme Court, it appeared, was not impervious to public opinion. The retrial of the original indictment did not take place until September, and it was anti-climactic. For the third time in three years, the jury returned a verdict of not guilty.

The Bourassa government stubbornly refused to acknowledge any implicit message in the three jury acquittals and initiated proceedings for still another trial on eight more outstanding charges. How long these prosecutions could have continued will never be known, for on November 15, 1976, the Parti Québécois swept to power in an emotional political landslide. A month later the new PQ Minister of Justice, Marc-André Bédard, sent a letter to Ottawa informing his federal counterpart that section 251 of the Criminal Code had become unenforceable in Quebec. The PQ government, Bédard announced, would no longer prosecute violators.

The simultaneous success of the Parti Québécois and Henry Morgentaler was not an accident. Both had ridden the same new tide of changing public opinion in Quebec. While political autonomy for Quebec was its first and foremost issue, the PQ represented much more than separatism. A part of the PQ heritage was the sexual revolution of the sixties and its acceptance of much more casual sexual relations. Indeed, the abortion issue had come to symbolize many of the cultural differences between the Quebec Liberals and the supporters of the PQ: the older versus the younger; practising Catholics versus those who had wandered away from the Church; those who were satisfied with the status quo versus those who wanted to reform it. In the *Morgentaler* case, all of these conflicts were compressed into one: judges versus juries.

The famous British jurist Lord Patrick Devlin once described the jury as "a little parliament." The jury is an essential institution for a free people, Devlin explained, because it keeps the administration of justice in touch with the views of the people. The Morgentaler juries were a political bellwether, indicating how far the Quebec Liberals had drifted from the man and woman in the street.

Ottawa never replied to Bédard's letter, and the PQ dropped the outstanding charges against Morgentaler. The new government's tacit approval of Morgentaler's clinic encouraged others, and free-standing abortion clinics were allowed to operate outside the guidelines of section 251. By the end of the 1970s, Quebec, the most Catholic province in Canada, was the only province with a *de facto* policy of abortion on demand. While Quebec's non-enforcement policy was probably illegal, the Trudeau government was in no mood to make an issue of it.[20] To do so would once again divide the Liberal caucus and further exacerbate the quickly deteriorating relationship between Quebec and Ottawa.

CHAPTER 10

Borowski Wins the
Right To Be Heard

By 1978, it was clear to Joe Borowski that things were not working out the way he had planned. Neither Alliance Against Abortion nor his civil disobedience was having any noticeable effect on Canada's abortion policy. He had petitioned, picketed, marched and gone to jail, but the number of abortions performed each year kept rising. Henry Morgentaler had gone to jail once and emerged a martyr and a media celebrity. Borowski had been to jail three times and the media had labelled him a crackpot. Frustrated, Borowski felt the need for a new plan of attack.

He turned to the small group of pro-life lawyers who worked with him in Winnipeg. Was there any possibility of launching a lawsuit against the abortion law? They researched the legislative history of the 1969 abortion reform law and found a statement by then Minister of Justice John Turner that the proposed amendments to the Criminal Code would not require government funding of therapeutic abortions. Perhaps, they suggested, Borowski could use this evidence to petition the courts for an injunction against any further public funding of abortions. This hardly satisfied Borowski. He wanted to stop abortions, not the funding of abortions. Where, he pressed his lawyer friends, could he find a lawyer that could mount a successful challenge to the abortion law itself? Someone suggested Morris Shumiatcher, the well-known constitutional lawyer from Regina, but cautioned that he was probably too expensive. Expense, said Borowski, was not the issue. Was Shumiatcher one of the best? When the lawyers nodded in the affirmative, Borowski telephoned Regina the next day. By week's end he was sitting in Shumiatcher's office discussing the possibilities of litigation.

Linking up with Morris Shumiatcher was a double win for Borowski. Without Shumiatcher's imagination, expertise, and perseverance, Borowski's court challenge to the abortion law may never have gotten off the ground. It was Shumiatcher who designed the elaborate "right to life" constitutional challenge and shepherded it through twelve long years of litigation. No less important was Shumiatcher's symbolic value. Shumiatcher's presence on the Borowski team was like "a badge of intellectual credibility."[1] Unlike his client, the media could not lightly dismiss Morris Shumiatcher as a crank.

Born and raised in Calgary's small Jewish community in the 1920s, Morris Shumiatcher had risen through the ranks to become a living legend of the Canadian bar. His father was a well-known lawyer in Calgary, and he constantly urged his son to follow in his steps. Young Morris did what any spirited young man would do, and vowed never to become a lawyer. He enrolled in the University of Alberta in 1934 as an English major, hoping to pursue a career of teaching and writing. But by the time he graduated, his interest in the academic life was waning and he "wanted to be more a part of the world."[2] After some soul-searching, he entered the faculty of law at Alberta. From that moment on, his life has been a love affair with the law.[3]

Upon graduating from Alberta, he travelled east to the University of Toronto where he did both a master's and a doctorate of law. One of his teachers at Toronto was the young Bora Laskin, the future Chief Justice of the Supreme Court of Canada. Shumiatcher's doctoral thesis was on debtor relief legislation in the western provinces, the knowledge of which he quickly put to work. In 1943, at the age of twenty-five, he argued his first case before the Supreme Court of Canada, successfully defending Alberta's Debt Adjustment Act. At the age of twenty-nine, Shumiatcher became the youngest lawyer ever appointed King's Counsel in the entire Commonwealth.

Growing up in Calgary, the young Shumiatcher was an eye-witness to the human suffering and sorrow of the grim depression years on the Prairies. As a teenager his political imagination had been fired by the searing oratory of Tommy Douglas, one of the founders of the

Co-operative Commonwealth Federation (CCF), the predecessor to the New Democratic Party. Shumiatcher recalls himself in those years as a "starry-eyed young socialist."

Douglas led the fledgling CCF to victory in the Saskatchewan elections of 1944, forming the first socialist government ever elected in North America. Shumiatcher was just leaving the Air Force, and Douglas's Attorney-General, John W. Corman, invited him to come to Regina to help draft and defend the new socialist policy agenda.[4] Shumiatcher agreed on the condition that he would only stay for twelve months. Instead, Shumiatcher went on to become one of the Premier's most influential legal counsellors, serving as an executive assistant to Douglas for five years before going into private practice.

During those five years he helped to design, draft, and defend much of the innovative social welfare legislation that was the trademark of Douglas and the CCF. He was one of the principal authors of the 1947 Saskatchewan Bill of Rights. This document preceded the United Nations Charter of Human Rights by one year and was the first such bill of rights in Canada. Shumiatcher also successfully defended Saskatchewan's then radical Farm Security Act and Trade Union Act before both the Supreme Court of Canada and then the Judicial Committee of the Privy Council. By the 1980s, he was one of only a handful of practising lawyers ever to have argued a case before the JCPC.

Shumiatcher eventually parted company with Tommy Douglas and the Canadian Left. Indeed, he became a vocal critic of too much state intervention. He published a book entitled *Welfare: The Hidden Backlash,* in which he attacked what he considered the suffocating effects of the modern welfare state. He still likes to explain the conservative evolution of his political views by citing the old saw: "If you're not a socialist at twenty, there's something wrong with your heart. If you're still a socialist at forty, then there's something wrong with your head."[5]

Notwithstanding the more conservative bent of his mature views, Shumiatcher remained a non-conformist. When an interviewer asked why he was considered "controversial," he replied: "I find that more often than not, the popular view is not the proper or honest view. . . . I like to think of myself as a sort of gadfly on the flank of the nation."[6] Finally, perhaps like all criminal lawyers, Shumiatcher still had time for the underdog. For him, abortion was the ultimate underdog issue.

Shumiatcher's first public involvement with the abortion issue came in the 1960s, when the Canadian Bar Association began to lobby for a more permissive abortion law. Shumiatcher spoke in opposition to this effort. He drew an analogy between the thalidomide babies tragedy and abortion. Thalidomide was a new sedative that came on the market in the 1960s. It was banned in North America but available in Europe. Within a year, the drug was linked to terrible deformities in the babies of women who had used it while pregnant. The affected women went to court and successfully sued Imperial Chemical, the manufacturer, for millions of dollars in damages.

Shumiatcher challenged his colleagues. If they believed that the accidental maiming of an unborn child by the distribution of thalidomide was a civil wrong, then surely the intentional killing of an unborn child was a criminal wrong. While he failed to persuade a majority of the Canadian Bar Association, Shumiatcher himself became morally certain that there was no difference.

Shumiatcher's concern for the unborn also reflected personal experiences. He still remembers as a child being aware of his parents' conversations about women who had abortions, especially one who died. He and his childhood friends even thought they knew the house – a small, one-storey, red-brick structure on Fourth Avenue East in Calgary – where illegal abortions were performed. His most vivid memory of this early awareness of abortion was that "it frightened me."[7]

The experience of the Nazi Holocaust had also made a deep and lasting impression. Later in his life, Shumiatcher could not help connecting the Holocaust with the growing campaign for abortion. To Shumiatcher, the fundamental issues were the same: the sanctity of each human life versus the state-supported extermination of that life. Indeed, Shumiatcher privately professed his astonishment at how Henry Morgentaler could reconcile his first-hand experience in the Nazi death camps with his role as Canada's premier abortionist. He speculated that perhaps Morgentaler's experiences at Auschwitz made human life seem cheap and disposable.[8] (Morgentaler, it will be recalled, said that his concentration camp experiences reinforced his atheism, and also made him suspicious of state authority.[9])

Finally, there was the effect of his own marriage. Shumiatcher and his wife Jacqui – whom he adored and faithfully telephoned every day when out of town – never had children of their own. He frankly conceded this made children – including the unborn – seem even more precious, indeed a gift. It thus pained him deeply to see the abortion statistics rise year after year beginning in the early 1970s. Never one to hold his tongue, this "gadfly on the flank of the nation" began to speak out on the abortion issue and by 1978 had become a board member of the Canada-wide Coalition for Life.

Borowski's phone call to Shumiatcher came as a complete surprise. Despite his previous involvement in the pro-life movement, Shumiatcher had never met Borowski. He knew him by reputation only – the former labour leader and NDP cabinet minister, now a pro-life activist, tough, unorthodox, outspoken, a fighter. But lawyers, especially good lawyers, are accustomed to receiving telephone calls from strangers. Shumiatcher was sufficiently curious about both Borowski and his project to invite him to Regina to discuss it further.

The meeting was a success. Despite their manifest differences, each man instinctively liked the other. Their differences complemented one another. Borowski quickly saw that Shumiatcher could provide the legal expertise and intellectual respectability that would be necessary to win. Shumiatcher liked Borowski's sincerity, frankness, and single-minded determination. These traits, plus a healthy bank account, would be necessary assets in the complex and protracted lawsuit that was beginning to take shape in Shumiatcher's mind.

The idea of using a lawsuit to challenge the 1969 abortion law had occurred to Shumiatcher before. The 1960 Canadian Bill of Rights begins by affirming the "dignity and worth of the human person," and then explicitly declares "the right of the individual to life" and "the right not to be deprived thereof except by due process of law." Shumiatcher had often wondered whether this right could be used to protect the unborn from unnecessary abortions. His noon-day conversations with jogging partner Dr. Donovan Brown, a Regina physician, had brought to his attention recent developments in the field of neo-natology, the science of the newborn child.

Through the use of ultra-sound, *in utero* photography, and other new techniques, modern science was steadily expanding human knowledge of conception and fetal development. Shumiatcher had contemplated the possibility of using the new evidence provided by modern science to prove the humanity and personhood of the unborn child in a court of law. But where was the plaintiff to bring such a case? Who could get standing? Who could afford the costs associated with bringing in the many expert witnesses that would be required to establish the scientific facts of human life? Enter Joe Borowski and his Alliance Against Abortion.

From this first meeting grew one of the more unlikely alliances in Canadian politics. Shumiatcher and Borowski were a true "odd couple." Shumiatcher is physically small, almost dainty; Borowski is a lumbering hulk. Shumiatcher's tiny, delicate hands and finely featured face remind one of a surgeon or orchestra conductor. Shaking hands with Borowski is like being gripped in a vice, and his heavy Slavic face could have been chiselled with the backside of a shovel. Shumiatcher is a dapper dresser with custom-tailored suits from London and Montreal; he is well-mannered, learned, articulate. Borowski wears off-the-rack suits from Sears – usually the same one, a pale blue number. He has only a grade six education, and often it shows. They were, to say the least, an unlikely pair. Yet working together, they produced the lawsuit that became a focal point of the anti-abortion effort in Canada in the 1980s, the pro-life response to Henry Morgentaler.

On September 5, 1978, Shumiatcher initiated Borowski's challenge to the abortion law by filing a statement of claim in the Court of Queen's Bench in Regina. They had agreed to try the case in Shumiatcher's home town to reduce expenses. Their case had two prongs. First, it sought a declaration that the therapeutic abortion provisions of the Criminal Code were invalid because they violated the Canadian Bill of Rights. Second, it sought an injunction (a legal order) prohibiting the further expenditure of federal funds on abortions.

The government response also had two prongs, but only one of them was carried out in the courtroom. The legal response was that Shumiatcher and Borowski were in the wrong court. The Court of Queen's Bench, they claimed, had no jurisdiction to hear Borowski's case, and his case should be brought in the Trial Division of the Federal Court of Canada. This was clearly a delaying tactic. By 1978, the question of where the jurisdiction of the Federal Court began and the jurisdiction of the provincial superior courts (e.g., Queen's Bench) ended had become one of the murkiest issues in Canadian law. The wording of the statute was unclear and there was a welter of conflicting precedents. The federal lawyers hoped that by throwing the Borowski challenge into this maelstrom of legal (and political) confusion, they could tie the case up for years. With their superior resources, perhaps they could wear down Borowski's endurance and drain his budget.

The second prong extended this strategy, but more directly. On November 16, 1978, Revenue Canada seized Borowski's new car (for which he had just paid $7,000) and then sold it for $3,200 to pay his back taxes. Less than two weeks later, Revenue Canada seized the $32,000 dollars that Alliance Against Abortion had raised to help pay for Borowski's lawsuit, claiming the money was really Borowski's and should also be used to pay his back taxes.

While Borowski later joked about it with the press – "The rats could have taken my old car but they waited until we got a new one" – he lost his temper when the Revenue Canada collection officers came to his store to serve the writs of seizure. Borowski grabbed one by the arm and "escorted" him out the front door, explaining, "I don't want Trudeau's bootlickers in this place." Borowski's version of an "escort" left some incriminating bruises on the arms of the collection agent, who subsequently complained to the police. When the police refused to lay assault charges, the tax collector brought a private prosecution and several months later Borowski was convicted and sentenced to fifty hours of community service.[10] No sooner had Borowski finished his community service than Revenue Canada dragged him into court again, where he pleaded guilty to failing to file income tax returns for a third time and spent the next three and a half months in jail.

Technically, of course, there was no connection between Revenue Canada and the Attorney-General's office. From Borowski's perspective, however, it was no coincidence: "I think there's no question the seizure is related to our lawsuit. They haven't bothered me for the last three years. But now that we've raised the money for our lawsuit, they're coming around again."[11] For a change, Borowski won this round. Faced with a threat of burglary charges and more public criticism, Revenue Canada returned the seized funds to Alliance Against Abortion on December 5, 1979.

As it turned out, the legal challenge to the abortion law would take longer. The Federal Court was created by Parliament in 1971 to replace the old Exchequer Court.[12] Like its predecessor, it would hear claims against the government for money or compensation. In addition, it was intended to strengthen judicial review of administrative decisions made by the rapidly growing federal bureaucracy and to relieve the Supreme Court from hearing routine appeals from the old Exchequer Court and federal administrative tribunals.[13] From its inception, the Federal Court was plagued by jurisdictional disputes with provincial superior courts. The *Borowski* case was an example, and lent credence to the old saying:

I am the Parliamentary draftsman;
I compose the country's laws,
And of half the litigation
I am undoubtedly the cause.[14]

Section 17 of the Federal Court Act states that "the Trial Division has original jurisdiction in all cases where relief is claimed against the Crown and, except where otherwise provided, the Trial Division has exclusive original jurisdiction in all such cases." Was the Borowski case a claim for relief against the Crown? The Crown said it was. Shumiatcher responded that it was not a claim for relief in the "intended" sense of material damages or financial compensation. Rather, it was essentially a challenge to the constitutional validity of a federal statute, the kind of case that superior courts had been deciding since Confederation. Who was right? There were a number of contra-dictory rulings in similar cases.[15]

On April 1, 1980, Justice Hughes of the Saskatchewan Court of Queen's Bench rejected the Crown's argument and ruled in favour of Borowski.[16] But before Borowski had time to celebrate, the Crown appealed this decision to the Saskatchewan Court of Appeal. The Appeal Court did not hand down its decision until November, 1980. By a vote of 2–1, the Appeal Court ruled that the Court of Queen's Bench did have jurisdiction to consider the validity of the abortion law, but that it lacked authority to issue an injunction against the Minister of Health.[17] While less than their trial victory, this result was still good enough as far as Borowski and Shumiatcher were concerned, but again the Crown appealed, this time to the Supreme Court of Canada. It took more than a year for the Supreme Court just to hear the appeal, and it did not deliver a judgment until December, 1981, more than three years after the case was initiated.

The Crown's appeal to the Supreme Court was complicated by the addition of a new issue. Having lost twice on the jurisdictional issue, the Crown lawyers were evidently casting about for a new legal argu-ment and hit upon the issue of *locus standi* or "standing." Standing is the right of an individual to bring a legal controversy to court for adju-dication. To establish standing, a would-be litigant must prove the existence of a *lis,* or legal dispute, and must also be a party to that dis-pute. Stated negatively, a court will normally refuse to answer legal questions brought to it by a party who would not be personally affected by the court's answers. Standing is usually an issue only in civil cases, since in a criminal prosecution the accused will obviously be affected by the outcome of the case.

The question of standing in the *Borowski* case was problematic. Where was the dispute? Where was Borowski's "personal stake" in the validity of the abortion provisions of the Criminal Code? Unlike Henry Morgentaler, he was not a doctor charged with violating a criminal law and subject to fines and imprisonment. Nor was he a woman who had been denied (or received) an abortion. Nor did he claim to be the husband or the father of a woman seeking an abortion. The plain fact was that Joe Borowski was just an ordinary citizen who disliked this particular government policy. Was a citizen's disapproval of government policy sufficient to acquire standing to challenge the policy in court? The government of Canada now said no, and the existing precedents seemed to support this contention.

Like questions of jurisdiction and mootness, standing is what is known as a "threshold" issue, a legal question that a judge must answer first – just as one must first cross the threshold of a house in order to enter – before considering the substantive issues raised by the case. In the Borowski case, it was thus necessary to determine if the Court of Queen's Bench (rather than the Federal Court) had the legal authority to hear this kind of case (jurisdiction), and whether Borowski himself had the legal right to engage the court (standing), before addressing the validity of Canada's abortion law. Mootness is a corollary to the doctrine of standing. It requires that the original dispute giving rise to the case continue to exist. For example, if the accused in a criminal case dies while the case is on appeal, or the litigants in a civil suit settle out of court, a judge will normally refuse to answer the legal questions raised and terminate the judicial hearing. The issue of mootness was not relevant at this stage of the *Borowski* case, but it took on great significance when he came to the Supreme Court for the second time in 1988.

These restrictions on access to the courts – jurisdiction, standing and mootness – can be traced to the traditional "dispute-resolving" function of courts in the common-law tradition. According to this tradition, the purpose of courts is to solve disputes by applying – and where necessary, interpreting – existing law. If no dispute exists, or if a person is not an actual party to a dispute, then there is no case. These rules follow from the premise that the courts are not in the business of making unilateral pronouncements on abstract legal questions – that is, giving legal advice. This is especially true in constitutional law, since the effect of a constitutional ruling is usually to condone or condemn some government policy. Such judicial intrusion on legislative turf is deemed undesirable precisely because it is unnecessary.

Normally, the rules of standing and mootness are legal technicalities mainly of interest to lawyers. But in the area of constitutional law they take on added significance since they influence the frequency of judicial intervention in, and thus influence over, the decisions of the legislature and the executive. Alexis de Tocqueville captured the political significance of the rules of standing in his analysis of judicial review in mid-nineteenth-century American politics. "The American judge," Tocqueville wrote, "only pronounces on the law because he has to judge a case, and he cannot refuse.... The political question he has to decide is linked to the litigants' interests, and to refuse to deal with it would be a denial of justice."[18] Judicial adherence to these traditional, strict rules of standing made it quite difficult for interest groups to use constitutional litigation to challenge laws they opposed. They could only engage the courts if they could contrive for someone to be prosecuted or harmed by the law. Thus what initially appears to be a legal technicality turns out to have significant implications for the political role of courts.

Tocqueville was describing the much more restricted role of the courts 150 years ago. In contemporary American politics, the development of the courts as an independent force for political change was largely the result of expanded rules of standing and interest groups' creative use of systematic litigation strategies. The former has facilitated the latter by making it easier for interest groups to get into court. Justice Potter Stewart, a former justice of the American Supreme Court, is alleged to have said that the most important judgment he wrote was in *United States v. SCRAP* (1973), which opened the doors of the federal courts to groups who wanted to challenge government decisions that did not affect them directly.[19] In that case, the Court granted standing to a group of law students (Students Challenging Regulatory Agency Procedures or SCRAP) in Washington, D.C. to challenge a new federal surcharge on railroad freight. The students alleged the higher costs incurred by the surcharge would discourage recycling and thus increase pollution of the environment. Since they breathed the air that would become more polluted, they claimed to suffer sufficient injury to gain standing to sue. The Supreme Court agreed.

The result was the emergence of an "oracular court" in the United States.[20] Unlike the adjudicatory court described by Tocqueville, which limited its decisions to cases where there was a live case or controversy and a party with a tangible personal stake in the outcome, the oracular court tends to issue constitutional edicts upon request. The oracular court derives from the premise that the government is obliged to obey the constitution and the proposition that only the Supreme Court can and should say for certain what the constitution allows. The function of judicial review became detached from its adjudicatory roots and the American Court began to resemble a true oracle, a shrine dispensing wise and authoritative decisions "at large." Its transition to constitutional oracle made the American Supreme Court the most politically powerful court in the world. With a stroke of the judicial pen, it was capable of blocking legislative majorities. The result was to encourage attempts by interested parties to shape this new locus of power, mainly via judicial appointments.

In Canada there was little enthusiasm for either interest-group litigation or the oracular court. Consistent with the attachment of Canadian judges to the more English, adjudicatory view of the judicial function, the rules governing standing in Canadian constitutional law were much stricter than in the United States. Until recently, they had not really changed much since the nineteenth century. In 1972, a trial judge had dismissed a suit by Joseph Thorson, an unhappy retired judge, challenging the constitutionality of the then recently enacted Official Languages Act of 1969. This Act represented a major policy initiative of the Liberal government of Pierre Trudeau to extend official bilingualism by requiring all federal institutions and Crown corporations to provide services in both English and French. Thorson sought to have the expenditure of funds to administer the Act declared invalid on the grounds that the Act itself exceeded the constitutional limits of Parliament's authority to legislate with respect to language. The trial judge dismissed the suit on the grounds that Thorson lacked standing. The basis for his reasoning was the 1924 precedent of *Smith v. A.-G. Ontario*, which held that "an individual has no status or standing to challenge the constitutionality of an Act of Parliament in an action of this type unless he is specially affected or exceptionally prejudiced by it."[21]

The authority of the 1924 precedent was confirmed by the Ontario Court of Appeal, which also ruled that Thorson lacked standing. It thus came as a surprise when the Supreme Court of Canada, led by the newly appointed Chief Justice Bora Laskin, reversed the lower courts and granted Thorson standing. According to Laskin, while the *Smith* precedent was still valid, the courts retain discretion to hear constitutional challenges to federal legislation in special circumstances. Laskin proposed the novel doctrine that there is a general "right of the citizenry to constitutional behaviour by Parliament."[22] By this, Laskin meant a right to have such constitutional questions answered by the courts. If the normal rules of standing, per *Smith,* operated to prevent judicial review of federal statutes, and there was no other way that the statute in question could be challenged in court, then the courts could exercise discretion to grant standing. *Thorson,* argued Laskin, was such a case. Because the Official Languages Act was "declaratory and directory" in nature – that is, it "created no offences and imposed no penalties"[23] – there were no persons who were so directly aggrieved that they could qualify for standing under the traditional rules. In these circumstances, Laskin persuaded the rest of the Court, standing should be granted.

The Supreme Court moved quickly to further broaden the rules of standing the following year in the case of *Nova Scotia Board of Censors v. McNeil* (1976).[24] The provincial Board of Censors had refused to grant the necessary permit to theatre owners to allow the showing of the 1974 Marlon Brando film, *Last Tango in Paris.* Gerry McNeil, the editor of a weekly newspaper in Dartmouth and a resident-taxpayer in the province, was offended by what he regarded as undue censorship and restrictions on freedom of expression. McNeil asked the Nova Scotia government to overrule the Board's decision or at least to refer the relevant portions of the Theatres and Amusements Act to the courts for a ruling on their validity. When the government refused, McNeil initiated his own taxpayer's lawsuit challenging the constitutional validity of the Act.

Again the issue of standing arose. The government argued that McNeil was not directly affected by the Act and so could not challenge its validity. McNeil's lawyers pointed to the *Thorson* precedent and claimed he could. The government's response was that McNeil was not in analogous circumstances to Thorson, since the Theatres Act was regulatory and *did* directly affect the economic interests of identifiable persons: theatre owners. Theatre owners clearly had standing to challenge the Act, but McNeil did not.

The Supreme Court disagreed. Again under the leadership of Chief Justice Laskin, the Court further expanded the rules of standing. While Laskin conceded that the business enterprises it regulated were the immediate focus of the Theatres Act, it was still true that "members of

100

the Nova Scotia public are directly affected in what they may view in a Nova Scotia theatre."[25] Indeed, sheltering the public, not regulating theatre owners, was clearly the ultimate purpose of the statute. "In light of the fact that there appears to be no other way, practically speaking, to subject the challenged Act to judicial review," Laskin concluded, the court should exercise its discretion to grant McNeil standing.[26]

McNeil clearly went beyond *Thorson,* since it granted standing to a third party even though there was a class of persons – the theatre owners – who were directly affected and did have standing to challenge the Act. It set the stage for *Borowski,* which clearly went another step beyond *McNeil.* In *Borowski,* not only was the statute being challenged the Criminal Code, but it was the clearest example yet of an organized, national interest group trying to use litigation to shape public policy. The Borowski appeal thus took on a significance that went beyond the abortion issue, since it had implications for all interest groups that might want to use the courts to challenge public policy. The potential was further heightened by the imminent proclamation of the new Charter of Rights and Freedoms, which was scheduled to take effect in several months. Thus there was more than casual interest in the Supreme Court's ruling in the Borowski case when it was released on December 1, 1981.

The ruling caught everyone by surprise. There was a general consensus that if the Court were to use the Borowski case to loosen still further the rules of standing – and it was hardly clear that it would – this could happen only through the leadership of Chief Justice Laskin, Shumiatcher's former law professor at Toronto. Contrary to expectations, the Supreme Court extended standing to Joe Borowski by a vote of 7–2, with Laskin (joined by Lamer) dissenting. Why had Laskin, who up to this point had been the leader on expanding standing – and thus the scope of judicial review – suddenly reversed directions?

Laskin's dissent carefully laid out the traditional policy on standing. "As a general rule," Laskin began,

> it is not open to a person simply because he is a citizen and a taxpayer . . . to invoke the jurisdiction of a competent court to obtain a ruling on the . . . validity [of legislation], when that person either is not directly affected by the legislation or is not threatened by sanctions for an alleged violation of the legislation. Mere distaste has never been a ground upon which to seek the assistance of a court.[27]

"The rationale for this policy," Laskin continued, is based on the "dispute-resolving" function of courts. In an apparent reference to Borowski, Laskin added that "Courts do not normally . . . answer questions in the abstract merely to satisfy a person's curiosity or perhaps his or her obsessiveness with a perceived injustice in the existing law."[28]

As the author of the *Thorson* and *McNeil* precedents, Laskin could hardly ignore them. These decisions, he explained, represent legitimate exceptions to the general rule. In the former, there was no other way in which the validity of the Official Languages Act could be tested in court. In the latter, McNeil, as a member of the public, was still the ultimate if indirect target of the censorship function of Nova Scotia's Theatres Act. Borowski, Laskin argued, was not similar to either. Unlike McNeil, Borowski could not claim to be even indirectly affected by the abortion law. And unlike the *Thorson* case, there were other parties – women, doctors, hospitals, husbands – who were affected and could establish standing.[29]

The Chief Justice concluded with a very "un-Laskin-like" warning. If Borowski were granted standing, the courts would probably have to grant intervener status to groups who would argue the opposite side of the abortion issue "with the same obsessiveness" as the plaintiff. "The result," Laskin warned, "would be to set up a battle between parties who do not have a direct interest [and] to wage it in a judicial arena."[30] The Chief Justice, heretofore the great champion of an increased political role for the Supreme Court, was suddenly cautioning against the dangers of going too far!

The majority opinion was equally incongruous. It was written by Justice Ronald Martland, the most senior English-speaking judge, whom Trudeau had passed over in 1974 when he appointed Laskin as the new Chief Justice. (Coincidentally, Martland had also had Shumiatcher as a student in law school at the University of Alberta.) Martland was renowned mainly for his antipathy toward American-style judicial activism, yet here he was authoring a new Canadian ruling of standing that would "out-American" the Americans!

Martland, writing for the majority, agreed with Laskin that the Court should exercise its discretion to allow standing if there is no other way for a law's constitutional validity to be tested in court. Unlike Laskin, Martland ruled that Borowski's case clearly fell into this category. He rejected Laskin's contention that the law could be easily challenged by other persons. Because section 251(4) made permissible what would otherwise be criminal conduct, the persons directly affected by it – women seeking abortions, doctors and hospitals providing abortions – were hardly likely to challenge a law that benefited them.[31] Martland described Laskin's example of a husband who might want to prevent his wife from having an abortion as "illusory." Given the time factor involved, the woman would either have had the abortion or had the baby, and the case would be moot.[32] The most "direct impact," Martland added, was "upon the unborn human fetuses whose existence may be terminated by legalized abortions," but "they obviously cannot be parties to the proceeding in court."[33]

According to Martland, there was no significant difference between *Thorson* and *Borowski*. The "issue as to the scope of the Canadian Bill of Rights in the protection of the human right to life is a matter of considerable importance. There is no reasonable way in which that issue can be brought into court unless proceedings are launched by some interested citizen."[34] As for *McNeil,* Martland pointed out that other persons could have challenged the Censor Board's ruling but McNeil still was granted standing. Borowski's claim to standing, Martland asserted, was "at least as strong." He concluded by formulating what is still the broadest rule of standing in any common-law jurisdiction:

> I interpret these cases as deciding that to establish status as a plaintiff in a suit seeking a declaration that legislation is invalid, a person need only to show that he is affected by it directly or that he has a genuine interest as a citizen in the validity of the legislation and that there is no other reasonable and effective manner in which the issue may be brought before the court.[35]

The *Borowski* decision was an enigma. What prompted Laskin the activist and Martland the apostle of judicial self-restraint to suddenly trade roles? Was it legal considerations or more personal predilections? There was certainly circumstantial evidence to suggest that Laskin was not fond of Joe Borowski and perhaps his cause. At oral argument the preceding May, Laskin repeatedly interrupted Shumiatcher's presentation and peppered him with aggressive questions. Borowski, then in the twenty-eighth day of a hunger strike, became so frustrated that he stood up and objected. Laskin promptly ejected him from the courtroom.[36] There was the intangible effect of Laskin's long friendship with Pierre Trudeau, the Prime Minister who had sponsored the 1969 abortion reform and later appointed Laskin to the Supreme Court. Finally there are the not-so-oblique references to Borowski as "obsessive" in Laskin's written dissent.

As for Martland, several passages in his majority judgment could be construed as conveying sympathy with the pro-life side of the abortion issue. Martland describes the legal ability of a husband to prevent his wife from having an abortion as "illusory," implying this is unfortunate. He also notes that section 251 has a "direct impact" on the fetus because it threatens to "terminate" its "existence," and goes on to declare that "the protection of the human right to life is a matter of considerable importance."[37] There may have also been an element of personal rivalry with Laskin, the man who was appointed Chief Justice instead of Martland. If Laskin was going to allow liberals like McNeil to challenge conservative censorship laws, then why shouldn't conservatives like Borowski be allowed to challenge liberal abortion laws? Was Martland taking the opportunity to get in a last lick at Laskin (or even Trudeau), only months before he retired from the Court?

Enigma or not, the *Borowski* decision dramatically increased the potential for judicial policy-making by Canadian judges. It removed the traditional requirements for "standing" and created a broad right for citizens to go to the courts and demand that the judges force the government to "behave constitutionally." When combined with the 1982 Charter of Rights and Freedoms, it made it much easier for the "losers" in the legislative arena to challenge government policy in the courts.

Borowski was of course happy to win, but he was not impressed by the process. "It took me three years and cost $100,000," he complained, "before we were even given the right to challenge the law of this country. Now that is outrageous. You can talk about democracy, you can talk about judicial process and freedom, but what freedom is it if . . . in order to exercise it you have to have $100,000?"[38]

Borowski was also puzzled by Laskin's behaviour. "When I was in the labour movement," he later explained, "Laskin was our hero." When it came time for arbitration, "we would appoint our stooge; they would appoint their stooge; and then there was the arbiter." When it was Laskin, "we were always happy because he was no more neutral than our guy. . . . He was on the side of the working people. I was shocked to learn he was no longer our friend."[39] For Borowski, the unborn child was every bit as much an underdog as the working man or working woman, and he never did understand how a person could side with one but not the other.

CHAPTER 11

Framing the Charter

The election of René Lévesque and his Parti Québécois in 1976 rekindled Canada's perpetual concern with national unity. The PQ triumph cast the ominous shadow of Quebec separation over all subsequent national politics and set in motion a seemingly endless process of constitutional reform in search of consensus. The creation of the Charter between 1978 and 1982 was a central element of a larger reform effort to defuse the threat of Quebec separatism.[1]

The year after the PQ victory, the federal government established a Task Force on National Unity. Similar efforts were mounted by several provinces and the Canadian Bar Association. Over the next three years there was a veritable flood of proposals for constitutional reforms from both levels of government. Federal proposals stressed "patriation" of the constitution from Great Britain and a new amending formula; the extension of official bilingualism; and a new, constitutionally entrenched bill of rights. Provincial governments were more interested in a reallocation of legislative jurisdiction over culture, telecommunications, and natural resources to the provinces. Both levels of government were interested in reform of the Senate and the Supreme Court, but with very different ideas. The predictable outcome of such a complex and fragmented process was stalemate. Already staggering under a stagnant economy and soaring inflation, the Trudeau government was driven from office by Joe Clark and the Conservatives in the spring of 1979.

The catalyst for renewed action on constitutional reform came in 1980 with the electoral defeat of the short-lived Clark government in February and the defeat of the "sovereignty-association" option in the Quebec referendum in May. Pierre Trudeau returned from the political graveyard and found a new opportunity to pursue his dream of a united, bilingual Canada. This coincided with the referendum on Quebec independence promised by René Lévesque. Trudeau, himself a Quebecer and life-long opponent of Quebec separatism, was now able to campaign for the "non" side not as a private citizen but as the Prime Minister of Canada. This allowed him to promise a federal initiative for "renewed federalism" if the voters of Quebec would reject the "sovereignty-association" option. When the "non" side triumphed in May, it was Trudeau's turn to deliver on his vague promise of "renewed federalism."

The day after the referendum victory over the PQ, the House of Commons was in a "climate of near celebration."[2] Trudeau rose to announce that he intended to pursue immediately extensive constitutional reforms in response to Quebecers' "massive support for change within the federal framework." Trudeau then laid out his minimum conditions:

> First, that Canada continue to be a real federation, a state whose constitution establishes a federal Parliament with real powers applying to the country as a whole and provincial legislatures with powers just as real applying to the territory of each province. Second, that a charter of fundamental rights and freedoms be entrenched in the new constitution and that it extend to the collective aspect of these rights, such as language rights.[3]

All other issues, Trudeau advised, were negotiable.

The Quebec referendum brought not only a new sense of urgency but also a new confidence and assertiveness on the part of Trudeau and his inner cabinet. Fresh from two spectacular political triumphs, Trudeau was in no mood to tolerate what he regarded as the bad-faith obstructionism of the provincial premiers. In his first twelve years as Prime Minister, Trudeau had seen several promising opportunities for constitutional reform torpedoed by the convention requiring the unanimous consent of all ten provinces. Presented now with an unexpected second chance, Trudeau was in no mood to see history repeat itself. If the provinces would not be "reasonable," perhaps it was time for Ottawa to proceed on its own – unilaterally – to break what Trudeau saw as Canada's potentially fatal constitutional deadlock.

Three weeks after the referendum, Trudeau called a conference with provincial premiers to discuss "renewed federalism" and constitutional reform. They tentatively agreed to a constitutional agenda of federal-provincial distribution of powers, a restructuring of the Supreme Court and the Senate, a new amending formula that would patriate the constitution,[4] and a charter of rights. This package was the focus of intense negotiations throughout the summer of 1980, culminating in a first ministers' conference in September.

At the nationally televised opening session of the conference, Trudeau, looking past the ten provincial premiers and speaking directly into the television cameras at the end of the horseshoe-shaped table, made it clear that the Charter was going to be the centrepiece of the federal proposal.

> There are some powers that shouldn't be touched by government, that should belong to the people, and that is why we call it the people's package because it isn't a quarrel or a quibbling of who can exercise what jurisdiction. It is a question of what basic fundamental rights of the people are so sacred that none of us should have jurisdiction in order to infringe these rights.[5]

Trudeau concluded by warning the provincial premiers not to attempt to "trade more powers for governments and politicians" against something that the people really want, "the right to have a Canadian Constitution made in Canada and which protects all their fundamental rights."[6]

The public opening session was the first and last show of civility for the remainder of the conference. As the proceedings moved upstairs to the private fifth floor of the Ottawa Conference Centre, Trudeau and Lévesque became like "two scorpions in a bottle."[7] At the end of a week of bitter confrontation, the conference collapsed in failure amid accusations of bad faith.

In retrospect, Trudeau's assertive opening remarks foreshadowed the subsequent failure of the September conference. Not only was Ottawa in no mood for compromise, but a leaked memorandum from Trudeau's top constitutional adviser indicated that the government had already mapped out a strategy of unilateral patriation and constitutional reform by going over the heads of the provincial governments and directly to the Canadian people. The key to this strategy was the presumed popularity of the proposed Charter, what Trudeau and his lieutenants loved to call "the people's package."

On October 2, Trudeau went on national television to announce that the federal government intended to proceed unilaterally, with or without the support of all the provincial governments. "It is a long and painstaking process, building a country to match a dream," he told Canadians. "But . . . every generation of Canadians has given more than it has taken. Now it is our turn to repay our inheritance. Our duty is clear: it is to complete the foundations of our independence and of our freedoms."[8]

Four days later the government introduced in the House of Commons a draft of the bill that was to become the Constitution Act, 1982. Its major features were anticipated by Trudeau's October 2 speech to the nation: patriation, a new amending formula that included a referendum option, and a Charter of Rights and Freedoms. While the Charter was only one part of the constitutional package, Trudeau unabashedly used the "people's package" to sell the rest of his proposals. This strategy represented a curious blend of principle, statesmanship, and old-fashioned political opportunism.

Trudeau had a long-standing personal interest in a charter of rights and the liberal political theory that infused it. Trudeau's commitment to "small l" liberalism can be traced back to his student days at Harvard University in 1945, where the sign on his door read, "Pierre Trudeau: Citizen of the World."[9] Individuals and equal rights, not race or culture, were the central categories of the young Trudeau's political vision. The same liberalism was much in evidence in his now famous 1958 article, "Some Obstacles to Democracy in Quebec." Trudeau argued that:

Historically French-Canadians have not really believed in democracy for themselves; and English-speaking Canadians have not really wanted it for others. Such are the foundations upon which our two ethnic groups have absurdly pretended to be building democratic forms of government. No wonder the ensuing structure has turned out to be rather flimsy.[10]

Trudeau's interest in repairing the "flawed structures" of Canadian democracy continued when he later entered federal politics. First as Justice Minister in the sixties, then as Prime Minister in 1971 and 1978,

Trudeau actively promoted the idea of a constitutional bill of rights as a means to strengthen Canadian democracy. His charter proposal in 1980 represented only the latest episode of a lifelong campaign.

Trudeau's interest in a charter was not just ideological. Like Diefenbaker before him, he also saw it as a potential nation-building process, as a way to enhance national unity by emphasizing what Canadians have in common rather than what divides them. A constitutionally entrenched charter would promote the idea that all Canadian citizens shared a defined set of civil, political, and human rights, regardless of where they lived or what language they spoke. A new rights consciousness hopefully would promote the national focus of Canadian public life and discourage the ugly politics of ethnic prejudice and regional chauvinism that had historically coloured Canadian politics.

Last but not least, Trudeau opportunistically used the rhetoric of the "people's package" to sell the more contentious elements of his constitutional reform package. He hoped that the popular appeal of the Charter to rank-and-file Canadians would counterbalance the opposition of provincial premiers to unilateral patriation (to which most Canadians were indifferent). The Charter was also used to divert attention from the extension of bilingualism, to which there was considerable popular opposition.

At the outset, it was far from clear that this strategy would succeed. Eight of the ten provincial governments – all but Ontario and New Brunswick – quickly announced their opposition. The "gang of eight" objected to the claim of the federal government's alleged unilateral right to amend the constitution in a way that could significantly affect their interests. Quebec was adamantly opposed to the language rights provisions of the Charter, which were clearly intended to override many of the protective education and cultural policies enacted under that province's Bill 101, "The Charter of the French Language." The Western provinces objected to Ottawa's failure to address either natural resources or Senate reform. All eight feared the potential of the Charter to place new restrictions on the law-making function of the provinces. The 1960 Bill of Rights applied only to the federal government. The proposed Charter would apply to both levels of government, and its constitutional entrenchment would presumably encourage a more aggressive exercise of judicial review, posing a new threat to provincial autonomy. The provinces' fear of the Charter was exacerbated by their perception that the Laskin-led court was covertly pro-Ottawa.

In the House of Commons, NDP leader Ed Broadbent was willing to go along with Trudeau, despite some backbench defections and the opposition of several provincial NDP parties. Joe Clark and the federal Tories, however, sided with the "gang of eight." The Tories claimed not to be opposed in principle to the Charter but refused to accept it if it came as the result of unilateral action. After three weeks of often bitter debate, the government invoked closure and referred the bill to a special House-Senate committee on the constitution. Initially the government had set a December deadline for the committee's report, thereby eliminating the possibility of any public hearings. Under intense criticism from the opposition and the press, Trudeau reluctantly agreed to public, televised hearings and extended the deadline to January.

The Joint Parliamentary Committee hearings turned out to be a pleasant surprise for the Liberals. Instead of becoming a lightning rod for provincial opposition, the hearings ended up mobilizing support for the Charter and, by extension, for the package of which it was a part. Only two of the dissenting provinces even bothered to testify. Instead, the Committee was deluged with submissions from an informal and impromptu coalition of human rights, feminist, and native groups. The common denominator of this otherwise diverse group was their lack of interest in the amending formula and provincial rights but commitment to a strong Charter.

Doris Anderson, president of the federal Advisory Council on the Status of Women (ACSW), made the priority of her constituency crystal clear: "Most countries do not get the chance to rewrite their Constitution, unless they have a war or a revolution, and here we have a heaven-sent opportunity to entrench a Charter of Rights in our Constitution."[11] Anderson went on to say that while her group strongly supported the principle of a constitutionally entrenched Charter, it had "grave and serious reservations" about this particular version.[12] This criticism was repeated by group after group that testified before the Committee during November and December. Various groups criticized the wording of specific sections of the proposed Charter and recommended much broader language. The attitude of these groups was summed up by J.S. Midanik, former president of the Canadian Civil Liberties Association (CCLA), when he told the Committee that if the October, 1980, version of the Charter was the best the government could offer, then his organization's response was "Thanks, but no thanks."[13]

The Trudeau government could not have been completely surprised by this turn of events. Despite his decision to proceed unilaterally, Trudeau was sensitive to provincial concerns about the impact of the Charter on their law-making function. To placate these concerns, the government had consciously revised the wording of the October, 1980, draft of the Charter to restrict future judicial discretion and thereby minimize the policy impact of the Charter. As Justice Minister Jean Chrétien admitted later, the original version of the Charter "was the result of compromises achieved . . . in negotiations between the federal government and the provinces" and thus contained "the type of compromise which weakens the effectiveness of constitutional protection of human rights and freedoms."[14]

As the hearings of the Joint Parliamentary Committee proceeded, it became clear that this tactic was backfiring. Not only did the "gang of eight" remain hostile, but the watered-down version of the Charter incurred the criticism of the interest groups who wanted a stronger document. From the failure of this first tactic, Trudeau and his advisers plucked the seeds of a new strategy. Ever opportunistic, Trudeau did a complete reversal. Over the Christmas recess, government draftsmen rewrote numerous provisions of the Charter to accommodate the criticisms of the pro-Charter interest groups. The new strategy would be to ignore the provinces and instead to bring these groups on side by giving them the Charter they wanted, thereby building support for the Charter and defusing criticism of unilateralism.

This new strategy was unveiled on January 12, 1981. Chrétien dramatically announced a series of amendments to the October, 1980, version of the Charter. In response to the criticisms leveled by the Canadian Civil Liberties Association, the government proposed to amend the section 1 "reasonable limitations" clause to place the burden of proof on the government and to strengthen the provisions dealing with search and seizure, illegal arrest, right to counsel, and illegally obtained evidence. "It's incredible," exulted Walter Tarnopolsky, CCLA president. "They've responded to just about everything that we . . . asked. . . . I will have to take a closer look [at the changes], but it appears that they have given us just about exactly what we asked for."

Native groups also fared well. The October, 1980, draft contained only a loose reference to the "rights or freedoms that pertain to the native peoples of Canada." This had been sharply criticized as inadequate by native groups. The government now responded by offering a new clause (section 25) stating that "aboriginal, treaty, or other rights" of native groups shall not be negated by anything in the Charter. When this failed to elicit a positive response, the government went even further two weeks later and proposed the addition (section 35) that "recognized and affirmed . . . the aboriginal and treaty rights of the aboriginal peoples of Canada." Native leaders and friends wept openly in the House of Commons as all three political parties agreed to this addition.

Perhaps no group received more than Canadian feminists. They, too, had lobbied for changes to section 1. More importantly, the government had incorporated almost verbatim feminist proposals for rewriting the "non-discrimination" rights in section 15. The government adopted the recommendations of the ACSW and the National Association of Women and the Law (NAWL) that it be renamed the "Equality Rights" section "to emphasize that equality means something more than non-discrimination." To do this, the government adopted feminist proposals to expand the scope of section 15 to include the right to equality "under the law" and "equal benefit of the law." To ensure maximum political mileage, the government leaked these changes to the press the day before they were announced. The *Globe and Mail* accommodated this tactic by running front-page headlines on January 12: "More Rights for Women in Changes to Charter."

The tactic worked. Commenting on the proposed changes, Doris Anderson described them as a "considerable improvement. . . . On the whole we're pretty pleased. . . . The women of Canada should be fairly pleased." The government subsequently consolidated feminist support by conceding to their primary remaining objective. After two months of private negotiations with members of the feminist Ad Hoc Committee on the Constitution, the government agreed in March, 1981, to an additional guarantee of sexual equality (now section 28) intended to take precedence over the "reasonable limitations" loophole of section 1. The strength of the government's new ally was demonstrated a month later when Parliament unanimously approved this addition.

One item on the feminists' Charter shopping list was not provided: the right to abortion, or at least an explicit rejection of a right to life for the fetus. Given the major role of the U.S. Supreme Court in American abortion politics, it was hardly surprising that the subject of abortion arose during the Charter-framing process. Indeed, it would have been surprising if it had not. Since the intended meaning of the framers is an important guide to future judicial interpretation of a constitution, the skirmishes over abortion-related language are of more than passing interest.

Most of the controversy over abortion and Charter wording occurred in the context of section 7, which states:

> Everyone has the right to life, liberty and security of the person and the right not to be deprived thereof except in accordance with the principles of fundamental justice.

Groups on both sides of the abortion issue had concerns about the meaning of the term "everyone" and also the implications of the concept of "principles of fundamental justice" for judicial policy-making.

Testifying before the Joint Parliamentary Committee on November 20, Lynn McDonald, representing the National Action Committee on the Status of Women (NAC), recommended that the term "everyone" be replaced by "every person" throughout the Charter, because the latter was "more specific" and "has been clearly defined by the courts in the *Persons Case*."[15] (The *Persons Case* is the landmark 1929 decision of the JCPC recognizing women as full legal persons.[16]) She made no reference, however, to the implications of this change for abortion. Later that day, Mary Eberts, legal counsel for the ACSW, also objected to the use of the term "everyone" because of its vagueness and lack of any prior legal definition. Eberts also recommended that the Committee replace "everyone" by the phrase "every person," but did not mention abortion. Two weeks later the identical recommendation was made by the NAWL. Again, the reason given was "possible problems of interpretation," but without mentioning abortion.[17]

The mystery over the difference between "everyone" and "every person" ended on December 12 when the Canadian Abortion Rights Action League testified. CARAL opposed the Charter "in its present form" because it threatens the "right [of women] to a medically safe abortion." CARAL also objected to the potentially broad scope implied by the use of the concept "everyone" in sections 7 and 12 (cruel and unusual punishment).[18] With the pending Borowski case in mind, CARAL representatives declared:

> Any lawyer worth his salt or her salt would of course take advantage of that phrase in this constitution. . . . [T]his language is completely open to litigation and to the argument that somehow Parliament intended to create rights in the fetus or embryo, and if Parliament does not intend that then we suggest they must include a section which explicitly states that.

To ensure that "section 7 cannot be misinterpreted," CARAL recommended the addition of a new section to the interpretive part of the Charter (sections 25-31) "that nothing in this Charter is intended to extend rights to the embryo or fetus nor to restrict in any manner the right of women to a medically safe abortion." CARAL also recommended the addition of "a special section which talked about reproductive rights, including the rights of women to a medically safe abortion."

Pro-life groups were also dissatisfied with the wording of section 7, but for the opposite reason. On December 9, the Coalition for the Protection of Human Life testified before the Committee, recommending that section 15 be amended to prohibit discrimination against the unborn and criticizing earlier feminist recommendations to replace "everyone" by "every person." "Women's groups," the Coalition added, "have made a big mistake in taking the pro-abortion decision [because] any opinion poll will show that more women than men are opposed to abortion."[19] A week later, representatives for Alliance for Life recommended to the Committee that section 7 should be amended to read that "everyone from conception until natural death has the right to life."[20] This request was repeated on January 7 by the Ontario Conference of Catholic Bishops[21] and on January 8 by Campaign Life.[22]

When Justice Minister Chrétien tabled his long list of Charter amendments on January 12, there were no abortion-related changes.[23] The intention behind the government's refusal to accept either pro-choice or pro-life recommendations was made explicit the following week by David Crombie, the Conservative MP from Toronto-Rosedale. "My concern," Crombie told the Committee, "was that I want the question of abortion to be dealt with by Parliament and whether or not one agrees with it, the question is who will decide it, Parliament or the courts." Bob Kaplan, the federal Solicitor-General, replied:

> I think that Mr. Crombie has put very well the position of the government that this is a matter which, in our view, the Charter does not touch and, therefore, does not put it within the competence of a court to determine whether an abortion or a non-abortion law is valid.[24]

Several minutes later NDP MP Svend Robinson asked Crombie if he was favouring the use of "everyone" rather than "every person" because of the testimony of pro-life groups. Crombie emphatically denied this:

That is why it was important that we not give any colour of legitimacy to either side of the question in the use of words. . . . That is
why it was important that there be no change which would give that
colour of legitimacy; that the question should be dealt with not by
the courts, but by Parliament.[25]

There were similar concerns that the other portion of section 7 –
"the principles of fundamental justice" – might affect the competence
of Parliament to deal with abortion. Earlier versions of Trudeau's Charter had employed the term "due process of law" rather than "principles
of fundamental justice." Provincial negotiators, especially those from
Saskatchewan, strenuously objected to the use of the "due process" ter-
minology. They feared it would encourage Canadian judges to import
the "substantive due process" jurisprudence fashioned by the American Supreme Court to strike down legislative efforts at social and economic reform. They demanded that Ottawa change "due process of
law" to "principles of fundamental justice" to ensure that judges would
restrict their interpretation to questions of procedural fairness and not
the substance of the policy in question.[26] This proposed change had
important connotations in the context of abortion, as the provinces'
preferred wording would also preclude courts from ruling on the rightness or wrongness of any abortion law.

When Ottawa unveiled its proposed constitutional package in
October, 1980, the "due process" wording had been replaced by "principles of fundamental justice." This change was one of many intended
to restrict the scope of judicial discretion under the Charter and thereby
placate provincial opponents of the Charter.[27]

Subsequent testimony before the Joint Parliamentary Committee
confirmed that the intention behind this change was to prevent judges
from using section 7 to review the "wisdom" of government policy. On
January 27, 1981, Svend Robinson proposed to amend section 7 by
adding the phrase, "including the principles of due process of law."
This addition was desirable, Robinson argued, "to permit some expansion by the courts if necessary of this concept [with respect to] the
questions of life, liberty and security of the person."[28] While he did not
say so, it appeared that Robinson, an outspoken advocate of both gay
rights and abortion rights, hoped to build into the Charter a foothold for
future judicial action on these topics.

Robinson's amendment was immediately opposed by Jean Chrétien
and his assistant deputy minister in charge of public law, Barry Strayer.

Strayer clarified the government's reason for replacing "due process" with the new wording:

> Mr. Chairman, it was our belief that the words "fundamental justice" would cover the same thing as what is called procedural due process, that is the meaning of due process in relation to requiring fair procedure. However, it in our view does not cover the concept of what is called substantive due process, which would impose substantive requirements as to the policy of the law in question. . . .
>
> This has been most clearly demonstrated in the United States in the area of property, but also in other areas such as the right to life. The term due process has been given the broader concept of meaning both the procedure and the substance. Natural justice or fundamental justice in our view does not go beyond the procedural requirements of fairness. . . . The term "fundamental justice" appears to mean to us to be essentially the same thing as natural justice.[29]

Crombie again asked the government to clarify "what effect will the inclusion of the due process clause have on the question of marriage, procreation, or the parental care of children?"[30] Strayer explained that the government was now opposed to using the term "due process" because "it could be seen to open the door to the courts dealing with the question of abortion, that sort of thing, contraception, which has been dealt with by the American courts. In other words, the courts would be making those policy decisions instead of Parliament." Chrétien strongly seconded his assistant deputy minister:

> The point, Mr. Crombie, that it is important to understand the difference is that we [pass] legislation here on abortion, *Criminal Code,* and we pass legislation on capital punishment; Parliament has the authority to do that, and the court at this moment, because we do not have the due process of law written there, cannot go and see whether we made the right decision or the wrong decision in Parliament.
>
> If you write down the words, "due process of law" here, the advice I am receiving is the court could go behind our decision and say that their decision on abortion was not the right one, their decision on capital punishment was not the right one, and it is a danger, according to legal advice I am receiving that it will very much limit the scope of the power of legislation by the Parliament and we do not want that; and it is why we do not want the words "due process

of law." These are the two main examples that we should keep in mind. [31]

Robinson's proposal to reinsert the phrase "due process of law" into section 7 was then voted on and defeated. [32]

The beefed-up Charter produced by the Joint Parliamentary Committee in February was much different from the one it received in November. [33] The government's October, 1980, draft was a "minimalist" Charter, one intended to placate suspicious provincial premiers by minimizing the potential for judicial nullification of government policies. What emerged from the Committee process was a "maximal" Charter, rewritten from start to finish according to the requests of the *ad hoc* coalition of civil liberties, feminist, native, and human rights groups. On the abortion issue, however, the government, supported by the opposition Tories, had remained scrupulously neutral.

While neither pro-life nor pro-choice groups were happy with Parliament's refusal to build their respective versions of justice into the Charter, most eventually accepted the fact of constitutional neutrality on abortion. Joe Borowski was a predictable exception. Borowski watched with growing anger as pro-life groups lobbied unsuccessfully to add a right-to-life clause to the Charter. For Borowski, whose own appeal to the Supreme Court was scheduled to be heard in the spring, the government's refusal to add such a clause was inexcusable. The Joint Parliamentary Committee would not allow him to make a presentation and his letters did not elicit any response. When both chambers of Parliament approved the new Charter in late April, Borowski's patience ran out.

On May 1, he began a ninety-day fast to protest the absence of a right to life for the unborn in the Charter. Nothing would stop him, he declared, except a pro-life amendment to the Charter or a call from the Pope telling him to stop. For the next four weeks, he proceeded to live on a diet of nothing but herb tea. Predictably, the press ignored him.

On May 27 Borowski travelled to Ottawa to be present for the oral argument of his appeal on the standing issue. Physically and emotionally weakened from twenty-eight days of fasting, Borowski could not cope with Chief Justice Laskin's aggressive questioning of Shumiatcher. To the inexperienced Borowski, it looked as though Laskin was intentionally disrupting his lawyer's attempt to present his case. With

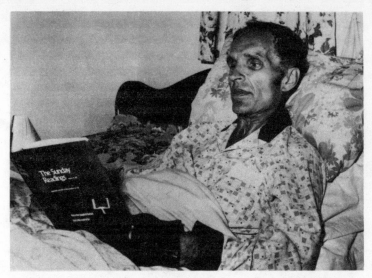

Borowski in the seventy-seventh day of his hunger strike protesting the absence of a right to life for the unborn in the proposed Charter of Rights, July 16, 1981. (*Napoleon Photography, courtesy Canapress Photo Service*)

Shumiatcher still in mid-sentence, Borowski suddenly rose from his seat and approached the elevated bench behind which the justices sat.

In a low but firm voice, he began to complain – half to Shumiatcher, half to the justices – that Laskin's questions were biased and he was not getting a fair trial. The tiny Shumiatcher tried to restrain his hulking client who – even after losing twenty-five pounds – still towered over his advocate. Laskin had had enough. The Chief Justice ordered Borowski removed from the courtroom and threatened him with contempt of court. It was the first (and still the only) time in the Supreme Court's history that someone has been evicted. Now the press took notice.[34]

Dejected, Borowski returned to Winnipeg to continue his fast. Days and then weeks passed. By mid-July he had reached a dangerously weakened condition. He had dropped from 190 pounds to 147. Too weak to walk, he stayed in bed and prayed, but there were still no phone calls from Ottawa or Rome. The doctors and his priest urged him to stop, but a sick Joe was just as stubborn as a healthy Joe. In the end, Borowski's life was probably saved by the intervention of his old boss and friend, Ed Schreyer. Unlike Borowski, Schreyer's political star had continued to rise, and he was now the Governor-General of Canada. Schreyer had stayed in touch with his former cabinet minister and his first-hand experience with Borowksi's stubbornness made him worry that Joe just might fast himself into the grave. Schreyer contacted the Vatican's emissary to Canada and persuaded him to intercede. As Borowski tells it, he received a phone call from the pro-nuncio telling him, "I've been in touch with the Holy Father and he wants you to stop."[35] It was July 19, 1981, the eightieth day of Joe's fast. He agreed to stop.

By this time the process of constitutional reform had passed Borowski by. The eight opposing provinces had gone to the courts to try to block Trudeau's plan. The governments of Quebec, Newfoundland, and Manitoba all launched references to their respective courts of appeal. Unilateral patriation, they argued, violated the (unwritten) constitutional convention of requiring the consent of all the provinces for constitutional amendments affecting provincial powers. The federal lawyers denied the existence of such a convention, or argued that even if it did exist, because it was a convention and not a written law, it could not be enforced by courts. The results of the first round of litigation confirmed that there was substance to both claims. Two courts of appeal (Manitoba and Quebec) ruled in favour of Ottawa and one (Newfoundland) supported the provinces. The thirteen appellate judges who heard these references were divided, seven to six, in favour of Ottawa.

The federal Conservative Party agreed with the "gang of eight" and was filibustering in the House of Commons, preventing final approval of the government's constitutional package. A deal was struck. The Conservatives agreed to stop their filibuster when the Liberals agreed not to proceed with final enactment until the Supreme Court heard a consolidated appeal from the three lower courts and ruled on the legality of Trudeau's unilateralism.

On September 28, all Canada stopped to hear the Supreme Court announce the most important decision in its 106-year history. Conscious that his court was for that moment the centre of the Canadian political universe, Chief Justice Laskin broke with tradition and allowed television cameras into the hallowed chambers. Ironically, the solemnity of the occasion was undermined when one of the justices tripped on a sound cable and disabled the audio portion of the broadcast. The Chief Justice's moment of glory was thus reduced to a somewhat comical "talking-head" without sound.

With Solomon-like balance, the Court declared that unilateral patriation was "legal but unconstitutional." That is, it did violate the unwritten constitutional convention of "substantial provincial consent," but conventions are not enforceable in a court of law.[36] In plain English, the Court was saying that Ottawa's unilateralism was legal but wrong. Both sides claimed victory, but in reality both sides won only half of what they claimed and risked losing even more depending on what happened next. The Court's "half-a-loaf-to-each" decision created strong incentives for both parties to compromise.

After a month of furious behind-the-scenes bargaining, all eleven governments met in Ottawa the first week of November to try again to reach an agreement. On November 5 a compromise was struck that gained the consent of every government except Quebec. Ottawa agreed to an amending formula that was more favourable to the provinces in return for provincial acceptance of the Charter. The provinces' acceptance of the Charter, however, was conditional on the addition of a *non obstante* or "notwithstanding clause," what is now section 33, which allows a government to protect a law from judicial nullification by inserting a clause stating that it shall operate "notwithstanding" the Charter. Trudeau reluctantly agreed, but only on the condition that those sections pertaining directly to democratic rights (sections 3-5) and his national unity objectives – language rights, minority education and mobility rights – be exempted.

The Court's decision in the *Patriation Reference* has been widely praised (outside of Quebec) for its "bold statecraft" – for facilitating the political compromise that eventually emerged. Most commentators failed to perceive that the decision had a second, more subtle but equally important effect. As Michael Mandel has pointed out, the decision previewed, and also legitimated, the new more overtly political role the Court would soon come to play under the Charter.[37] Overlooked in what the Court did for the process of constitutional reform was what the Court did for itself. It became the first court in any English common-law jurisdiction (and presumably in the world) to rule on the existence of an unwritten political convention. Despite the fact that there was no precedent of any court ever doing so, the Supreme Court did so unanimously.

While pragmatists might shrug this off with an "ends-justify-the-means" attitude, the fact remains that the Court "acted outside its legal function and [attempted] to facilitate a political outcome."[38] In other words, it "intervened as another political actor, not as a court of law."[39] Not only did the Court intervene as a political actor, but the majority did so for clearly partisan reasons: to deter the federal government from proceeding unilaterally. Why else would the six-judge majority break with all precedent just to tell the nation that even though unilateralism was legal it was still "unconstitutional"?

Given such an overtly political purpose, it was not surprising that the voting of the judges almost perfectly followed political and regional lines.[40] The three judges from Quebec all agreed that unilateralism was unconstitutional. The two judges who said that Trudeau's plan was both unconstitutional and illegal were Diefenbaker (i.e., Tory) appointees from provinces that were opposed to the Liberal plan (Alberta and Nova Scotia). The three judges who took the other extreme – that unilateralism was both legal and constitutional – were all Trudeau appointees, two from Ontario, a province that supported the Trudeau initiative. Of the seven-judge coalition that held unilateralism was legal, six were Trudeau appointees. This "political logic" is hardly surprising. When judges jump into the political arena their decisions will be driven by partisan consideration, not legal principles. "If we were paying attention," wrote Mandell, this "gave us a good idea of what Canada could expect with the Charter."[41]

It was surprising that no one – especially the federal government – publicly criticized the Supreme Court for being so transparently political. The six-judge coalition that handed down the verdict of "unconstitutional" had derailed, perhaps permanently, the plan that would have culminated Trudeau's lifelong political ambition. Yet, there was nary "a peep of political criticism."[42] Why? Because "the whole Charter enterprise depended for its success on reverence for the Court." In Trudeau's grand scheme, the Court would one day drive the Charter, striking down the anti-English language laws of the PQ government in Quebec and reforming the not-so-benign neglect of French-speaking minorities in other provinces. "How could [Trudeau] criticize the Court for going too far today when he needed it to go all the way tomorrow?"[43]

This was the final irony in the *Patriation Reference* decision. The Court jumped four-square into the political arena to facilitate the adoption of a constitutional reform – the Charter of Rights – that would in turn support more of the same "political jurisprudence." All nine judges broke with tradition to facilitate the adoption of a constitutional amendment of which the Supreme Court was the most immediate beneficiary. "It would have been strange indeed," Mandel has observed, "for the Court, standing on the threshold of its new era, to have been too prudish to engage in the very kind of activity that would characterize that era, or to have been criticized for so doing."[44] In effect, the Court performed the rather remarkable feat of serving as midwife at the birth of its new self.

This was how the Charter came to be. It established a new regime of constitutional supremacy, but, because of section 33, not necessarily a regime of judicial supremacy. In this respect, the Charter represented elements of both continuity and change. A number of important individual and collective rights were now entrenched in the constitution, but most of these had existed and been respected in other forms prior to the Charter. The real achievement of the Charter was not so much the creation of new rights, but a new way of making decisions about rights, a process in which the courts now had a much more influential voice.[45] The Canadian tradition of parliamentary supremacy was qualified but not discarded.

How great a change the Charter effected would be largely a function of how the judges used it. To the discerning, the *Patriation Reference* suggested that the Supreme Court was more than ready to abandon the cautious self-restraint and British-style legalism that had characterized its interpretation of the 1960 Bill of Rights. In his 1975 *Morgentaler* decision, Chief Justice Laskin had written that the Court could never exercise an American-style judicial review under a "statutory instrument" such as the Bill of Rights. Now Laskin had a constitutionally entrenched Charter of Rights. Was the implication that a more assertive exercise of judicial review was now acceptable?

Changing personnel would also be a factor. On February 10, 1982, Justice Ronald Martland retired. Martland was not particularly fond of Trudeau, Laskin, or the Charter. He had never forgotten the events of December, 1973, when Trudeau had snubbed him by appointing Laskin as Chief Justice despite Martland's seniority. In two of his last decisions, Martland had, perhaps, exacted some revenge. In September, he had helped to form the six-judge majority that held Trudeau's plan unconstitutional. (Martland went the extra mile, in dissent, and ruled it was also illegal.) In December, he had written the majority judgment in the first Borowski case, granting standing over the futile protests of Bora Laskin. Now Martland was gone.

On March 4, 1982, less than a month before the Charter was to be officially proclaimed, Pierre Trudeau appointed Bertha Wilson as the first woman to sit on the Supreme Court of Canada. While there was a great deal of fanfare attached to this historical first, the fact was that very little was known about the new Justice. Bertha Wilson had spent most of her legal career in the obscurity of a corporate law office and had only recently been appointed to the Ontario Supreme Court. What would be the effect of her replacing the departed Martland? Would the new Justice Wilson prove to be an ally or a foe of the judicial activism associated with Chief Justice Laskin? Only time would tell.

As for abortion, the government maintained its official position that the Charter was scrupulously neutral. When the Catholic bishops personally requested Trudeau to add a clause to the Charter stating that "the Charter would not prejudicially affect the rights of the unborn," Trudeau responded that such a clause was "completely unnecessary."[46] "[N]o provision of the Charter," Trudeau declared, "is reasonably capable of an interpretation that would either enshrine a right to abortion or a right to life for the unborn or deny the ability of Parliament to legislate on the matter in the context of the Criminal Code." Trudeau reaffirmed this position after the historic accord of November 5.[47]

The official government position of complete Charter neutrality was disputed by Professor Peter Russell, a constitutional expert at the University of Toronto. Speaking at a public forum on the Charter in Toronto in March, 1980, Russell gave a more prudent – and in retrospect, prophetic – response to the question about the affect of the Charter on abortion policy: "At this point no one can predict what the court would rule."[48]

CHAPTER 12

Return to Battle

The Charter of Rights and Freedoms was proclaimed amidst pomp and ceremony on April 17, 1982. Fourteen days later, Henry Morgentaler announced his intention to open abortion clinics in Toronto and Winnipeg. Was the former the cause of the latter? Yes, but there were other reasons as well.

Several weeks after his third jury acquittal in 1976, Morgentaler was asked about his own role in the future of the pro-choice struggle to change Canada's abortion law. "After six or seven years of legal battles," Morgentaler wistfully speculated, "I think that I have done my part. I hope that other people will take it from here."[1] Morgentaler's desire to step aside was understandable. He was physically and emotionally exhausted, and in debt. At his own expense, he had shown the way, and he had ended the enforcement of the abortion law in Canada's second largest province. It seemed reasonable to assume that others would now pick up the banner of reform. But this was not to be. Seven years later, he was once again leading a legal assault on the abortion law. His return to battle resulted from both public and private reasons.

First and foremost, there were no significant changes in abortion policy outside of Quebec. The PQ government's refusal to prosecute Morgentaler had encouraged other Quebec doctors to offer private abortion services. In 1980, Jeanne St. Amour, a doctor working for a CLSC (Centres Locaux des Services Communitaires), one of the government-sponsored community health clinics, approached Morgentaler. The CLSCs emphasize prevention and community education, and tend to attract younger, more liberal doctors. Dr. St. Amour asked Morgentaler to train her to perform abortions at her CLSC. Morgentaler did so, and soon other young CLSC doctors came to him as well. By year's end, abortion services were being offered in government-sponsored clinics across the province, in clear violation of the Criminal Code. When the story broke, the provincial Justice Minister's response was low-key. After three jury acquittals, abortion had become "a grey zone" in the law, he observed, and the government's top priority was to protect the health and lives of Quebec women. Morgentaler himself astutely summed up the law and politics of the situation: "You could say that the Quebec government was violating the federal criminal law, [but] of course nobody was going to prosecute the Quebec government."[2]

In the rest of the Canada, however, nothing had changed. The Trudeau government, still sharply divided by the issue, had succeeded in playing pro-life and pro-choice activists off against one another, and also had deflected much of the criticism concerning lack of access onto provincial governments. The nine other provinces, as Joe Borowski had learned, wanted no part of the abortion issue. They responded that abortion was a matter of federal criminal law and that they were bound to enforce it. In the context of this political stalemate, many abortion rights activists felt that the situation had deteriorated from 1976 to 1982. A growing number of pro-life groups were mounting increasingly effective grassroots campaigns to close down therapeutic abortion committees (TACs) at local hospitals and to cut off provincial and United Way funding to pro-choice groups. Finally, Borowski's victory on standing in the Supreme Court of Canada – the same court that had sent him to prison – infuriated Morgentaler and prompted him back into action.

There were also more private causes. Morgentaler's 1976 victory had turned out to be a mixed blessing. Emotionally and physically exhausted, he found it difficult to return to private life. His relationship with Mireille Lafortune, his companion and confidante through the three-year legal odyssey, withered and came to a bitter end. Separated for years from his first wife, Morgentaler now sued for divorce and had to part with a generous share of his depleted resources. In an attempt to deal with a growing sense of anger, Morgentaler turned to primal therapy. In the words of his friend and biographer, Eleanor Pelrine:

It was difficult for Henry Morgentaler, who had become instantly recognizable to virtually every Canadian, to go back to being an ordinary man.... He was a man suddenly without a cause, and without a grand plan.[3]

Several years later, in response to the question of why he had resumed his civil disobedience, Morgentaler seemed indirectly to confirm Pelrine's analysis.

It's just in a sense a continuation of a struggle. I always felt that it was almost that fate placed this thing on my shoulders. This is my destiny. I don't really believe in destiny. You create your own destiny to a certain extent. You choose something to do. If you're logical, in consequence it has some effect – this action has to lead to some kind of resolution of the problem.... It's like looking for a role in history. Nobody wanted that role.

The seventies witnessed growing dissatisfaction on all fronts with the 1969 abortion reform. The number of abortions being performed under the new law had risen from 20,000 annually to 65,000 in 1981. To pro-life forces this figure was much too high, to pro-choice advocates, too low. The number of pro-life groups across the nation had also increased in the early seventies – from seventy-five to 230.[4] These groups sharply criticized the dramatic increase in the number of abortions. In May, 1975, the Alliance for Life delivered to Parliament the largest petition in Canadian history – with one million signatures – demanding that the government do more to protect the unborn. From the other side, CARAL and other pro-choice groups criticized the law for impeding access to abortion services. Doctors, caught in the middle, first demanded that the government clarify the meaning of "health" in section 251. Eventually the Canadian Medical Association endorsed the complete elimination of abortion from the Criminal Code. The effect of the Morgentaler trials was like throwing gasoline on an already explosive situation.

In September, 1975, the Trudeau government finally responded: it appointed a special commission to study the problem. Like governments before and since, the Liberals hoped that the symbolic impact of an official inquiry would defuse the political situation, at least temporarily. The Committee on the Operation of the Abortion Law was chaired by Robin Badgley, a sociologist from the University of Toronto. Its mandate was to investigate the nature and extent of abortion practices under the existing law. The Badgley Report, released in February, 1977, paralleled many of the findings presented in the CCLA and CARAL factums to the Supreme Court in 1975:

> sharp disparities in the distribution of and accessibility of therapeutic abortion services; a continuous exodus of women to the United States to obtain this operation; and delays in women obtaining induced abortion in Canada.[5]

While pro-choice activists were gratified by the findings of the Badgley Commision, they were bitterly disappointed in its recommendations. The Report studiously avoided blaming these problems on the abortion law and thus the Liberal government. Instead, the problem was said to be caused by the spiralling number of unwanted pregnancies. Responsibility for this was laid on Canada's health institutions, the medical profession, and the Canadian people's general ignorance of modern birth control measures. The solution, concluded the Report, was not more abortions but more effective family planning. The Report ended by calling for co-ordinated federal-provincial programs of "public education and health promotion."

Most pro-choice critics of the Badgley Report were not surprised by its bland recommendations. The creation of the Committee was seen by many as a political act from the start, designed not to improve access to abortion services but "to deflect the political controversy away from the government and on to a 'neutral' commission." According to one insider, the cabinet itself was deeply divided by the decision even to appoint the Committee.

> There was blood in the halls over what it [the Committee] would actually do. No way would Justice allow it to find fault with the law. The government was not about to blame itself. That's why the supporting studies are still locked up in the vaults.[6]

The month after the Badgley Report was released, the federal government made its first and last attempt to implement its recommendations. Minister for Health and Welfare Marc Lalonde announced that his Family Planning Division would adopt a more aggressive interventionist policy of disseminating birth control information to the Canadian people. This new federal effort, he explained, would have to be matched by new provincial initiatives, possibly including women's health clinics that, among other services, might provide abortions.

The negative reaction of pro-life groups was immediate, loud, and effective. The speech provoked over half a million letters to the federal Department of Health and Welfare, almost all of them negative. Lalonde, the consummate politician, immediately back-pedalled and eventually scrapped the federal initiative. Seeing the political storm that Lalonde had created, his provincial counterparts wanted no part of it. Indeed, to many provincial leaders the Lalonde initiative smacked of the old game of minimizing federal exposure and shunting off the bulk of policy responsibility – and political flak – onto provincial politicians.[7] The net impact of the Badgley Report was pointedly summarized several years later by committee member Marion Powell: "Nothing happened. Absolutely nothing."[8]

This was hardly surprising. An opinion poll conducted by the Committee found that "there was no strong mandate either to 'tighten' or to 'reform' the existing legislation. . . . [M]ost persons implicitly endorsed the status quo."[9] If the political protest was coming only from the two extremes of the abortion conflict, it did not take a political scientist to predict that the Trudeau government – like any democratically elected government – would not disturb the status quo.

In December, 1981, the Supreme Court of Canada announced that Joe Borowski was entitled to legal standing to challenge the abortion law. Less than four months later, Henry Morgentaler announced plans to open abortion clinics across Canada. The two antagonists, as Ann Collins observed, were like "boxers in opposite corners of the ring. A blow from one naturally leads to a blow from the other."[10] Morgentaler called Borowski's Supreme Court victory "the last straw . . . [an attempt] to take away all the rights to legal abortion . . . by challenging the whole law."[11]

Frustrated by the political stalemate, angry at the Supreme Court's *Borowski* decision, Morgentaler felt himself being drawn closer and closer to renewing his campaign of civil disobedience. On the one hand, he was confident that no jury in Canada would convict him. His three acquittals in Quebec plus public opinion polls convinced him that there would always be at least one juror who could be counted on to refuse to vote for conviction regardless of the facts. The worst-case scenario would be a series of hung juries.[12] But this calculation ignored the human and financial costs of renewed civil disobedience. He was ten years older now, almost sixty, and the constant pressure of the threat of arrest, trials, and possibly jail could seriously harm his health. His new wife, Carmen, was adamantly opposed to his breaking the abortion law, as were his brother and all his friends. Time, mental energy, and financial resources would also be put at risk.[13]

Morgentaler was still wrestling with these arguments when fate intervened to make his decision for him. On February 12, 1982, he had gone to New York on business. That evening he and some friends were eating at a small restaurant off Times Square. Morgentaler excused himself to go to the washroom, which was located on the floor below. As he stood in front of the urinal, he was attacked from behind by a mugger. The assailant grabbed Morgentaler around the throat, wrestled him to the ground, and strangled him until he passed out. Morgentaler's last thought, as he lost consciousness, was that he was about to die. When he regained consciousness a few minutes later, the first thought that came into his mind was, "I'm alive! I can still do something with my life!" As he later recounted, "It occurred to me that the thing that I could do that nobody else wanted to do, or was able to do, was to again challenge the laws in the other provinces and bring about access to abortion across the country, as I had done for Quebec."[14] Two months later he publicly announced his intention to open abortion clinics in Toronto and Winnipeg.

Recalling the personal and financial costs of his first round of civil disobedience, Morgentaler first sought to solicit political support for a legislative change in the law. He wrote Prime Minister Pierre Trudeau, who replied that he had passed Morgentaler's letter on to his Justice Minister, Mark MacGuigan. One of MacGuigan's assistants wrote Morgentaler that she would meet with him, but Morgentaler wanted MacGuigan or nobody. Morgentaler also wrote Monique Bégin, Trudeau's Minister of Health, but again could get no further than her assistant. Stonewalled by the federal government, Morgentaler turned to the provinces (precisely what the feds had hoped). He wrote all nine provincial attorneys-general that he planned to open abortion clinics in their provinces. He explained what had happened in Quebec since 1976 and asked them if they also would consider not prosecuting. There were no takers.

Spurned by the political authorities, Morgentaler decided once again to turn to the courts. This decision was made more palatable by the proclamation of the new Canadian Charter of Rights and Freedoms on April 16, 1982. Unlike the 1960 Bill of Rights, the Charter was not just a federal statute but part of the written constitution. The new constitution explicitly authorized judges to interpret and enforce the Charter of Rights, giving them the power to declare conflicting statutes void. While the framers of the Charter had adamantly resisted attempts to insert any pro-choice (or pro-life) language into its text, the Charter invited closer judicial scrutiny of legislative policy choices. Morgentaler and other pro-choice activists hoped that the Charter would serve as a catalyst for more aggressive judicial review of Canada's abortion law.

Morgentaler's first assault on Canada's abortion law was basically an *ad hoc,* one-man show. By contrast, his second assault had all the trappings of a well-oiled political campaign. Legal strategy, media strategy, finances, and co-ordination with both national and local pro-choice groups were all carefully mapped out in advance.[15] Morgentaler's objective was to force the other nine provinces to follow the example of Quebec: to set up – or at least to permit – free-standing abortion clinics. To force the government's hand, Morgentaler planned to come into a designated province and set up an abortion clinic. At this point, he envisioned a two-step strategy, the first legal, the second illegal. The legal strategy involved asking the province to declare the clinic an official "hospital," thereby bringing it within the scope of section 251. This strategy had the obvious advantage that it might keep Morgentaler out of jail and avoid the costs of going to trial. And if a province declined his invitation, Morgentaler could claim that the government, by "refusing to co-operate," was the aggressor.

If a provincial government refused his offer, Morgentaler was prepared to force the issue by performing abortions. At this point he could still hope that local pro-choice groups could organize a sufficiently impressive show of public support for his clinic to persuade the government not to lay charges. Failing this, Morgentaler had two legal defences. First, he could argue that the abortion law violated the new Charter of Rights and was therefore void and unenforceable. Failing that, he could once again put the defence of necessity to a jury.

This type of civil disobedience, Morgentaler had learned, can be an expensive undertaking. As a first step, he sought and received assurances from CARAL president Norma Scarborough that her association would mount a nation-wide effort to raise half a million dollars for a Morgentaler Defence Fund. In addition, his brother Mike formed a new company, Gestions Habal, Inc., to purchase and manage the properties that would house the proposed clinics.

Finally there was the question of where to strike first. Toronto was an obvious first choice. A victory in Toronto, an urban centre of four million people – the largest in Canada – and the nation's media capital, would be decisive. And there were reasons to be sanguine about success. Outside of Quebec, there were already more abortions performed in Toronto than any other Canadian city. (In 1981, seventeen Toronto hospitals accounted for 16,000 of the 65,000 abortions reported to Statistics Canada.) In English-speaking Canada, Toronto was the centre for both feminists and abortion rights activists. Both groups, whose memberships were overlapping, possessed extensive networks and resources that could provide public support and private pressure to help a Morgentaler clinic.

This kind of grassroots support would be needed to offset the negative side of a Toronto campaign: Ontario Premier Bill Davis's "Big Blue" Tory machine. The Progressive Conservative Party had governed Ontario without interruption for almost forty years and was skilled at avoiding "no-win" political issues like abortion. Perhaps more importantly, the Tory instinct for law and order was deeply embedded in the history of central Canada. The people of Ontario could not be expected to look favourably on Morgentaler-style civil disobedience. In response to Morgentaler's announcement that he would open an abortion clinic in Toronto, Ontario Attorney-General Roy McMurtry had repeatedly asserted that the law would be enforced.

Morgentaler's second choice was much less obvious. Vancouver, the hub of Canada's free-wheeling west coast society, would have seemed more receptive to Morgentaler's tactics. Instead, he chose Winnipeg. According to Morgentaler, the decision was based primarily on the hope that Premier Howard Pawley's New Democratic government would not prosecute a Morgentaler clinic. The federal NDP endorsed removing abortion from the Criminal Code, and Morgentaler hoped that Pawley and his government – the only socialist party in power besides the Parti Québécois – shared this view. A contributing factor was the NDP Attorney-General, Roland Penner, a well-known civil libertarian who was on record as supporting the decriminalization of abortion. Morgentaler hoped that Penner might champion the cause of "non-prosecution" in the Pawley cabinet. Finally, was it coincidental that Morgentaler chose Joe Borowski's home town for his first clinic outside of Quebec? While he has never admitted it, the challenge and temptation of starting a clinic in his arch rival's backyard must have appealed to Morgentaler's pugnacious personality.

CHAPTER 13

Trial for Life

In February, 1983, Borowski received a letter from Shumiatcher. It brought good news and bad news. A trial date had finally been set – May 9 in the Court of Queen's Bench in Regina. This was overshadowed, however, by the bad news. Shumiatcher could not even consider going to court unless Borowski posted a $350,000 guarantee to cover expected court costs. Borowski was stunned. He had only $100,000 in the Alliance Against Abortion bank account. If he could not raise a quarter of a million dollars in the next sixty days, all his efforts of the past five years would be wasted.[1]

Borowski called a news conference to launch an appeal for contributions. Unlike his old glory days as an NDP firebrand, Borowski and his cause were no longer a press favourite. Only three reporters bothered to come. Desperate, Borowski called his friend Larry Henderson, editor and publisher of *The Catholic Register.* He needed help. Henderson obliged by running a front-page story on Borowski's predicament, reinforced by an editorial urging contributions.[2]

What happened next exceeded Borowski's wildest imagination. Money began to pour in. For the first time in Borowski's decade-long crusade, the Catholic Church actually provided some support. Sharelife, a Church-sponsored campaign, quietly kicked in $10,000. Local chapters of affiliate groups like the Knights of Columbus and the Catholic Women's League also contributed money for the first time. There

131

were also thousands of individual contributions. But the most remarkable story was the response to Borowski's barnstorm fund-raising campaign through small farm communities in the Prairies. At an evening meeting in North Battleford, Saskatchewan, an audience of 450 people filled the hat with $19,000. Within two weeks, they had raised another $8,000. A cheque for $16,000 came in from Macklin, Saskatchewan, "over $16 for every man, woman and child of that community," exclaimed a beaming Borowski.[3]

Contributions soon exceeded the $250,000 that Borowski needed, and – still the paragon of frugality and integrity – he actually published a message for people to stop sending money. Nothwithstanding, money was still trickling in five months after the trial. When pressed to explain such success, Borowski said it could only be "a miracle" since it certainly was not his eloquence as a speech-maker. (He was right about the latter!) But he also had a secular explanation: Henry Morgentaler, or more precisely, the fear and loathing that Morgentaler inspired among pro-life Canadians.

> Morgentaler is the biggest asset the pro-life movement has. . . . If you talk to any [pro-life] group in the country, they'll say that they never received so much money as since Morgentaler started his campaign on these clinics. . . . I hope he keeps going, shooting his mouth off in every city in the country.[4]

In the days leading up to the Borowski trial, the normally sleepy Regina airport was abuzz with the comings and goings of luminaries from both camps of the abortion battle. Borowski himself had flown in from Winnipeg, temporarily abandoning his mobile-home command post in front of the new Morgentaler clinic on Corydon Avenue. From Toronto came Norma Scarborough, president of the Canadian Abortion Rights Action League. CARAL was not going to let the Borowski trial proceed without a sign of protest. Distrustful of the government's will to defend a woman's right to abortion, CARAL had requested intervener status but had been turned down. (Judge W.R. Matheson rejected similar requests from the CCLA and Campaign Life.) Barred from the courtroom, CARAL took to the streets. The local chapter planned demonstrations in front of the courthouse on Victoria Avenue. Scarborough had come in from Toronto to do some open-line radio talk shows and to rally the troops.

Even more unusual was the arrival of foreign luminaries. From Auckland, New Zealand, came Sir William Liley, the celebrated

Borowski and lawyer Morris Shumiatcher arrive at the Court of Queen's
Bench in Regina to begin their "Trial for Life," May 9, 1983. (*Courtesy
Canapress Photo Service*)

inventor of amniocentesis and the first doctor to administer blood
transfusions to a fetus still *in utero*. From Paris, France, came Dr.
Jérôme Lejeune, the world famous geneticist who was the first to
unlock the chromosomal defect that produces Down's Syndrome.
From the United States came Dr. Bernard Nathanson, the former
"Abortion King" of New York City but now an active pro-life cam-
paigner.

These celebrities were only part of a cast of expert witnesses that
Shumiatcher had assembled for the Borowski trial. Shumiatcher's
research had persuaded him that modern science was on the side of the
unborn, but he worried that a dry recitation of "the facts" would
not persuade a judge. Something more compelling was needed. That

something more, Shumiatcher concluded, was *viva voce* evidence – to bring the leading experts from around the world to Regina to testify in person. Shumiatcher had interviewed over sixty such experts before finally choosing nine. As Shumiatcher later explained, "Such cases require counsel to assume the role of innovators. Counsel creates the case. . . . The first burden is to exercise ingenuity and imagination."[5] Ingenuity and imagination, however, do not come cheaply. The $350,000 price tag that Shumiatcher sent to Borowski in February nearly put an end to the case.

The other novel element in the Borowski challenge was its use of the new Charter of Rights and Freedoms. When Shumiatcher first filed his statement of claim in 1978, his legal arguments were based on the 1960 Bill of Rights. While the Supreme Court had not yet interpreted the Charter (its first Charter decisions were handed down in the spring of 1984), it was expected that the constitutionally entrenched Charter would elicit a more activist exercise of judicial review. This, of course, was just what Borowski would need if he were to succeed. As for Shumiatcher, he saw the adoption of the Charter as creating a whole new ball game. "Under the Charter," he observed, "lawyers must become philosophers and judges philosopher-princes." The addition of the Charter to his legal arsenal further fired Shumiatcher's enthusiasm for Borowski's case. It is, he declared, "the kind of case that lawyers dream of."[6]

On May 9, 1983, three days after the Morgentaler clinic opened in Winnipeg, Shumiatcher began unfolding his dream before Judge Matheson of the Court of Queen's Bench in Regina. The first issue was a procedural matter but one with great import for Shumiatcher. The Saskatchewan Evidence Act limits to five the number of expert witnesses a lawyer may call, unless the judge gives permission for more. Shumiatcher had lined up nine expert witnesses and thus needed permission. Judge Matheson appeared open to the request to exceed the normal limit and requested the opinion of the federal Crown Attorney, Ed Sojonky.

Sojonky strongly objected. The issue before the court, he responded, is "a strictly legal one" – whether the fetus is a person *in law*.[7] The testimony of medical experts is neither "germane nor relevant," he told the judge. This type of evidence is for legislatures, not courts. Matheson did not seem persuaded: "Without having heard it [the experts' testimony]," he responded, "how is one to determine that?"[8]

Sensing an opening, Shumiatcher launched a theme that he would hammer away at for the remainder of the trial. Prior to 1982, he conceded, Sojonky was probably correct. But the proclamation of the Charter had changed this:

> What Parliament has enacted is certainly not the last word. . . . [The question is] are the provisions of subsections (4) (5) and (6) of section 251 in conflict with the higher law of Canada . . . the Charter of Rights and Freedoms? [T]hat is, under our constitution, a matter peculiarly and exclusively reserved for this court.[9]

Sojonky persisted that the testimony of the experts would be both "predictable" and "irrelevant," and Judge Matheson became impatient. "Maybe you can [anticipate the medical evidence] but I don't know how I can without even knowing who these people are."[10] Sensing that he was fighting a losing battle, Sojonky gave up: "I have nothing further to add." The judge perfunctorily thanked him and announced that all nine experts would be allowed to testify. Shumiatcher smiled. Round one was his.

Shumiatcher began by outlining his argument. While its execution would be lengthy, his basic strategy was elegantly simple: "to wed the principles of law with the knowledge of science." Modern medicine, he declared, had discovered that the so-called "fetus" is indeed a human person. Section 7 of the Charter declared that "everyone has the right to life." Since section 251 of the Code permitted the aborting – indeed, the killing – of an unborn human child for no compelling reason, it violated section 7 and was therefore invalid.[11] The linchpin of this argument was the claim that the unborn child is indeed a person and thus protected by the Charter. This would be proven by the testimony of the nine experts, who would reveal how new "scientific inventions . . . now make it possible to see and examine . . . the growth of a human being in the mother's body."[12]

Shumiatcher urged Judge Matheson to approach the trial not as a narrow, legalistic exercise, but rather as a scientific expedition in search of the truth. "In this case," he intoned,

> we shall be embarking upon a voyage of discovery, My Lord; a voyage into the distant stages of our early life . . . that modern science and medicine are now charting with such precision that fancy is being overtaken by fact and our never-ending wonderment over the

nature of human life is elevated by the proofs of human knowledge and human understanding. [13]

Such flights of rhetoric notwithstanding, Shumiatcher knew that he was in a court of law, not a medical laboratory. He would need more than scientific facts. It was one thing to persuade a judge that the unborn child is a human being. It would be another to persuade the same judge to elevate this view into constitutional law and thereby overrule Parliament's collective judgment. He needed a legal lever that could serve as a catalyst for the judicial leap of faith that would be required to win the case. For Shumiatcher, that legal lever was to be the celebrated *Persons Case.*

After women gained the right to vote in federal elections in 1918, Canadian suffrage leaders began to agitate for the appointment of women to the Senate. A cautious federal government responded that this might not be allowed under the present wording of section 26 of the British North America Act, 1867. Section 26 authorized the appointment of "qualified persons" to the Senate. The legal issue was whether women could be considered "persons." In 1927 five women activists, including Henrietta Muir Edwards from Alberta, successfully petitioned the federal government to refer this question to the Supreme Court of Canada for an answer. In 1928 the Supreme Court replied negatively: women were not "persons" for the purposes of section 26. Their reasoning was simple and orthodox. The words of the constitution must be interpreted to mean what they meant at the time of their enactment. Since women neither voted nor held political office in 1867, certainly the framers of the constitution did not intend them to be eligible for appointment to the Senate! Legislative enactment, not judicial decision, was the only proper way to "update" the Senate appointment provision.

Edwards and her co-litigants appealed this decision to the Judicial Committee of the Privy Council. Under the leadership of Lord Sankey, the JCPC gave a very different answer. With respect to the strict judicial fidelity to legislative intent that underlay the Canadian decision, Lord Sankey wrote these historic words, which have influenced the interpretation of the Canadian constitution ever since they were first penned:

The *British North America Act* planted in Canada a living tree capable of growth and expansion within its natural limits. . . . Like all written constitutions, it has been subject to development through usage and convention. Their Lordships do not conceive it to be the duty of this Board – it is certainly not their desire – to cut down the provisions of the Act by a narrow and technical construction, but rather to give it a large and liberal interpretation. . . ."[14]

The "living tree" metaphor has encouraged judges to adapt constitutional language to new social, economic, and scientific change, thereby keeping the constitution in tune with the times. With respect to section 26, wrote Lord Sankey, "The exclusion of women from all public offices is a relic of days more barbarous than ours. . . ." He continued:

> The word "person" may include members of both sexes, and to those who ask why the word should include females, the obvious answer is why not? In these circumstances the burden is upon those who deny that the word includes women to make out their case.[15]

Following this reasoning, Lord Sankey concluded that women were indeed "persons" and thus eligible for Senate appointment. Over the years, the *Persons Case* has come to be celebrated both as a model of flexible, pragmatic constitutional interpretation, as well as a model of judicial promotion of human rights. According to Shumiatcher, both aspects were present in the *Borowski* case. "The battle that women fought and won in the first two decades of this century to establish their status and personhood," declared Shumiatcher, "is today renewed in the *Borowski* case. . . . Edwards confirmed the status of women as persons; *Borowski* seeks to establish the personhood of unborn children. The issues are the same."[16]

The first prong of Shumiatcher's attack was to discredit the present abortion law, especially its claim to limit abortions to pregnancies threatening the life or health of the mother. Shumiatcher sought to prove that in the real world, the TACs operated as nothing more than a rubber stamp for abortion requests. To this end, Shumiatcher called Dr. Donald Carnduff, the Administrator of Medical Care at the Regina General Hospital, to the stand. Dr. Carnduff was responsible for all medical committees at Regina General, including the TAC. Shumiatcher had issued a *subpoena duces tecum* to Dr. Carnduff, ordering him to come to court and to bring specified TAC documents with him.

Shumiatcher spent the remainder of the first day of the trial questioning an uncomfortable Dr. Carnduff about the operation of the TAC at the Regina General Hospital. No, there is not actually a formal meeting of the three-to-five doctor committee to discuss the applications. Each member reads the requests independently and then indicates approval or disapproval on a printed form. The acting chairman then counts up the votes (a simple majority decides) and, without any further discussion, indicates the reason for approval by ticking off one of the pre-designated codes: medical, psychological, or socio-economic. No one is designated to represent the interest of the fetus or to assess independently its condition. How many requests had the TAC received in 1982? 460. How many had it granted? 447.[17] A review of a number of actual TAC files (with the names of the women deleted) indicated that while all of the cases involved "unwanted pregnancies," none posed any threat to the physical health of the mother. Were these cases repesentative? Yes, conceded Dr. Carnduff, the largest percentage of TAC approvals are for socio-economic reasons, then psychiatric reasons, and least common are medical reasons. Shumiatcher later noted that threat to the "health or life" of the mother, not socio-economic reasons, is what section 251 explicitly authorized as a justification for abortion.[18] Then, he zeroed in on how the TAC defined "health." Carnduff allowed that it was a "very broad and all-encompassing" definition, along the lines suggested by the World Heath Organization.

> Shumiatcher: When you say "very broad," could you be a little more specific?
> Carnduff: In general terms . . . it says something to the effect that health shall be defined as a sense of physical, mental and social well-being.
> Shumiatcher: Do you think any of us in this courtroom would qualify as being healthy on that definition?
> Carnduff: No sir.[19]

A satisfied Shumiatcher brought the questioning to an end. Dr. Carnduff's answers had provided all the ammunition Shumiatcher needed for the first stage of his argument. Whatever section 251 purported to do in theory, in practice it meant abortion on demand. Pro-choice observers in the courtroom were shocked and angry when Crown Attorney Sojonky did not bother to challenge this implication.

The entire second day of the trial was devoted to the testimony of Dr. William Liley, the eminent physician from New Zealand. Twice knighted by the Queen, Liley had earned his reputation as the "Father of Fetology" through his pioneering work in the field of perinatal medicine – the methods of treating the unborn, the being-born, and the newly born. Shumiatcher drew on Liley's experience to demonstrate how separate and distinct the unborn child is from the mother. He began by covering the obvious possible differences: hair colour, skin colour, blood type, and sex. Liley recounted experiments indicating the ability of the fetus to experience taste, light, sound, and pain – all independently of the mother's experience. Most importantly, Liley explained to the judge how he and other doctors now diagnosed and treated an unborn child within but apart from the mother, just like any other patient. The implication was clear. If modern medicine views and treats the unborn as a separate patient, why shouldn't the law? The law did not give anyone else the power of life or death over others. Why should it be exercised by a mother over her unborn child?

This theme was reinforced by Liley's testimony about the continuity of human development. Responding to Shumiatcher's carefully rehearsed questions, Liley explained that in biological and medical terms there was no such thing as a "potential human being."[20]

> [I]n biological terms, it is simply a continuum. There are no particularly arbitrary points in it where anything dramatic or different happens. It is just part of an ongoing stream and although one uses terms like zygote or morular or blastocyst or embryo or fetus, one uses these no more technically . . . than you would talk about someone being a newborn or an infant or a toddler or an adolescent or a septuagenarian. These are simply names given to particular stages or ages of development.[21]

Liley emphasized the importance of the earliest stages of human development. A typical human spends only three-quarters of a year (nine months) in utero and three-quarters of a century outside of it. In chronological time, this means that less than 1 per cent of a person's life is spent in utero. But in terms of biological development, Liley continued, more than 90 per cent of a person's life takes place prior to birth. Each individual begins as a single cell and reaches approximately 30 trillion cells as an adult. This process consists of forty-five generations of cells. Eight of these occur within the first four weeks of life. "Thirty, or two-thirds of them, have occurred by eight weeks gestation . . . and forty-one by the time we are born. So you see," Liley concluded,

> looking at things on a developmental scale . . . we spend ninety per cent of our life in utero and indeed the die is very far cast as to the

type of person we are going to be.... This concept ... underpins the importance of ... perinatal medicine ... since events going wrong during that dramatic period of development can then cast a shadow so far into our chronological future.[22]

Shumiatcher carefully connected modern science's new understanding of fetal development back to the legal issues facing Judge Matheson. For several centuries, the law on abortion in English-speaking societies was tied to "quickening," that time in her pregnancy – approximately twelve to fourteen weeks – that a mother begins to feel her baby moving inside her body. Blackstone, in his *Commentaries* (1768), records that abortion prior to quickening was not a crime. Under questioning, Liley explained that this view was based upon the "popular ignorance" of the time, namely, that "the first perception of fetal movement was ... attributed to the baby coming to life at that moment." Liley explained how, like other internal organs, the uterus is insensitive to stimulus other than stretching. Modern techniques such as ultrasound, an echo-sounding device, show that a fetus begins moving its limbs about six weeks after conception. Only when it is large enough to stretch the surrounding abdominal walls does the mother become aware of this movement.[23] Blackstone's eighteenth-century view was based on archaic assumptions and a medical science that was only in its infancy. The inference for Judge Matheson was clear: use modern science and apply newly discovered facts to reform the law.

The dialogue between Shumiatcher and Liley occupied the entire second day of the trial. When Crown Attorney Ed Sojonky began his cross-examination the next morning, his strategy was evident. He began and ended with the same line of questioning: What were Liley's personal views on abortion? He pressed Liley to concede that medical views varied as to when life begins and that some views disagreed with his.

Liley was not without a rejoinder. In the 1950s and 1960s, "before abortion became a social issue," he told the judge, his hospital received a number of first-class antenatal [pre-birth] teaching films from the United States, England, Canada, and Europe. All of them unequivocally taught that human life begins at the time of conception. The technical credits on these films, he continued, "read like a 'Who's Who' of obstetric and gynecological specialists in the country in which they were made."[24] Now, years later, some of these same specialists have repudiated their earlier position. "[It] is [in] my opinion," Liley concluded, "a redefining of human life in the terms which will suit their present purpose, which is that of justifying abortion."[25]

Sojonky was not deterred and continued to press his original game plan.

> Sojonky: Well, that is your personal view, that abortion is immoral, criminal and arbitrary, isn't it?
>
> Liley: As one who looks after babies before birth, yes.
>
> Sojonky: Yes. And by using the term immoral you concede, Dr. Liley, that a moral issue is involved, is interwoven throughout this, isn't it?
>
> Liley: It is in all medical care, sir."
>
> Sojonky: Thank you. I don't think I have any further questions My Lord.[26]

Sojonky confidently returned to his seat, satisfied that he had impugned the "scientific" character of Liley's testimony by connecting it to his personal views on abortion. As for Liley, his testimony at the *Borowski* trial soon took on added significance. Several weeks later, upon his return to New Zealand, Sir William Liley suffered a heart attack and died. His testimony in the Regina courtroom became his last act in a life dedicated to helping and curing the very young.

Shumiatcher's next witness was a "Mrs. K," a twenty-seven-year-old woman who recounted a sad personal story of how she had been pressured by her mother to have an abortion when she was sixteen and had subsequently suffered three miscarriages. The putative purpose of Mrs. K's testimony, according to Shumiatcher, was to illuminate further the relationship of the Regina General Hospital's TAC with its patients. His questions, however, suggested a less factual objective.

> Shumiatcher: Do you see any relationship between this sad story of how you had these births, all ending in disaster . . . [and] the abortion you first had when you were sixteen?
>
> Mrs. K: Yeah, I think it has everything to do with it. . . . Like when I delivered my first one, you know, I just – as soon as I looked at her I wondered what the other one would have been like.
>
> Shumiatcher: The one that was aborted?
>
> Mrs. K: That's right. And I just think that it is a way of paying me back for what I did to that one.
>
> Shumiatcher: What did you do?
>
> Mrs. K: Well I killed it literally. I took its life and I don't think,

142

you know, anybody has that right. And I think by doing what I am doing now, maybe it is a way of – you know, like making – not – you will never make up, but help, you know.

Shumiatcher: Is that why you volunteered to come here today?

Mrs. K: Yes, because I think with any young girl at sixteen, there is nothing more than confusion. You know a lot of these girls don't know and they don't realize what it will do to them later, psychologically especially.[27]

Sojonky strongly protested that Mrs. K's autobiography was "not at all relevant," and Judge Matheson agreed. But like much irrelevant testimony, it had probably already had its intended emotional effect.

For the remainder of the third day, Shumiatcher put his client on the stand. Borowski briefly recounted the events of his decade-long struggle against the 1969 abortion law and then spent most of the afternoon identifying – and thus entering into evidence – his voluminous correspondence urging government leaders to stop funding and permitting abortions. The addresses on the stack of letters read like a "Who's Who" of the political leaders of the day: Prime Minister Trudeau and his Solicitor-General Warren Allmand, Finance Minister John Turner, Justice Minister Ron Basford, Robert Stanfield, leader of the Opposition Tories, David Lewis and Réal Caouette, leaders of the NDP and Créditiste parties, and members of the Schreyer cabinet in Manitoba. It made for a dull afternoon, although there were snippets of vintage Borowski. A letter dated July 31, 1976, was addressed to his old boss, Premier Schreyer. In it Borowski berates Schreyer's "tightwad government" for spending a million dollars on diseased elm trees but not giving a penny to "Pregnancy Distress Service," a pro-life group that counselled and assisted women with unwanted pregnancies. The letter ends as follows:

So Mr. Premier I am appealing to your sense of justice – fair play – common decency and baby-lingualism to allocate funds to this most worthy and deserving life-saving organization. The life they may save may be a MINDSZENSKY – or A FUTURE PREMIER OF MANITOBA. THINK WHERE YOU WOULD BE IF YOUR DEAR OLD MOM BELIEVED IN ABORTION DURING THE HUNGRY DIRTY THIRTIES????

With Kind Personal Regards, I am,
your friend and critic,
Joe P. Borowski[28]

A bored Ed Sojonky asked a few perfunctory questions and the third day came to an end.

Day 4 was again devoted entirely to the testimony of one of Shumiatcher's medical experts, this time Dr. Jérôme Lejeune, the world-famous geneticist from Paris. Lejeune's claim to fame was his pioneering work in the field of chromosomes, in particular, the discovery of the extra chromosome that causes Down's Syndrome (or "mongolism") in human children. Lejeune's achievements had been recognized by various awards and honours in England, Argentina, the Soviet Union, and the United States. This last award was conferred personally by President Kennedy just months before his assassination.

Shumiatcher's line of questioning had the potential for a mind-numbing, day-long lecture on genetics. Fortunately, Lejeune had the gift of all good teachers, the ability to illustrate complex subject matter with easily grasped examples. Chromosomes, Lejeune analogized, are like "tiny roads," easily seen under the modern microscope and resembling a series of "little sausages." Every human being has exactly forty-six chromosomes, twenty-three received from the mother and twenty-three from the father. (The cause of Down's Syndrome is an extra, forty-seventh chromosome.) Each chromosome is constituted by a long thread of DNA – "one meter long in a tiny spermatozoa and carefully coiled so that it could fit neatly upon the point of a needle." The relation of the DNA threads to the chromosome is analogous to the way a music tape plays in a cassette. Just as the music from a symphony is magnetically coded onto the tape, so all the genetic information from the parents is coded onto the threads of DNA. To be used, however, a tape has to be carefully wound and coiled inside a cassette.

> Chromosomes are just the minicassettes of life, the DNA perfectly coiled so that it can be used and read without making knots and fuss about it.
> Now, in human beings, we have twenty-three of those minicassettes as a basis and we receive twenty-three from our father and twenty-three from our mother. . . . At fecundation [fertilization], twenty-three plus twenty-three make forty-six; and forty-six is the basic number of those minicassettes in which the symphony of life begins to be played according to what is written on those tables of the law of life. . . . [A]t the very moment that the mechanism is triggered, what is played is a new human life. It's new because when we receive those informations on the minicassettes from father and . . .

144

from mother, we are not receiving exactly what have our parents because each of them gives us half of what they had and they choose it on a random manner. The result is that any conceptus is, by itself, carrying a new constellation of genes which has never been produced and will never be reproduced again.[29]

Lejeune repeatedly described this genetic constellation as the "table of the law of life," from which flows the uniqueness of each individual.

[T]his genetic make-up tells exactly what will be the colour of the eyes, the colour of the skin, the colour of the hairs, the form of the nose, the form of the ears, and even it spells out the weak and the strong – the strongness – of the person. . . . [O]nce this pre-mortal information has been gathered, every quality which makes an individual recognizable, as he will be later called Peter or Margaret or Mary . . . are entirely spelled out in its own personal genetic constitution.[30]

Lejeune supplemented his testimony with several films, slides, and pictures, all graphically illustrating various aspects of prenatal human existence. Prompted by Shumiatcher's careful questions, Lejeune explained to Judge Matheson that despite the fact that the secret of DNA was discovered only in the early 1970s, it is now standard information in all medical textbooks. The implication was again clear: the 1969 abortion law is out of step with modern science.

On cross-examination Sojonky tried to discredit Lejeune's testimony. As he did with each expert witness, Sojonky began by asking Lejeune his religion ("Catholic") and whether he was "personally opposed to abortion" ("yes"). Lejeune solemnly countered that in the unlikely event that the Pope declared abortion permissible, then he, Lejeune, would leave the Catholic Church!

Sojonky confronted Lejeune with testimony given before the American Senate Judiciary Committee in 1981 (before whom Lejeune had also testified) that while a fertilized human egg has the "potential" for human life, modern science cannot tell us "when human life begins." This question was said to involve "complicated ethical and value judgments," and is a matter of ethics and philosophy.[31] Lejeune refused to retreat. "Philosophy cannot be built out of the air," the Frenchman retorted. Ethical judgments require facts, true facts, and these are supplied by science.

[B]iology can only tell us this yellow man is a member of your kin, this white man is a member of your kin, this tiny human being is a member of your kin; but biology cannot tell you . . . you have to respect them. That is the moral, that's the ethics who has to tell us that; but first we have to know whether the man in question is really a member of our kin, and that is scientific.[32]

There followed a long and somewhat tedious debate between Lejeune and Sojonky about when the fertilized ovum becomes a human being and whether this is a matter of "science" or "ethics." While both agreed that the fertilized egg is a "living cell," a "human cell," and thus "human life," consensus broke down on whether or when it could be described as a "human person" or "human being." Lejeune insisted that there was no distinction. Sojonky's questioning suggested that the moral and legal connotations attached to the concept of "human person" were a matter of ethical judgment, not science.

Sojonky's persistent cross-examination of Dr. Lejeune carried over to Friday morning. Predictably, what had not been resolved by society was not resolved in the courtroom that day. Shumiatcher called several other witnesses Friday afternoon, but the energy of both sides was clearly depleted. At 3:10 p.m. a weary Judge Matheson mercifully adjourned proceedings until Monday.

The second week began with the testimony of the best-known and most controversial of Shumiatcher's witnesses: Dr. Bernard Nathanson from New York City. Nathanson had come into prominence as an abortion rights activist. He was a co-founder of NARAL (the American equivalent of CARAL) in the 1960s. From 1971 through 1972 he was director of the largest abortion clinic in the Western world. This New York clinic operated from eight in the morning until midnight, 364 days of the year. (It closed Christmas Day.) During Nathanson's tenure as director, he testified that approximately 60,000 abortions were performed, earning him the reputation as the "Abortion King of America." Ironically, he was probably the only man in North America with as much first-hand experience with abortion as Henry Morgentaler, and yet here he was testifying on behalf of the unborn at Joe Borowski's trial.

Nathanson's bizarre background made him not only the most famous but also the most effective witness called by Shumiatcher. Having been on "the other side," Nathanson spoke authoritatively about how he and other pro-choice doctors used to fake medical reports about their patients' psychological health to qualify them for abortions. He testified that in the early 1970s the TACs in New York state used to be stacked with pro-choice doctors who rubber-stamped all abortion requests.[33] Sojonky protested – with some success – that this was irrelevant to the operation of TACs in Canada in the 1980s.

Nathanson was also a compelling witness for the exponential growth of knowledge flowing from the development of new technologies. One by one, Nathanson ticked off and explained each of the new technologies that has broken down the walls of scientific ignorance about the unborn: real time ultrasound, electronic fetal heart monitoring, immunochemistry, fetoscopy, and hysteroscopy. The impact of these technologies was to create an entirely new medical specialty known as fetology – the science and care of the fetus or unborn child.

Ironically, Nathanson observed, fetology came into its own in the very years that the American Supreme Court was deciding *Roe v. Wade*. Had that appeal been heard a year or two later, Nathanson suggested, there could have been a very different result. Shumiatcher asked Nathanson about fetal "viability," a concept that played a crucial role in the Court's reasoning in *Roe*. Viability – the ability of the fetus/unborn child to live outside its mother's womb – Nathanson replied, is "a slippery concept." It was "in vogue" in the sixties and early seventies, but the "velocity of technology now has made such previously reliable concepts unreliable."[34] Nathanson reinforced this image of scientific revolution by citing chapter and verse from recent medical journals. The April, 1983, issue of the *American Journal of Obstetrics and Gynecology,* he told the judge, reports how developments in fetal therapy may require a physician to regard the fetus as a separate patient from the mother and even give rise to lawsuits if a mother refuses to consent to necessary fetal surgery.[35] An article from the prestigious *New England Journal of Medicine,* Nathanson continued, reported an experiment in which a group of women seeking abortions were first given the opportunity to observe their pregnancies by way of real time ultrasound shown on a screen. They subsequently all changed their minds.[36]

Shumiatcher saved the best for last: "Now, Doctor Nathanson," he purred, "would you tell His Lordship why you abandoned your practice of aborting babies, to take up the practice of saving them?" Nathanson replied:

Yes . . . my reasons for changing my viewpoint stem from purely secular bases. I have no religious convictions. . . . In the late 1960's . . . abortion on demand seemed to be necessary for women trapped in a difficult social situation . . . but most important . . . there was no countervailing moral force in the balance. Nothing of value, according to our perception in the 1960's . . . was being destroyed, but with the advent of Fetology, in 1973 . . . over the next four years . . . it became unmistakably clear to me that the person inside the uterus was a human being, indistinguishable from any of us, validated by all these new technologies . . . [and] that the continued destruction of this person was impermissible. . . . I could not continue to advocate or practice the destruction of what was now unmistakably, unarguably an identifiable human person, an unborn child in the uterus.[37]

Shumiatcher could not have dreamed up a better witness. Nathanson provided a human model for exactly the kind of "scientific conversion" that Shumiatcher hoped to elicit in Judge Matheson (and, ultimately, the Supreme Court of Canada).

Outside the courtroom, Borowski was so pleased with Nathanson's role in his trial that he could not stop from boasting and making jokes. "We could have gotten the Pope to testify but so what? People would say, 'What do you expect from the Pope?' So instead we got this atheist!"[38] One of his favourite "trial stories" was that when Nathanson arrived in Regina, Borowski explained to him that his prayer group normally prayed for the conversion of atheists. Recently, however, Borowski confided to Nathanson, they had excluded him from their prayers. "You're too valuable as you are!" Borowski roared with a laugh.

Shumiatcher called five more expert witnesses over the course of the second week. Some were more effective than others, but none added anything particularly new to Shumiatcher's thickening plot. Dr. Harley Smyth, an expert in neurosurgery and medical ethics from Wellesley Hospital in Toronto, sought to debunk the alleged "psychological harm" to the mother that was frequently used to justify abortions. Dr. Patrick Beirne, Head of Obstetrics and Gynaecology at St. Michael's Hospital in Toronto, and Dr. Robert Kudel, a radiologist from Saskatoon, both pioneers in the use of ultrasound in Canada, testified as to the early anatomical development and agility of the fetus. Dr. Heather Morris, a specialist in obstetrics and gynecology at the

Women's College Hospital in Toronto, reinforced earlier testimony as to the "rubber-stamp" character of the TAC process.

Sojonky's cross-examinations were all variations on the same theme: What is your religion? Isn't it your *personal belief* that abortions are morally wrong? Are there not other equally learned doctors who disagree with what you have said? Is not this whole matter, in the final analysis, a matter of values, not facts, personal judgment and not science?

At noon on Friday of the second week, Shumiatcher's last witness completed her testimony. After quietly suffering ten long days of the pro-life perspective, pro-choice observers in the Regina courtroom eagerly anticipated the Crown's witnesses. The time for rebuttal was at hand! Or so they thought. To their shock and dismay, Ed Sojonky rose to announce that the government did not intend to call any witnesses. The Crown did not dispute the accuracy of the plaintiff's evidence, he explained, only its relevance.[39] Instead, Sojonky sought only to introduce into evidence three documents: the 1977 Badgley Report on the operation of the abortion law, the 1980 and 1981 annual therapeutic abortions reports compiled by Statistics Canada, and the two-volume record of the 1981 U.S. Senate Judiciary Committee's hearings on the Human Life Bill. When Sojonky was unable to cite any Canadian rules of evidence that supported the use of foreign government documents, Judge Matheson refused to allow the American materials to be entered as legal evidence. A shaken Sojonky requested that proceedings be adjourned until the following Wednesday to allow time to prepare for final argument. This time Judge Matheson accepted his request.

Pro-choice observers left the courtroom shaking their heads in disbelief. Outside, an upbeat Borowski told the press that it looked like the government was "folding up their tents."[40] CARAL's worst suspicions about the government's willingness to defend effectively the right of women to choose abortions seemed to have been realized.[41]

Final arguments began on Wednesday, May 25. Following normal practice, Shumiatcher as counsel for the plaintiff went first; Sojonky as respondent followed; and then Shumiatcher was given a final opportunity to respond. With all his evidence in place, it was now time for Shumiatcher "to wed the principles of law with the knowledge of science."

Shumiatcher began with the legal prong of his attack. Citing Bracton, Coke, Blackstone, and other historical pillars of the common law,

Shumiatcher stressed the primacy of respect for human life in the liberal democratic tradition and the long-standing recognition of the right of the unborn to some form of legal protection. In addition to the criminal prohibition on abortion after quickening, Shumiatcher also noted the protection afforded the unborn in capital punishment cases involving pregnant women. In such cases, the punishment of the felon / mother had to be postponed until the birth of her child, so that "the hand of the executioner in no way harmed the unborn child."[42] He also argued that the 1969 abortion law was radically inconsistent with other fields of Canadian law. Child welfare acts have been interpreted to allow state intervention to protect an unborn child from the damaging behaviour – such as alcohol or drug abuse – of the pregnant mother. Canadian tort law recognizes the right of a child to sue for injuries suffered while still inside the mother. Similarly, property law allows unborn children to be named as inheritors in a will or trust. But without the right to life, Shumiatcher emphasized, these other rights become meaningless.

The second prong consisted of reminding Judge Matheson what he had heard for the past two weeks: that modern medical science has shown that the fetus/unborn child is biologically and genetically no different than the newborn, and that the 1969 reform thus rested on a mistake of fact. Nine expert witnesses had testified as to the findings of this "new art." This was "not opinion evidence," urged Shumiatcher, "but evidence of basic but complex facts" that were "not available ten years ago" or in 1969. Had it been, he suggested, Parliament "might well have taken a different view."[43] The quixotic Shumiatcher then surprised the judge (and offended some spectators) by reciting a poem he had written to characterize the treatment of the unborn under the 1969 reform:

We are the little nobodies,
Not dog, nor fowl, not cat.
We cannot meow or bark or cry.
De minimus lex not curat.
[The law takes no account of trifles.][44]

"The law, certainly under [section] 251, takes no cognizance of the unborn, and they are treated like trifles," declared a suddenly agitated Shumiatcher. "But that was before ultrasound, before we could see who and what they were and watch them live their intra-uterine life."[45]

The Crown, Shumiatcher reminded Judge Matheson, did not call "a single witness to contradict the facts." Why? Shumiatcher demanded. Because they are "beyond contradiction."[46]

Shumiatcher's emphasis on new technology was an integral part of his strategy. By emphasizing the recentness of these discoveries he hoped to finesse the problem of a direct confrontation between courts and legislatures, precisely the charge made by Sojonky. From Shumiatcher's perspective, he was not asking Judge Matheson blatantly to substitute his personal judgment for that of Parliament's, but only to find that Parliament in 1969 had acted on incomplete and inaccurate information. He was not asking the judge to overrule Parliament, only to correct its earlier mistaken judgment based on new scientific facts.

This aspect of Shumiatcher's strategy paralleled that used by the National Association for the Advancement of Colored People in the landmark American school desegregation case, *Brown v. Board of Education* in 1954.[47] NAACP lawyers believed that both the "framers' intent" and earlier precedents dealing with the Equal Protection Clause of the U.S. Constitution were against them. To counter these considerations, NAACP lawyers emphasized the "new" discoveries of modern social science: that racially segregated schooling had a negative impact on the educational opportunities of black students. The strategy worked. The American Supreme Court relied on the new social science evidence of "unequal effects" to support their ruling that racial segregation violated the right of black school children to the "equal protection of the law." With this line of reasoning, the Court and its defenders could claim that it was not overruling precedents or ignoring the framers' intent, but only adopting the meaning of "equal protection" to new and unforeseen facts. Shumiatcher hoped the same strategy would work for the unborn in Canada.

Shumiatcher concluded his soliloquy by invoking yet again the *Persons Case*. Just as Lord Sankey and the Privy Council had adopted a "large and liberal" approach to constitutional interpretation to extend new rights to Canadian women in 1929, so now it was time to extend new rights to the unborn by recognizing that they, too, are "persons."[48] To those who objected to the inclusion of the unborn in word "everyone" in section 7 of the Charter in 1983, the response was the same as it was in 1929: Why not?

Sojonky's closing statement was much shorter. He repeated yet again that the Crown did not contest the accuracy of the medical testimony, only its relevance. The question of what constitutes a human person "goes beyond medicine and biology" and is based on personal beliefs.[49] Under cross-examination, each of Shumiatcher's expert witnesses had conceded that they were personally opposed to abortion. They also conceded, Sojonky noted, that abortion may still be appropriate in certain circumstances. While their personal beliefs may lead them to conclude that these circumstances are extremely rare, others – and most particularly Parliament – are equally free to conclude that more flexible access to abortion services is desirable. This latter policy has been embodied in the exculpatory provisions of section 251. After all, Sojonky reminded the judge, section 251 still makes abortion a crime, and thus protects the fetus, unless a TAC, staffed by medical experts, approves the request. Parliament has adopted a policy that is neither pro-life nor pro-choice, but rather a compromise middle ground. This policy may offend the personal beliefs of the expert witnesses or Mr. Borowski, Sojonky exclaimed, but this hardly makes it illegal.

Sojonky also worked through a randomly ordered, point by point rebuttal of many of Shumiatcher's legal arguments. Most importantly, he tackled the analogy to the *Persons Case* head on. Sojonky cited chapter and verse from the minutes of the 1980-81 Parliamentary Committee on the Constitution that section 7 of the Charter was intended to have a purely procedural meaning and did not affect the abortion issue one way or the other. Sojonky's message was clear: the "constitutional tree" was much too young for judicial grafting and Judge Matheson was obliged to respect the meaning intended by the framers.

Judge Matheson had listened passively during Shumiatcher's and now Sojonky's closing statements. He had asked the occasional question but they were usually just to clarify what counsel meant. This now changed. Matheson began to challenge Sojonky with hypothetical questions that clearly put the Crown on the defensive. What if, the judge speculated, "one concludes that the unborn child is part of everyone, do you think the [TAC's] non-legal process that you have described is in accordance with fundamental justice?"[50] The question trapped Sojonky, who had already stated that because the TAC "was not a legal process in any shape or form," it did not have to meet the usual criteria of procedural fairness.

Before Sojonky could wiggle off the hook, Matheson raised the ante. "Take it one stage further," said the judge. "If . . . you have a three-year-old child whose activities are such that the mother is in imminent danger of both a mental and physical breakdown and medical opinions

152

so certify that, does that justify terminating the life of the child?"[51] Sojonky protested that this was not at all analogous to the situation contemplated by section 251, but he was clearly on the defensive. Fortunately for Sojonky, it was time for the afternoon break. A somewhat more subdued Ed Sojonky returned to complete his rebuttal, which spilled over to the next morning.

Shumiatcher now had the opportunity to respond. If he had properly gaged Judge Matheson's new inquisitiveness he might well have passed. But it is an occupational liability of all lawyers – even the good ones, perhaps especially the good ones – that they cannot resist a platform. Shumiatcher had barely begun before the judge interrupted. If a TAC consisted of Dr. Beirne, Dr. Smyth, and Dr. Morris, queried Matheson, "what do you think the result would be in view of their testimony?"[52] Shumiatcher tried repeatedly to lead the discussion away from the obvious answer, but Judge Matheson persisted. Quite clearly, a TAC consisting of Shumiatcher's medical witnesses would approve few requests for abortions. Why, demanded Matheson, do other doctors give such different answers? Cornered, Shumiatcher spoke from his heart:

> I think the reason is very, very simple. I think it's part of the whole consumerism concept of our society, My Lord. The customer is always right. If you want it, you can have it. If you want to buy, I'll sell. It just comes down to that. And it's part and parcel of the casual relationship that we have towards the most important values [that] traditionally we have had in society, [so that now] little kids don't count. That's why. . . . You're not supposed to endure any discomfort; you're not supposed to have any burdens or obligations to bear in this society. You're just supposed to have fun. Well, if that's the kind of society – with this kind of law, we guarantee that sort of future, I submit.[53]

People on both sides of the abortion debate could find more than a little truth in Shumiatcher's answer,[54] but in an odd way it probably weakened his legal argument. Quite clearly, from the pro-life perspective the problem was not the law *per se* but the general state of public opinion that allowed, perhaps encouraged, the (generally) permissive application of the criteria set out in section 251. A judge could hardly declare that public opinion violated section 7 of the Charter! Realizing the implication of what he had said Shumiatcher tried to backtrack, but the damage had been done. He went on to several other topics for another twenty minutes, but with flagging energy and lack of direction. At one p.m., his monologue ground to an anticlimactic end.

Justice Matheson quietly announced that he would reserve judgment and adjourned the court. The courtroom emptied quickly, as did the downtown hotels. Outside, a confident Borowski joked with Ed Sojonky. "Look, Ed," Borowski grinned, "what the government is asking you to do is to prove the earth is flat. Now they may belong to the Flat Earth Society but the judge does not."[55] As Regina slipped into another hot, boring summer, attention shifted to Winnipeg and then Toronto, where the abortion conflict was soon to reach the boiling point.

CHAPTER 14

Abortion Wars:
The Spring of '83

On May 5, 1983, the Morgentaler clinic in south-central Winnipeg was set to open its doors. The opening of the two-storey, white stucco building at 883 Corydon Avenue had been delayed for several costly months because of legal manoeuvring by local pro-life groups. Opponents had used every imaginable tactic to block the opening of the clinic. They had challenged the zoning allowance, building permit, occupancy permit, and certification from the Manitoba College of Physicians. One by one, the Morgentaler clinic cleared these legal hurdles under the supervision of Greg Brodsky, Morgentaler's new lawyer.

Soon after choosing Winnipeg as the site for his clinic, Morgentaler had hired Brodsky, Winnipeg's best known and highest paid criminal lawyer. Local feminist leaders regarded Brodsky as too closely associated with the defence of murderers and rapists and had advised against hiring him. But Henry Morgentaler had spent time in prison and wanted to make sure it did not happen again. Brodsky was his insurance policy. Brodsky had worked closely with Morgentaler on all aspects of the clinic project. In anticipation of eventual criminal charges, Brodsky had advised the clinic to keep extensive and accurate records of the circumstances of each patient, information that could be used later to develop another "defence of necessity" similar to the Verona Parkinson case. He also counselled against mounting any prochoice counter-demonstrations in front of the clinic. Let the media show the people of Winnipeg how pro-life protesters hassle and insult clinic staff and patients, he said. Let the media show us as the good guys and them as the troublemakers. This public relations strategy, he said, would pay handsome dividends when it came time to choose a jury.[1]

Brodsky was paying a price for his association with Morgentaler. Someone shot a hole through the back window of his son's Bronco as well as the front door of the family house. Obscene and threatening phone calls had become routine. Brodsky also learned first hand what Morgentaler's previous lawyers already knew: the doctor was not an easy man to work with. The day before Brodsky and Morgentaler were to appear before the board of the Manitoba College of Physicians, Morgentaler publicly referred to the board members as "hyenas." Another morning Brodsky picked up the newspaper to read that Morgentaler was telling the Toronto press how he intended to instruct Brodsky in the handling of his Manitoba charges. Brodsky telephoned his client immediately: "Look, Henry, if you want to tell me something, tell me directly, not through the *Globe and Mail*."[2] Still, Brodsky admired Morgentaler's tenacity and commitment. "Henry," Brodsky observed, "was willing to go to jail for his beliefs."[3] To a person whose career consisted of keeping his clients out of jail, this was the mark of a very unusual man.

To protest the clinic opening, Joe Borowski had summoned his troops with a full-page ad in the *Winnipeg Sun*. Several hundred pro-lifers responded, and Borowski directed them from the leased mobile home he had parked on a supportive neighbour's front yard. Hymns, prayers, speeches, and a free lunch were served from the trailer. Morgentaler "made a mistake" in choosing Winnipeg, Borowski half-predicted, half-threatened. "He's going to find out Winnipeg isn't Montreal. There's a great difference in the morality of people here."[4]

Ironically, the success of the pro-life demonstrators was undermined by one of the bureaucratic hurdles they had encouraged – the delay of an "occupancy permit." The permit arrived too late in the day for the clinic to open. The following day the clinic opened quietly, picketed by only Borowski and a handful of protesters. Borowski's frustration was further compounded when the city informed him that he was violating municipal zoning by-laws by parking his mobile home in a front yard. He was given forty-eight hours to move it or face a $5,000 fine. Never at a loss for words, the disappointed Borowski threw reporters one of his typical screwball metaphors. The current protest, he declared, was "the last hurrah" of the anti-abortion movement. "If we can't stop an illegal clinic, how are we going to stop abortions in hospitals? It's like Custer's last stand. Either I'm Custer or he [Morgentaler] is Custer."[5]

While Borowski's own protest turned out to be anticlimactic, there were other indications to support his claim that Winnipeg was not Montreal. The anticipated benign neglect of the NDP government never materialized. Morgentaler had written the Attorney-General, Roland Penner, asking him to "stand on principle" and refuse to prosecute. He explained how the Quebec government had simply stopped enforcing section 251 and now asked the Manitoba Attorney-General to do likewise. Penner flatly refused. It was his legal duty as Attorney-General, Penner wrote back, to uphold the law, regardless of his personal beliefs about abortion. The Manitoba Court of Appeal had recently ruled that the Attorney-General did not possess any general discretion to suspend the enforcement of a section of the Criminal Code.[6] To allow each province to select which provisions of the Criminal Code it would enforce would be to subvert Parliament's unquestioned jurisdiction over criminal law. This could result in a "checkerboard" criminal law, where what was legal in one province was illegal in the next.

Predictably, Morgentaler was not impressed with such legal niceties. If Quebec had done it in the seventies, why couldn't Manitoba do it in the eighties? Penner patiently pointed out that Quebec only suspended prosecution *after* three separate jury acquittals. If a similar scenario developed in Manitoba, Penner suggested, it was certainly possible that his government would consider suspending enforcement of section 251 for the same reason that Quebec had given: that it was no longer enforceable. But this would take time.

Patience was not one of Morgentaler's virtues, and he was growing increasingly irritated with what he perceived as Penner's overly cautious "wait and see" approach. Morgentaler's frustration boiled over a few weeks later when both he and Penner were invited to address a small conference of leftist lawyers in Toronto on consecutive days. Penner went first and not only gave his reasons for turning down Morgentaler's request but also revealed their correspondence. Morgentaler addressed the same group the following night. Thinking that the correspondence had been confidential, Morgentaler became angry and publicly declared that Penner was either a coward or was sacrificing his

Borowski and Morgentaler debate the abortion issue at the University of
Toronto, 1984. (*Courtesy Canapress Photo Service*)

socialist principles to keep his new political office.[7] Penner was not
pleased when Morgentaler's accusations leaked into the press.

Relations between the two were further poisoned in the wake of a
January 28 debate between Morgentaler and Borowski at the University of Manitoba (interrupted for an hour by an anonymous bomb
threat). Morgentaler told an overflow audience of 2,100 that he had
recently performed an abortion on the girl friend of the son of an Attorney General in whose province he planned to open a clinic. While Morgentaler said professional secrecy prohibited him from revealing the
boy's name, the implication to many was that the Attorney General was
Roland Penner. An angry Penner quickly denied the implication and
called Morgentaler's tactics "shamefully exploitive" and "intolerable."[8]

Subsequent public and private requests to Penner not to prosecute
were turned down. Privately, Penner did not think that the abortion law
would survive Morgentaler's Charter challenge. If it did, he told his
closest friends, he would resign rather than proceed with the prosecution.[9] Publicly, however, Penner simply repeated that to grant immu-
nity from prosecution to Morgentaler "would mean in effect the end of
criminal law in Canada."[10]

In fact, the Morgentaler clinic had seriously divided the NDP

158

caucus. The feminist vote was an important part of the NDP majority coalition and had outspoken representatives, such as MLA Myrna Phillips. But there were also influential Catholics and pro-life supporters, including Minister of Health Larry Desjardins. Desjardins, in May, rejected Morgentaler's application to have the clinic classified as a hospital, an administrative ruling that could have brought the Morgentaler clinic within the letter of the law. He had also threatened to resign if Morgentaler wasn't prosecuted. Desjardins had delivered the St. Boniface riding for the NDP government, and their slim majority made keeping him a high priority. Desjardins's threat to resign also brought back memories of Joe Borowski's resignation from a different NDP government ten years earlier. Ellen Kruger, spokeswoman for the Winnipeg Coalition for Reproductive Choice and an NDP supporter, described the NDP's dilemma. "We have the dichotomy on the Prairies of groupings of people who are very progressive on economic issues, but because of religious socialization, and so on, are less progressive on the social issues."[11]

The abortion issue has been hard on the "old Left" coalition. The ascendancy of the pro-choice position among the "new Left" is witnessed by the growing number of NDP refugees in the pro-life ranks – Joe Borowski and Morris Shumiatcher being only the best known.

Less than a week after his Winnipeg clinic opened, Morgentaler told reporters that its first abortions had been performed. The clinic is ready for business, Morgentaler went on. "I don't think that any woman asking the clinic in Winnipeg for an abortion will have to wait longer than five to six days."[12] Once again Henry Morgentaler had thrown down the gauntlet to provincial law enforcement authorities. Borowski and others launched a public relations campaign to force the government to respond, including publishing in the *Winnipeg Free Press* a petition signed by 37,000 Manitobans protesting the Morgentaler clinic. In a province the size of Manitoba, no government can safely ignore a petition with 37,000 names.

On June 3, the inevitable occurred. Cheered on by the pro-life picketers, the Winnipeg police raided the Morgentaler clinic and took away eleven people for questioning. One woman who was in the process of being aborted had to be taken to the hospital. Borowski himself arrived on the scene shortly after the raid began and congratulated the police for a job well done. Those arrested included the clinic staff, several patients, and Dr. Robert Scott, the medical director of the the clinic.

Scott, a doctor from Alexandria, Ontario, near Cornwall, had been trained by Morgentaler in his Montreal clinic. When no suitable Manitoba doctors stepped forward to help with the Winnipeg clinic, Morgentaler persuaded Scott to take on the role of medical director. Morgentaler himself was in Montreal at the time of the raid.

For almost a week, no charges were laid. Pro-choice groups grew cautiously optimistic, while Borowski and his supporters feared that Attorney-General Penner was obstructing the laying of charges. Both sides tried to exert pressure on the government. The suspense ended June 9, when the Winnipeg police laid charges of conspiracy to violate section 251 against Morgentaler and Scott, the four registered nurses, and two social workers who worked in the clinic. The announcement touched off another round of demonstrations in the struggle for public opinion and the government's ear. Six hundred Morgentaler supporters protested that night in front of the legislature.

The conspiracy charges caught Morgentaler and Brodsky offguard and posed serious problems for their defence. Brodsky had been quietly co-operating with the Chief of Police for several months. In what is presumably the first time in the history of Canadian criminal law, a lawyer had actually gone to the police and explained that his client wanted to be arrested and charged with violating the Criminal Code. According to Brodsky, he had told the police that "if you let me know ten minutes in advance [of a raid] I'll get out whatever you want. We don't want any technically tricky defences. We don't want any fooling around. We want to face a direct charge head-on and deal with it. We don't want to hide anything."[13]

All these careful plans went out the window with the conspiracy charge. The crime of conspiracy consists of the intention of two or more people to break the law, plus proof of an agreement actually to carry out the planned illegal action. It would be much more difficult to persuade a jury that the defence of necessity applied to a plot to perform illegal abortions. The success of the defence of necessity rested with presenting a jury with a moving case of a real woman with a real need for an abortion. In anticipation of this defence, Brodsky had instructed Morgentaler's nurses to keep careful case histories for each patient, detailing both why they wanted the abortion and why the doctor thought it was necessary.[14] These records would be little help in a conspiracy trial.

Brodsky later insisted that the conspiracy charge was a mistake – that he and Winnipeg's chief Crown attorney, Wayne Myshkowsky, had been preoccupied with an important murder case, and that the Morgentaler file had been delegated to a junior Crown attorney not privy to their agreement.[15] The latter had decided to lay the conspiracy charge because it seemed the easiest way to tie together the doctors, nurses, and social workers who together ran the clinic. More important still, the conspiracy charge was broad enough to include Henry Morgentaler, who had not yet performed an abortion at the Winnipeg clinic at the time of the raid.[16]

The day after they were charged, Dr. Scott and the rest of the clinic staff appeared determined to continue their work. Emerging from a hearing at the Winnipeg courthouse arm-in-arm with four other defendants, head nurse Lynn Crocker told cheering supporters and television cameras, "The clinic is open. We're on our way back to work." While this public show of defiance may have bolstered the morale of the pro-choice supporters, it angered the Winnipeg police department. Crocker's "back-to-business" speech was all they needed to get another search warrant, and two weeks later the police raided the clinic for the second time. Equipment was seized, including Morgentaler's vacuum aspirator, and six persons were arrested and charged. Morgentaler, who was not present, was again named as a co-conspirator. Five of the six arrested spent the weekend in jail because they refused to consent to a judicial order not to return to the clinic.

This time the clinic did not re-open. It would be expensive to replace the vacuum aspirator and other equipment seized by the police. Even if they did, another police raid seemed likely. For several of the nurses and social workers, the romance of being martyrs was waning and the reality of being treated like criminals was sinking in.[17] Morgentaler had opened his Toronto clinic on June 15, and events there soon overtook those in Winnipeg. After the preliminary inquiry in October, the entire Morgentaler prosecution was put on hold, pending the outcome of similar litigation in Toronto. This no doubt pleased Howard Pawley and Roland Penner, who were more than happy to pass the Morgentaler "hot potato" to Bill Davis and Roy McMurtry, their Ontario counterparts. They could now hope that the outcome of Morgentaler's Toronto trial and his constitutional challenge before the Supreme Court of Canada would relieve them of responsibility for subsequent events in Manitoba.[18]

On June 7, less than a week after the first police raid on his Winnipeg clinic, a defiant Henry Morgentaler announced that he would open his

Toronto abortion clinic the following week. He also disclosed the location of the clinic, hitherto a closely guarded secret. The Morgentaler Clinic, as it was named, would be on Harbord Street just west of the University of Toronto, several blocks south of the Bloor-Spadina subway station. Morgentaler told the press conference that "the only way to change the law and provide this service is to open clinics across the country." While he once again urged the Ontario government to ignore the clinic, Morgentaler said he expected charges to be laid, and plans were already under way to establish a $500,000 legal defence fund.[19] The next day Morgentaler gave the media a guided tour of his new facility. Obviously proud of the $100,000 worth of renovations, he walked reporters through various offices, waiting and reception areas, and two fully equipped operating rooms. An undercover policeman posing as a reporter took careful notes.

Contrary to appearances, the opening of the Morgentaler Clinic was not a one-man affair. It culminated almost a year of careful planning and co-ordination with two Toronto-based abortion-rights groups: the Committee for the Establishment of Abortion Clinics (CEAC) and the Ontario Coalition for Abortion Clinics (OCAC). CEAC was formed by a group of women activists to facilitate the establishment of a freestanding abortion clinic in Toronto. CEAC respected Morgentaler's medical expertise and consulted with him on technical matters. However, it also considered Morgentaler to be a political liability in its dealings with Queen's Park and initially planned to open the clinic quite independently of the Montreal doctor. Working with Dr. Leslie Smoling (whom Morgentaler had recommended), CEAC had rented space for a clinic at LuCliff Place, a high-rise office building on Bay Street. Smoling had invested $14,000 in renovations. By late October the clinic was within weeks of opening when the landlord learned of its intended use and cancelled the still unsigned lease.[20] CEAC and Smoling subsequently joined forces with Morgentaler, in large part because he had the financial backing (his brother's company) to purchase a building outright, now considered a necessity after the Bay Street fiasco. CEAC spearheaded the very secretive search for a new clinic building. In the end, however, it was a lawyer hired by Morgentaler and his brother who located the Harbord Street property.[21]

OCAC was formed in September, 1982, and had a complementary but distinct purpose: to lobby Queen's Park and "educate the public on the issue."[22] During the six months preceding the opening of the clinic, OCAC had conducted a low-key but sustained campaign to persuade

162

the people of Ontario that existing abortion facilities were inadequate. As plans for the Morgentaler Clinic crystallized, OCAC also mobilized support for it. Both efforts purposely emphasized the concept of "freedom of choice" in order to attract even individuals who were personally opposed to abortion. This tactic bore fruit – as in the Ontario Federation of Labour's endorsement of the clinic. It also reflected the growing political sophistication of the pro-choice movement. Like other mature political interest groups, it had come to realize that cultivating favourable public opinion was a full-time operation.

The final and perhaps the most important member of Morgentaler's Toronto braintrust was his lawyer, Morris Manning, one of the top criminal lawyers in English-speaking Canada. After graduating from the Law School at the University of Toronto in 1965, Manning had spent nine years honing his courtroom skills as a lawyer for the Attorney-General of Ontario, including numerous appearances before the Supreme Court of Canada. Six years as a Crown prosecutor helped him to become one the country's leading criminal law experts by the tender age of thirty-five. Three years as one of the top civil and constitutional litigators for Queen's Park had helped him develop a keen sense of the growing role of empirical evidence in constitutional litigation. After the Charter was adopted in 1982, Manning was one of a small group of legal experts chosen by the Canadian Institute for the Administration of Justice to tour the country conducting seminars on the new addition to the constitution. This Charter "road show" crisscrossed the country explaining the Charter to both federal and provincial judges. The following year Manning published one of the first book-length treatises on the Charter, a work that achieved "authority" status almost on its release.[23]

Morgentaler first came to Manning in November, 1981, only weeks after the historical constitutional accord of November 5. With the adoption of the Charter now certain, Morgentaler disclosed his intention to open a clinic in Toronto and asked Manning if he was interested in being his lawyer. Manning replied that he would gladly handle Morgentaler's case, but counselled caution. "Wait a couple of years," he advised, "[and] let the Charter develop." It was "still too early" to tell what effect the Charter would have.

Morgentaler replied that he was not interested in waiting. He could not believe that a jury would convict him or that a judge would uphold the abortion law under the new Charter. After several more unsuccessful attempts to persuade Morgentaler to wait, Manning did what his professional ethics required. "Henry, as your lawyer, I have a legal duty to inform you that you would be breaking the law." "Fine," replied Morgentaler, "let's get on with it."[24]

Manning was a leading example of a new breed of Canadian lawyers – "Charter free-lancers" – sought after by those who wanted to turn their legal cases into political causes, or vice versa, as in the case of Henry Morgentaler. There was an almost romantic "hired gun" charisma attached to Manning. A modern-day constitutional alchemist, Manning's "Charter magic" seemed capable of transforming the most ordinary case into the defence of a noble-sounding Charter principle. At the same time he was defending Morgentaler, for example, he had been hired by Mississauga tavern owners to defend nude dancing. The Charter's right to freedom of expression, Manning argued, gave dancers the constitutional right to discard their g-strings.[25]

Manning was quick to point out his involvement in other high-profile cases involving "progressive" causes. He defended the owners of Gay Bath House and the Church of Scientology in Toronto, and has worked for native land claims and the environment. Manning's critics label him as an opportunist and emphasize the work he has done for conservative business clients. Political consistency aside, these cases all contributed to Manning's booming reputation and an equally robust cash flow. When Manning's association with the Merv Lavigne anti-union case was announced – incorrectly, as it turned out – the *Globe and Mail* estimated that it would cost the National Citizens' Coalition $500,000 "to hire Canada's top constitutional lawyer."[26]

Manning, however, was on the Morgentaler case for much more than the money. An avowed civil libertarian, Manning was married to Dr. Linda Rapson, one of the founders of the pro-choice Doctors for the Repeal of the Abortion Law (DRAL). Rapson had been Norma Scarborough's doctor, and it was through Rapson that Scarborough had first become active in CARAL. As CARAL president in 1983, Scarborough had hired Manning to direct CARAL's Charter challenge of the abortion law. For Manning, the Morgentaler case thus represented the happy coincidence of moral conviction and professional expertise. In terms of media exposure and potential political impact, it was the biggest case of his career, and one that would help to build his "Charter superstar" billing.

As promised, the Morgentaler Clinic opened its doors on June 15, as several hundred supporters, followed by almost as many reporters and camera crews, demonstrated in front. In the Toronto media fishbowl, the Morgentaler story dominated the news in a way that few ostensibly non-political stories can. Taking the *Globe and Mail* as a barometer, in the five-week span from the opening of the Winnipeg clinic (June 3) through the week of the police raid on the Toronto clinic (July 5), the Morgentaler story was on the front page seven times, the third page six times, and on page five six times. Television coverage was more extensive and – with mass demonstrations, police raids, fires, and assaults – even more dramatic. Morgentaler seemed to enjoy the "free" media exposure that political consultants dream of, but Manning was concerned about the "backlash" effect it might have on future judges or jurors.

The media were initially disappointed with the lack of "opening day" drama. No organized right-to-life picketers showed up. (Their leaders, it turned out, had intentionally discouraged any confrontation for fear of "bad press.") Not until Morgentaler arrived early that afternoon did the media get the kind of action they were looking for. As Morgentaler made his way from the car toward the clinic, a man suddenly rushed toward him shouting and brandishing a large pair of garden shears. Judy Rebick, an OCAC activist, blocked the attack, and the man fled around the corner. No one was hurt, and police later arrested the man – Augusto Dasilva Dantas – at his Robert Street house. According to Dantas, he had told Morgentaler, "You want to butcher children? Butcher kids? I'll butcher you!" He also claimed that he only intended to frighten Morgentaler, not harm him.[27]

With the clinic open, reporters once again pressed Attorney-General McMurtry to explain how he planned to deal with Morgentaler. McMurtry had obviously run out of patience on this question. "The Attorney-General does not lay charges," he retorted, "the local police does." The police had consulted the local Crown officers, McMurtry continued, and the Morgentaler case would be handled in normal fashion. "One man," McMurtry concluded, "not even Dr. Morgentaler, will not change the nature of the justice system."[28]

By now there was no doubt that the police would raid the Morgentaler Clinic; the only question was when. Police investigators hung around the clinic trying to gather information from patients. To protect the latter and frustrate police, OCAC organized "escort services" for patients, making it difficult for police to distinguish clients. Manning took the unusual step of asking the Supreme Court of Ontario to issue an interim injunction prohibiting the police from raiding the clinic. The abortion law, he pointed out, was already being challenged by CARAL (with Manning as lawyer) as a violation of the Charter of Rights. If the court decided that section 251 was unconstitutional, then it could not be enforced. The police, he argued, should be enjoined from raiding the Morgentaler Clinic until the validity of the abortion law could be decided. The Court turned down Manning's request, but the police had not waited in any case. On July 5, ninety minutes before the Court announced its decision, the police moved in.

The actual raid resembled a Hollywood movie set. It was a steamy, still, and hot Toronto summer morning. The sweet aroma of malt from the nearby Molson's lakeshore brewery wafted over the Spadina neighbourhood. The usual contingent of clinic supporters, the press, and the curious continued their vigil, watched over by several bored policemen. Television film crews patiently stood by. A distraught-looking couple, who turned out to be undercover police, entered the clinic. Once inside, they said they had come from out of province and wanted an abortion for the woman. They had just finished paying their consultation fee when the raid began. Police cruisers suddenly appeared at both ends of Harbord Street, blocking off traffic. Three ambulances and two ambulance buses swooped down on the clinic. A dozen policemen and detectives rushed into the clinic.

Inside the clinic the receptionist's phone rang. An anonymous media supporter told her that the raid had started. As she jumped up to warn the rest of the clinic staff, the undercover policeman grabbed her and identified himself. Dr. Robert Scott was in an operating room with a patient. She had already been sedated when they were alerted to the raid. Scott's first instinct was to stop. But then he decided to hell with the police, locked the door, and completed the abortion.[29]

As the raid progressed things grew tense outside the clinic. An OCAC telephone network had alerted clinic supporters to the police raid. Within an hour several hundred angry supporters milled around the clinic, heckling police and chanting: "Stop . . . stop . . . stop police harassment!" Anger mounted when police led several wobbly-legged patients – their faces covered with towels to avoid the television cameras – down the back fire escape. Two plainclothes policemen carried out a green plastic garbage bag and a paper-covered tray to a car marked "Forensic Pathology Branch, Ministry of the Solicitor-General." Heckling spilled over into confrontation as the police began to carry out boxes of client files and clinic equipment, including both vacuum aspirators, without which the clinic could not operate.[30]

Television camera crews had patiently waited three weeks for this event, and now they eagerly captured all three hours of it. That night the network news programs played back the "highlights" to Canadians across the country. Morris Manning, who came to the clinic soon after the raid began, provided colour commentary. If Henry Morgentaler had wanted more national exposure for his cause, he now had it in spades. Ironically, the mastermind missed his own show. He was vacationing in California the day of the raid.

CHAPTER 15

Charter Superstar Courts
the Reluctant Judge

In the weeks and then months that followed the police raid on the Toronto clinic, both sides continued to jockey for position vis-à-vis public opinion and the government of Ontario. On July 6, 1983, the day after the police had raided the Harbord Street clinic, OCAC mounted an impressive demonstration of 4,000 pro-clinic supporters who marched from Queen's Park down Bloor Street and past the clinic. "Roy McMurtry will rue the day he decided to move against the women of this province," clinic representative Judy Rebick told a cheering crowd.[1] The clinic again found the front pages at the end of July, when an arsonist tried, unsuccessfully, to burn it down. (Police later arrested an unemployed twenty-nine-year-old man who was not connected to any pro-life organizations and was already charged with another unrelated arson.) After being released on bail, Morgentaler spent the rest of July "playing himself" in the making of a National Film Board movie that documented his earlier run at the abortion law in Quebec.

Toronto-area pro-life organizations had been uncharacteristically silent during the early months of the Morgentaler Clinic. As it turned out, this was intentional, part of their own media strategy. Like their adversaries, they had come to realize how important the battle for public opinion was and the crucial role of the media in shaping the public's perception of issues and events. The pro-life leaders were extremely distrustful of the media, whom they perceived as being heavily biased in favour of the pro-choice position. With this in mind, the Right to Life Association of Toronto and Area, the largest such group in Canada, had decided that public confrontation would play into the hands of the pro-clinic forces. Toronto was not like Winnipeg, explained the president, Laura McArthur.

> In Winnipeg, you had a government that as part of its party platform has abortion on demand. . . . So the pro-life forces there had to go directly to the people and say, "Hey, this is our problem," and they had to rally . . . demonstrate . . . and advertise.
>
> Here we didn't have to go to the people. We knew the law would be upheld, the police would step in. There was absolutely no reason to move, except to satisfy the pro-abortionists, who would just love a counter-demonstration so they could scream at us. We don't go for that. We're non-violent, peaceful people.[2]

McArthur initiated this strategy almost a full year before the Morgentaler Clinic even opened. On June 18, 1982, she sent a strategy memo to other Toronto-area pro-life groups:

> We must *not* fall into the trap [Morgentaler] is setting. We must *not* contribute to the controversy by responding publicly. Our response to the media, if pressured, must be low keyed. We should simply state that "it is the responsibility of the provincial Attorney-General to enforce the law." Period.[3]

Quietly but effectively, in January, 1983, the pro-life organizations inundated Attorney-General McMurtry with letters demanding that he enforce the law against any Morgentaler clinics in Ontario. It was not until October 1, 1983, that the pro-life leaders finally called their troops into the streets. Forty thousand pro-lifers, the largest abortion-related demonstration ever in Canada, rallied at Queen's Park and then marched in silent protest down Harbord Street and past the Morgentaler "abortuary." From the second storey of the Clinic building, above the burned out Women's Bookstore, fluttered a small banner: GONE TO CITY HALL. BE BACK MONDAY. signed CHOICE.[4]

Several blocks away at City Hall, clinic supporters had organized their own demonstration as part of the October 1 "National Day of Action for Choice." Only a thousand or so supporters filled Nathan Phillips Square that afternoon, and there was a noticeable sense of disappointment and uneasiness on the speakers' platform. The heady days of June and July were now memories, and there was growing dissension within the OCAC-CEAC leadership about the wisdom of their alliance with Henry Morgentaler. A few had begun to see his reputation as more of a political liability than an asset. Others had simply found him difficult to work with or had tired of his style.[5]

But if there were signs of strain within Morgentaler's Toronto coalition, there was good news for pro-choicers from the Prairies. On October 13, 1983, Judge Matheson handed down his decision rejecting Borowski's claim that the unborn child is protected by the Charter.[6] Shumiatcher's double-barrelled, science-law strategy had only fired on one barrel. Judge Matheson accepted most of the scientific evidence regarding the development and status of the fetus, but then refused to take the legal leap of faith and strike down the abortion law. Matheson's judgment accepted that "the fetus is a genetically separate entity" and that "it [is] possible for a fetus to be treated separate from its mother and, although not sufficiently developed for normal birth, to survive separate from its mother." He also concluded that an abortion "results in the termination of the fetal life, which . . . is an existence separate and apart from that of the pregnant woman" and thus "cannot be therapeutic for both the pregnant woman and the fetus."[7]

Notwithstanding his findings of fact, Matheson did not find any conflict between the Charter and the abortion law. Rather than defining the scope of section 7 of the Charter with reference to the scientific evidence and then using it to overrule section 251, Matheson defined "everyone" in terms of existing usage in the Criminal Code, thus precluding any possibility of conflict.

> Although rapid advances in medical science may make it socially desirable that some legal status be extended to fetuses, irrespective of ultimate viability, it is the prerogative of Parliament, and not the Courts, to enact whatever legislation may be considered appropriate to extend to the unborn any or all legal rights possessed by living persons. Because there is no existing basis in law which justifies a conclusion that fetuses are legal persons, and therefore within the scope of the term "everyone" utilized in the Charter, the claim of the Plaintiff must be dismissed.

While disappointed, Shumiatcher and Borowski remained optimistic about their chances on appeal. The issue of standing had already been decided in their favour. The trial judge had now accepted much of the factual evidence concerning the status and development of the fetus. As is the case with all trial court records, these findings of fact would be legally binding on both the Saskatchewan Court of Appeal and the Supreme Court of Canada. Finally, Judge Matheson had been extremely cautious in his interpretation of the new role of judges under the Charter. By measuring the meaning of the Charter in terms of existing statutes and case law rather than vice versa, Shumiatcher noted, "his conclusion was written as though . . . the Charter never existed."[8] Shumiatcher had good reason to believe that the Supreme Court would interpret its new Charter mandate much more aggressively. The coincidence of these various factors made him optimistic: "So far as I know," Shumiatcher told an audience in London, Ontario, "these facts never had been established in a court of law. Coupled with the Charter, they bespeak the unborn's right to life."[9]

Such optimism notwithstanding, it would be two more years before Shumiatcher would have the opportunity to re-argue his case before the Saskatchewan Court of Appeals. With the *Borowski* case bogged down in the appeal process, it was now Morgentaler and Manning's turn to take on Canada's abortion law. A week before the trial began, their effort got a $50,000 boost from a fund-raiser at a downtown Toronto hotel. A thousand people paid $50 each to hear two leading American feminists, Gloria Steinem and Flo Kennedy, recount the pro-choice struggle to expand and protect access to abortion in the United States and praise Morgentaler for his challenge to the Canadian law.[10]

The Toronto trial of Morgentaler, Scott, and Smoling began on November 21, 1983, before Associate Chief Judge William Parker of the Supreme Court of Ontario. (The trial division of the Supreme Court of Ontario is equivalent to the Court of Queen's Bench in other provinces.) The Ontario Crown prosecutor, Alan Cooper, had charged all three with conspiracy to perform abortions in violation of the Criminal Code. After arraignment but prior to entering any pleas of not guilty, Manning made a pre-trial motion to quash the indictment on constitutional grounds. A pre-trial motion launches a sort of "trial within a trial." Until the question of the constitutionality of the abortion law was determined, there could be no jury trial. If the abortion law was ruled invalid, the charges laid under it would have to be dropped. Because the constitutionality of one of its laws was being challenged, the federal government was allowed to intervene. Ottawa sent down veteran federal Crown counsel Arthur Pennington to defend the constitutional validity of section 251.

The pre-trial motion was expected to last one to two weeks. In the end, it took eight months.[11] Manning, perhaps determined to outdo Shumiatcher's performance in Regina six months earlier, summoned nineteen expert witnesses during the first four weeks of the hearing. The end result – 3,000 pages of courtroom transcript – was a veritable encyclopedia of the pro-choice critique of Canada's abortion policy.[12]

Access to abortion services in Ontario was inadequate and growing worse, testified several Toronto social workers and family planning counsellors. This was confirmed by American witnesses from abortion clinics in Buffalo and Duluth, Minnesota, who testified that the number of Canadian women coming to their clinics was increasing. Quebec's experience contrasted sharply with the problems in Ontario. Four doctors and a social worker from Quebec testified to the medical success and political acceptance of the Parti Québécois abortion policy. Not only did the PQ government permit private free-standing abortion clinics such as Morgentaler's, but it had also set up public clinics. Other doctors testified that the present practice of requiring TACs to approve abortions was medically unnecessary and only caused extra delays, costs, and frustration. The pro-life position that human life begins at conception was rejected by several leading Canadian and American obstetricians and gynecologists. A widely published American psychologist testified that there was no empirical evidence to support the cliché that women who chose abortions were either more selfish or more irresponsible than those who carried pregnancies to term. He also cited a study from Czechoslovakia that suggested that "planned" children turned out to be more successful and happier than children born from "unwanted" pregnancies.

These submissions took four long weeks, and some observers thought that Manning was wasting time. What trial judge was going to rule the abortion law unconstitutional before the trial had even begun? These armchair quarterbacks overlooked the strategic value Manning gained by introducing his factual critique of section 251 at this stage. Manning was looking down the road to an eventual hearing before the Supreme Court of Canada. Such facts would not be admissible *de novo* at the appeal stage, nor would they be relevant to his defence to the conspiracy charge. The pre-trial motion allowed Manning to lay the

172

factual foundation for his subsequent constitutional challenge to the abortion law.

At the end of the first four weeks, it was the Crown's turn to submit evidence. The government response caught many of the pro-life court-room spectators by surprise. Neither Cooper nor Pennington called any witnesses of their own. All of Manning's evidence, said both Crown attorneys, was irrelevant. It addressed the wisdom of the law, not its legal validity. Judges, even under the Charter of Rights, were not authorized to strike down a law simply because they found it to be poor public policy. Unless there was a violation of a specific and identifiable Charter right, maintained the Crown, Manning's evidence was legally irrelevant, regardless of its substantive merit. For those familiar with the Borowski trial six months earlier, the Crown's response had a familiar ring: law reform is the business of the legislatures, not the courts. If you have evidence that a law is bad or not working, take it to your MP, not to a judge.

Manning's evidence, concluded the Crown, would become relevant only if he could show that somewhere in the Charter there was a right to abortion. Only then could he use his evidence to argue that the section 251 "limitation" of that right was neither "reasonable" nor "justified." This was the gist of the second part of Manning's strategy, his legal arguments. But by now it was almost Christmas, and Judge Parker adjourned his court until January 18, 1984.

The Crown's refusal to challenge Manning's "evidence" highlights one of the novel, and problematic, aspects of Charter litigation: the role of "social facts." Social facts refer to "the recurrent patterns of behaviour" that serve as the basis of public policy.[13] Social facts are the kind of evidence that legislators want to see when they consider adopt-ing and designing a new law or program. Since the lawmakers' goal is to design a policy that will efficiently accommodate future behaviour, they need accurate evidence of general trends of past behaviour. To ascertain "the lay of the land," legislators usually commission studies, hold hearings, compile statistics, and so forth. An example of this fact-finding process was the special commission appointed by the Trudeau government in 1976 in the wake of the first Morgentaler trial: the Com-mittee on the Operation of the Abortion Law. The mandate of the Badg-ley Committee was to gather accurate statistical data on how the TAC-based abortion policy was actually operating. Parliament could then consider amendments to the law based on these findings. (As noted earlier, however, the government chose not to act.)

Social facts are contrasted with "historical facts," the events that occurred between the parties in a legal dispute. Historical facts are particularistic not general, backward-looking not forward-looking. Their purpose is to determine guilt or innocence, not to serve as a guide for future-oriented debates over general policy questions. The original dispute-resolving function of courts meant that they were interested only in historical facts – who did what to whom, how, when, and so forth. The adversary system of presentation – examination and cross-examination, the rules of evidence – is designed to flush out what actually happened. The self-interest of each party can be safely relied on to bring forward all the relevant facts that favour his or her side and to challenge any contradictory facts put forward by the other side.

By contrast, under the Charter, the focus of judicial inquiry is often the fairness or the effectiveness of the law being challenged, not the guilt or innocence of the accused. This draws the courts into the new enterprise of collecting and judging social facts rather than historical facts. In the Morgentaler trial, for example, neither party disputed the accuracy of the historical facts – namely, that Morgentaler, Scott, and Smoling performed abortions outside of an accredited hospital and without any approvals from a TAC. What was at issue was the very legality of these requirements. While the validity of section 251 was technically a legal question (the position of the Crown), the normative character of the legal issue tended to raise broader policy questions. It was difficult to separate the purely legal question of validity from other questions pertaining to the fairness of the abortion law and the means used to achieve its purpose. This was Manning's contention, and it explains why he took so much time presenting social facts to the court through his expert witnesses and other non-adjudicative sources, such as the Badgley Report. Shumiatcher, of course, had done the same thing, but for opposite ends, in the Borowski trial.

The problem with cases like *Morgentaler* and *Borowski* is that the judges are presented with kinds of evidence that neither they nor the procedures of their courts are particularly well prepared to deal with. The judicial process was designed to determine what happened in the past in one particular case, not what will usually happen in thousands of future "cases." The rules of evidence designed to flush out historical facts may not elicit, and can even discourage, the introduction of relevant social facts. Books, articles, and studies that present social facts relevant to a policy issue are normally not admissible as evidence under the traditional rule against "hearsay" or second-hand information. Unlike a legislative committee or a royal commission, a court cannot call its own witnesses, generate independent studies, or hire in-house policy specialists. A court has to accept whatever the lawyers bring and then sort out the contradictory "expert" testimony by itself.

Even when judges allow exceptions to such rules, as they did in both the *Morgentaler* and *Borowski* cases, there are no procedural safeguards to ensure either comprehensiveness or accuracy. Reliance on expert witnesses is problematic, since the experts typically disagree, and both sides hire experts whose testimony supports their case. Judges are left to their own devices to determine which of the competing "pictures of reality" is most accurate. This problem may be further exacerbated in the frequent instances when the social facts are presented in the form of statistical evidence. Statistical results are notoriously malleable, and very few judges have the training to make an informed choice between competing statistical analyses.

Historically, Canadian judges have been reluctant to admit or to use "extrinsic evidence," the technical legal term for social facts. The "dispute-resolving" nature of the judicial function and the tradition of judicial deference to Parliament made social facts seem inappropriate, if not illegitimate. Social facts were for lawmakers, not for law-interpreters. This attitude began to change under the tenure of Chief Justice Laskin[14] and has been further eroded under the Charter. Cases such as *Morgentaler* and *Borowski* tended to address the fairness of a law, not the guilt or innocence of the litigants. Charter cases challenged judges to go beyond historical facts and to use social facts through greater receptivity toward extrinsic evidence. In general, Canadian judges responded to this challenge, but in so doing they have had to face the new problem of how adequately to collect and assess the relevant social facts.

The Charter thus created a dilemma for the courts concerning evidence. If judges discouraged the introduction of extrinsic evidence or ignored it when it was presented, they were open to the criticism of sterile legal formalism and flying blind – making decisions without any knowledge of the real-world context of the case or the probable policy impact of the decision. Alternatively, judges could encourage the introduction and use of extrinsic evidence. But there was no assurance that the facts they received were either comprehensive or accurate, and judges themselves were usually ill-equipped to sort out social facts from social fictions.

Manning launched the second prong of his attack on the abortion law on January 19, 1984. The length of his legal arguments testified to their complexity. His factum filled thirteen volumes, and his oral presentation took eighteen mind-numbing days.[15] He attacked the abortion law on various fronts, but the most important part of his argument addressed the new role of judges under the 1982 Charter of Rights.

The Charter of Rights, Manning began, has fundamentally altered the relationship of judges and legislators in Canada. Section 52 made it clear that the recently patriated constitution, and not Parliament, was now supreme:

> The Constitution of Canada is the supreme law of Canada, and any law that is inconsistent with the provisions of the Constitution is, to the extent of the inconsistency, of no force or effect.

Section 24 of the Charter, Manning continued, was equally explicit that responsibility for enforcing constitutional supremacy was vested in the courts.

> Anyone whose rights or freedoms, as guaranteed by this Charter, have been infringed or denied may apply to a court of competent jurisdiction to obtain such remedy as the court considers appropriate and just in the circumstances.

The net result, Manning reasoned, was a fundamental change in the Canadian political system, from "Parliamentary supremacy at first instance" to "judicial supremacy at first instance." Manning's qualification of "first instance" was important. It alluded to section 33 of the Charter, the legislative override. A last-minute concession to provincial premiers who feared the Charter would erode provincial rights, section 33 allowed a legislature, provincial or federal, to re-enact a law that the courts had declared to violate one of the Fundamental Freedoms (section 2 of the Charter), Legal Rights (sections 7-14), or Equality Rights (section 15). Section 33 has been aptly described as a form of "legislative review of judicial review." "If Parliament or the legislative body doesn't like the way the courts are interpreting the Charter," explained Manning to Judge Parker, "then in these areas . . . they can change the law" to override the judicial decision.[16]

While section 33 was born of a distrust of judicial lawmaking,

Manning cleverly transformed it into an invitation for judicial activism. Unlike their American counterparts, said Manning, Canadian judges need not worry about making an irreversible error in constitutional interpretation. Specifically, Judge Parker need not worry about the kind of negative political reaction that occurred with the *Roe v. Wade* decision in the U. S. If Parliament thought that he or any other Canadian judge had misinterpreted the Charter as far as the abortion law is concerned, the government could simply invoke the section 33 override to undo the damage. Section 33 thus provided a "safety-factor or cushion" for judges who gave a novel and broad interpretation to the Charter.[17]

Having reassured Judge Parker that he had the right to strike down any law of Parliament that violated the new Charter of Rights, Manning turned his attention to the abortion law. Manning advanced ten different legal arguments against the validity of section 251, six of them based on the Charter of Rights.[18] Of course, not all of them were of equal weight. Manning was using a tactic he describes as "playing cards." By presenting Judge Parker with many alternatives, Manning hoped to facilitate at least one choice. In his hand, Manning held ten different cards, each representing a plausible legal argument supported by evidence. In effect, he was saying, "Pick a card, any card."[19]

In truth, however, both Manning and the Crown recognized that the real weight of his case rested on the scope of a woman's "liberty" and "security of the person" interests that were protected by section 7 of the Charter.

> Everyone has the right to life, liberty and security of the person and the right not to be deprived thereof except in accordance with the principles of fundamental justice.

Carefully, Manning led Judge Parker through the key concepts of section 7. "Security of the person," Manning suggested, meant much more than just bodily security and freedom from arbitrary arrest or physical restraint. Rather, it referred to the *whole* person, "soul as well as body, and therefore . . . psychological security as well as bodily security."[20] While Manning did not develop it further, the implications for a woman's freedom to abort a pregnancy were obvious.

Next Manning dispatched an objection that both Crown attorneys had already raised: that section 7 was limited to a procedural meaning, not a substantive one. "Procedural due process" denotes the traditional common-law protections afforded an individual whose life, liberty, or property are threatened by the state: the right to be notified of charges; the right to a hearing before an impartial judge; the right to be represented by counsel; the right to compel witnesses; and the right to appeal. These procedural rights are essential safeguards of individual freedom, and their absence is a reliable indicator of an authoritarian regime. However, they do not touch the substance of the law. An "unjust law" could still be enforced against an individual so long as the procedural safeguards were observed.

"Substantive due process" connotes judicial review that goes beyond assuring that procedural safeguards are observed and actually addresses the substance or wisdom of the legislation being enforced. While the idea of a mechanism by which unjust laws can be identified and nullified is appealing, it raises an equally fundamental problem: Who should decide whether a law is unjust? Democracy is based on the principle of government by the consent of the governed. In practice this means laws are made by the elected representatives of the people, who are held accountable through periodic elections. To the extent that substantive due process allows non-elected, non-accountable judges to overrule the policy choices of elected representatives, it is undemocratic.

There was clear evidence that the framers of the Charter intended to avoid any connotation of substantive due process.[21] The historical record showed that Trudeau's top adviser on the drafting of the Charter had told the Special Joint Committee, "We thought that this [section 7] was to be confined to procedural matters only – at least that's what we intended. We didn't want a broad expansive view."

Undaunted by such legislative history, Manning argued that what the framers intended wasn't what they got.[22] The phrase "in accordance with the principles of fundamental justice" was new and had no clearly established legal meaning, Manning argued. If they had intended to limit section 7 to procedural guarantees, why hadn't they been more explicit? Certainly the common-sense meaning of "principles of fundamental justice" suggested just laws as well as fair procedures.

Manning then turned to the heart of his Charter argument: the concept of individual liberty.

The word "liberty" as found in Section 7 is a broad concept – broad enough to include more than freedom from bodily restraint. And it's broad enough to encompass the right to freedom to govern one's family affairs . . . the freedom to have children or not, the freedom to practise birth control or not, as one sees fit. And it's broad enough to determine whether one will continue a pregnancy.[23]

At this point Judge Parker interrupted. "Aren't you asking me to make law?" Manning answered yes, but tried to lead the judge back to familiar territory.

What I'm asking your lordship to do is to make law in a traditional sense . . . not in any radical or innovative sense, but to look at the words actually used by the drafters of the Charter to determine whether the rights described in the particular provision are capable of supporting a particular meaning and if so then to apply that meaning.

And that's no different from interpreting an ordinary legislative enactment – the *War Measures Act,* the *Criminal Code* – save for the fact that the words are found in a constitutional document.

In effect, Manning was trying to induce Judge Parker into discovering a constitutional right to abortion within the potentially broad contours of section 7. Manning's interpretation of section 7 was certainly plausible linguistically and logically, but it was far from conclusive in a *legal* sense. Because it was untested, this broad interpretation lacked the string of legal precedents, the judicial track record, that would give it legal authority. Judges, especially trial judges like Judge Parker, want to see that legal pedigree before they accept an interpretation with such obvious political consequences.

Manning of course knew this and gave Judge Parker precedents – only they were American precedents. Decisions of American courts are not binding on Canadian judges, but they have what is termed "persuasive value." To the extent that Canadian judges find an American precedent relevant and helpful to a problem in Canadian law, they can use it to support their rulings. With the advent of the Charter, Canadian judges have been deluged with American precedents.

In preparation for the Morgentaler trial, Manning had read hundreds of American law review articles analysing the evolution of the right to privacy and its culmination in *Roe v. Wade.* Now he selectively presented Judge Parker with the story of the development of the "right to privacy." Despite the fact that there was no explicit mention of a right to privacy in their Constitution, he explained, the American Supreme Court had found such a right to be implied by the principle of individual liberty protected by the Fourteenth Amendment. Manning started with the early cases that struck down state statutes that interfered with parents' freedom to educate their children. This "zone of privacy" that surrounds the family was further extended in the birth control cases of the sixties. State laws prohibiting the distribution of birth control materials to married[24] and then unmarried[25] persons were declared unconstitutional. Justice Blackmun for the majority wrote:

> If the right of privacy means anything, it is the right of the individual, married or unmarried, to be free from unwarranted governmental intrusion into matters so fundamentally affecting a person as the decision to bear or beget a child.[26]

While written to address a law prohibiting the sale of contraceptives, this reasoning became the foundation of the Court's ruling on abortion the following year. While conceding that "the Constitution does not explicitly mention any right of privacy," the American Supreme Court went on to cite the string of privacy precedents and concluded:

> This right to privacy . . . whether it be found in the Fourteenth Amendment's concept of personal liberty . . . or in the Ninth Amendment's reservation of rights to the people, is broad enough to encompass a woman's decision whether or not to terminate her pregnancy.

The concepts of "individual liberty" in section 7 of the Charter also supported a right to privacy, Manning urged. Indeed, he suggested that the Charter's additional protection of "the security of the person" – psychological as well as physical – made the individual liberty protected by section 7 even broader than the American Fourteenth Amendment. For Manning, the American right to privacy precedents were a road map to help guide Judge Parker through the uncharted contours of section 7. For Manning, *Roe v. Wade* showed the way. All Judge Parker had to do was follow.

It was a telling sign of how the Charter has Americanized Canadian law that the Crown also called on American experience to rebut Manning. But Pennington's and Cooper's version of American experience was a far cry from Manning's. They recounted for Judge Parker the controversial legacy of substantive due process in American constitutional law. The Fourteenth Amendment declares that, "No State shall deprive any person of life, liberty, or property, without due process of law." Prior to 1937, the American Supreme Court had used the due process clause of the U.S. Constitution to strike down progressive state laws that protected workers and consumers. The most infamous substantive due process case was *Lochner v. New York,* a 1905 decision striking down a New York state health law that restricted to sixty the number of hours per week that could be worked in a bakery. This legislation was struck down by the American Court because it was alleged to violate workers' "liberty of contract" without due process of law. In similar cases, the American Supreme Court ruled minimum wage and child labour laws unconstitutional. Critics of these decisions protested that conservative judges were simply using the due process clause to strike down liberal legislation that restricted the power and the profits of employers. Dissenting in the *Lochner* decision, Justice Oliver Wendell Holmes declared that, "A constitution is not intended to embody a particular economic theory [such as laissez-faire]. . . . It is made for people of fundamentally different views."[27] Holmes and many others considered substantive due process to be a serious anti-democratic abuse of judicial authority, since non-elected judges could use it to substitute their political preferences for the policy outcomes of the democratic process.

Substantive due process contributed to the "court crisis" of 1937. In 1932, in the depths of the Great Depression, Franklin D. Roosevelt and his Democratic Party captured both the White House and Congress from the Republicans. Their mandate was to reverse the economic collapse that was crippling the nation. Roosevelt's response was the New Deal – a series of dramatic economic and social policy initiatives that extended government regulation of the economy to an extent never before attempted. However, much of Roosevelt's New Deal legislation was subsequently struck down by the American Supreme Court. The majority of judges on the Court were politically conservative appointees of previous Republican administrations, and they ruled twelve different pieces of New Deal legislation to be unconstitutional. The Court's actions infuriated Roosevelt and the Democrats, who argued that the Court was abusing its power. This confrontation reached a crisis in 1937 when, after being re-elected in 1936 by an even larger majority than in 1932, President Roosevelt proposed to expand the number of judges and then to "pack the Court" with appointees who supported his New Deal. Recognizing its vulnerability, the Supreme

Court retreated, and the doctrine of substantive due process was discredited and disappeared from American constitutional law – until the 1973 *Roe v. Wade* decision.

The dissenters in *Roe v. Wade* had been quick to denounce what that they saw as the return to "the bad old days" of substantive due process. Justice White described it as "an exercise of raw judicial power . . . improvident and extravagant." Justice Rehnquist elaborated this criticism:

> While the Court's opinion quotes from the dissent of Mr. Justice Holmes in *Lochner v. New York* . . . the result it reaches is more closely attuned to the majority opinion. . . . As in *Lochner* and similar cases applying substantive due process standards to economic and social welfare legislation [the majority's opinion] will inevitably require this Court to examine the legislative policies and pass on the wisdom of these policies. . . . The decision here . . . partakes more of judicial legislation than it does of a determination of the intent of the drafters of the Fourteenth Amendment.[28]

While *Roe v. Wade* was widely praised by feminists and abortion rights reformers, it contributed to a backlash among conservatives and some moderates who thought the judges were simply using the power of judicial review to impose their own policy preferences on the country. In 1980 Ronald Reagan and the Republicans successfully campaigned for the presidency on a platform that included a commitment to appoint federal judges "who respect the traditional family values and the sanctity of innocent human life." Once in office, Reagan acted to fulfil these promises by appointing three "strict constructionists" to the Court and elevating Rehnquist to Chief Justice. Reagan's "court-packing" was alternately praised or denounced depending on one's politics. But regardless of perspective, there was no question that *Roe v. Wade* had contributed to a growing politicization of judicial appointments and the Court.[29]

This was the lesson Pennington and Cooper wanted Judge Parker to draw from American experience. Substantive due process had been a political and legal disaster – both in the thirties and now again with abortion. They recounted the numerous attempts of both state and federal authorities to avoid compliance with or to reverse *Roe v. Wade*. Canadian judges, they declared, must avoid making the same mistakes. Indeed, Pennington and Cooper made the issue a matter of Canadian sovereignty and identity. The Charter, they argued, was a Canadian document, not an American one. It had evolved out of the Anglo-Canadian legal tradition, which had never accepted the *American* practice of judges overseeing the wisdom of parliamentary lawmaking. In the end, the Crown's response to Manning's section 7 argument was simple and direct: "Don't Americanize the Charter."[30]

Oral argument finally ended on April 5, 1984, and Judge Parker reserved judgment. Manning's strategy had been to bolster his plausible but untested Charter arguments with factual evidence of the inadequacies and inequities of the 1969 law. Judge Parker seemed visibly impressed by the latter but was unmoved by Manning's flattering invitations to play the new judicial role of philosopher-statesman created by the Charter. Sixty-nine years old and near the end of a distinguished judicial career, William Dickens Parker had lived most of his professional life under the guiding assumptions of parliamentary supremacy. He was an unlikely candidate to succumb to Manning's constitutional flattery. By contrast, Pennington's dire warnings of an American-style "government of judges" seemed to have struck a responsive chord. Three months after the pre-trial motion had ended, Judge Parker released his judgment refusing to strike down the abortion law.

For Manning to succeed with his Charter arts, he would have to find a younger, more innovative audience, one less attached to the British rule-of-law tradition. For this very reason, perhaps Morris Manning was already looking forward to his next audience: the jury of twelve men and women, all strangers to the law, who would sit in judgment of Morgentaler, Scott, and Smoling in the next stage of this legal marathon.

CHAPTER 16

The Toronto Jury: Voice of the People or a Stacked Deck?

Nearly three months passed before the same cast of characters reconvened on Monday, October 15, 1984. There were surprisingly few spectators on hand to view the trial of Henry Morgentaler and his associates for conspiracy to perform illegal abortions. Those who did show up were disappointed. Parker, Manning, and Crown Prosecutor Allan Cooper spent almost the entire day in the judge's chambers haggling over the rules that would govern the selection of jurors. By outward appearances, it was a nothing day. As it turned out, it may have been the most important day of the trial.

Manning had arrived with a list of twenty-five different questions that he wanted to ask prospective jurors. Initially caught off guard, Judge Parker resisted. While American lawyers usually have a free hand in examining prospective jurors, Canadian practice restricts questioning to the bare essentials. Only questions relevant to discovering potential juror prejudice for or against the accused are permitted. The allowable questions are fairly standard. Is anyone related to a police officer or to anyone employed in law enforcement? Is anyone personally acquainted with or related to the accused, or does anyone have any trouble understanding English? A "yes" answer to any of these questions is a free pass out of the courtroom. In the Morgentaler case, Judge Parker put these questions to the jurors at the outset, and they eliminated seven people.

It is also standard for lawyers in Canada to ask prospective jurors their names, occupations, and whether they know anything about the case or have discussed it. Judge Parker had no problems with these questions. But the other questions on Manning's unusual list troubled him: Do you belong to a church? Which one? How often do you attend church services? and so on. The relevance of such questions was far from clear to Judge Parker, and six hours of bargaining did little to remove his initial scepticism. In the end, Manning found himself on the defensive. His own list of questions was rejected, and he was lobbying for a few changes to the Crown's questions. The result was a mutual agreement that he (or Cooper) could ask the following three questions:

1. Do you have any religious, moral, or other beliefs relating to abortion such that you would convict or acquit regardless of the law or the evidence? Answer yes or no.
2. Have you, because of religious or moral beliefs or because of what you have read or seen in the media, formed any opinion as to the guilt or innocence of the accused? Answer yes or no.
3. Despite any beliefs or opinions, would you be able to set aside those beliefs or opinions and reach a verdict of guilty or not guilty solely on the evidence and the law you receive in this courtroom? Yes or no.

The jury selection process began with each prospective juror being questioned by both the Crown and the defence lawyers. Based on his or her responses, the prospective juror was then screened by two other jurors known as "triers." The triers were chosen initially at random from the panel of prospective jurors, and subsequently, as jurors were selected, by the two most recently selected. The triers listened to the potential juror's answers to the questions and then determined if the potential juror's responses indicated that he or she was sufficiently impartial to serve. If the triers approved, both the Crown and the defence still had the option to reject the juror. The defence was entitled to thirty-six peremptory challenges and the Crown to four. The Crown was also entitled to forty-eight "stand asides" – a sort of temporary rejection that sent the prospective juror back into the pool for possible reconsideration if more suitable jurors were not found.

With the ground rules settled, jury selection began in earnest on Tuesday. It quickly became apparent that it was not business as usual. Juror after juror was rejected by the triers, often for no apparent reason.

An increasingly frustrated Judge Parker finally remarked that "excellent" jurors were being lost "for some reason we don't know about." Manning immediately objected, and a private conference ensued. Manning tried to reassure Judge Parker that nothing was amiss with the triers: "It's their gut reaction, my lord." By the end of the day, fifty jurors had been examined. Five had been chosen.

Manning's indulgence of the triers' scepticism was consistent with his own conduct. In addition to asking the three established questions, Manning began his questioning of each prospective female juror by asking, "Is that Miss, Mrs., or Ms.?" He also asked some prospective jurors if they were married or if they had children, what jobs they held, and if they had previously discussed the case. Cooper objected to Manning asking other than the agreed-upon questions, but Judge Parker allowed him to continue.

It also became apparent that Manning was being assisted by two unidentified women sitting with him in the counsel's box. After each juror was quizzed, Manning would return to his bench and huddle with the two women and the three doctors before announcing his decision to accept or reject the juror. At a break, curious reporters questioned the women. They refused to identify who they were or what they were doing, other than "working for Mr. Manning." Manning also refused to answer a reporter's questions about the two women.

As the parade of jurors continued, a fairly clear pattern emerged. Manning automatically rejected anyone who said he or she had previously discussed the case.[1] Female jurors who said they preferred to be addressed as "Mrs." or had more than two children also tended to be rejected. Some prospective jurors, apparently confused by the disjunctive character of the questions, responded only to the first part with comments like, "Yes, I have moral beliefs," or "Yes, I'm Catholic." They were rejected, if not by the triers, then by Manning.

The next day the mystery over Manning's two female assistants was ended. Bill Walker's story in the morning edition of the *Toronto Star* identified the two women as Marjorie Fargo and Catherine Marks, jury selection experts from the United States. Walker reported that Fargo operated Jury Services, Inc., a Washington, D.C., firm that specialized in "scientific" jury selection techniques. The *Star* indicated that Fargo had worked in more than 200 criminal cases in the U.S. since 1973. Earlier that year she had helped to select the California jury that acquitted businessman John DeLorean on cocaine charges. This revelation sharpened spectator interest in Manning's questions and the exercise of his peremptory challenges.

The day did have some light moments. When Manning noticed that one of the jurors was wearing a red rose lapel pin, he moved quickly to confront the man: "What is that?" Manning demanded, pointing to the pin. The stunned juror stammered back, "It's for Right to Life. It means that I believe in the right to life of the unborn child." The triers quickly rejected him as not impartial. The next prospective juror was a woman wearing a large brooch. Imitating Manning, Cooper leaped forward and menacingly demanded, "What is that brooch you have on?" The nervous gallery of spectators burst into laughter. By the end of the day, another thirty-seven jurors had been examined but only three chosen. Manning had now exercised seventeen of his thirty-six vetoes.

Thursday was different. Four more jurors were needed, and the supply of potential jurors had dwindled. Conscious of their narrowing options, both Cooper and Manning now weighed their decisions carefully. Manning would huddle for long periods with his clients and the two jury selection experts before making his decisions. By 4:15 that afternoon, three more jurors had been selected, bringing the total to eleven. However, all 132 of the potential jurors impanelled for the case had now been questioned.

With no more unexamined candidates available, Cooper was forced to go back and choose from the four potential jurors he had previously "stood aside." Tension in the courtroom mounted as he peremptorily challenged the first two. With only two remaining, a rejection of the third would have forced him to accept the fourth and last juror. He then accepted the third, a female mailroom clerk.

The jury was now set. It included six men and six women. Six jurors were married, six unmarried. Seven of the jurors appeared to be less than thirty years old. Occupations included a sausage casing inspector, a cashier, a mailman, two former company managers, a computer operator, an electrical engineer, and a marketing manager. By outward appearance, the jury seemed balanced and representative.

But what were the invisible effects of the selection process? In the end, the twelve jurors were chosen from 132 prospects – a rejection rate of more than 90 per cent. What did these twelve have that the other 120 did not? Manning used thirty-one of his thirty-six peremptory challenges; Cooper only two, plus five stand asides. The triers, jurors themselves, had rejected eighty of their fellow citizens. Had the jury been emotionally or ideologically shaped by this winnowing process?

Joe Borowski thought so. He had come to Toronto for the Morgentaler trial. During the first week he established a ritual of shaking hands with Morgentaler during the Court's morning recess. On Friday, Borowski surveyed the jury and predicted: "Henry will go scot-free."[2] Not surprisingly, Crown Prosecutor Cooper disagreed. After the jury selection had been completed, he remarked, "That was probably the most important thing we will do here."[3] But Cooper rejected suggestions of possible unfair advantage resulting from Manning's use of jury selection experts. "Gut instinct," Cooper said, was the most reliable way to choose a juror. While they had no way of knowing it at the time, Borowski and Cooper had already touched upon what was to become a major post-trial issue.

On Friday, the trial proper began with the opening address to the jury by Crown Prosecutor Allan Cooper. Jury selection experts believe that jury trials are often won or lost on these opening statements, not by witnesses or final addresses. Jurors tend to make up their minds in the opening stages of a trial and then filter all that follows through the lens of their initial reaction. An effective opening statement must establish "psychological anchors," impressions that the jurors will remember even if they forget everything else. There are two kinds of anchors: factual and emotional. The essential ingredient of a factual anchor is that it be simple. The key to the emotional anchor is for the lawyer to win the trust, if not the affection, of the jurors for himself or his client.[4]

Cooper's strategy was simple and straightforward. This was not a trial about either abortion or the abortion law, he told the twelve jurors. It was simply a conspiracy case: Did Dr. Morgentaler and his colleagues conspire to perform illegal abortions? "A conspiracy," he explained, "simply means an agreement to commit a crime." Using the records seized from the clinic and tape-recordings of Morgentaler's public speeches announcing his intention to open a clinic in Toronto, Cooper told the jury that he would prove beyond any reasonable doubt that such a conspiracy did indeed exist.

As for the "emotional anchor," Cooper carefully steered clear of the abortion issue, thus avoiding the mistake made by the Quebec Crown prosecutor a decade earlier. Instead, Cooper tried to paint a picture of Henry Morgentaler as a greedy crime boss who was only in it for the money. The clinic's records showed that its standard charge for an abortion was $300. Of this amount, only $75 went to the physician, while $225 went to the clinic, which was jointly owned by Morgentaler and his brother.[5] In addition, the clinic paid Morgentaler himself $2,165 a month in "consulting fees." The Morgentaler Clinic, said the Crown, was no more than a "robbery" in which Smoling and Scott were the triggermen, while Morgentaler supplied the guns and took a cut of the loot.

Manning also had a two-prong strategy: a legal one aimed at the head and an emotional one aimed at the heart. The legal strategy was once again based on the common-law defence of necessity. What Morgentaler and his associates did, Manning told the jury, was necessary to avoid still greater harms – the intolerable and dangerous delays in Ontario's abortion system. Manning characterized it as "the great Ontario telephone lottery" – a lottery full of delays and therefore dangers to the pregnant women forced to play it. By comparing the policy in Ontario to those in Quebec and the United States, where abortions are readily available, the defence would demonstrate that "it was necessary to open the Morgentaler Clinic in Toronto."

The substance of Manning's defence paralleled his earlier motion before Judge Parker, only now he substituted the defence of necessity for the Charter. He called many of the same witnesses and they testified to essentially the same facts. Instead of arguing that the abortion law was itself illegal, he now argued that his clients' performance of abortions was not illegal, thanks to the defence of necessity. Rather than persuading a judge to make a ruling of constitutional invalidity, this time Manning would try to persuade a jury to deliver a verdict of not guilty.

While Manning no doubt welcomed replacing the judge by the jury, his task was complicated by the Crown's decision to charge the doctors with conspiracy to commit the crime rather than actually commiting it. The conspiracy charge meant that the Crown did not have to put any women who had actually had abortions at the clinic on the witness stand. This was a shrewd tactical move, because it deprived Manning of using the personal story of the "patient/victim" to win over the hearts of the jurors. This time there was no Verona Parkinson, the lonely, impoverished foreign graduate student whose story figured so prominently in Morgentaler's first jury acquittal. Manning could not get away with proving the "necessity" of giving an abortion to this or that particular woman. Rather, he was faced with the much more difficult task of proving that it was necessary *in a general sense* for Morgentaler to open a clinic in Ontario. Manning's expert witnesses could paint the same picture of overcrowding and delay they had presented to Judge

Parker ten months earlier. But Manning knew this was largely a cerebral message, one that lacked the emotional impact of a Verona Parkinson story.

He compensated for the lack of a tragic heroine by creating a new hero and new villains. The hero, of course, was Henry Morgentaler, who was presented to the jurors as the caring and compassionate friend of the underdog. Manning called witness after witness to testify to the generous character and pure motives of Morgentaler. When Morgentaler himself finally took the stand as the last and perhaps best witness for the defence, he spilled out his life story. From the Jewish ghetto in Lodz to the Nazi concentration camps to the women "butchered" by illegal abortions in post-war Canada, he told the jurors that he knew suffering first hand and had dedicated his life to fighting it. He summarized his actions by invoking the metaphor of the modern-day Good Samaritan. He was driven, Morgentaler said,

> by the image of someone drowning in a river or a lake, and all you had to do was stretch out your arm to save them. Would you do it if there was a sign there saying, 'It is forbidden to help'? I knew I could not obey that sign; I would obey a higher morality."[6]

The villains in Manning's story were the politicians and the police. The former were painted as hypocrites, the latter as brutes. Under cross-examination, Manning grilled the police officers who had been called as witnesses by Cooper. Why did they raid the clinic if they already had enough evidence? Why did they raid it while they knew abortions were being performed? Why was there only one female officer assigned to the raid? Why was the only police gynecologist a male? Had the police no respect for the dignity and privacy of the women involved?

As for the politicians, Morgentaler himself testified that their wives and mistresses had been quietly coming to him for abortions for years, at the same time that the politicians refused to change the laws under which he and his colleagues were being prosecuted. "These [abortions] were done in secrecy and I'm not going to give any names," declared Morgentaler. "I'm just bringing out the hypocrisy of the whole thing." Of course, all of this was quite irrelevant to the legal issue of the guilt or innocence of the accused. But Manning knew full well that he was not going to win his case on technical points of law. His carefully orchestrated version of the Morgentaler "mini-drama" was aimed at the hearts, not the heads, of the jurors.

By the end of the third week, both sides had examined all the witnesses they intended to call. On Friday, November 2, 1984, they began their closing addresses to the jury. The Crown led off with a predictable appeal to the jurors to be neutral on the abortion issue. The trial was not about whether the fetus is a person or whether the law is a good law, Cooper lectured the jurors. These questions are the responsibility of duly elected legislators. The jury's duty was narrow and simple: Was there a conspiracy? Cooper solemnly cautioned the jury not to abuse their power:

> You are a high stoop of land between two stormy seas. Follow the path of the law and you can do no wrong. If you step off that path or lean over to one side you will fall into the stormy sea. And I say the consequences of that are disastrous. . . . If you acquit, this is an invitation to anarchy. . . . Breaking the law in an attempt to change a law one doesn't like is like plunging a knife into the very heart of democracy. I say the ends do not justify the means.

Manning's closing address was equally predictable. All the carefully crafted pieces of the puzzle now fell neatly together: hypocritical politicians, insensitive police, a bad and unworkable law, suffering women, and the Good Samaritan, Henry Morgentaler. The accused must be acquitted, Manning advised the jury, because their "crime" prevented even greater harm from occurring. This is what the defence of necessity permits, indeed requires. But Manning did not stop at even this simplified version of the law.

> You have become for Canadian women, the twelve most important people in this country. You have become the key to a locked door, a door that is locked for many women.
>
> . . .
>
> Send a message to Mr. McMurtry saying "stop prosecuting doctors for trying to help people." You are the only independent body that can do this. Politicians can't. They are dependent on votes. You can say we won't stand for this any more.
>
> . . .
>
> You are this country. An independent country. A country which is not tied to any political party bosses. You can bring freedom, as the jury is the lamp by which freedom is lit.
>
> . . .
>
> These doctors are here on behalf of Canadian women. On their

behalf, I ask you to bring back the right and just verdict – that of not guilty.

...

The judge will tell you what the law is. He will tell you about the ingredients of the offence, what the Crown has to prove, what the defences may be or may not be, and you must take the law from him. But I submit to you that it is up to you and you alone to apply the law to this evidence and you have a right to say it shouldn't be applied.

By now it was late Friday afternoon. Judge Parker's charge to the jury would have to wait until Monday. The jurors were sent to their hotel rooms for the weekend with Manning's impassioned plea still ringing in their ears.

On Monday morning, Judge Parker picked up where Manning had ended, but to the opposite end. For four long hours, Judge Parker sought to undo Manning's "mistakes." He outlined a much narrower and more stringent version of the "defence of necessity." There was no evidence, he emphasized, of any woman who was actually denied an abortion in Ontario. There was evidence of reasonable legal alternatives to breaking the law – the availability of abortions in both Quebec and New York. Morgentaler's earlier attempt to change the law through lobbying was overly impatient, inadequate, and not relevant to the defence. Nor were the three jury acquittals in Quebec of any relevance to the present case. But most of all, Judge Parker condemned Manning's suggestion to the jurors that they could ignore the letter of the law and acquit the doctors because they were supplying a necessary service.

I think it is improper for a lawyer to suggest to a jury that they should break the law. . . . Your duty is to decide the facts and then apply the law. You are not here to judge the law and you have no right to do so. . . . Mr. Manning implies you can do whatever you want because you are not accountable. . . . I'd ask you to disregard those comments of counsel.

At 3:20 that afternoon the jurors retired to begin their deliberations. Ninety minutes later they were told to suspend their talks until the judge spoke to them again the next day. Unbeknownst to them, no sooner had the jurors left the courtroom than Manning rose to challenge Judge Parker's charge. "It is my submission," said Manning dryly, "that your lordship's charge completely and utterly takes away the defence." Judge Parker responded by sending orders to the jury to halt their deliberations pending further instructions.

Those instructions were slow in coming. When the Court reconvened Tuesday morning, Manning resumed his attack, ticking off a long list of complaints about the charge. But he complained most bitterly about the judge's comment that civil disobedience was not a defence in the case and that the jury would be breaking the law if they brought back a verdict of not guilty. This was simply wrong, said Manning. "Canadian and British juries have always had the right to bring back a verdict that some might consider perverse, that is contrary to all the evidence and contrary to all the law." He repeatedly alleged that the judge's instructions had wrongly undermined his defence and amounted to an order to the jury to convict. Cooper, on the other hand, had only two minor complaints about the charge, but publicly criticized Manning for trying to manipulate the judge into making a more favourable re-charge to the jury. The jury, of course, was not allowed to be present for any of this, and spent most of Tuesday confined in a small jury room adjacent to the courtroom, wondering what in the world was going on.

It was not until Wednesday morning that the jurors were summoned to the courtroom and re-charged by Judge Parker. Parker had stayed up until 4:30 a.m. reviewing the case, and it showed. A tired Judge Parker – frequently halting, stumbling, and once even apologizing – re-instructed the jurors. His two and one-half hour re-charge covered the same ground, adding little that was new. Manning said he was still dissatisfied, but he saw no point in yet another re-charge. The jurors were dispatched once again to decide upon a verdict.

The jury deliberated for six hours. During their deliberation, they asked for copies of the Criminal Code, the Charter of Rights, and the latest Supreme Court of Canada decision on the defence of necessity. Judge Parker provided only the first. He told the jury they must accept his version of the defence of necessity and that the Charter was irrelevant to their task. Thursday morning they sent a message that they had reached a unanimous verdict. Judge Parker reconvened the trial.

Which story had been more convincing – the greedy crime boss or the modern-day Good Samaritan? Manning had certainly been a more compelling storyteller than Cooper, but then, maybe Cooper did not need to tell stories, his case was so open and shut. From the outset of the trial, the equipment used by Morgentaler to perform abortions – the nitrous oxide and vacuum-aspirator machines – had been prominently

Morgentaler and lawyer Morris Manning celebrate the doctor's jury acquittal, Toronto, November 8, 1984. (*Wasserman photo, courtesy* The Globe and Mail, *Toronto*)

displayed just to the side of Judge Parker. Was it possible that the jury could ignore such palpable evidence?

As the jurors filed back into the packed Toronto courtroom, they avoided looking at the three accused doctors – behaviour interpreted by some observers as indicating a conviction. The courtroom bristled with tension as the jurors took their seats across from the prisoners' box. At 12:15, Judge Parker asked the foreman, Tom Green, for the jury's decision. As in all trials, at this split second, any prior optimism on either side evaporated. All bets were off as Green rose to announce the verdict, but then juror Susan Bishop telegraphed the result by suddenly looking up at the Morgentaler contingent with a widening grin.

"Not guilty," pronounced Green, as twenty reporters bolted for the door. Morgentaler stretched out and hugged Manning. Morgentaler asked Judge Parker if he could say something to the jury. Parker tersely rejected the request and told Morgentaler, "Just keep quiet." As they left the courtroom, Manning struggled, unsuccessfully, to suppress his client's exuberance. Morgentaler, wearing a wall-to-wall grin, shouted excitedly: "a victory for the women of Canada, for the system of democracy, for reason . . . long live the jury system . . . in spite of all the judges."

Reaction to the jury's acquittal was predictable. Pro-choice partisans jubilantly celebrated the decision as a blow for democracy and "a message to the politicians." On the steps of the courthouse following the acquittal, Morris Manning declared:

> This is a clear message from the jury to the politicians of this province and this country that this is what the people want. . . . I hope that people in positions of power like Roy McMurtry, who wants to be premier of this province, listen.

Morgentaler seconded Manning:

> The jury's decision shows that the people of Ontario are ready for the establishment of free-standing abortion clinics. . . . [The abortion law] is obsolete already in Quebec, now it has been shown to be obsolete in Ontario and by extension across Canada.

Pro-life leaders bitterly disagreed. They attacked the decision as "a perversion of justice" and pointed to the jury selection process as the culprit. Pro-life groups had attended the trial and closely monitored its progress. From the very first day they were upset by a jury selection process that they felt was dominated by Manning and resulted in a jury biased in favour of Morgentaler. When the jury acquittal came down on November 8, their worst fears were realized. It didn't help matters when one of the jurors was spotted participating in a pro-choice victory rally shortly after the verdict.

Laura McArthur, president of the Right to Life Association of Toronto and Area (the largest such group in Canada), said the jury selection process had made "a mockery of the jury system. [Manning] was obviously trying for . . . the transient, roving young type of people who, in his mind, would be for abortion." Borowski complained to the press that Manning "did everything but administer saliva tests" to the prospective jurors.

Initially these charges might easily have been dismissed as the whining of sore losers. They took on a new seriousness, however, the day after the acquittal, because of a front-page article in the *Toronto Star*. Only inches below the headline announcing Morgentaler's acquittal was a second article entitled, "Religion key factor in defence jury selection." It detailed for the first time "the secret system used to help select the jury in the Morgentaler abortion trial."

In a telephone interview from her Washington, D.C., office, Marjorie Fargo had told the *Star* that she and Catherine Marks had conducted a survey of past Toronto-area jurors' attitudes toward abortion and then used it to create a profile of sympathetic and unsympathetic jurors. Based on these profiles, she advised Manning to try to exclude "regular church goers, housewives, young people and older professionals" from the Morgentaler jury. According to Fargo,

> Religion was very important. . . . It was probably the key factor. It wasn't so much what religion but how active you were in your particular church. . . . Generally speaking, here in this country, the more frequently one attends church services the more likely they are to be anti-abortionists.

Their recipe for a "pro-Morgentaler" jury, she added, was a jury with "several working women in their 30s who didn't attend church regularly."

Fargo revealed that Judge Parker had thwarted much of their original game plan. They had prepared twenty-five questions for Manning to ask potential jurors, but Parker had disallowed them on the opening day of the trial. Instead, Parker allowed only the three "yes or no" questions that the public had observed.

The judge's decision to restrict questioning was partially offset by other techniques. Fargo said they also used the potential jurors' "body language" to "weed out jurors unfavourable to Morgentaler." She explained that if a potential juror stared intently at either Morgentaler or Manning, shifted nervously during questioning, or gave flippant responses, they recommended rejection. The use of the "Miss, Mrs., or Ms?" opening line had been Manning's idea, she added, but one she heartily endorsed. Also, jurors who referred to Morgentaler as "Mister" rather than "Doctor Morgentaler" were considered suspect. Fargo said that she and Marks were "thrilled" to learn of Morgentaler's acquittal, adding, "We felt good about the jury that we helped pick."[7]

These revelations gave a new seriousness to the pro-life charges of jury-stacking. Letters of protest poured into the Toronto area papers.

The president of the Canadian Bar Association, Claude Thomson, indicated that his association would be examining the issue. "If we have no rule of law, we have no properly regulated society," he told the *Globe and Mail*. "Why is it perfectly alright to disrupt society as long as you think it's morally right?" Eddie Greenspan pointed to the danger of "jury lawlessness." The danger, he elaborated, is that juries can end up being tools for interest groups and "create a great deal of uncertainty in the law." Even Ontario Attorney-General Roy McMurtry observed that while there had been nothing illegal about the jury selection process, "the acquittal created the impression that jury members in general could come to the task with some bias."

Comments like these added further credibility to the criticisms from the pro-life camp about a stacked jury, and began to erode the initial boost that Morgentaler's acquittal had given the pro-choice movement. Almost overnight, the issue had been transformed from the "jury's message to the politicians" to Manning's alleged manipulation of the jury. This reversal of momentum frustrated Morgentaler supporters, and no one more than Morris Manning.

By mid-December, 1984, Manning had had enough. He published a long letter in the *Toronto Star* rebutting his critics and defending his jury selection tactics. He pointed out that he had not chosen the jury single-handedly. The jurors themselves, serving as triers, had rejected more people than he had, and the prosecutor had the final say on each juror. Judge Parker had prevented him from asking the questions he wanted to ask, especially questions about religion or church attendance. As for the three questions that were asked, they were intended "to expose bias in persons on *both sides* of the issue." He defended his use of the American jury selection experts as necessary in order to find "truly impartial" jurors, not just jurors who said they were impartial. Last but not least, the jury was a true cross-section of the community – half men, half women; ranging in age from their twenties to their fifties; from working-class to businessmen; from high school dropouts to university-educated. "Those who have attacked the Morgentaler jurors as . . . unrepresentative of the community, and who have made scurrilous and libelous statements about the selection process," Manning concluded, "speak in utter ignorance."[8]

The dispute over the Morgentaler jury in Toronto is only the most recent chapter – albeit the first Canadian one – in a growing controversy over the use of jury selection experts. Like many recent innovations in Canadian law, this practice originated in the United States and has been carried across the border by television and enterprising lawyers.

The origins of "scientific" jury selection techniques are recent, a product of an alliance between anti-war professors and activists during the Vietnam War. In 1972 two Catholic priests, Philip and Daniel Berrigan, and five other anti-Vietnam War activists were charged with conspiring to destroy draft board offices and records and to kidnap then Secretary of State Henry Kissinger. Jay Schulman, a New York sociologist, was a strong supporter of the anti-war movement and wanted to help the Berrigans. He hit upon the idea of using his expertise in surveying public opinion to help find an impartial jury.

Schulman and his graduate students conducted a telephone survey of residents of Harrisburg, Pennsylvania, the site of the trial. They asked questions about the Vietnam War, the upcoming trial, and the demographic characteristics of the persons being interviewed – age, gender, race, religion, education, occupation, and political party. They entered this information into a sophisticated computer program that correlated positive and negative attitudes with personal characteristics. The result was demographic profiles of jurors with sympathetic and unsympathetic attitudes toward the "Harrisburg Seven."

Their lawyers then used these profiles to question, reject, and accept prospective jurors. For example, Schulman found that, contrary to the hunch of the lawyers, college-educated people in the Harrisburg area tended to support the government's Vietnam policies and to dislike the Berrigan brothers. On the other hand, the survey data indicated that women in the Harrisburg area were generally more "open-minded" toward anti-war protesters than men. (Interestingly, a similar survey done for a subsequent trial of Vietnam protesters in Miami found the opposite. This demonstrates the importance of surveying the attitudes of the community in which the trial is held and not depending on national trends.) The lawyers subsequently used their peremptory challenges to exclude people with college degrees from the jury. In a decision that attracted national attention, the jury acquitted the Harrisburg Seven and a significant new approach to jury selection was born.[9]

The success of the Harrisburg Seven led to the adoption of scientific jury selection in several other celebrated trials of the American Left in the 1970s: the Vietnam Veterans Against the War trial in Miami, the Attica Prison rebellion trial in New York, and the Wounded Knee trial of Indian activists in South Dakota. The high costs incurred by the survey of local attitudes were paid by "legal defence funds" using direct mail campaigns for financial contributions. These fund-raising campaigns used select mailing lists from organizations known to be sympathetic to "the cause" represented by the accused. In each case, the accused were either acquitted or found guilty of lesser charges.

While scientific jury selection was pioneered by the political Left, its success quickly led to its adoption by the Right. In the Watergate trial of Maurice Stans (President Richard Nixon's fund-raiser) and John Mitchell (Nixon's former Attorney-General), the defence team identified "good" jurors as working-class Catholics with moderate income who read the *Daily News* (the New York City equivalent of the *Toronto Sun*). "These sociological characteristics [were] associated with conservative politics, respect for authority, and suspicion of the media."[10] The profile of the "bad" juror was college-educated, Jewish, and a reader of the *New York Times* or *New York Post*. The defence lawyers succeeded in choosing a jury in which all twelve jurors matched the desired profile. Several weeks later, this jury acquitted Mitchell and Stans.

The Morgentaler trial was not the first time jury selection experts had been used in Canada. In 1979, Neil Vidmar, then a psychology professor at the University of Western Ontario, conducted a community opinion survey in preparation for a widely publicized fraud trial in London, Ontario. He found widespread knowledge of the case and strong feelings against the accused, a local building products company that was perceived to have cheated many local residents. Vidmar's study was the basis for a successful request for a change of venue, that is, to have the trial conducted in a different city. In 1983 American jury expert Jay Schulman was brought to British Columbia for the trial of the "Squamish Five," a left-wing group accused of planting bombs on the Lower Mainland. Schulman used a survey of public opinion in the Vancouver area to persuade the trial judge that extensive pre-trial publicity had created widespread prejudice against the accused. Based on this finding, the judge then allowed extensive questioning of prospective jurors.

Unlike the Morgentaler acquittal, the employment of jury selection experts in these earlier cases did not spark any public controversy. In the United States, however, the use of jury selection experts in high-profile political cases has led to charges of jury-stacking. In one case a defence attorney actually bragged to the media after the acquittal that he "bought" the verdict with his huge "defence fund."[11] Are these new jury selection techniques really this effective? Do they undermine the integrity of the jury function?

While there is no definitive answer to the first question, researchers believe that jury selection guided by a pre-trial survey of community attitudes is a more effective method of discovering juror bias than the "gut instinct" of trial lawyers. This is especially true of certain types of cases: "when the evidence is ambiguous, when the jury pool is heterogeneous, when demographic variables are strongly related to reactions to the case, and when the trial contains political or other issues likely to polarize jurors."[12] Of course, this does not guarantee a verdict of "not guilty." And even in cases where it results in such a verdict, there may be other more important factors, such as the facts. Still, the record is impressive. Schulman claims to have won seven out of ten jury trials in federal courts, when the norm is only two out of ten.[13] Litigation Services, another U.S. jury consultant, advertised a 95 per cent success rate.[14]

As to the second question, there are two common defences against the charge that scientific jury selection undermines and perverts the administration of justice. The first, used by Manning in his letter to the *Star,* is that all these techniques ensure is truly impartial jurors, not just people who claim to be impartial. While it is true that jury experts may detect subtle prejudice *against* the accused, this answer begs the important question of where the search for impartial jurors ends and the search for jurors with prejudice *for* the accused begins. Off the record – which is to say, not in front of judges or reporters – what any defence lawyer really wants is not just an impartial jury but one that will acquit his or her client. Winning, not fairness, is the real goal. The more that professional jury selectors can deliver this, the more money they can make. The desire of the defence for a favourable jury is especially strong when, as in the Morgentaler trial, the case turns not on the jurors' assessment of the facts but on their view of the crime.

The other defence of the use of jury selection experts is that they do what trial lawyers have always done, only more systematically. This is true, but it points to yet another problem – the weakness of the adversary process when the two sides are not evenly matched. The real problem is not that survey-driven jury selection works, but that only one side is allowed to use it. Precisely because it does work – at least under certain circumstances – the use of jury selection experts by only the defence can create an unequal contest and thereby impugn the integrity of the jury's verdict. The appearance, if not the reality, becomes "the best justice money can buy," a long-standing criticism of the adversary process in general.[15] In criminal trials this cannot be easily remedied, since public opinion would not tolerate the Crown's use of these techniques against the accused. Because of this, some experts claim that the ancient common-law tradition of trial by jury is at a dangerous crossroads and that its future is far from certain.

Did Henry Morgentaler and his associates go free because the jury was "scientifically stacked"? There are certainly good reasons to doubt this. He was acquitted by three Montreal juries a decade earlier without the help of jury experts, albeit on different charges, so there is no gainsaying that a "normal" Toronto jury might well have done the same. The problem, of course, is that the Toronto jury was not "normal" in the sense that it was chosen with the assistance of the American jury experts. We can never know for sure what might have been.

While no one can definitively say that Morgentaler could not have won without Jury Services, Inc., it also seems fair to conclude that their use by Manning probably helped win his clients' acquittal, which, it should be remembered, was his first responsibility. To begin with, the trial had most of the ingredients that favour the use of jury selection techniques: massive pre-trial publicity, emotional issues, a polarizing political issue, and a heterogeneous jury pool.[16] Judge Parker's restrictions on questioning negated some of the advantages of jury selection techniques, but the fact remains that before the final twelve jurors were chosen, 120 were rejected, and only seven of these by the prosecutor.

There is also the impact of the selection process on the dynamics of the jury itself. Studies indicate that judges and juries agree on the proper outcome of a trial three out of four times.[17] It is safe to assume, based on his closing address to the jury, that Judge Parker alone would not have acquitted Henry Morgentaler. The Morgentaler trial is thus an exception, one of those 25 per cent of trials where judges and juries part ways. When this occurs, it is usually because the jurors are influenced by extra-legal considerations that do not affect a judge. This can and does happen because jurors are "non-rule minded," as compared to judges, who are trained to see all their decisions in terms of rules. In the *Morgentaler* case, it seems likely that the extra-legal factor that came into play was the jurors' attitudes toward abortion and Canada's abortion law. Through his skilled use of the defence of necessity, Manning was able to persuade the jurors that what was really on trial was not the accused but the law itself. Each juror's attitude toward abortion thus took on added importance. Manning sought to transform disapproval of the law into the basis for an acquittal of the accused. He succeeded. In the end, the jurors excused not the criminal but the crime.

From this perspective, we can identify the advantages that Manning gained through his use of jury selection experts. At a minimum, he probably succeeded in excluding from the jury persons with even moderate pro-life views. If such a person (or persons) had been on the jury, it would have been that much harder for the jurors to achieve a unanimous verdict of "not guilty." A "hung" jury might have resulted. At a maximum, Manning may have succeeded in selecting a majority of jurors who actually held pro-choice views. Studies show that when such an initial majority exists at the outset of the jury's deliberation, it usually can pressure the rest of the jurors to join them in the obligatory drive for unanimity.[18]

Is this what happened in the Morgentaler jury? We will never know. Unlike judges, juries are not required to give reasons for their decisions. The only people who know for sure are the twelve Morgentaler jurors, and they are sworn to silence.

The final say belongs to Morris Manning. "If I had another case like this one – a controversial social issue or a big murder – I'd definitely use jury selectors," he told a reporter the month after the trial.[19]

CHAPTER 17

Déjà Vu

The Toronto acquittal remobilized both sides of the abortion controversy. Pro-choice forces sensed an important new opening for their campaign for free-standing abortion clinics and took the initiative. On the Saturday following the acquittal, 700 people rallied at Queen's Park, where pro-choice speakers further amplified the "message to the politicians" theme. Morgentaler upped the ante by announcing that he would reopen his clinic in several weeks and once again offered to allow the Ontario government to use it as a "pilot project for the training of doctors in the best abortion techniques." The *Globe and Mail* added its editorial voice to the swelling pro-choice chorus. Invoking the memory of Morgentaler's earlier acquittals in Quebec, the *Globe* urged the federal government to take "the necessary next step" – to place the decision to abort in the hands of women and their doctors. "How many juries must speak before Parliament is prepared to act?"[1]

Pro-life leaders sensed their new vulnerability and launched a counter-offensive. They bitterly attacked the jury as biased and unrepresentative, and demanded that the government appeal the decision. They promptly organized a "Jury for Life" project that soon sent over one-million postcards to the Prime Minister opposing "the choice to kill." They remobilized the pro-life pickets in front of the Morgentaler Clinic, which once again became the focal point of bitter verbal clashes between pro-choice and pro-life activists. All of this was duly captured and replayed by the ever-present television camera crews, further escalating the sense of conflict. Caught in this crossfire, the effect on elected politicians was one of paralysis. Federal and provincial politicians who could not escape interviews fell back on their favourite dodge: the problem was the responsibility of the other level of government.

The two politicians most directly on the spot were the federal Justice Minister, John Crosbie, and Roy McMurtry. As the Attorney-General of Ontario, McMurtry was the top law enforcement officer in the province, and it was his responsibility to decide whether the Crown should appeal the jury's acquittal. His decision was complicated by the fact that he was in the midst of a four-way leadership campaign to succeed his old boss, Bill Davis, as the leader of the Progressive Conservative Party of Ontario. The timing could not have been worse. The usually outspoken McMurtry begged off with the comment that it would be "irresponsible" for him to comment on the case before he had time to consult with Cooper and his other legal advisers. He promised a decision within a week.

As the Mulroney government's Minister of Justice, John Crosbie was ultimately responsible for the Criminal Code, and thus section 251. He was immediately challenged by the Opposition and the press as to what he intended to do in the wake of the Morgentaler acquittal. The political veteran from Newfoundland had little trouble (and probably fewer qualms) in deflecting the issue back on his provincial counterparts. Rather than being an issue of "uneven application of the law," he suggested that it was a matter of "an uneven application of medical and hospital facilities," which, he emphasized, "is a provincial responsibility." "The present law is a compromise," he patiently explained. "I have no plans at this time for any changes."

For Roy McMurtry, the next month was a politician's nightmare. In addition to having to decide whether to appeal the jury's acquittal, he had to deal with Morgentaler's decision to reopen the clinic on Harbord Street. He was heavily and publicly pressured by pro-life groups not just to proceed with the appeal, but also to seek an injunction prohibiting the reopening of the clinic and to lay new criminal charges if it did. Pro-choice groups were just as adamant on these issues, but in the opposite direction.

Matters were further complicated by a public quarrel between Morgentaler and the Archbishop of Toronto, Emmett Cardinal Carter. Two weeks after the Morgentaler acquittal, Carter had authorized a pro-life pastoral message to be read in all of Toronto's 196 Catholic parishes. The Cardinal's letter called abortion "the killing of innocents" and urged Catholics "to work together to curb and, if possible, eliminate this abomination." Morgentaler immediately accused the Cardinal of indirectly inciting violence against him and the clinic, and called for "peace talks." This was dismissed by the Church as a cheap "publicity stunt," further poisoning public debate.

Not surprisingly, it took Roy McMurtry not one week but one month to make his decision. Rarely has a politician come down so squarely on the fence. On December 4, with Morgentaler watching from the public galleries at Queen's Park, McMurtry announced that the government would appeal the jury's acquittal, but that there would be no injunction and no new charges if the clinic reopened.

McMurtry tried to downplay the abortion issue. "The issue here," he said, "has nothing to do with personal convictions on the issue of abortion; it has everything to do with the proper administration of criminal justice...." The main focus of the appeal was Manning's appeal to the jury to disregard the law. "If this verdict stands unchallenged," explained McMurtry, "it would be open to defence counsel in any case to urge the jury that the law was wrong and that the jury should disregard the law." The same option, he noted, would be open to the Crown in an attempt to secure convictions. It was the unanimous opinion of his legal advisers, he explained, that an appeal "was necessary to protect the integrity of the jury system and the duty of a jury to uphold the law."[2]

This attempt at compromise was quickly denounced by both sides. To his further chagrin, McMurtry was almost immediately contradicted by Ontario's Solicitor-General, George Taylor, who said that the police probably would raid the clinic if it reopened. In the midst of the ensuing confusion, the clinic reopened on Monday, December 10.

Tension and confusion escalated in the week that followed. Pro-life groups upped the ante by picketing the clinic and threatening civil disobedience. If the government would not stop illegal abortions, pro-lifers would, said Laura McArthur. McMurtry and Taylor tried to settle their differences with the surprise announcement that responsibility for laying new charges belonged to the Metro Toronto police, not them. This attempt to pass the buck quickly backfired when a planned police raid on the clinic was cancelled, resulting in damaging allegations of "political interference" with police law enforcement. McMurtry's final *faux pas* was to publicly ask Morgentaler to close the clinic pending the outcome of legal appeal. Morgentaler of course refused – I've already been closed for a year and a half, he retorted. Pro-life leaders were quick to denounce as "ludicrous" the sight of the province's highest law enforcement officer pleading, unsuccessfully, with a private citizen not to break the law.

Pro-life picketers returned to the clinic the day it opened. Initially they marched quietly in a circle on the Harbord Street sidewalks. The longer McMurtry procrastinated, however, the more militant they became. By the end of the week, they began to block the steps leading to the clinic in an attempt to prevent women from entering. When some protesters ignored police warnings, they were arrested under the Trespass Act. Infuriated with what they saw as police protection of an illegal abortion clinic, pro-life demonstrators escalated the level of their civil disobedience and more were arrested.

Stung by the accusation that they were protecting a law breaker and abandoned by the Attorney-General's office, the police finally moved against the clinic. As Dr. Robert Scott left the clinic on the evening of December 20, he was arrested and charged with conspiring to perform illegal abortions. Morgentaler had been vacationing somewhere in the U.S. for the past week and had once again missed his own party. He arrived at Pearson International Airport later that night and proceeded to the Metro Toronto police station at Dundas near University Avenue. There he surrendered to police, was photographed, fingerprinted, and released on his own recognizance.

Morgentaler blamed the Catholic Church for the new arrests and promised to reopen the clinic in the new year. The Archdiocese sniffed that "such statements will not be dignified with a response." Manning sniped at a more familiar target, cowardly politicians, who received only lukewarm support from the pro-life camp. Laura McArthur said that her group was "surprised it took so long" and then blasted the government for not finishing the job by closing down the clinic with an injunction. So it was that on the eve of Christmas, 1984, "Toronto the Good" found itself more bitterly divided than ever over the abortion issue.

While there were no clear winners in this round of the abortion wars, there was one clear loser: Attorney-General Roy McMurtry. McMurtry, who began as the favourite, went on to lose the PC leadership race to the dull and plodding Frank Miller. Miller subsequently lost to

David Peterson and the Liberals, bringing to an end forty-two years of Tory rule in Ontario and putting the once invincible "Big Blue Machine" on the road to political oblivion. For the second time in as many decades, Henry Morgentaler's crusade left a defeated government in its wake.

On December 4, 1984, the Ontario Attorney-General filed his notice of appeal from the acquittal. There were three legal grounds for the appeal: that Judge Parker should not have allowed the defence of necessity; that he incorrectly instructed the jury as to relevant evidence; and, finally, that a mistrial should have been declared after Manning told the jurors they had the "right not to apply the law." Manning responded the following day with a motion to quash the appeal, and, in addition, raised seventy-four grounds of cross-appeal on Judge Parker's original ruling on the constitutional validity of section 251. The following month the Attorney-General of Canada was granted leave to intervene to defend the validity of its abortion law. In announcing his decision to appeal, McMurtry had commented that the unusual jury selection process may have left some impression of "bias," but that there was nothing illegal about it. Accordingly, it was not one of the grounds for appeal.

The post-trial revelations by and about the American jury selection experts had infuriated pro-life leaders. They believed that the only reason Morgentaler had been acquitted was because of jury-stacking, and they were dismayed to learn that the government was not appealing the jury selection issue. In April, four different pro-life groups – Hamilton Right to Life, Alliance for Life, Coalition for the Protection of Human Life, and Catholic Women's League of Canada – filed for intervener status to raise the jury selection issue. Their petition argued that "it is in the public interest that the issue of the jury selection process in this case be considered." If the Crown was not willing to represent the public's interest in this matter, then they would.

The main thrust of the interveners' petition was that the jury had been improperly chosen. They alleged that the selection process gave the appearance of bias against Catholics and other religious groups, and that the judge had mismanaged the jury selection process. "The fact that a juror has views about abortion is not a proper ground of challenge for cause, just as jurors are not excluded from trial involving murder, rape or robbery just because they believe that murder, rape and robbery are morally wrong."[3]

It appears from the questions asked, the percentage of prospective jurors excluded, and the media coverage of the trial that the accused, with the consent or acquiescence of the Crown and Trial Judge, searched for and was ultimately tried by a favourable jury rather than an indifferent one made up of a cross-section of the community.[4]

According to Dr. Janet Ajzenstat, who represented Hamilton Right to Life, this was precisely what Manning had wanted – jurors who would excuse not the criminal but the crime. "Because his client had admitted – indeed, boasted of – breaking the law, Manning knew that he had to have not a jury that would favour Morgentaler under the law, but a jury that would vote down the law."[5]

Both the Attorney-General of Ontario and Manning strongly opposed the pro-life motion for intervention. They argued that appeals were limited to questions of law alone and that the issue of jury selection did not raise an issue of law alone. The Crown also said that to allow interveners to appeal a new issue would usurp the role of the Attorney-General. Several days later, Chief Justice Howland agreed. In rejecting the petition, he wrote:

In a criminal proceeding, the Crown represents the public interest and it alone is given the right to appeal from an acquittal. To permit a third party to intervene to raise an additional ground of appeal would enlarge the scope of a Crown appeal from an acquittal beyond that contemplated by Parliament. . . . I know of no case in which such a right has previously been granted.

Privately, pro-life leaders were disappointed that the jury selection issue would not be part of the appeal. Publicly, they pointed out that the Court had not rejected their claim of a stacked jury but only their right to press the claim in court. They consoled themselves that they had kept the public's attention on the jury issue, thereby, they hoped, eroding the integrity of the Morgentaler acquittal.

The Ontario Court of Appeal heard the Morgentaler appeal the first week of May, 1985. There was a new factor in the Morgentaler appeal and it did not bode well for the three doctors. The jury acquittal and the ensuing controversy over jury selection had overshadowed an important Supreme Court of Canada decision released only days before Morgentaler's jury trial was to begin in Toronto. At first glance, *Perka et al.*

v. The Queen[6] appeared to have nothing to do with Morgentaler or abortion. It involved the prosecution of drug smugglers under the Narcotics Control Act. But a closer reading revealed ominous news for Morris Manning and his clients.

On May 22, 1979, William Francis Perka and the other crew members of the ship *Samarkanda* had been stopped by the RCMP in No Name Bay on the west coast of Vancouver Island. When the RCMP discovered thirty-three tons of marijuana on the beach, they arrested Perka and his shipmates and charged them with importing narcotics into Canada. Notwithstanding such evidence against them, Perka and his friends were subsequently acquitted by a jury. Their defence was the defence of necessity.

Evidence presented at trial showed that the *Samarkanda* was nearing the end of a three-week voyage from Colombia to Juneau, Alaska, when engine trouble and stormy seas threatened to swamp the boat off the coast of Canada. Fearing for the safety of both the ship and his crew, the captain decided to seek refuge along the shoreline of Vancouver Island. The *Samarkanda* subsequently ran aground in No Name Bay, and, fearing that his ship was about to sink, the captain ordered the cargo of marijuana offloaded. It was at this point that the RCMP arrived.

At trial the crew of the *Samarkanda* pleaded the defence of necessity. They told the judge and jury that they had no intention of importing their marijuana into Canada but had only stopped to escape being lost at sea and to make repairs. Documents were produced indicating that they had planned a rendezvous with another ship, the *Julia B,* 200 miles off the coast of Alaska at the end of May. Several individuals with marine experience were called as expert witnesses and testified that under the circumstances the captain of the *Samarkanda* made the right decision. The Crown contested the alleged "necessity" of landing on Vancouver Island, but the jury believed Perka's story and acquitted.

The Crown successfully appealed to the Court of Appeal of British Columbia, and Perka then appealed that decision to the Supreme Court. Thus, for the first time since its 1976 *Morgentaler* decision, the Supreme Court was being asked to define more precisely the defence of necessity. Since 1976, the defence of necessity had been successfully invoked in several subsequent trials – including Morgentaler's second and third trials in Montreal – but had also been ruled inapplicable in several other trials. Chief Justice Dickson described the resulting law of necessity as "ill-defined and elusive." Such uncertainty cried out for clarification, and *Perka* presented the opportunity to provide it.

What made *Perka* different, however, was the pending Morgentaler trial in Toronto. While Manning's defence strategy would not be known until the trial began, it was clear to anyone with knowledge of the case that Manning would try to use some version of the defence of necessity as a back up to his Charter challenge. *Perka* was thus decided in the shadow of *Morgentaler,* and the justices knew very well that how they defined the defence of necessity for Perka would directly influence its availability to Manning and Morgentaler.

The majority opinion in *Perka* was written by Chief Justice Dickson, who was joined by four of the other five justices.[7] It could hardly have been worse for Morgentaler. Precedent and scholarly opinion had identified two different theories of the defence of necessity: excuse of illegal conduct and justification of illegal conduct. This latter possibility – that conduct which by itself is illegal can become legal if it is done to honour a higher obligation – was rejected as having no application in Canada. "It is still my opinion," wrote the Chief Justice, quoting from his 1976 *Morgentaler* judgment, "that 'no system of positive law can recognize any principle which would entitle a person to violate the law because on his view the law conflicted with some higher social value.'" In so saying, Dickson destroyed any possibility of Morgentaler defending his conduct as being required by moral conscience.

To make matters worse, Dickson then narrowed the "excuse" branch of the necessity defence. It was no longer enough that for otherwise illegal conduct to be excused it would have to be done unwillingly, in an emergency, in order to avoid a still greater harm. Dickson added one more – and for Morgentaler, fatal – requirement: only in the absence of "a reasonable legal alternative to disobeying the law" can the defence be invoked. The judge must instruct the jury to determine, "Was there a legal way out?" If there was, necessity is no defence.

For Perka and his associates this meant a new trial, since the first trial judge had not properly instructed the jury. For Morgentaler and his associates, whose trial was scheduled to start only four days after the decision was released, *Perka* seemed to strip them of any chance of winning with a defence of necessity. As it turned out, because of the close timing, the *Perka* decision was not a major factor at the October, 1984, trial. The decision had not yet been reported, much less discussed in the law journals. Judge Parker was on his own, armed only with the pink "judge's copy," an advance transcript of the decision. Parker had read verbatim selected portions to the jury. The jury, confused, had requested a copy for themselves. Parker refused. Manning objected. Parker read the decision to the jury again. In the end, the jurors had been left to sort out the meaning of *Perka* by themselves. By the time of the appeal hearing six months later, however, *Perka* had been widely reported and discussed. It was little wonder that the Crown attorneys were eager to appeal their trial defeat to Ontario's highest court.

The Chief Justice of the Ontario Court of Appeal, William Howland, selected a panel of five judges, rather than the customary three, to hear the Morgentaler appeal. In addition to the Chief Justice, there were Justices Charles Dubin, G. Arthur Martin, B.J. MacKinnon, and John Brooke. The importance of the case was further underscored by the fact that these were the five most senior judges on the court. In a scene strongly reminiscent of the Quebec Court of Appeal a decade earlier, Morgentaler and his lawyer were given a cool reception that only became frostier as the hearing progressed. [8]

The Crown led off the hearing by laying out the three grounds for its appeal. Manning had no sooner started his rebuttal when the judges began to pepper him with questions. How could the doctors invoke the defence of necessity when they had planned in advance to perform abortions on almost all women who came to the clinic, regardless of whether they had been rejected by a TAC or had even applied for an abortion? "The Emergency feature is missing," observed Justice Brooke. Justice Dubin was even more sceptical: "This whole defence seems to be . . . misconceived. If you are right, then any doctor can do [an abortion] in his office at any time."

Justice Dubin also chided Manning for going far beyond the real issue in the case. When Manning asked, "What issue is that?" Dubin shot back: "The issue of guilt or innocence of the accused. Not about the issues that you have introduced at this trial." Dubin also challenged Manning's contention that the only purpose of section 251 was to protect the health of the mother, not the fetus. When Manning persisted in his interpretation, Dubin cut him off: "That's not what [the Supreme Court] said. I suggest that you re-read the judgment."

Manning took three days to present his arguments. In addition to rebutting the Crown's appeal, he also presented his cross-appeal – that the abortion law itself was unconstitutional because it violated nine different provisions of the Constitution. These were the same arguments that Manning had put to Judge Parker in his pre-trial motion. Morgentaler's prospects took a turn for the worse when the Chief Justice told Crown counsel Bonnie Wein that four of Manning's nine legal arguments were so lacking in merit that she need not even address them. Well before the hearing ended there was a discernible new sense of pessimism in the Morgentaler camp. The pro-life contingent, by contrast, was encouraged. "We do not presume to second guess the outcome of this appeal," said the pro-life monthly, *The Interim,* "but for some days pro-lifers had an unaccustomed pleasure in reading the headlines."

Seven months later, on October 1, 1985, the Ontario Court of Appeal handed down a unanimous and unsigned opinion. It allowed the Crown's appeal of the jury acquittal on all three grounds and rejected all of Manning's constitutional challenges to section 251.[9] For Morgentaler and Manning, it was a complete and total defeat.

Although the appeal had been brought by the Crown, the Court first dealt with Manning's constitutional challenge to section 251. This was dictated by legal logic and economy. If the Court were to find that the abortion law violated the Charter, then deciding the Crown's appeal would become unnecessary. Morgentaler would be free because the law was invalid, regardless of the legal propriety of the jury's acquittal.

The main thrust of Manning's constitutional challenge was that the abortion law violated a woman's "right to privacy" as protected by section 7 of the Charter. The problem with this argument was that the term "right to privacy" nowhere appears in section 7 or anywhere else in the Charter. Section 7 speaks of the "right to life, liberty and security of the person," and the right not to be deprived of any of these rights "except in accordance with the principles of fundamental justice." This did not necessarily mean that a judge might not find such a right to be implied or included by the broad language of section 7, but traditionally judges are reluctant to add new meaning unless there is a good reason to.

One of the most accepted reasons for judges to add non-explicit meaning is evidence that such meaning was intended by the framers of the constitution – that is, that it really is not new at all. The most commonly used evidence of "original understanding" or "framers' intent" is *Hansard* (the official record of parliamentary debate) or the minutes of parliamentary committees. The same type of evidence can be used to rebut claims of implied rights.

Unfortunately for Morgentaler, there was clear evidence from the minutes of the 1981 Joint House-Senate Committee on the Constitution that section 7 had been revised specifically to prevent the kind of "substantive" interpretation asked for by Manning. The Crown had presented this evidence to rebut Manning's claim for a section 7 "right to privacy," and the Court had clearly been impressed. In its reasons for judgment, the Court noted that the original wording of section 7 – "due process of law" – had been changed to "principles of fundamental justice" in the final draft. The two top officials in the federal Department of Justice had both testified before the Committee that the purpose of this change was to prevent judges from giving an American-style "substantive due process" interpretation to section 7.[10]

Faced with such a clear record of the intended meaning of section 7, the Court concluded that it could not accept Manning's invitation to engage in "substantive review" and find an implicit "right to privacy" lurking in the shadows of section 7. For good measure, the Court added its endorsement to the framers' intention to prevent judicial review of substantive legislative policy choices. Not once but twice, the Court asserted that "the policy and wisdom of legislation should remain first and foremost a matter for Parliament and the Legislatures."[11]

The Ontario Court of Appeal also firmly rejected any use of the defence of necessity by the accused doctors. Drawing from the Supreme Court's recent precedent of *Perka v. The Queen,* the Court ruled that the defence of necessity was available only "when compliance with the law is demonstrably impossible," when there is "no legal way out." This was clearly not the case, the Court observed, when the three doctors agreed in advance to open a clinic to provide abortions outside the law. "Planning, deliberating, relying on legal precedent – all of these are incompatible with the uncalculated response essential to 'involuntary conduct,'" which is the core element of the defence of necessity.

> With respect, the defence of necessity is not premised on dissatisfaction with the law. The defence of necessity recognizes that there are certain factual situations which arise and which may excuse a person for failure to comply with the law. It is not the law which can create an emergency giving rise to a defence of necessity, but it is the facts of a given situation which may do so."[12]

Judge Parker's misconception of the defence of necessity, the Appeal Court continued, led him to make another mistake in his charge to the jury as to what evidence they should consider relevant. Judge

Parker erred in allowing the jury to consider "the merit of the law" as relevant to the defence of necessity. "He confused an over-all need for medical services with the defence of necessity."[13] All the evidence led by Manning with respect to the former was irrelevant to the latter.

The Appeal Court also blasted Manning for telling the jury they had "a right" to refuse to enforce the law. This constituted "a direct attack on the role and authority of the trial judge and a serious misstatement to the jury as to its duty and right in carrying out its oath." They commended Judge Parker for directing the jury to ignore this statement by Manning, but said that the damage was already done and a mistrial should have been declared.

The Appeal Court's judgment in the Morgentaler case was eighty-three rambling, single-spaced pages, but its final disposition of the appeal was clear and concise: impermissible defence, impermissible evidence, and impermissible misstatement of the law to the jury: "Accordingly, the appeal is allowed, the verdict of acquittal is set aside, and a new trial directed."

Morgentaler denounced the decision, and Manning announced they would appeal to the Supreme Court. The Supreme Court would be obliged to hear the appeal since, as a jury acquittal reversed on appeal, the case fell into that small category of cases that enjoyed an appeal by right. The fact that they were now on their way to the Supreme Court could not disguise the fact that Morgentaler and Manning had suffered a serious defeat, one that did not bode well for the future. In Canadian legal circles, the Ontario Court of Appeal is second only to the federal Supreme Court in prestige and authority. It was also establishing itself as one of the more "pro-Charter" provincial courts of appeal and one with an excellent record of having its Charter decisions upheld on appeal by the Supreme Court.[14] In short, the Ontario Court of Appeal was usually a dependable legal barometer. On October 1, 1985, the forecast for Morgentaler, Scott, and Smoling suddenly did not look promising.

It was December 18, 1985, six weeks after the Ontario Court of Appeal had rejected Manning's constitutional arguments. A light snow was falling outside the Regina courthouse. Inside, Morris Shumiatcher and Joe Borowski were also fighting an uphill battle before the Saskatchewan Court of Appeal. For the past two days, Shumiatcher had been arguing that those sections of the Criminal Code allowing therapeutic abortions violate the "right to life" of the unborn child/fetus as protected by section 7 of the Charter. Once again, legislative history was proving to be a major stumbling block.

Justices Cameron and Wakeling repeatedly pressed Shumiatcher to offer some evidence that the framers of section 7 intended the term "everyone" to include the unborn. Crown counsel Ed Sojonky was quick to offer evidence to the contrary. Shumiatcher tried to deflect the judges' questions with the observation that constitutional documents such as the Charter are typically written in broad, generic terms, terms flexible enough to encompass the changes that time inevitably brings. Switching to the offensive, Shumiatcher invoked Lord Sankey's "living tree" doctrine of constitutional interpretation and quoted *obiter dicta* from the Supreme Court's early Charter decisions urging a "large and liberal" judicial interpretation of the Charter. It all sounded very familiar. If you shut your eyes, replaced "right to life" with "right to privacy," and Shumiatcher's tenor with Manning's baritone, you could just as easily have been in the Osgoode Hall courtroom on Queen Street in Toronto six months earlier.

Shumiatcher's seductive rhetoric seemed to be having some influence. At one point, Justice Cameron challenged Crown attorney Sojonky to tell him why the court should not adopt the "living tree" approach and expand the section 7 right to life to include the unborn. Sojonky curtly responded that the constitutional "tree" was too young for judicial shaping and that the original intention of the framers was still binding on the judges.

It was the third and last day of the hearing, and Shumiatcher was making his closing statement before the three-judge panel when one of his assistants scurried into the courtroom clutching a document. Stopping in mid-sentence, Shumiatcher eagerly scanned the document and then excitedly announced to the Court that he had just received a copy of a Supreme Court decision handed down in Ottawa the previous day. This new decision, he told the Court with obvious satisfaction, would totally negate the Crown's extensive use of "framers' intent." The three judges were now free, Shumiatcher exclaimed, to adopt the "living tree" approach and to expand the meaning of section 7 to include the unborn. He proceeded to quote selectively from Justice Antonio Lamer's judgment in the *Reference re British Columbia Motor Vehicle Act*.[15]

The *B.C. Motor Vehicle Reference* was relatively unimportant with respect to the policy issue at stake but very significant in terms of constitutional interpretation and development. Section 94(1) of British

Columbia's Motor Vehicle Act made it an offence for a person to drive if his or her licence had been revoked or if that person had been legally prohibited from driving. Section 94(2) made it an absolute liability offence; that is, guilt was established by proof of driving, whether or not the driver knew of the prohibition or suspension. The offence was punishable by a fine and a minimum term of imprisonment.

At issue was whether the absolute liability provision violated the "principles of fundamental justice" set forth in section 7 of the Charter. The Attorney-General of British Columbia argued that the meaning of section 7 was limited to "procedural fairness" alone and that section 7 did not authorize judges to pass judgment on the "substance" of impugned legislation. Speaking for a unanimous court, Justice Lamer rejected a strict dichotomy between "substantive" and "procedural" interpretations of section 7. The two could not be so easily separated. The entire array of procedural safeguards enumerated in sections 8 through 14 of the Charter constitute the substance of "principles of fundamental justice" articulated in section 7. More to the point, Lamer wrote, "A law that has the potential to convict a person who has not really done anything wrong offends the principles of fundamental justice. . . . In other words, absolute liability and imprisonment cannot be combined." To justify this interpretation of section 7, Lamer proceeded to discount the importance of "framers' intent."

While conceding the admissibility of the "framers' intent" as relevant to determining the proper interpretation of Charter rights, Justice Lamer characterized legislative history as "inherently unreliable" and cautioned against granting it anything more than "minimal weight." To attach any more significance to the so-called "original understanding" of Charter rights, he cautioned, "would in effect be assuming a fact which is nearly impossible of proof, i.e., the intention of the legislative bodies which adopted the Charter." Moreover, Lamer continued,

> If the newly planted "living tree" which is the Charter is to have the possibility of growth and adjustment over time, care must be taken to ensure that historical materials, such as the Minutes of the Special Joint Committee, do not stunt its growth.[16]

Shumiatcher could not have obtained a more helpful, more timely precedent if he had written and delivered it himself. As he later observed, "What had been the three contentious points urged against us by the Attorney-General were answered directly and completely, and in each instance, in favour of Borowski."[17] This is the stuff courtroom lawyers dream of. The three judges eagerly asked for copies, as did a glum, disbelieving Ed Sojonky.

The *B.C. Motor Vehicle Reference* marked the triumph of what is known as "noninterpretivism" over "interpretivism" in Charter jurisprudence. Both of these approaches to constitutional interpretation recognize the truth of the "living tree" metaphor – that constitutional meaning must be flexible enough to keep up with social change – but draw very different conclusions about the permissible scope of "judicial updating." The interpretivists stress judicial fidelity to the text and the original understanding of that text as illuminated by evidence of the framers' intent. They readily concede that new circumstances may require novel applications of that original meaning. However, the new meaning may not contradict or overrule the original meaning.[18]

The noninterpretivists do not accept this limitation. They are less attached to the concept of judicial fidelity to original understanding and framers' intent. As reflected in Justice Lamer's opinion in the *B.C. Motor Vehicle Reference,* they believe that the framers' intent is too obscure to be a reliable guide to present-day interpretation. Who counts as a "framer"? What if different groups of framers had different understandings of what a constitutional clause means? What one person "speaks" for all the framers?

Even if the original understanding of a constitutional clause is clear, noninterpretivists may still support a contrary judicial interpretation if it is required to reach a "just" result under present circumstances. The present generation should not be blindly controlled by past generations. It does not make sense, they argue, for judges in effect to punish the living in order to appease the dead. For the noninterpretivist, the judge's ultimate responsibility is to keep the constitution in tune with the times, not to keep the times in tune with the constitution.

Because it officially sanctioned the noninterpretivist approach to Charter interpretation, the *B.C. Motor Vehicle Reference* has become one of the most important and most cited Charter precedents. By freeing constitutional law (i.e., the judges) from constitutional text (the meaning intended by the framers), the Court had granted itself and all other Canadian judges wide discretion to read new meaning into the Charter. Future litigants could now invoke the symbol of the Charter as a "living tree" and argue that even if the meaning they attributed to a Charter right was contrary to its original meaning, the judge was still free to adopt it.

It was difficult to assess what effect the timely arrival of the *B.C.*

Motor Vehicle Reference would have on the Saskatchewan Court of Appeal's handling of the Borowski case. It clearly helped, but was it enough? Shumiatcher certainly thought so, since it kicked the legal support out from underneath the Attorney-General's three principal arguments. Whatever the outcome of the Saskatchewan appeal, it did not take a crystal ball to predict that the Supreme Court of Canada was going to hear a great deal more about the *B.C. Motor Vehicle Reference* when Morris Manning arrived with the Morgentaler appeal. The doctrine that up to now had served the Crown as an effective checkmate to Manning's Charter attacks on the abortion law had suddenly disappeared. It was as much a Christmas present to Morris Manning in Toronto as it had been to Morris Shumiatcher in Regina.

CHAPTER 18

Return to
the Supreme Court

Henry Morgentaler returned to the Supreme Court building on October 7, 1986. Outwardly it looked no different from the building he had walked away from a decade earlier. Inside, however, was a very different Court indeed. The Court was now well on its way into "Charterland" and bore only a faint resemblance to the self-restrained Court that had cautiously avoided the abortion issue and sent Morgentaler to prison a decade earlier. Part of the change was new personnel. Justices Beetz and Dickson were the only remaining judges from the Court's 1975 *Morgentaler* decision. For the first time there was now a woman on the Court – Madame Justice Bertha Wilson – appointed by Pierre Trudeau only weeks before the Charter became law. With this important exception, however, the new justices were not very different – in social background, education, and experience – from the judges they replaced. The important difference was the Charter of Rights.[1]

By the time the Morgentaler appeal arrived, the Supreme Court had handed down twenty-two Charter decisions. Both in word and deed, the Court had begun to carve out a bold new path of judicial activism. The Court had repeatedly stressed the difference between the Charter and the statutory 1960 Bill of Rights. "The task of expounding a constitution," wrote Chief Justice Dickson, "is crucially different from that of construing a statute."[2] Justice Le Dain spoke of the Charter as providing a "new constitutional mandate for judicial review."[3] Justice

Wilson was even more blunt. "The adoption of the Charter," she had declared, "has sent a clear message to the courts that the restrictive attitude which at times characterized their approach to the Canadian Bill of Rights ought to be reexamined."[4]

In its first Charter case, Justice Estey set the tone for the Court's "new mandate" by invoking Lord Sankey's "living tree" doctrine from the *Persons Case* and urging a "large and liberal interpretation" of the Charter.[5] This theme was carried forward by Chief Justice Dickson, who urged his colleagues "not to read the provisions of the Constitution like a last will and testament lest it become one."[6] Charter interpretation, according to the Chief Justice, "should be . . . generous rather than . . . legalistic."[7] This judicial creativity and boldness had reached a peak in the Supreme Court's decision in the *British Columbia Motor Vehicle Reference.*[8]

The Supreme Court matched the boldness of its words with its decisions. In its first twenty-two decisions, the Supreme Court had ruled in favour of the individual Charter claimant twelve times. This success ratio of 55 per cent was quadruple the win ratio of only 14 per cent (five out of thirty-five) under the Bill of Rights from 1960 to 1982.[9] In only two years the Supreme Court had nullified portions of six statutes, compared to just one such instance of judicial revision during the first twenty-two years of the Bill of Rights.[10] Another telling measure of the Supreme Court's new activism under the Charter was its treatment of Bill of Rights precedents. In the five cases where the Crown relied on pre-Charter precedents to support its case, the Supreme Court explicitly overruled three of its previous decisions and found in favour of the individual litigant.

No case better exemplified the Court's new course of judicial activism than its decision in *Big M Drug Mart v. The Queen.*[11] The Supreme Court ruled that the Sunday-closing requirements of the federal Lord's Day Act violated the freedom of religion provision of the Charter. This holding directly overruled the Court's own 1961 Bill-of-Rights precedent of *Robertson and Rosetanni v. The Queen,* which had upheld the Lord's Day Act on the grounds that it did not violate freedom of religion. The *Big M* ruling also went further than the U.S. Supreme Court, which has upheld similar Sunday-closing laws. The Court's new willingness to overrule pre-Charter precedents and strike down legislation was a good omen for Morgentaler, as he would need the Court to do both in order to win his own appeal.

The Morgentaler appeal also exemplified one of the other important changes brought about by the Charter – interest group use of litigation as a political tactic. The Charter created a new forum in which interest groups could press their claims. Historically, Canadian interest groups had concentrated their lobbying activities at the cabinet and senior levels of the bureaucracy. Unlike their American counterparts, they avoided lobbying parliamentary committees and rarely had used litigation as a political tactic.

This pattern of Canadian interest group activity was explained by the "closed" character of the Canadian policy-making process.[12] Unlike the American separation of powers system, in the parliamentary system there was little opportunity to influence public policy in either parliamentary committees or the courts. Party discipline negated the independence and thus any real power of parliamentary committees. Prior to the Charter, the tradition of parliamentary supremacy relegated the courts to a secondary political role and a more legalistic exercise of the judicial function. As a consequence, the substance of Canadian public policy was hammered out mainly within the party and the bureaucracy, which ultimately came together in the cabinet.[13] Interest groups accordingly concentrated their efforts at this single "access point" of the policy process. The Charter of Rights changed this situation by creating a new access point in the decision-making process. Interest groups that failed to achieve their policy objectives through the traditional political party and bureaucratic channels could now turn to the courts.

While the Morgentaler and Borowski cases were two of the purest, earliest, and best-known examples of interest group use of the Charter, they were hardly alone. In the highly publicized case of *Operation Dismantle v. The Queen,*[14] a coalition of peace and anti-nuclear groups unsuccessfully challenged the testing of the American cruise missile in Canadian territory as a violation of the rights to life and security of the person protected by section 7 of the Charter. A more successful example was the 1984 challenge by the National Citizens' Coalition to the Canada Election Act, which prohibited independent third-party expenditures for federal elections. These restrictions were deemed to violate the right to "freedom of expression" protected by the Charter.[15] Another success story was the Quebec Protestant School Board's challenge to the education provisions of Bill 101, which severely restricted access to English-language education in Quebec.[16]

Interest group use of Charter litigation was further encouraged by the federal government's new "Court Challenges Program," announced in September, 1985. The government allocated $9 million over the next five years to fund litigation arising under the equality rights, language rights, and multiculturalism provisions of the Charter. Applications for financial support were screened according to the criteria of "substantial importance . . . legal merit . . . [and] consequences for a number of people." The Canadian Council on Social Development, a privately administered but publicly funded organization chosen to administer the program, stated that its selection of cases would "emphasize the setting of social justice priorities."[17] Selected cases were eligible for $35,000 at each stage of litigation – trial, provincial appeal court, and, for those who were granted leave, the Supreme Court of Canada.

While success had been confined to only several cases, the sudden increase in the amount of interest group litigation, combined with the new policy of government funding, constituted a major departure from past practice. Prior to the adoption of the Charter, interest group use of litigation as a political tactic was widely perceived as illegitimate and a tactic of last resort.[18] The accuracy of this analysis had been seriously challenged by the first five years of Charter experience. How the Supreme Court would dispose of the Morgentaler appeal – one of the purest examples of an attempt to litigate social change – would decide whether there was any truth left to this perception

Surprisingly, there were no interest groups participating as interveners as there had been in Morgentaler's 1975 trip to the Supreme Court. Intervention at the appeal level offered interest groups a timely and less expensive way to participate in the new game of Charter politics. After some initial reluctance, the Supreme Court has adopted an open-door policy of granting intervener status to interest groups in Charter appeals. The result has been a dramatic 70 per cent increase in the number of cases with non-government interveners, a change reflecting the new, more political role of the Court.[19] Here, however, in the most political Charter case yet to come before the Court, there were no interveners. Why?

There were several explanations. Pro-life groups had decided not to intervene because they were already heavily committed financially to the Borowski case. They also thought that they would get their opportunity when the Borowski appeal arrived in Ottawa. This turned out to be a bad tactical error. As for the pro-choice groups, CARAL was already backing Morgentaler financially and was satisfied with Manning's legal plan of attack. The CCLA, which had intervened in the

1975 *Morgentaler* hearing, had offered to intervene, but Manning had turned them down. CCLA general counsel Alan Borovoy wanted to argue the section 15 "equity of access" issue but not the section 7 liberty-right to privacy claim. Manning wanted support for both. More generally, Manning feared that interveners supporting Morgentaler would provoke an equal reaction from the other side. Manning was happy that there were no interveners on the pro-life side and wanted to keep it that way. He thought that the government lawyers had not made the strongest possible defence of the abortion legislation and feared that pro-life interveners might bring in new facts and arguments that would strengthen the Crown's case.[20]

The most publicized and controversial case in the Charter's brief history was scheduled to start at 10:30 a.m., Tuesday, October 7. Supporters, opponents, and the curious began lining up at 8:30 to be assured of a seat inside. Television camera crews from the major national networks jockeyed for strategic positions. By ten o'clock, a small mob stood on the front steps of the Court. There could be no better evidence of the Court's new and powerful role in Canadian politics.

The doors were opened at ten, and after passing through a double security check, including a metal detector, the spectators quickly filled the small public seating area. Dr. Scott and his wife had arrived early and were seated in the front left row that had been reserved for the Morgentaler entourage, immediately behind Manning. Morgentaler arrived in a dramatic flurry at the last minute, ensuring maximum media coverage. As he made his way down the centre aisle to take his seat next to the Scotts, he was warmly greeted and even hugged by several spectators. His friends clearly outnumbered his enemies.

At 10:33, three minutes late, the Court clerk announced the entrance of the judges. This provided the first and only surprise of the day. Because of the controversy and publicity surrounding the appeal, it was expected that Chief Justice Dickson would marshal a full panel of nine justices rather than the usual seven. The Court usually sits as nine in politically controversial cases, as this places the authority of the entire court behind its eventual decision. It also pre-empts speculation that the outcome might have been different with different judges.

This morning, however, only seven judges appeared from behind the tall, maroon curtains to take their seats. Le Dain and Chouinard were missing. Court officials later explained that Chouinard was too ill to sit (he subsequently died of cancer) and that to avoid the possibility of an evenly divided court, Le Dain had been dropped. At the time it was not clear if Le Dain volunteered or was asked by the Chief Justice to step down.

Whatever the reason, it was an auspicious beginning for Morgentaler. Chouinard and Le Dain (especially the latter) were identified with an emerging faction on the Court, led by Justice William McIntyre, that leaned toward a less activist exercise of Charter review. Earlier in the year both were part of five-judge majority in a language rights decision that held that the courts should leave such politically sensitive issues to the elected legislatures.[21] This disposition toward judicial self-restraint was not receptive to Manning's vision of the judges' role under the Charter. Manning was not upset when he saw that Le Dain and Chouinard were absent.

The cast was rounded out by the various Crown counsels. Bonnie Wein was still representing the Attorney-General of Ontario but had been joined by James Blacklock. (Ironically, both Wein and Blacklock had articled for Manning back in the 1970s when he worked in the Ontario Attorney-General's office.) The federal government had been granted intervener status and was represented by Ed Sojonky, the same federal Crown prosecutor who was arguing Ottawa's position in the Borowski case.

There were two prongs to Manning's appeal: the constitutional attack on section 251 and then the issues arising from the trial itself. The latter included the availability of the defence of necessity; the issue of a mistrial because of Manning's closing statement to the jury; and whether the right of the Crown to appeal from a jury verdict was itself a violation of the Charter. The constitutional issues were the same as before: Did the abortion law violate freedom of conscience (s. 2(a) of the Charter), the liberty and security of the person (s. 7), the right against cruel or unusual punishment (s. 12) or the equality provisions (s. 15 and s. 28)?[22] Political attention was focused on these Charter issues. Not only would a positive answer by the Court set Morgentaler and his associates free, but it would also strike down the abortion law across the entire country. Thus, as Morris Manning rose to present his arguments, a hushed audience leaned forward in keen anticipation.

What followed was a great disappointment. What should have been one of the most exciting and engaging legal debates of the decade turned out to be one of the greatest bores. Once Manning began, he did not stop for two days. He read almost verbatim from an abridged version of his factum, copies of which the judges had received over a month before. Not only the audience but even the judges seemed to lose interest. As he passed uninterrupted from one issue to the next – each raising controversial issues that begged to be debated and probed by the give and take of questioning – the judges slumped ever more deeply into their plush, high-backed chairs. Manning later said that he was surprised – almost disappointed – by the passive behaviour of the judges.

By now, the constitutional arguments for both sides were well rehearsed. As he had twice before, Manning mounted a broad Charter attack on the abortion law, claiming violations of sections 2, 7, 12, and 15. He sharply criticized the Ontario Court of Appeal for its over-reliance on pre-Charter precedents, especially the first *Morgentaler* decision, and for ignoring the U.S. precedents, especially *Roe v. Wade.* In his factum, Manning cited seventy-one American precedents and twenty U.S. law review articles.[23] The Ontario Court of Appeal had failed to grasp the significance of the new Charter era, which, according to Manning, made *Roe* relevant and the 1975 *Morgentaler* decision irrelevant. Crown counsels Wein and Sojonky countered with the same arguments they had won with twice before: avoid the mistakes of the U.S. Supreme Court, don't add unintended meaning to the Charter, and don't meddle in political issues reserved for Parliament.

There was one new card in Manning's deck, and he played it repeatedly: the *B.C. Motor Vehicle Reference* decision. Decided only weeks after the Ontario Court of Appeal's decision, Manning argued that this precedent now paved the way for the Supreme Court to find a right to abortion in section 7 of the Charter. It sanctioned judicial departure from the legislative history of section 7 and thus a substantive interpretation of the rights to "life, liberty and security of the person." This "emancipated" version of the right to liberty was broad enough, Manning told the Court, to "include . . . the right to be let alone in making fundamental decisions such as whether to marry, divorce, bear children, . . . not to bear children, [or] to . . . terminate an unwanted pregnancy."[24] Manning was clearly gambling that the *B.C. Motor Vehicle Reference* would trump what had previously been the Crown's strongest suit: the legislative history indicating that the framers of the Charter intended it to be completely neutral on the abortion issue.

On Tuesday, Manning spoke almost without interruption for four hours. The judges had asked only ten simple questions. Not surprisingly, the audience had thinned considerably when the Court reconvened Wednesday morning. Manning continued for three more tedious hours. At the end of the afternoon, the judges finally woke up from their intellectual slumber when Manning turned to the issue of his remark to the jury that they had "the right to ignore the law."

"What is the juror's oath?" queried the Chief Justice. "Isn't it to uphold the law?"[25] Manning tried to sidestep the question by replying that he was not sure, but Justice Estey jumped in to cut him off. To tell jurors they have a right to refuse to apply the law is contrary to their oath, Estey declared. Justice Lamer chimed in next: "What is the point of a judge's instruction to the jury, if the jury has a right to ignore them? . . . If juries feel they don't have to obey the law, might they not convict [an innocent person] contrary to the law?" Manning tried to fend off these attacks through repeated references to Lord Devlin's celebrated defence of the jury as "the conscience of the community," but without much success. While it is true, Justice McIntrye reminded him, that juries have on occasion refused to enforce the law, and that some of these occasions are justly celebrated, "this is a very different thing from instructing a jury that they are entitled to ignore the law."[26] The Chief Justice returned to the fray in an effort to pin Manning down on the source of his authority.

> C.J. Dickson: You have four large volumes of hundreds of cases. Can you take us to any one that says a jury has the right not to apply the law?
>
> Manning: Only one. *Bazelon.*
>
> C.J. Dickson: So your best authority is a dissenting opinion of an American court? Do you have no Canadian or British cases?
>
> Manning: Only Devlin. . . .
>
> C.J. Dickson: What page?
>
> Manning: Pages 160 to 165.
>
> C.J. Dickson: What specific passage?
>
> Manning: No specific statement. It is implicit in the "conscience of the community function."

For Manning, this was a sour note on which to end his oral presentation. The aggressive and pointed questioning from five of the seven justices suggested that Manning had badly overplayed his hand on the jury issue. If he was going to win, it would have to be on his Charter challenges.

The remainder of the week was taken up by the three Crown attorneys, then closing statements. Wein and Sojonky defended the abortion law against Manning's Charter attacks, while Blacklock presented the Crown's position on the jury-related issues. Like Manning's, the oral presentations of the three Crown attorneys were cautious, rarely departing from their factums. The seven justices also lapsed back into a relatively passive mode, seeming content to listen to the three Crown counsels more or less read from their factums. The only aggressive questioning from the bench concerned certain factual issues – the uneven administration of the *TAC*s and the resulting problems of access to abortion services in some regions of the country. As with Manning's presentation earlier in the week, the judges allowed the Crown's central constitutional claims to pass relatively unchallenged and untested.

The *Morgentaler* appeal raised many of the most fundamental issues confronting the Court in its new role under the Charter of Rights. Should the broadly worded section 7 guarantee that "life, liberty and security of the person" can be infringed only "in accordance with the principles of fundamental justice" be limited to procedural meaning or does it allow the courts to review the substance of legislation? How much weight should be given to the legislative history – the "framers' intent" – in interpreting section 7 as well as other sections of the Charter? If the judges are free to add substantive non-explicit meaning to section 7, is there any compelling reason to prefer the "right to privacy" of a pregnant woman to the "right to life" of the fetus/unborn? Should the "reasonable limitations" criterion of section 1 be interpreted in a way that defers to legislative judgment or should the burden of proof be placed on the government? Would the latter simply amount to "judicial second-guessing" of legislative choices? Do the section 15 equality rights simply prohibit laws that discriminate unfairly between individuals, or do they create a positive obligation for governments to remedy private inequalities? Cumulatively, the Supreme Court's answers to these questions could reshape the institutional contours of Canadian politics, redefining the balance of power between courts and legislatures as well as affecting provincial rights.

These were important questions that the Court should have confronted. They were all present in the appeal, but they never were really explored during oral argument. The various counsel made their respective assertions, but, in the absence of any systematic and probing questioning by the judges, their arguments were like ships passing in the night. With the exception of the jury issue, there was never any real intellectual engagement, no confrontation of competing constitutional claims. What should have been a constitutional seminar of the highest order ended up as a series of unconnected and unchallenged soliloquies.

This anticlimactic portion of the hearing highlighted one of the traditional, and increasingly criticized, elements of Supreme Court procedure: the absence of any time limit on oral argument. This practice of unlimited oral argument was a legacy of the British tradition in Canadian law. It reflected the British view that the primary responsibility of courts, even appeal courts, was the adjudication of disputes, and thus the need to grant the adversarial process – which is to say the opposing lawyers – as much time as is necessary. As at trial, the lawyers, not the judges, dominated the appeal hearing.

This practice, which is still the rule in the United Kingdom, contrasts sharply with that of the American Supreme Court. The American Court strictly limits oral argument to thirty minutes per side. There is even a system of warning lights to indicate to the lawyer how many minutes and seconds remain. It is not unheard of for an American lawyer to be cut off in mid-sentence!

The American practice evolved initially as a practical response to time limitations but has come to be seen as having certain inherent virtues. The limitation on time encourages the American justices to take the initiative and to examine the counsel appearing before them on the weaknesses of their arguments. The judges are not expected to sit passively and leave the conduct of the appeal to the lawyers. Rather, the American justices aggressively question what they deem to be the pivotal issues of the appeal. These sharp and probing exchanges are an efficient way to determine how strong or weak an appeal is. Occasionally a case is won or lost on how well the lawyers involved can satisfy their judicial interlocutors. By contrast to traditional Canadian Supreme Court practice, it is a more judge-dominated process.

In the years following the adoption of the Charter in 1982, the Supreme Court of Canada fell badly behind in its work. Since becoming the final court of appeal in 1949, the Court had averaged well over 100 written judgments a year. In 1983 this figure dropped to eighty-three, then fell to only sixty-three judgments the following year. While the illnesses of Laskin and Chouinard had contributed to this decline in productivity, the flood of new Charter appeals was also a factor.

Critics were urging the Court to reform some of its procedures to cope with its new workload. The Court had accepted some of these criticisms. It had imposed a sixty-page limit on factums (subsequently lowered to forty pages) and was in the process of eliminating the time-consuming practice of giving lawyers an oral hearing to request leave to appeal. The Court had balked, however, at recommendations to limit oral argument on the merits of the case.

In the *Morgentaler* case, the Court took its first step in this direction. Manning had requested five days to present his arguments but had been turned down by the Court. He was limited to two days, but even this proved to be too long. After Manning had taken the first two days, the presentations by the three Crown attorneys and then the closing statements by both sides took up the remainder of the week. The Court had thus devoted almost an entire week to hearing oral argument in one case. No wonder its productivity was plummeting. What was worse, almost nothing new had been presented or uncovered. With precious few exceptions, the seven judges had sat sphinx-like on their thrones, rarely challenging counsel to defend their claims. This judicial reticence could be traced to the lingering influence of the neutral, passive role of the judge in the adversarial process. While this practice may have worked well at the trial level, its efficacy in constitutional appeals before the Supreme Court was doubtful. It was time-consuming and inefficient, not to mention terminally boring.

There is a positive case to be made for imposing a strict time limit on oral argument. This would force both the judges and the attorneys to focus on the truly core issues of a case. There would be no time to repeat – or to listen to – arguments and facts already available in the written factums. Time limits would also shift control of the appeal hearing to the judges. A judge who had done his or her homework would come to the appeal armed with a list of "hard questions," the answers to which could make or break a counsel's case; questions would drive the appeal hearing. While the winnowing process elicited by strict time limits can be impolite, it would better serve the interests of the Court and the country by uncovering the strengths and weaknesses of competing constitutional claims. The case for time limits on oral argument rests not just on efficiency but on the promise of an improved constitutional jurisprudence.

One year after the *Morgentaler* appeal was argued, the Supreme Court announced that henceforth, "in order to increase efficiency," it would allocate two hours per appeal with time to be equally divided between appellant and respondent. This was a much needed reform and it did improve the calibre of oral argument. It was too late, however, to salvage the *Morgentaler* hearing.

Other aspects of the *Morgentaler* hearing encouraged doubts about the wisdom of turning over major issues of public policy to the courts for resolution. The sombre judicial robes, scarlet with white ermine trim, evoked a medieval atmosphere. The modes of address between counsel and the justices – "My Lord" and "My Lady" – were foreign to the discourse of modern democracy. Last but not least was the "legalese" spoken by the participants but unintelligible to the 99.9 per cent of Canadians without legal training but who must live with the results of the Court's decisions.

Imagine a group of "average Canadians" visiting Ottawa on October 7, 1986. Our citizen-tourists first visit Parliament Hill for Question Period. There are many empty seats and few reporters. As they listen to the spirited give and take across the centre aisle, they readily understand what is being said and equally quickly realize that most of it is political posturing and not very important. As they continue down Wellington Street, they arrive at the Supreme Court, just in time for the first day of oral argument in the *Morgentaler* case.

The swarm of media on the front steps alerts them that something important must be happening inside. A reporter tells them that the Court is deciding the validity of Canada's abortion law. Eagerly they enter the building and take their seats (if they can find any), anticipating an articulate and enlightening debate on the divisive abortion issue. After listening to several hours of abstract and dreary legal monologues, they give up and leave. There has been much talk about "section seven" . . . "security of the person" . . . "principles of fundamental justice" . . . "substantive interpretation" . . . but the abortion issue seems to have disappeared. While something important is indeed being decided, it is being done in a foreign language, incomprehensible to our citizen-tourists.

The public cannot understand, much less participate in, the constitutional debate over abortion or any other public policy issue that becomes entangled in the Charter and the courts. Public understanding depends on – and is thus shaped by – "translation" of Supreme Court proceedings and decisions by the national media into ordinary English or French. There are thus two stages of interpretation in Charter politics: the judges' interpretation of Charter text and then the media's interpretation of judicial text. By now it is obvious how much discretion, and thus political influence, the first stage has conferred on judges. The second confers almost as much on the media.

This helps to explain why on Wednesday evening, at the conclusion of Manning's two-day soliloquy, Henry Morgentaler was entertaining selected members of the press at his posh downtown hotel. It was a small, almost intimate gathering. In addition to Manning and Dr. Scott, there were Norma Scarborough, president of CARAL; Selma Edelstone, long-time friend and supporter; and Svend Robinson, an NDP member of Parliament and an outspoken gay rights activist, who was also a long-time advocate of the complete decriminalization of abortion. (Earlier he had taken Morgentaler to dinner at the private Parliamentary Restaurant.) Last but far from least were the handful of reporters who were covering the Supreme Court hearing for the national press.

The tone was informal. The reporters chatted and joked with Morgentaler and his entourage as they helped themselves to the free drinks and snacks. At one point Morgentaler spoke up. "So, what does the media think the verdict will be?" he demanded, half-seriously, half-playfully. Scarborough quickly provided the answer: "We're going to win, of course." The relaxed smiles around the room indicated general sympathy, if not the same degree of optimism.[27]

Behind this casual facade, however, was a serious purpose. Manning and Morgentaler clearly understood that they were fighting both a legal and a public relations campaign, and the distance between the two was not that great. They understood the crucial linkage role of the press between the Supreme Court's eventual decision and the public's understanding of that decision. They knew the political importance of media "spin" – the favourable or unfavourable light the media can cast on public personalities and issues by their choice of words and pictures, by what they report and what they leave unsaid.

While any decision by the Supreme Court was at least a year away, here were Manning and Morgentaler carefully cultivating favour with the handful of men and women who eventually would present most Canadians with their first and most lasting impression of that decision, whatever it might be. As the distinction between courtroom and pressroom, law and public opinion, blurred, the art of Charter politics was being taken to a new level of sophistication.

CHAPTER 19

The Decision That
Rocked the Country

On January 21, 1988, the Supreme Court issued a press release announcing that it would hand down its *Morgentaler* decision the following week. The practice of alerting the press to upcoming decisions was initiated by Bora Laskin during the 1970s to remedy what he criticized as the press's lack of coverage of important Supreme Court decisions. With the advent of the Charter, lack of media attention was no longer a problem. Were he still alive, Laskin no doubt would have smiled at the scurry of activity and speculation set off by the Court's January 21 release.

It had been sixteen months since the Court had finished hearing oral argument in the *Morgentaler* case. This longer than usual delay led to speculation that the Court was having difficulty agreeing on a decision. In what was clearly going to be the Court's most important and controversial Charter decision to date, Chief Justice Dickson no doubt would have liked the protection of a "united front." In politically controversial cases it is not unusual for the Court to seek out a common middle ground that all the justices can support. Judicial unanimity amplifies the authority of the Court's decision and serves to deflect the inevitable criticism from the losing side. The Court had used this "united front" tactic in 1982 when it rejected Quebec's claim that the new Constitution Act violated its historical right to a "constitutional veto,"[1] and again in 1984 and 1985 when it struck down major language laws in Quebec[2] and in Manitoba.[3] The judgments in all three of these cases were unanimous and anonymous. "The Court," as these judgments were signed, had spoken in unison, and there was no doubt.

Unanimity in the *Morgentaler* decision would have been nice, but it was not to be. On Thursday, January 28, a divided Court handed down its decision. By a margin of 5–2, the Court ruled that the abortion law violated section 7 of the Charter. In addition to the two dissents, the five-judge majority divided three different ways on why the law was invalid. Only one justice out of seven – Justice Wilson – explicitly declared a constitutional right to abortion, and even she acknowledged a legitimate state interest in protecting the life of the fetus/unborn child at some point.

The other four judges who ruled against the abortion law did so because they said that it violated the procedural fairness required by section 7, not because there is any independent right to abortion. These four disagreed among themselves on just how serious even the procedural violations were. Two, Dickson and Lamer, said that the requirements of the current law, such as approval by a therapeutic abortion committee, were inherently unfair and would have to be scrapped. The other two judges, Beetz and Estey, defined the procedural problems more narrowly and thus remediable. While certain requirements as currently written, such as the TAC approval, created unfair delays and burdens, a revised version of the TAC might be acceptable. Specifically, Beetz and Estey ruled that in principle there was no legal problem with the requirement of the current law that abortions be permitted only when the continuation of a pregnancy "would threaten the life or health of the mother" or with the requirement of an independent and impartial third party to be the judge of this issue – the purpose of a TAC.

The two dissenters, McIntyre and La Forest, looked behind the text of the Charter to the original understanding of its meaning. They found that the history of the debates surrounding the framing of the Charter in 1980-81 shows that it was intentionally neutral on the abortion issue. They reasoned that judges have no authority to create rights (for either the fetus or the mother) that were not intended to be included in the text of the Charter. When the Charter is silent on an issue, they concluded, so, too, must be the judges. Finally, all seven justices explicitly recognized the legitimate interest of the state in protecting the life of the fetus/unborn child. They disagreed – four different ways – on when and how.

This division within the Court, not to mention the other nuances and subtleties of its decision, quickly disappeared as the media relayed the news across the country. It was perhaps predictable that early television and radio broadcasts did not even mention the two dissenting judges. More surprisingly, the CBC's evening news program, *The National,* did not report the dissent, much less the division within the majority. The following day's *Globe and Mail* did a better job but still minimized the divided nature of the decision. Its two-inch headline was somewhat misleading:

ABORTION LAW SCRAPPED;
WOMEN GET FREE CHOICE

While the follow-up article presented short summaries of all four judgments, the *Globe* did not reprint any portions of the dissenting judgment as it did for the three majority opinions.

The *Morgentaler* decision is as interesting for what it says about the Supreme Court's approach to interpreting the Charter as for what it says about abortion policy. Indeed, the two cannot really be separated. The Court's four different judgments were not just technical legal disagreements over the meaning of the Charter but also disagreements over the new role of the Court vis-à-vis Parliament. While the entrenchment of the Charter was clearly intended to empower the Court to strike down offending statutes, it did not spell out the precise rules governing the judicial exercise of this awesome new power. This was a question that the Court would have to work out for itself. Under what circumstances should unelected judges overrule the policy judgments of the democratically elected Parliament and provincial legislatures?

There is, of course, an easy answer to this question: activist judicial intervention is justified whenever Parliament or a provincial government makes a clear mistake and enacts a law that obviously violates the Charter. The problem is that the case of the "clear mistake" is rare. Neither level of Canadian government is likely to enact laws that violate the core meaning of Charter rights, for which there is consensus and support. Nor are individuals or groups likely to waste their money going to court to challenge statutes that clearly do not violate the core meaning of a right. The example of the "clear mistake" allows us to justify the judicial veto in theory, but it is rare in actual practice.[4]

More common is the case that contests the peripheral meaning or

234

"outer limits" of a Charter right. The *Morgentaler* and *Borowski* cases are both typical examples. No fair person can reasonably claim that the right to abortion for the mother or the right to life for the fetus/unborn is *clearly* included in section 7 of the Charter. (The text and its legislative history all dictate otherwise.) But at the same time, no one can reasonably deny that such meanings might be implied by the broadly worded rights to "life, liberty and security of the person." That is, it is plausible to interpret section 7 as including either of these specific rights as falling within its outer limits.

To say that Manning's (or Shumiatcher's) Charter claims are plausible, however, is not to say that a judge should accept them and declare the abortion law invalid. To say that a claim is plausible is to say that it might be right or it might be wrong. It is a matter of personal opinion, an issue over which reasonable people can reasonably disagree. But if it is essentially a matter of opinion and not a "clear mistake," why should the opinion of several unelected, unaccountable judges take precedence over the collective judgment of democratically elected representatives of the people? To do so risks placing the Court above Parliament and undermining Canadian democracy.

These doubts about the undemocratic character of judicial review underlie and shape every judicial interpretation of the Charter. This institutional issue of the relationship of the Court to legislatures can be reduced in practice to the question of how deferential a judge should be toward Parliament's (or a provincial legislature's) collective judgment. Predictably, judges in Canada (and also in the United States) have disagreed among themselves on this difficult question.

One school of thought, described as judicial self-restraint, takes very seriously the anti-democratic problem of judicial review. A judge committed to self-restraint is reluctant to strike down legislation and tries to minimize this problem by deferring to legislative judgment unless there is indeed a "clear mistake." In cases where the constitutional claim against a statute is only plausible, these judges characteristically reject the invitation to extend the scope of a right to embrace a new meaning. In the *Morgentaler* decision, Justice McIntyre's dissenting judgment is a textbook example of judicial self-restraint.

The opposing school of thought, known as judicial activism, animates the solo judgment of Madame Justice Wilson. The judicial activist tends to minimize the anti-democratic problem and stress the importance of protecting and even promoting rights. The activist judge tends not to limit the exercise of the judicial veto to the case of the "clear mistake." The judicial activist is more willing to accept the invitation to extend the boundaries of existing rights and, if necessary, to strike down laws that infringe the newly discovered boundaries of these rights.

Judicial self-restraint and judicial activism are distinct from but related to the interpretivist and noninterpretivist approaches to determining the meaning of constitutional text. The interpretivist approach, it will be recalled, stresses judicial fidelity to the original meaning of a constitutional right or power, as revealed by the text and evidence of what the framers intended such text to mean. The noninterpretivist approach, which was adopted by Justice Lamer in the *B.C. Motor Vehicle Reference* decision, attaches only "minimal weight" to the original understanding and intent of the framers and allows the judges a much freer hand in updating the meaning of constitutional rights and powers.

While it is theoretically possible for noninterpretivism to produce judicial self-restraint (especially in federalism cases), in practice a noninterpretivist approach to the Charter usually produces judicial activism, while the interpretivist approach normally results in judicial self-restraint.[5] Not surprisingly, there have been very few incidents of governments violating the meaning of Charter rights as they were understood in 1982. Much more typical is the case, as illustrated by *Morgentaler* and *Borowski,* where an interest group wants to change a policy by challenging it as a violation of the Charter. For such Charter challenges to succeed, the groups must persuade judges to "find" new meaning in the Charter right. Noninterpretivism thus becomes the prerequisite for the judicial activism that many Charter litigants are trying to encourage.

While both judicial activism and judicial self-restraint have the virtue of theoretical consistency, they also have their attendant practical vices. The self-restrained judge risks providing inadequate protection for the legitimate rights of individuals or groups. The judicial activist runs the risk of harming the public good by undermining citizens' respect for the democratic process and sense of political obligation. Too much judicial activism also risks provoking a political backlash against the courts, such as occurred in the United States after *Roe v. Wade.* Not surprisingly, many judges opt for a practical balance between activism and restraint rather than theoretical consistency. The

236

judgments of Chief Justice Dickson and Justice Beetz, which form the centre core of the *Morgentaler* decision, reflect this ambivalent and cautious use of the Court's new power.

Madame Justice Wilson's judgment was one of the purest examples of noninterpretivist judicial activism under the Charter. While the four other judges who voted to nullify the abortion law limited their decision to procedural violations of section 7, Wilson said this would be wasting Parliament's time. The government might spend months redrafting the procedural aspects of the abortion law only to be told in a subsequent case that it also violated a woman's substantive right to abortion. To address only the procedural issues, wrote Wilson, "begs the central issue in this case . . . [Does section 7] confer on the pregnant woman the right to decide for herself whether or not to have an abortion?"[6]

Wilson was technically correct in this assertion, but she obviously did not share the concern of her four colleagues that the Court would be well advised *not* to confront Parliament on "the central issue." What they saw as a danger to be avoided, Wilson saw as an opportunity to be seized. For her it was more important to use the *Morgentaler* case to declare a constitutional right to abortion for women than to finesse the "central issue" by limiting the judgment to procedural grounds.

As she proceeded to map out the contours of a woman's substantive right to liberty and security of the person, Wilson never once referred to legislative history or the framers' intent. Knowing full well that these sources of interpretive guidance would point in the opposite direction from the one she preferred to take, she chose simply to ignore them. While ignoring the framers' intent, however, Justice Wilson was happy to invoke a "purposive" approach to interpreting section 7.

In Justice Wilson's mind, the purpose of section 7 turned out to be broad indeed. She wrote that the rights to liberty and security of the person had the purpose of protecting and promoting "human dignity and worth." Her "purposive" interpretation of section 7 led her to conclude that "the right to liberty . . . guarantees to every individual a degree of personal autonomy over important decisions intimately affecting their private lives." Did "this class of protected decisions" include "the decision of a woman to terminate her pregnancy?" "I have no doubt that it does," declared Wilson.[7]

Her support for this conclusion combined a broad appeal to history with a narrower appeal to anatomy, and quickly became the most praised – and most criticized – portion of her judgment. According to Wilson, the struggle for abortion rights was only the culminating stage of the much larger historical struggle for human rights. Men won their rights in the eighteenth and nineteenth centuries. In the twentieth century, women successfully struggled to win their rights against discriminatory laws and "to achieve a place for women in a man's world." The time had now come to redefine that "man's world" into a truly human world, in which "women's needs and aspirations are translated into protected rights." The "right to reproduce or not to reproduce," Wilson asserted, "is one such right and is properly perceived as an integral part of modern woman's struggle to assert *her* dignity and worth as a human being."

Thus, by her own analysis, Wilson was using the Charter to strike a blow for the "modern woman's struggle," to help history fulfil its true destiny. For those who would question her theory of history, Wilson had a pointed rejoinder: "It is probably impossible for a man to respond, even imaginatively to such a dilemma," wrote Wilson, "not just because it is outside the realm of his personal experience (although this is, of course, the case) but because he can relate to it only by objectifying it, thereby eliminating the subjective elements of the female psyche which are at the heart of the dilemma." To feminists this was the new gospel, pure and simple. That it had now received judicial consecration was reason to celebrate. To those who did not espouse this new gospel, it was a breathtaking assertion of raw judicial power.

Wilson went on to give an equally broad interpretation to "security of the person" and found that it, too, was violated. The "essence" of section 251, she proclaimed, was:

> that the woman's capacity to reproduce is not to be subject to her own control. It is to be subject to the control of the state. She may not choose whether to exercise her existing capacity or not to exercise it. This is ... a direct interference with her physical "person".... She is truly being treated as a means – a means to an end which she does not desire but over which she has no control. She is the passive recipient of a decision made by others as to whether her body is to be used to nurture a new life. Can there be anything that comports less with human dignity and self-respect? How can a woman in this position have any sense of security with respect to her person?[8]

These were bold words indeed. The American Supreme Court's ruling in *Roe v. Wade* seems timid and pale by comparison. Justice Wilson in effect read almost the entire pro-choice perspective on abortion into five words of section 7, their legislative history notwithstanding. It would be difficult to find a clearer example of noninterpretivist judicial activism.

Justice Wilson's desire to use the *Morgentaler* case as an opportunity to influence any new abortion legislation by Parliament was also evident in her handling of the section 1 "reasonable limitations" issue. Wilson begins by identifying the purpose of section 251 as the protection of the fetus, which she described as "a perfectly valid legislative objective." "The question," she continued, was:

> at what point in the pregnancy does the protection of the fetus become such a pressing and substantial concern as to outweigh the fundamental right of the woman to decide whether or not to carry the fetus to term? At what point does the state's interest in the protection of the fetus become "compelling" and justify state intervention in what is otherwise a matter of purely personal and private concern?[9]

Wilson's answer was "that the value to be placed on the fetus as potential life is directly related to the stage of its development during gestation." This "developmental view" of the fetus, she concluded,

> supports a permissive approach to abortion in the early stages of pregnancy and a restrictive approach in the later stages. In the early stages the woman's autonomy would be absolute; her decision . . . not to carry the fetus to term would be conclusive. Her reasons for having an abortion would, however, be the proper subject of inquiry at the later stages of her pregnancy when the state's compelling interest in the protection of the fetus would justify it in prescribing conditions.[10]

Justice Wilson was admirably frank in admitting that this was only "my view," but this raised the troublesome issue of why "her view" should be preferred to the collective view of Parliament. This problem was made more acute by her concession that "the fetus is potential life from the moment of conception,"[11] a fact that supported a non-developmental view. Presumably it was to avoid this appearance of judicial second-guessing that the other four judges for the majority limited their decision to procedural grounds.

Justice Wilson might still have avoided the appearance of overt judicial lawmaking had she left her decision at this. Her vague talk of "early stages" and "later stages" left considerable room for Parliament to work. Perhaps conscious of how closely she was working the law/politics distinction, Wilson herself at one point declared that it is up to "the informed judgment" of Parliament to determine "the precise point in the development of the fetus at which the state's interest in its protection becomes 'compelling.'" In the end, however, she could not resist suggesting her own solution. "It seems to me," she concluded, "that it might fall somewhere in the second trimester."[12]

The casual fashion in which it is presented – almost as an afterthought – could not disguise the very political purpose of this closing remark. As it was quite unnecessary to her section 1 analysis, it can only have been intended to influence subsequent deliberations in Parliament. Wilson was suggesting that if Parliament enacted a new abortion law, this was what she would accept. Wilson commended this approach by noting more than once that it was essentially the "trimester" policy adopted by the American Court in *Roe*. Since about 90 per cent of abortions in Canada were being performed in the first trimester, her recommendation, if followed, would have represented a significant triumph for the pro-choice side of the abortion battle.

Just as Justice Wilson's opinion represented the activist end of the judicial spectrum, so the McIntyre-La Forest opinion represents the opposite end. McIntyre's decision was a model of judicial self-restraint based on an interpretivist approach to the Charter. According to McIntyre the Court should never have allowed itself to be drawn into the abortion controversy by the *Morgentaler* case. The abortion issue, he noted, dealt with the respective rights of women and the unborn, none of whom were present in this case. The appellants were all doctors charged with conspiracy to violate the Criminal Code. None of the doctors could claim that they have been denied a therapeutic abortion. The Court's grappling with the section 7 issues was thus on a purely "hypothetical basis" and should have been avoided.[13]

In polite but unmistakable terms, McIntyre was chastising the majority for being more concerned about addressing a public policy dispute than adjudicating the legal dispute that was before them. Since the rest of the Court had decided the case on these issues, McIntyre reluctantly concluded that he must address them also. Significantly, however, he prefaced his section 7 analysis with a lengthy discourse on the new political role of the Court under the Charter. For McIntyre, Charter interpretation could not be divorced from its institutional context.

Although McIntyre agreed with Chief Justice Dickson's observation that the Court was now responsible for "ensuring that the legislative initiatives pursued by our Parliament and legislatures conform to the democratic values expressed in the Charter," he insisted that, "the courts must confine themselves to such democratic values as are clearly found and expressed in the Charter and refrain from imposing or creating other values not so based."[14] The responsibility of the Court, McIntyre continued, is "not to solve or seek to solve ... the abortion issue" but to determine whether section 251 violates any "clearly expressed" rights in the Charter. "If a particular interpretation enjoys no support, express or reasonably implied, from the Charter, then the Court is without power to clothe such an interpretation with constitutional status." "The Court must not," McIntyre warned, decide the *Morgentaler* case "on the basis of how many judges may favour 'pro-choice' or 'pro-life.'"[15]

This was a clear application of the interpretivist approach to determining the meaning of the Charter. It emphasized judicial fidelity to the text of the Constitution and the intent of the framers that lay behind it. While it did not preclude the judicial extension of Charter rights to new circumstances, it would restrict such innovation by insisting that it be consistent with the original meaning.

While McIntyre's approach to Charter interpretation is the antithesis of Wilson's opinion, both relied heavily on American constitutional authorities. Unlike Wilson, however, McIntyre marshalled lengthy quotations from American justices to demonstrate the dangers of judicial attempts to enact the judges' views of enlightened public policy in the name of constitutional interpretation. Drawing from Justice Harlan, McIntyre condemned the "current mistaken view of the Constitution and the constitutional function of this Court ... that every major social ill in this country can find its cure in some constitutional 'principle,' and that this Court should 'take the lead' in promoting reform when other branches of government fail to act."

The Constitution is not a panacea for every blot upon the public welfare, nor should this Court, ordained as a judicial body, be thought of as a general haven for reform movements.... This Court ... does not serve its high purpose when it exceeds its authority, even to satisfy justified impatience with the slow workings of the political process. For when, in the name of constitutional interpretation, the Court adds something to the Constitution that was deliberately excluded from it, the Court in reality substitutes its view of what should be so for the amending process.[16]

With this warning against judicial amendment of constitutional meaning still ringing in his readers' ears, McIntyre quickly disposed of the Wilson view: "The proposition that women enjoy a constitutional right to have an abortion is devoid of support in the language of s. 7 of the Charter or any other section."[17] McIntyre notes that while other controversial rights were specifically mentioned, "the Charter is entirely silent on the point [of abortion]." Drawing on the legislative history ignored by his fellow judges, McIntyre emphasized that this silence was no oversight. Parliamentary debate and the minutes of the Special Parliamentary Committee on the Constitution showed that the framers deliberately excluded abortion from the Charter.[18]

As for the alleged procedural violations of section 7, McIntyre was sceptical of the evidence, which was drawn primarily from the Badgley and Powell reports, policy studies commissioned by the federal and Ontario governments. While conceding the Court had become more receptive to this kind of "extrinsic evidence" in constitutional cases, McIntyre maintained that he would still "prefer to place principal reliance upon the evidence given under oath in court."[19] This preference for sworn testimony that can be tested by the heat of cross-examination is another characteristic of McIntyre's traditional view of the courts as adjudicators, not policy-makers. Of those who so testified, he noted, not one doctor or woman claimed to have ever had a TAC application for an abortion rejected. For McIntyre, this conflict between extrinsic evidence and sworn testimony made it "anything but clear" that the procedure mandated by section 251 made the section 251(4) defence "illusory."[20] Ironically, a report commissioned to assist possible legislative reform of the abortion law was now being used by courts to accomplish the same task. The majority's frank use of legislative facts was a clear indicator of the legislative character of the Court's new role under the Charter.

On other procedural issues, McIntyre conceded that the defence provided by section 251(4) was a narrow one, but that the narrowness or breadth of the defence reflected Parliament's judgment of when "the disapprobation of society is not warranted." It was not for judges to "second guess" Parliament's choices in these matters. As for the claim (accepted by three other justices) that the meaning of the word "health" in section 251(4) was so vague as to render it invalid, McIntyre noted that this claim was unanimously rejected by the Court in its 1975 *Morgentaler* decision. If the meaning of "health" was sufficiently clear in 1975, it was still acceptable in 1988.[21]

McIntyre concluded by emphasizing that he was expressing "no opinion" on the abortion issue. His decision was based exclusively on the fact that "no valid constitutional objection to s. 251 of the Criminal Code has been raised."

> If there is to be a change in the abortion law, it will be for Parliament to make. This is not because Parliament can claim all wisdom and knowledge but simply because Parliament is elected for that purpose in a free democracy and, in addition, has the facilities – the exposure to public opinion and information – as well as the political power to make effective its decisions.[22]

The core of the *Morgentaler* decision was found in the Dickson-Lamer and Beetz-Estey judgments. While there were important differences in reasoning between these two opinions, together they defined a middle ground between the Wilson and McIntyre positions. Unlike McIntyre, their "bottom line" was to strike down section 251. Unlike Wilson, however, they limited their rulings of invalidity to procedural violations.

Manning had invited the Court to interpret the section 7 right to liberty as creating a "a wide ranging right to control one's own life and to promote one's individual autonomy . . . [including] a right to privacy and a right to make unfettered decisions about one's own life." This, wrote Dickson, "is neither necessary nor wise. . . . I prefer to rest my conclusions on a narrower analysis." Dickson concluded that it "will be sufficient to investigate whether or not [section 251] meets the procedural standards of fundamental justice."[23]

Justice Wilson was right in claiming that the majority's reliance on procedural grounds amounted to ducking the issue. Yet in the traditional adjudicative courtroom, ducking the issue was often considered a virtue rather than a vice. There is a well-established canon of construction that constitutional cases should be decided on the narrowest legal reasoning possible. This rule is based primarily on respect for the duties of the legislative branch and the desire to intrude as little as possible on those duties. It also reflects a degree of institutional self-interest based on the perception that it can be dangerous for the Court to become prematurely or unnecessarily embroiled in volatile political issues. The Canadian justices – with the memory of American court-packing plans still fresh in their minds – were well aware of the high price the American Supreme Court was paying for its attempt to take the political lead on the abortion issue. For the Dickson-Lamer and Beetz-Estey opinions, both principle and prudence dictated avoiding Wilson's "central issue." They sought to minimize the Court's role in shaping Canada's abortion policy, while she sought to maximize it.

The two middle-ground opinions thus did not address the question of whether the Charter created a right for women to decide for themselves whether to have an abortion. Provisionally accepting the authority of Parliament to prohibit non-therapeutic abortions, they focused on whether the defence allowed by section 251(4) – the certificate of approval from a TAC – restricted the section 7 right to "security of the person" in a manner inconsistent with "the principles of fundamental justice." That is, given Parliament's decision to allow a defence to the crime of abortion, was this defence in fact available in a timely and reasonable manner? Both the Dickson and Beetz opinions concluded that *in practice* it was not.

The key to this finding was extensive reliance by both justices on extrinsic evidence drawn from the Badgley Report (1977) and the much more recent (1987) Powell Report. The latter was a study commissioned by the Peterson government after it had upset the Tories in the Ontario provincial elections in 1986.[24] Conducted by Dr. Marion Powell, the study surveyed the availability of abortion services in Ontario.

The Badgley Report found uneven access and delays to abortion services and attributed both to the haphazard implementation of the TAC requirements. These delays increased the threat to the health of pregnant women seeking abortions, the judges concluded. The Powell Report found that the eight-week average delay reported by Badgley had been reduced to one to three weeks in areas, such as Toronto, where there were hospitals with functioning TACs. Not all of Ontario was served by such hospitals, however, and even the reduced delay was said to contribute to additional psychological stress and medical complications. Like the Badgley Report, Powell found that the delays were an inevitable consequence of the procedural requirements of section 251.

Section 251 stipulated that abortions must be performed in

"accredited or approved" hospitals. Only larger hospitals that provided a certain minimum number of specified services were eligible for accreditation. Similarly, a hospital could offer abortions only if it had at least four doctors to authorize and perform them. The combined effect of these two requirements, according to the 1977 study, was that 58.5 per cent of Canadian hospitals were ineligible to perform abortions. The Powell Report confirmed similar statistics for Ontario in the 1980s. Furthermore, of the 559 general hospitals that were qualified, the Badgley Report found that only 271, or 20 percent of the total, had chosen to create TACs, and most of these were in the larger metropolitan areas. The Powell Report found that 54 per cent of accredited hospitals in Ontario had TACs. Finally, the Badgley Committee reported considerable inconsistency in how different TACs applied the "threat to health" criteria. What qualified for abortion certificates in some hospitals was unacceptable in others.

For Chief Justice Dickson, the problem lay in Parliament's failure to define "health," thus leaving the TACs without an adequate standard to determine when lawful abortions should be permitted. Some TACs interpreted "health" to encompass mental and psychological health, while others limited it to threats to physical health. The former definition made it relatively easy to get abortions while the latter made it more difficult. This administrative inconsistency, declared Dickson, was "a serious procedural flaw."[25]

"The combined effect of all these problems with the procedure stipulated by s. 251," concluded the Chief Justice, "is a failure to comply with the principles of fundamental justice. One of the basic tenets of our system of criminal justice," he continued, "is that when Parliament creates a defence to a criminal charge, the defence should not be illusory or so difficult to attain as to be practically illusory."[26] This, both he and Justice Beetz concluded, was presently the case under the section 251 regime, which therefore violated section 7 of the Charter.

While the Dickson-Lamer and Beetz-Estey opinions agreed on this point, they were divided over the seriousness of the "procedural flaws" of section 251. Dickson defined "security of the person" very broadly as a right against "state interference with bodily integrity and serious state-imposed psychological stress." Section 251 infringed this right by "forcing a woman, by threat of criminal sanction, to carry a fetus to term unless she meets criteria entirely unrelated to her own priorities and aspirations."[27] This very broad definition of "security of the person" was almost identical to Justice Wilson's, and suggests that any third-party, TAC-style determination of a woman's decision to abort her pregnancy would be unacceptable.

Justice Beetz gave a narrower interpretation of "security of the person." He repeatedly stressed that it was the threat of criminal sanctions, not restrictions on access to abortion, that created the section 7 violation. Unlike Dickson and Lamer, Beetz and Estey rejected the claim that "threat to health" was unconstitutionally vague. Indeed, they explicitly accepted the principle of limiting abortions to "therapeutic" reasons (reasons of health), and also the use of some sort of third-party determination to ensure "a reliable, independent and medically sound opinion in order to protect the state interest in the fetus."[28] This implied that a revised section 251 with a "streamlined" determination process would be acceptable. In sum, for Beetz and Estey, section 251 violated section 7 because it imposed "unnecessary rules [that] impose delays which result in additional risk to women's health."[29] The problem with section 251 was not what it tried to achieve, but how it went about it. Beetz and Estey would require some procedural retooling of section 251(4), but not as much as Dickson and Lamer.

A final point of importance in the Beetz-Estey opinion was its not-so-subtle criticism of Justice Wilson's *obiter dicta*. Like Wilson, these judges affirmed that the state had a legitimate interest in protecting the fetus because it is "potential human life." They also agreed with Wilson that this interest could not justify a complete prohibition of abortion. The crucial question was when and under what circumstances could the state prefer the interest of the mother to the interest of the fetus? Wilson had endorsed the "developmental approach" adopted by the U.S. Supreme Court, suggesting that this point was "somewhere in the second trimester," as the fetus becomes viable or capable of living outside the womb. Beetz and Estey now countered by quoting from a dissenting judgment by Justice Sandra Day O'Connor, the first woman ever to serve on the American Supreme Court:

> The difficulty with this [developmental] analysis is clear: potential life is no less potential in the first weeks of pregnancy than it is at viability or afterward. . . . The choice of viability as the point at which state interest in potential life becomes compelling is no less arbitrary than choosing any point before viability or any point afterward. Accordingly, I believe that the state's interest in protecting potential human life exists throughout the pregnancy.[30]

Justice Beetz's digression on this point was no less gratuitous than Justice Wilson's. Both were pure *obiter dicta*. They revealed the political calculations that sometimes underlie judicial opinion-writing. By quoting from another female Supreme Court justice, Beetz sought publicly to challenge Wilson's claim to privileged knowledge by virtue of her gender. Like Wilson, Beetz anticipated a response by Parliament to the Court's decision. Wilson tried to send one type of message to Parliament, Beetz and Estey responded with a different one.

To summarize, while five of seven justices held that the section 251 abortion law violated section 7 of the Charter, they disagreed on why. There was no single, unified decision of the Court. Only one justice out of seven declared a constitutional right to abortion. The other four members of the majority coalition found only procedural violations of the Charter and were further divided on their seriousness. The reasoning of a majority of the seven justices – Beetz and Estey, plus McIntyre and La Forest – would have supported a reformed version of the current law. Finally, all seven justices explicitly recognized the legitimate interest of the state in protecting the life of the fetus/unborn child. They disagreed – four different ways – on when and how. It was now up to the Mulroney government to decipher the meaning of the Court's 196-page ruling and to decide what, if any, new abortion legislation to bring to Parliament.

Pro-life activists were shocked and disappointed by the *Morgentaler* ruling. Even though the majority judgments (Wilson's excepted) were technically narrow and procedural, their practical effect was to put the Morgentaler clinics in both Toronto and Winnipeg back in business and to pave the way for more. Nor did the Court's decision exactly encourage high hopes in the pro-life camps for the success of the *Borowski* appeal scheduled to be heard later that year. It seemed clear that Borowski was not going to get any support from Bertha Wilson. While McIntyre and La Forest did not appear to share Wilson's pro-choice perspective, there was no reason to think they harboured any pro-life sympathies. Even if they did, consistency presumably would require them to give the same answer to Borowski that they gave to Morgentaler: that the Charter was silent on the issue of abortion. Any support for Borowski's Charter claims would have to come from the two middle judgments. Pro-life lawyers poured over the Dickson-Lamer and Beetz-Estey judgments searching for some sign of support.

One of these lawyers was Gwendolyn Landolt, who has been described as "the Phyllis Schlafly of Canada: smart, tough, physically imposing, a potent politician."[31] She graduated from law school at the age of twenty-two (one of three women in a class of 110), worked as a full-time lawyer for seventeen years (including four in Ottawa with the federal government), then married and had five children.[32] Landolt served as legal counsel for both Campaign Life and the Right to Life Association of Toronto (which she had founded in 1971), and she was also instrumental in founding REAL Women in 1983.

Landolt had the 196-page Morgentaler decision faxed to her the morning it was released. As she read the Dickson and then the Beetz judgments, her jaw dropped in disbelief when she saw their extensive reliance – six and nine references, respectively – on the social facts drawn from the Powell Report. The reason for her disbelief: the Powell Report was not released to the public until January 27, 1987, three months *after* the *Morgentaler* hearing before the Supreme Court. A subsequent trip to the Supreme Court archives to review the *Morgentaler* docket confirmed that the Powell Report was not mentioned once in the thousands and thousands of pages of official court records. Of course, this was not surprising. The report did not even exist at the time of the hearing. Landolt was incensed. How had the Court acquired the Powell Report? More importantly, how could they use it as evidence when it had not been subject to examination by all parties in court?

Landolt communicated her discovery to Laura McArthur, president of the Toronto-area Right to Life Association. Their options seemed limited. They were certain that the press (whom they regarded as overwhelmingly pro-choice) would not pay any attention to the issue. Complaining directly to the Supreme Court also seemed self-defeating. In the end, they decided that McArthur would lay an official complaint to the Canadian Judicial Council, the watchdog agency that deals with allegations of judicial misconduct. While they were not optimistic about receiving a positive response (Chief Justice Dickson also served as the president of the Judical Council), at least they would create an official record of what they regarded as a serious breach of judicial ethics and a mistake in law by the High Court.

McArthur's two-page letter to the Council alleged that what the Court had done was "contrary to long-established procedural rules of accepting evidence off-the-record."[33] By using social facts "not admitted as evidence at the time of the hearings," McArthur argued, the

Court had deprived the Crown and other interested parties of the right to challenge the "impartiality of the document." She went on to suggest that its impartiality was very much in question, as Dr. Powell "has a long history (dating from 1972) of pro-abortion activism" and that her findings were biased and "could not be considered an *accurate reflection of the abortion situation in the province of Ontario.*"[34] McArthur concluded that "this unorthodox manner of approaching the Court renders Court procedures meaningless, since it provides no protection for those litigants who are unaware that the Court is considering a document to which they cannot form a rebuttal, or provide information." If the Court continued to receive evidence in this fashion, McArthur argued, the public "will cease to have confidence that the Court's decisions are balanced and reasonable and based on credible evidence."

The complaint had some validity, but as McArthur and Landolt already sensed, it was not really addressed to the right forum. The disciplinary oversight function of the Canadian Judicial Council was restricted to allegations of judicial bias or blatant misconduct. An evidentiary *faux pas* did not fall within this scope. The Court's use of the Powell Report was more a questionable procedural decision than misconduct. Perhaps if a lower court had accepted and then relied on off-the-record evidence, it might have been grounds for an appeal as a mistake of law to a higher court. But there was no appeal from the Supreme Court of Canada. As an American Chief Justice once said with some irony, "We are not final because we are infallible. We are infallible because we are final."[35]

A prompt reply from the Judicial Council informed McArthur that her complaint "raises no issue of judicial misconduct for investigation by the Council pursuant to its mandate under the Judges Act."[36] McArthur's complaint, the Council said, "concerns the practices and procedures of the Supreme Court of Canada." McArthur was of course free to criticize these practices, the reply continued, but the Council had no mandate to deal with such criticism. The Council's reply concluded by suggesting that "it is not unheard of" for the Supreme Court "to cite articles, books or other publications which might not have been referred to by the parties to the litigation."[37]

In this last remark, the Council was referring to the practice of "judicial notice" – a convention that permits judges on their own initiative to "take notice" of relevant social facts that are widely recognized and uncontroversial. Judicial notice is a useful technique that allows judges to include in their decisions relevant facts that were not previously introduced as evidence. The qualifier is that the facts must be widely recognized and uncontroversial. To justify the Court's use of the Powell Report as an exercise of judicial notice was to stretch the concept beyond its normal scope. While it was not impossible to justify the Court's behaviour as an exercise in judicial notice, the Court had exercised poor judgment in doing so. Dr. Powell's uncontroverted record as a pro-choice activist inevitably gave her report a partisan appearance to those who disagreed with its findings. In choosing to use her findings, the Court unnecessarily invited criticism and charges of unfairness.

This criticism could be justified on the Court's own terms. The Court had ignored the spirit of one of its own constitutional norms: the right to a fair hearing. In the earlier case of *Singh v. The Minister of Employment and Immigration,* [38] the Supreme Court struck down Canada's refugee determination process because it said the lack of an oral hearing deprived the applicant of the opportunity to challenge the accuracy of the hearing officer's report. This, said the Court, violated the right to a fair hearing and thus the "principles of fundamental justice" required by section 7 of the Charter. If a right of reply exists in routine administrative hearings, then surely it should be respected in constitutional controversies before the highest court in the land.

By using evidence received off the record, the Court appeared to violate the principle articulated in *Singh.* If the justices had obtained and used an analogous pro-life study in the same off-the-record manner, there would have been howls of protest from the pro-choice camp, and justifiably so. Perhaps the Chief Justice was embarrassed by the appearance of bias, a possibility that might explain the Court's more generous treatment of various pro-life parties in the next round of abortion litigation, much to the consternation of LEAF and CARAL. The venerable practice of "evening up" is not limited to the hockey rink.

CHAPTER 20

Borowski's Dilemma:
No Law Left to Challenge

The Supreme Court's *Morgentaler* decision set in motion two different political dramas, one public, one private. The public drama was the Mulroney government's promise of a prompt legislative response to the nullification of section 251, followed by the reality of division and paralysis. For three months the caucus was so divided that the government did nothing.

In May the government tried to introduce a package of resolutions designed to measure the "sense of the House" on new abortion legislation. A main resolution proposed a compromise policy that would have reinstated the existing policy minus the TAC requirement. Only the opinion of a doctor (or in later stages of pregnancy, two doctors) would be required. MPs who believed this policy was too permissive could vote for a "pro-life amendment" that would have required two independent doctors to agree that a woman's life would be endangered, or her health "seriously and substantially" endangered, by continuing the pregnancy. This amendment specifically excluded the effects of stress or anxiety, as well as social or economic considerations. MPs who thought the compromise policy was too restrictive could vote for an alternative "pro-choice amendment" that essentially made abortion the choice of a woman in consultation with her doctor. The idea was to hold a free vote on these three proposals to determine "the sense of the

House." The government would then draft legislation that reflected the outcome of the free vote.

This plan collapsed almost as soon as it was introduced. Because the proposals did not represent legislation, the government planned to limit debate and prohibit amendments altogether. The Liberals and New Democrats denounced these procedures as anti-democratic, unprecedented and even illegal. They also denounced the government for its lack of leadership. Despite this criticism, the government introduced the motion on May 25. The opposition parties then threatened to bring a procedural point of order if the government tried to pursue its plan. Realizing it would lose the procedural ruling, the government sheepishly withdrew its proposal.

In July the government tried again. This time a single proposal was put forward and amendments were allowed. The government proposal basically set out a two-prong policy that made it relatively easy (the agreement of one doctor) to get a therapeutic abortion "during the early stages of pregnancy" but made it more difficult (two doctors and stricter criteria) "during the subsequent stages of pregnancy."[1] For three days at the end of July, the House of Commons debated this motion. No party discipline was enforced, and twenty-one amendments were proposed. On July 28, every proposal was defeated.

The House soundly defeated the government's motion by a vote of 147–76. Two strong pro-choice amendments and one strong pro-life amendment were defeated by even larger margins. The amendment that came the closest to passing (it was defeated by a vote of 118–105) was a pro-life amendment that would have prohibited abortions except when two doctors thought the continuation of the pregnancy would endanger the life of the mother. While the voting crossed all party lines, female MPs from all parties voted consistently for the pro-choice positions. Following the defeat of his government's main proposal, Prime Minister Mulroney announced that his government would take no further action until after the Supreme Court had dealt with the *Borowski* appeal.

The private drama launched by the *Morgentaler* decision concerned LEAF. Pro-choice groups had closely monitored the *Borowski* case from the start. Not trusting the government to defend its interests, CARAL tried to participate in Borowski's Regina trial in May, 1983, but an application for intervener status was turned down by Judge

Matheson. The trial hearing confirmed the group's suspicions about the government's ability or desire to defend abortion rights, but they were relieved when Judge Matheson subsequently rejected Borowski's Charter challenge. They took further comfort in the April, 1987, decision of the Saskatchewan Court of Appeal rejecting Borowski's appeal, but they knew this was not the end of the matter. When the Supreme Court of Canada granted Borowski leave to appeal in September, 1987, Mary Eberts, a LEAF founder and senior litigator, promptly filed LEAF's own request for intervener status, easily meeting the Court's thirty-day deadline.[2] (This later took on importance as the pro-life interveners applied long after the deadline but still received permission.)

LEAF was confident that its petition would be granted. While the Supreme Court had been initially unreceptive to intervener requests in Charter cases, LEAF seemed to be an exception.[3] Four out of their five prior requests had been granted, and they were not disappointed this time. "Twenty minutes and twenty pages," was the Court's affirmative response. Eberts would have preferred more, but LEAF counsel had become expert at decreasing the margins and setting the line-spacing at one and a half on the word processor.[4]

In December, 1987, shortly before the *Morgentaler* judgment was released, Justice McIntyre set out the five legal questions that the Court would address in the *Borowski* appeal.

1. Does a child *en ventre sa mere* have the right to life as guaranteed by section 7 of the Canadian Charter of Rights and Freedoms?

2. If the answer to question 1 is "yes," do subsections (4), (5), and (6) of section 251 of the Criminal Code violate or deny the principles of fundamental justice, contrary to section 7 of the Canadian Charter of Rights and Freedoms?

3. Does a child *en ventre sa mere* have the right to the equal protection and equal benefit of the law without discrimination because of age or mental or physical disability that are guaranteed by section 15 of the Canadian Charter of Rights and Freedoms?

4. If the answer to question 3 is "yes," do subsections (4), (5), and (6) of section 251 of the Criminal Code violate or deny the rights guaranteed by section 15?

5. If the answer to question 2 is "yes" or if the answer to question 4 is "yes," are the provisions of subsections (4), (5), and (6) of section 251 of the Criminal Code justified by section 1 of the

Canadian Charter of Rights and Freedoms, and therefore not inconsistent with the Constitution Act, 1982?

Questions one and three were somewhat unusual in that they were posed in an abstract fashion, without any reference to the statute being challenged. At the time, however, this seemed inconsequential.

When the *Morgentaler* decision was announced on January 28, 1988, it seemed like a double victory for the pro-choice forces. Not only did Morgentaler win, but the decision also appeared to pull the legal rug out from under the *Borowski* appeal. In legal parlance, the *Borowski* case appeared to become "moot" since the law it sought to challenge no longer existed. Without a law there was no longer a "live dispute," and without a dispute the Court would normally lose jurisdiction. LEAF and CARAL fully expected the Court to announce that it would no longer hear the *Borowski* case. At CARAL's annual meeting, Morgentaler confidently predicted, "You don't have to worry about Borowski now."[5]

But February and then March passed and nothing happened. Becoming uneasy, CARAL hired Morris Manning to write a letter to the Minister of Justice forcefully requesting that the Solicitor-General move to have the appeal dismissed for mootness. "I am most disturbed," wrote Manning, "by the fact that the Court appears to be hearing a moot case, dealing with hypothetical constitutional questions, without any statutory authority to do so. . . . the Supreme Court of Canada . . . has no jurisdiction to deal with matters that are moot unless a reference is directed by an Attorney General."[6] Manning demanded that the government explain "why you have not moved to strike this appeal," adding that the the failure to do so suggested that the Tories were taking "inconsistent positions" vis-à-vis Borowski and Morgentaler.[7] When the letter did not elicit a positive response, pro-choice groups, including LEAF, became suspicious of the Mulroney government's intentions. Why had they not moved to quash the appeal as moot? Did they want the Supreme Court to hear the *Borowski* appeal? And if so, why?

At this point Justice McIntyre's unusual phrasing of the questions on appeal took on a new and, from LEAF's perspective, disturbing significance. Since the two abstractly worded questions did not refer explicitly to section 251 of the Criminal Code, they were not affected – in a technical sense – by the *Morgentaler* ruling. This was certainly Morris Shumiatcher's reading of the situation. Eberts was now troubled why McIntyre had phrased the questions in this abstract fashion. She took this question to a meeting of the LEAF case committee that was preparing the group's Borowski factum. (When LEAF takes a case, its standard practice is to create a case committee consisting of lawyers, law professors, and staff to canvass options, strategize, and hammer out a final factum.) Members of the case committee conjectured that McIntyre may have already known in December the outcome of the *Morgentaler* case, which was subsequently released in January. Presumably he would have also anticipated the issue of mootness that the *Morgentaler* decision was going to create for the *Borowski* appeal. Had Justice McIntyre, the author of the dissenting opinion in *Morgentaler,* purposefully phrased the constitutional questions in an abstract fashion to protect Borowski's appeal?

LEAF's anxieties further escalated the following month when REAL Women, a conservative women's group espousing traditional, pro-family policies, suddenly asked the Supreme Court for intervener status in the *Borowski* case. Since REAL's affidavit came six months after the filing deadline, LEAF assumed that it would be dismissed without a hearing. When the Supreme Court set a hearing date of May 19, LEAF was horrified. Why was the Supreme Court bending its own rules to accommodate REAL Women?

LEAF was also disturbed by another aspect of REAL Women's request. Both in form and substance, its written affidavit closely paralleled LEAF's own affidavit for intervener status. For the first four pages, the REAL affidavit tracked LEAF's paragraph by paragraph and often word for word. On page four, however, the difference was made explicit. LEAF, declared REAL's affidavit, "does not speak for all women of Canada. It represents a position which makes no allowance for balancing the interests of mother and child even when the child is full-term." Repeating that there was "no single 'women's' perspective," REAL Women argued that these issues would not be properly addressed unless it was allowed to intervene.[8]

Eberts and others became convinced that the similarity was calculated and intended to trap the Supreme Court. From their vantage point, it strongly resembled an earlier coup of REAL Women that involved public funding. The federal government's "Women's Program" doles out more than $13 million a year, all of it to feminist groups. The greatest share goes to the largest feminist lobby group in the country, the National Action Committee on the Status of Women (NAC).[9] From its inception in 1983 to 1985, REAL Women had, as a point of principle, relied exclusively on private donations. As a result, the group was starving financially. In 1985, REAL president Gwen Landolt told her executive that REAL would have to ask for government funding if it were to compete effectively with the feminist NAC. They did, but to their astonishment, they were not even sent an application form. Repeated requests were ignored. (Subsequent access to the files of the Women's Program revealed that this non-response was intentional.)[10]

This bureaucratic brush-off confirmed REAL Women's suspicion that the federal Women's Program was really a "feminist guerrilla camp on Parliament Hill." They changed tactics. This time they contacted the Women's Program claiming to represent an organization called "The National Association of Lesbian Mothers." In no time, they received a funding application form and "a warm, hand-written note, welcoming them to the world of government funding." They filled in the form, requesting $92,000 in operating expenses for REAL Women. The Women's Program turned them down. REAL Women, the rejection said, stood for the "promotion of a particular family model [that] is not within the spirit of the objectives of the program."[11] This is all REAL Women needed to go to the press. Why, they demanded, was the government giving away taxpayers' dollars to groups promoting homosexuality while denying it to a group that promoted traditional family values? The resulting scandal produced a parliamentary investigation into the funding policies of the Women's Program and put NAC on the defensive for the next two years.[12]

Eberts and others on the LEAF litigation committee now smelled a rat. They suspected REAL Women was setting a similar trap for the Supreme Court. If the Supreme Court rejected REAL Women's petition after accepting LEAF's, they would be open to the same charge of political bias and double standards.

LEAF decided to challenge REAL Women's request for intervener status. REAL Women had justified their status as interveners in part on the basis of "expertise" in the relevant policy areas. LEAF thought they were vulnerable on this point, and so Eberts filed an affidavit requesting permission to cross-examine Gwen Landolt, who had sworn REAL's affidavit, on the nature of her and REAL's expertise.

The hearing for REAL's intervener request was held on May 19 before Justice Lamer. Since Eberts had sworn the affidavit requesting cross-examination, she could not represent LEAF. Instead, one of her law partners from Toronto, John Laskin (a nephew of the late Chief Justice), represented LEAF. The hearing quickly turned into a disaster for LEAF. REAL Women was granted permission to intervene despite missing the filing deadline by more than six months. Still more ominous was Justice Lamer's treatment of the LEAF motion. Lamer was furious to the point of trembling that LEAF had even sought such a motion. The Court, he sternly told Laskin, was very capable of deciding for itself whether REAL Women or any other interveners had the requisite expertise. LEAF had no business meddling in the Court's business, and it had been presumptuous to assume otherwise.[13] REAL Women was granted intervener status, and LEAF was sent packing back to Toronto.

Laskin's report of these events shocked the LEAF case committee. The suspicion that had been subtly building for weeks now burst into full-blown paranoia. "What the hell was going on?" they asked one another. Why had McIntyre framed the questions so abstractly? Why had the government consented? Why, after the *Morgentaler* decision, had the government not moved to dismiss the appeal as moot? And now, why had the Supreme Court departed from its own rules to allow REAL Women to participate in the *Borowski* hearing? LEAF lawyers sent out feelers to well-placed contacts in Ottawa asking what was going on inside the Court. When this network failed to yield any "intelligence," more formal requests were sent to government lawyers working on the case. When these, too, failed to elicit any responses, members of the case committee began to imagine a silent conspiracy stretching from the cabinet to the Justice Department and perhaps even into the Supreme Court itself. As Eberts put it later, "We were the only ones playing by the rules, and we had the feeling we were getting hosed!"[14]

LEAF felt compelled to do something to stem the turning tide, but their options seemed limited. They considered submitting a "motion for directions" to the Supreme Court asking for guidance on the scope of issues to be argued in the *Borowski* hearing. Such a motion, some suggested, would serve to warn the Court of the "Pandora's box" that the fetal rights issue would open up and perhaps dissuade them from hearing the appeal, at least in its present form. Others pointed to the Court's hostile reaction to LEAF's most recent motion and argued that another would amount to a "kamikaze motion." The latter sentiment prevailed, although the "Pandora's box" argument was subsequently used in LEAF's factum for the October hearing.

More direct political action also had its risks. To criticize the Court publicly would be self-defeating. Criticizing the government made more sense, but this could have jeopardized LEAF's tax-exempt status, which rested on the educational character of its activities and prohibited it from partisan political action. To avoid this, LEAF decided to go underground. Some of the lawyers on the case committee prepared a "no name" report that detailed the government's failure to respond to the mootness issue, and then distributed the report to its political allies for propagation. Copies were sent to the Canadian Labour Conference, the National Association of Women and the Law, the Canadian Abortion Rights Action League, and the National Action Committee. LEAF also sent the report out through its informal network of "free lance agitators."[15]

As part of this same strategy, LEAF worked with Senator Lorna Marsden, former president of NAC, to press the issue in the Senate. During Question Period on June 28, Senator Marsden challenged Tory minister Lowell Murray: Why had the government not asked the Supreme Court to dismiss the *Borowski* appeal now that it was moot? She also asked why it had not opposed the petition for intervener status from REAL Women despite its clear violation of Supreme Court rules regarding filing deadlines. Murray adroitly sidestepped both questions. The intervener issue, he sniffed, was "a matter for the Court to decide." As for the alleged mootness issue, the Attorney-General was currently preparing the government's response in keeping with the timetable established by the Court. Senator Marsden and other interested parties would learn the government's position "at that time."[16]

The government did respond two weeks later, but not in the fashion LEAF had hoped for. The government dusted off the obscure "rule 6" of the Supreme Court, which was basically a housekeeping procedure. It authorized a single judge to hear motions to postpone and reschedule hearings. The government, however, sought to use it for a larger purpose. Its petition requested an "indefinite adjournment" of the *Borowski* hearing until after Parliament had dealt with the abortion issue. Once there was new abortion legislation on the books, then the *Borowski* hearing could proceed, suggested the government.

This was hardly what LEAF wanted. The government motion, if accepted, would resuscitate what they (happily) viewed as the already comatose *Borowski* appeal. For the Court to allow the appeal to continue on this unorthodox basis, LEAF lawyers agreed, would be to circumvent the mootness issue in an unprecedented and improper way.

The government's proposal certainly was unorthodox and unprecedented. Whether it was also improper was harder to say. The *Borowski* case was already so "hypothetical" that to substitute a new abortion law for the original (but now invalidated) section 251 would simply have made a strange case stranger. Moreover, as it had already demonstrated by its use of the Powell Report in its *Morgentaler* decision, when it came to procedural decisions, the Supreme Court had the discretion to do pretty much as it chose.

LEAF decided to oppose the government's motion, and Eberts telephoned the registrar of the Court to request permission to participate in the hearing. To her horror, she was told that the Chief Justice intended to hear the government's motion privately in his own office. Rule 6 motions, the registrar explained, dealt with mundane scheduling matters and as a matter of efficiency were always held "in chambers," that is, in the office of the presiding judge.

This development further heightened the paranoia in the pro-choice camp. The idea of Shumiatcher and the Crown attorneys meeting privately with the Chief Justice to discuss the *Borowski* appeal rekindled fears of some sort of dark conspiracy against them. LEAF tried hard to interest the *Globe and Mail* in the story but it would not bite. To LEAF's relief, David Vienneau, the Court reporter for the *Toronto Star,* did.

Vienneau proceeded on two fronts. Publicly, he wrote a series of three articles – based on an unnamed source – announcing Justice Minister Ray Hnatyshyn's intention to "quietly" ask the Court to postpone the *Borowski* hearing and then covering the ensuing furore.[17] Privately, he was able to use his position as the head of the court committee of the parliamentary press gallery to contact Bob Sharpe, the Chief Justice's administrative assistant. Citing a previous agreement between the Court and the press gallery concerning "in chambers" hearings, Vienneau requested that reporters be allowed to attend the Chief Justice's scheduled hearing with the federal lawyers.

The headline's of Vienneau's first article – "Ottawa trying to shelve appeal on fetus rights" – elicited angry responses from just about every party involved. Shumiatcher immediately protested that the effect of the government's motion would be "to delay the case until God knows when."[18] Liberal MP Robert Kaplan jumped on the government for attempting to "stage manage" the Court's agenda. Kaplan's criticisms were seconded by an unlikely source – pro-life Tory backbenchers.

John Reimer (PC – Kitchener) complained that Hnatyshyn should not allow "his department's bias to prejudge the case and . . . [should] allow the case to be heard." Jim Jepson (PC – London) added that "he and thousands of other Canadians are distressed" by Hnatyshyn's request. He was "particularly disturbed," Jepson declared, "to have learned of the government action from the newspaper."[19]

The government tried in vain to extinguish the political firestorm unleashed by the Vienneau articles. Hnatyshyn denied that there was any "bias" in the Justice Department or that the request for postponement was motivated by his government's concern that abortion not become an issue in the federal elections that were anticipated for later that year. It was his own decision, Hnatyshyn patiently explained, and it was motivated simply by the desire to prevent all parties, including the Supreme Court, from dealing with a challenge to a law that no longer existed. "Rather than be negative," Hnatyshyn protested, "I have taken an action which is supportive of having the *Borowski* case heard at an important time in the future when Parliament has spoken on this very sensitive issue."[20] Future events would later make the Justice Minister's explanation look more credible, but at the time he persuaded absolutely no one, including the Supreme Court.

The public exposure of the government's private meeting with the Chief Justice also had its intended effect. Chief Justice Dickson opened the hearings to the public and heard arguments not just from Shumiatcher and the government lawyers but also from any of the interveners who so desired. At the hearing, Dickson pressed the Crown to explain why it had not brought a motion to quash the *Borowski* appeal on grounds of mootness following the *Morgentaler* decision. (Court rules required that this type of motion be brought before a panel of five judges, so Dickson, sitting by himself on the June 19 hearing, could not consider such a motion.) Crown counsel responded – not terribly persuasively – that the government's tabling of its abortion resolutions in May was a new circumstance that explained its prior inaction.

The July 19 hearing on postponement turned out to be a dress rehearsal for the October hearing on the merits. There was a carnival atmosphere of the press, the partisan, and the curious. Joe Borowski had come all the way from Winnipeg. Stationed at the front door with his predictable blue suit and wide grin, he appeared like a friendly innkeeper, welcoming the guests to a banquet. David Vienneau, the anonymous architect of this latest "Charter happening," was of course there, too, busily taking notes on what only weeks before was intended to be a private meeting between the Chief Justice and a handful of government lawyers.

At the end of the hearing, when Chief Justice Dickson announced, "I am in no way persuaded this is a case which should be postponed," Borowski was quick to claim victory. "If there is a message in this," declared an ecstatic Borowski, "it is that the courts have their agenda and they are not going to be told or bullied by Parliament [about] when to have trials or hearings."[21] Ironically, Mary Eberts and LEAF were also pleased with this outcome. It was the first time Eberts had felt encouraged since early that spring.[22] Hnatyshyn was philosophical in defeat. "You win some, you lose some," he said. "The court has decided that it will go ahead and we'll be prepared." With that, the television camera crews packed their bags and scurried off, while the various combatants returned to their base camps to prepare for the October showdown.

CHAPTER 21

The Supreme Court Decides Whether To Decide

Writing in dissent in the 1981 *Borowski* decision, then Chief Justice Laskin warned that if Borowski were granted standing, "other persons with an opposite point of view might seek to intervene and would be allowed to do so, [and] the result would be to set up a battle between parties who do not have a direct interest [and] to wage it in a judicial arena."

On October 3, 1988, Laskin's fears seemed to have been realized. Joe Borowski was back, and with him were three different interest-group interveners – despite the fact that there was not even a valid abortion law left to challenge. In this respect, the case was even more abstract than before. There was still no woman complainant who had been denied an abortion (as in *Roe v. Wade*), nor any doctor charged with performing an illegal abortion (as in *Morgentaler*). The case had become a double hypothetical. In the absence of either real litigants or even a real law, the Court – the constitutional oracle – was being asked to pronounce on the rights of the fetus. This was Charter politics in its purest form.

Borowski's legal argument was deceptively simple. Section 7 of the Charter declared that "everyone has the right to life, liberty, and security of the person." The unborn child, he claimed, was included in the concept "everyone." If the legal question seemed simple and narrow, its potential policy consequences were anything but. This explained the packed courtroom. In addition to Shumiatcher and Crown counsel, Ed Sojonky, there were counsel for three intervener groups. Opposing Borowski was LEAF, represented by Mary Eberts, one of its founders and most able advocates. Supporting Borowski were REAL Women and the Interfaith Coalition, a diverse alliance of Catholic, Protestant, Jewish, Islamic, Hindu, evangelical, and native Indian groups.

The supporting casts for both sides were duly assembled in the public benches at the rear: top brass from LEAF, the National Action Committee on the Status of Women, and the Canadian Abortion Rights Action League on one side; their counterparts from REAL Women, Alliance for Life, and Toronto Right to Life on the other. Both groups were symbolically seated on opposing sides of the centre aisle: the Borowski supporters behind their champion, to the right of the judges; the anti-Borowski camp to the left. Students and other curious onlookers grabbed seats on whichever side they could find them. Reporters had filled all the side seats reserved for the press, and the media overflowed into the adjacent press room where there was a closed-circuit monitor.

When Borowski began his case back in 1978, the government had argued that he lacked legal "standing" and that his claim should be dismissed. Borowski spent three years and $150,000 to defeat the government's claim. Only the precedent-setting 1981 Supreme Court decision dramatically expanding the law of standing allowed him to begin his abortion challenge. Now, after a second trial, another appeal, seven more years, and another $200,000, he was back in the Supreme Court. Once again, the government was arguing that he had no business being there.

Borowski's new problem was, of course, the Supreme Court victory in January of his long-time adversary, Dr. Henry Morgentaler. Even though Morgentaler had challenged the abortion law for the opposite reasons, the Court's invalidation of section 251 had robbed Borowski's claim of any legal grounding. How could he challenge the constitutionality of a law that no longer existed? According to Crown attorney Ed Sojonky, Borowski's case was now "moot" and should be dismissed.

From a legal perspective, Borowski barely had a leg to stand on. But in a broader sense, he seemed to have earned a right to a hearing by the Court. He had resigned his Manitoba cabinet position and sacrificed his political career because of his opposition to abortion. He had gone to jail three times for refusing to pay his income taxes and had nearly killed himself with an eighty-day hunger strike. In 1978 Borowski had hired Morris Shumiatcher to turn his cause into a case. Now, after ten years of litigation and $350,000 in expenses, Borowski was back in the Supreme Court. How, Shumiatcher implored the Court that Monday morning, could the seven justices tell "poor Joe" that they would not even hear his case?

All this was, of course, legally irrelevant. As Justice Antonio Lamer reminded Shumiatcher, "It's not just a question of pleasing or displeasing Mr. Borowski. It's a question of this Court taking a very big step as regards its jurisdiction in relation to Parliament. . . . I am very concerned about judges gnawing away at Parliament's jurisdiction. . . ."[1] If the Supreme Court functioned strictly as a court of law, the jurisdictional issue would probably have disposed of the *Borowski* case at the outset. But the justices knew they were not just dealing with Borowski the individual but with Borowski the symbol – the symbol of the pro-life cause and the millions of Canadians who actively supported it. Borowski was the symbolic counterpart to Morgentaler. To hear one but not the other might have given the appearance of bias. The modern Supreme Court has become sensitive to the political environment in which it works. In its role as umpire of Canadian federalism, the Court has gone out of its way to appear evenhanded in its treatment of competing federal and provincial claims. Dr. Morgentaler received his day in Court. Should Borowski have his?

The Court spent almost the entire first day deciding whether to decide. The justices took turns pressing Shumiatcher with jurisdictional questions. In the absence of any law, began Chief Justice Dickson, wouldn't any answer by the Court be a case of "blatant legal legislation?"[2] Justice Antonio Lamer elaborated:

> There is no law prohibiting abortions and there is no law prohibiting pregnancy and ordering abortions as in some countries. Where are we going to latch onto . . . a proper judicial function as distinct from a policy pronouncement?. . . I can't relate to a law, I can't apply a law, I can't strike a law down, I can't uphold it, I can only express an opinion as to what maybe the law should say.[3]

Shumiatcher, a veteran of forty years of legal sparring, tried valiantly to slip the question.

> My Lord, with all respect, I don't think that Your Lordship should have difficulty. What is the law that bears upon this case? I'm not

looking to a statute. . . . I've got something much better before the Court and that's the supreme law of Canada, I've got the Charter of Rights and Freedoms.[4]

Sensing the vulnerability of his position, Shumiatcher quickly mounted a second line of defence. "No law is a kind of law," he countered. "To fail to hear this [case] now is to make a decision. It is to make a decision against Mr. Borowski."[5]

Shumiatcher alternated his legal arguments with pleas for moral leadership from the Court. "[T]he situation here is a desperate and urgent one," he told the Court. "[T]he people of Canada are looking to this Court as never before, not just for guidance in respect of legal matters, but in respect of moral conduct."[6]

This tack met with only limited success. Madame Justice L'Heureux-Dubé countered: "An easy answer to your query would be that it is up to the state to decide rather than the courts. You say [the fetus] has no rights. Well, it is up to the state to decide, the legislators, is it not?"[7]

Shumiatcher refused to retreat. The legislators had acted, he reminded the Court, and they had given some protection to the unborn until the *Morgentaler* decision in January of this year. "I put it to you that the responsibility for there being no abortion laws in Canada to protect the unborn is the result of a decision of this Court,"[8] declared Shumiatcher. His implication was clear: you created this problem, now it is your responsibility to fix it.

Still, Shumiatcher had not directly met the Court's central concern, which was best articulated by Justice Lamer: ". . . if this Court [proceeds with the case], then it is an acknowledgement . . . that it has the power to tell Parliament that it should enact a law, and that if it doesn't, Parliament is in violation of the Charter of Rights."[9] Shumiatcher initially responded with a discourse on how, with the adoption of the Charter, "the whole jurisdiction of this Court has expanded enormously" and created "new perceptions in the relationship between" courts and legislatures.[10] But this theoretical reflection tailed off into a dangerously frank and ill-advised conclusion: ". . . let's face it, this Court is telling the legislature what to do or what not to do all the time."[11]

While Shumiatcher was technically correct in this assessment, it was hardly the right time or place to say it. In its earlier Charter decisions, the Court had repeatedly denied that it ever made public policy

– especially in cases where it clearly was. Shumiatcher's candour touched a raw nerve.

Sensing the potential damage incurred by Shumiatcher's blunt response, Claude Thomson, counsel for one of the pro-life interveners, tried to narrow the scope of the case. "This is not a case in which the Court is being asked to direct Parliament to pass a law," Thomson reassured the justices. The Court, he continued, is merely being asked to clarify the meaning of section 7 of the Charter: Is the unborn child included in the concept of "everyone" used in section 7? The Court, he concluded, is not being asked "to strike down in advance any proposed legislation [or] to get into the difficult question of balancing whatever rights the unborn may have against the rights of women. . . . what we have here is [only] . . . a question of declaratory relief."[12]

Mary Eberts, the counsel for LEAF, urged the justices not to be seduced by Thomson's narrowing of the issue.

The Charter may have circumscribed the doctrine of parliamentary supremacy, but it did not create an environment where there are no guidelines about the proper relations between this Honourable Court and Parliament. . . . this Court . . . is not an actor of first instance, but . . . a reviewing actor, and what Mr. Borowski asks you to do in this Court today is to be an actor of first instance. . . . The proper role for this Court under the Charter . . . is to review legislation and not to to be a pronouncer in the first instance.[13]

The Court clearly was uncomfortable with Borowski's request, but it soon became apparent that they were not too happy with the Crown, either. In July, the Mulroney government had requested the Court to postpone the *Borowski* hearing until it had enacted new abortion legislation. The Chief Justice had flatly refused. Judicial independence, Dickson had declared, protected the Court's agenda from being rearranged to suit the political convenience of the government.

Crown counsel Ed Sojonky began by renewing his request that the case be postponed. He had just begun his attack on the mootness issue – that the Court should not hear the case until there was a law – when Justice L'Heureux-Dubé interrupted him. "Counsel, I am surprised [by your] stand," she observed dryly. "I would have suspected that since you did not ask for quashing that you would be happy that we hear it."[14]

Sojonky backpedalled. It is true, he conceded, that the Crown had not asked that the appeal be quashed, but his authorities "could well be used in support of such a motion."[15] Justice La Forest shot back impatiently: "[But] none was made, and in the meantime, the parties on all sides have prepared for a question that was at least part of the original question."

Sojonky politely conceded the point and quickly tried to steer the Court back to the issue of mootness. He was cut off again, this time by Justice Lamer. "Mr. Sojonky, I realize that you follow instructions," Lamer dryly observed. "I understand the position. . . . In other words, you would like us to quash it, but you do not want to ask for it."[16] Muffled laughter rippled across the previously sombre courtroom. Sojonky replied somewhat meekly: "With the greatest of deference, My Lord, the word quash does not appear in the factum."[17]

The exchange continued, but it was clear that the Court was exasperated with the government's tactics. The Mulroney government did not want the Court to hear the *Borowski* case – at least not before the federal election set for November 21 – but it did not have the political courage to say so. In May, Morris Manning, on behalf of CARAL, had written the Attorney-General requesting that he move to quash the appeal on the grounds that it was moot. No doubt this was discussed at the highest levels – probably cabinet – and rejected. The government recognized the symbolic meaning of Borowski. They did not want to alienate the pro-life vote by asking the Court to close its doors to him. Sojonky had indeed been given instructions – to persuade the Court to quash the appeal but not to ask for it directly. The government was trying to get the Court to do its dirty work and take the political heat that went with it.

The Court took the unusual step of recessing not once but twice to decide whether to continue. During the second recess on Monday afternoon, the betting in the press room was that the justices would not continue. Shumiatcher's moral rhetoric had been powerful, but he had not directly answered the Court's legal concerns. The Court returned at three o'clock, and the Chief Justice rose to announce their decision: "We will reserve decision on these matters [of jurisdiction]," and continue to hear the remainder of the case.[18] There was an audible sigh of relief from the Borowski side of the courtroom.

Shumiatcher picked up where he had left off. The most important aspect of his case, he reminded the Court, was the evidence that the unborn child is a human being. He summarized the evidence given by the nine expert witnesses he had brought from around the world to

Regina in 1983 for the initial trial. These experts in genetics, embryology, and perinatal medicine testified to the "individuality, the separateness, and the uniqueness" of the human qualities and characteristics of the unborn. Their testimony ranged from the technical – thirty divisions, or two-thirds, of the forty-five cell divisions that occur in a lifetime take place in the first eight weeks after fertilization – to the homespun:

> [E]ach of us may say and none of us may deny that I am the fetus that was. There has never been a time when I was not the same individual. . . . There was a time when I couldn't walk and a time when I couldn't speak and a time when I couldn't articulate my claim upon you as my brother, but there has never been a time when I was not the same individual. [19]

In an unusual move for a court whose function was to review questions of law, not questions of fact, Shumiatcher was then granted permission to show a series of ultrasound videotapes of life in the womb. The tapes showed the development and activities of the fetus/unborn child from six to fifteen weeks after gestation. For most right-to-lifers, these videos were the ultimate rejoinder – the proof of just how human the fetus is. At first all seven justices paid rapt attention to the television screens in front of them. But the flickering images were hard on the eyes, and soon the justices' – and the audience's – attention waned. At four o'clock, Chief Justice Dickson, somewhat sleepily, suggested that this had been enough for one day and adjourned the Court until the next morning.

Shumiatcher completed his presentation Tuesday morning. His strategy was evident. On top of the factual base already constructed, he now added a long string of legal precedents. Criminal law, property law, torts, family law, and the civil law all recognized rights in the unborn child. How unfair it was, Shumiatcher declared, that the unborn child be deprived of the one right that is a prerequisite for the enjoyment of all the others – the right to be born alive. And how ironic, Shumiatcher continued, that society took away this right just at a time when modern medical science was discovering how distinctively human the unborn child really was. While a "primitive society [lacks this knowledge and] cannot be expected to accord to the unborn the care and concern that are bestowed upon children once they are born," Shumiatcher observed, there was no such excuse for a modern society. [20]

Shumiatcher concluded with an emotional appeal for the Court to temper the administration of the law with compassion. "In our advanced society," observed Shumiatcher, "it is both the mother and the unborn child within her who are deserving of the compassion of which Chief Justice Dickson [recently] spoke . . . ." In what has become a favourite tactic of lawyers appearing before the Supreme Court, Shumiatcher quoted the Chief Justice back to himself:

> It is common now for individuals to assert their rights and liberties [under] the Charter. But we all must recognize that there is another side of the coin . . . that we must have . . . a sense of obligation [and] responsibility . . .; [that] we must retain a profound respect for the rights of others. . . . compassion is not some extra-legal factor. . . . Rather, compassion is part and parcel of the nature and content of that which we call 'law'.[21]

Imitation may remain the sincerest form of flattery, but would it be sufficient to persuade the Court?

Shumiatcher was followed by counsel for the interveners who supported the Borowski motion, REAL Women and the Interfaith Coalition. They had been allotted fifteen minutes each, and the Court held them to it. After a brief lunch recess, the Court reconvened to hear Sojonky's presentation of the Crown's position. The justices listened intently but asked few questions. Sojonky was finished in less than an hour. There was a growing impression that, unlike the day before, the justices were more interested with finishing the case than in the issues it raised.

The Crown's position was predictable and prosaic. Sojonky repeated the government's preference that the Court postpone any decision on the merits pending new abortion legislation. If, however, the Court insisted on proceeding, there were sound legal arguments for rejecting Borowski's claims. Sojonky plodded through a careful, point-by-point rebuttal of Shumiatcher's legal arguments. There had never been an absolute fetal right to life in English or Canadian criminal law. The interests of both the mother and the fetus had always been recognized. Canada's 1969 abortion law reform was consistent with this tradition, continuing the criminal prohibition on abortion but allowing it for therapeutic reasons under specified circumstances.

As for the various legal rights vested in the fetus by tort, property, and family law, these had always been understood as depending on live birth and in no way implied such a right. Sojonky reminded the justices that the framers of the Charter had been asked to include the right to life for the unborn and had refused. Surely the Court would not be justified in adding to the Charter what its authors had rejected. Sojonky finished with a flourish and appeared to brace himself for an onslaught of questions from the bench. Instead, the Chief Justice quietly asked Eberts to make LEAF's presentation.

Eberts opened with an impassioned plea for the justices not to be seduced into thinking that the only issue before them was the rights of the fetus. Mr. Borowski and Mr. Shumiatcher like to show films of the fetus happily bouncing around, she began. "But where is that fetus?" she demanded. "It is in a grainy blur. That grainy blur is a woman. . . . Broaden your focus," Eberts implored the Court. The woman is there and she is not just a "grainy blur." You cannot and must not separate the fetus from the mother, or the discussion of a right to life from abortion.

LEAF had been allocated twenty minutes. Eberts used most of the remainder of this time to reinforce some of the legal arguments advanced by the Crown. She ended with a caution that the Court should refrain from changing the status quo. Parliament is now trying to frame a law that balances the "rights" of the mother with the "interests" of the fetus. An affirmative answer to the *Borowski* case would change the equation from an issue of "rights versus interests" to "rights versus rights." "The legislative context must be free from judicial interference," she admonished.

Eberts's plea was good law but somewhat hypocritical, coming from LEAF. The organization was a leading example of the new breed of interest groups that routinely ask courts to overrule legislative policy choices. More importantly, Eberts's closing remarks suggested what really was at stake in the *Borowski* case – the battle for public opinion.

Supreme Court decisions may settle legal cases but they rarely "solve" political issues. Just as the abortion issue had survived the *Morgentaler* decision, so it would outlive whatever the Court decided in Borowski. Pro-choicers were no more likely to pack up their bags and go home if Borowski won than the pro-lifers had after Morgentaler's victory in January. This is not to say that the Court's decisions have no consequences. They do. The consequence is the creation of a new political resource for the winning side. The victor in the judicial arena returns to the larger political arena armed with a new weapon – the favourable judgment of the Court and the moral authority that carries. In the abortion debate after Morgentaler, pro-choice activists had the advantage of being able to claim that the Charter protected a woman's right to abortion. While such claims were typically over-stated, legislators and other public officeholders could not safely ignore them. *Borowski* had the potential to give to pro-lifers a similar "moral club."

This is what Borowski, Shumiatcher, and their pro-life supporters wanted from the Court: a declaration that the unborn child was indeed a human person and thus entitled to the protection granted by section 7 of the Charter. Armed with such a statement, they could return to Parliament and aggressively lobby for a much more restrictive abortion law. It was unthinkable that they could persuade Parliament to outlaw all abortions. But it was undeniable that a favourable ruling would strengthen their position. At a minimum, it would allow them to argue that a just abortion policy must balance "rights against rights."

This is what Eberts, LEAF, and their pro-choice supporters wanted to prevent. While the legal basis of *Morgentaler* was a narrow, proce-dural ruling, its practical consequence was to suspend the enforcement of the law until Parliament "fixed" it. Symbolically, it also defined the abortion issue as a conflict of "rights versus interests." The ensuing political paralysis in the House of Commons had produced a policy of "no law." From the pro-choice perspective, "no law" was a good law as far as abortion goes, thus the defence of the status quo.

A poignant incident at the end of the second day suggested why the battle for public opinion was an uphill one for Joe Borowski and his pro-life followers. Oral argument concluded at about four o'clock Tuesday afternoon. As expected, the Court reserved its judgment, meaning that their decision would not be announced for several months. The courtroom emptied quickly, but Borowski remained behind to speak with Shumiatcher and a few supporters. By the time Borowski left the Supreme Court building at about 4:15, only the guards were left in the lobby. Outside, however, a scrum of reporters and television camera crews was waiting at the bottom of the front steps. The group included Neal MacDonald from CBC television, David Vienneau from the *Toronto Star,* Kevin Newman from CTV, among others.

"Where are the fetuses?" they demanded. "Show us your fetuses." Joe grinned with almost childlike glee. "They're gone," he replied. Subsequent questioning disclosed that Borowski had arrived at the Supreme Court building that morning carrying a blue airline travel bag. Inside were two large glass jars, one containing a ten-week-old fetus and the other a seven-month-old fetus. Borowski earnestly explained to the impatient reporters how he had hoped to present the two jars to the judges. If the judges could only have seen them, he began to lecture, and "pass them hand to hand," it would be "very convincing evidence."[22]

Borowski had hatched this bizarre strategy without consulting Shumiatcher. When the advocate learned what was afoot, he ordered his client to take the fetuses from the courtroom immediately. "They were gruesome," Shumiatcher later remarked, and totally inappropriate to bring to court.[23] Later, two nuns were seen leaving the building with the blue travel bag, but not before Borowski had shown the fetuses to at least one reporter. Now the rest of the pack wanted to see them, but Joe had nothing to show.

Suddenly, the tone of the interview turned ugly. Aggressive questioning provoked sharp replies. Within seconds, the interview degenerated into a shouting match. "Why won't you show us the fetuses?" "Are you ashamed?" "What are you trying to prove?" "Don't you think women can think for themselves?" Borowski responded with a few choice epithets of his own, then turned and walked away, suddenly a very lonely figure. Trading insults with the press was hardly a recipe for cultivating good public relations. When contrasted with the light-hearted reception that Morgentaler and Manning had laid on the press two years earlier, it showed why the pro-life cause was having so much trouble projecting a positive image in the press.

As it turned out, his day in court was all Joe Borowski received. Five months after the end of oral argument, the Supreme Court announced its decision. It concluded that the *Borowski* case had indeed become moot, and refused to address the substantive issue of whether the unborn child was included in the concept of "person" and thus protected by section 7 of the Charter. To do so in the absence of any law, wrote Justice Sopinka for a unanimous court, would be like answering a "private reference," and could result in the appearance that the Court was trying to "preempt a possible decision of Parliament by dictating the form of legislation it should enact." Such unnecessary judicial pronouncements about the rights of the unborn would be "a marked departure from the traditional role of the Court."[24] Thus the Court decided not to decide.

Borowski was bitter when he heard the news from Ottawa. As far as he was concerned, he had not so much lost as been denied his day in court. Nor was he coy about the way he felt. "Had I been there," he told reporters, "I probably would have gone into the court and punched the judges in the nose." Fortunately, he was in Winnipeg.

From a political perspective, this second act of the Supreme Court's abortion drama was anticlimactic. From a legal perspective, the "non-result" in *Borowski* was predictable. Six out of the seven judges who participated in the *Morgentaler* decision only nine months earlier had indicated their wish to avoid becoming embroiled in the substance of abortion policy. The *Borowski* decision simply reaffirmed the majority's sense of judicial self-restraint. Sensitive to the public's perception of fairness, they had given Joe Borowski his day in court, just as Henry Morgentaler had had his. But they refused to go further. In the wake of the *Morgentaler* decision, the ball was in Parliament's court, and the Court did not intend to act until there was a new abortion law. Justice Sopinka's opinion anticipated – correctly – that the abortion issue would return to the Court soon enough. What the justices did not anticipate was just how soon and how explosively.

CHAPTER 22

The Court Plays Solomon

The Court's next encounter with abortion was by accident not design. Morgentaler and Borowski were point men for well-organized and well-financed political movements trying to use the courts to change public policy. Morgentaler and Borowski came before the Supreme Court because they chose to. This was not the case with Chantal Daigle, whom fate dragged from the obscurity of private life across the judicial stage of abortion politics in the summer of 1989.

The *Daigle* case burst upon a political scene already simmering with abortion controversy. Since the fiasco of the preceding June, the Mulroney government had still not introduced new abortion legislation. The government's inaction gave rise to several surprising new developments in the abortion battle.

While the November, 1988, election became a virtual referendum on the Mulroney government's free trade agreement with the United States, abortion politics did not disappear completely. Several party nominations turned into contests between pro-choice and pro-life candidates, and pro-life groups mounted direct-mail campaigns to elect (or defeat) candidates in thirteen ridings. In the end, the *Globe and Mail* estimated that at least seventy-four explicitly pro-life MPs were elected.[1]

The policy vacuum at the federal level opened the door for innovations and initiatives at the provincial level. While criminal regulation

273

of abortion remained the exclusive jurisdiction of Parliament, the provinces could influence the availability of abortions through their jurisdiction over health policy. By attaching conditions to public health insurance funding of abortions and by permitting or prohibiting abortion clinics apart from hospitals, each province could influence the availability of abortion services. Predictably, within a year there were ten different provincial policies.

In British Columbia, outspoken pro-life Premier Bill Vander Zalm announced that his Social Credit government would "de-insure" – that is, no longer pay for – abortions except for pregnancies that threatened the life of the mother. This policy was immediately challenged in court by the British Columbia Civil Liberties Association and was subsequently declared invalid on a procedural technicality. Rather than appeal this ruling, the B.C. government launched a $20 million campaign to facilitate alternatives to abortion.[2] Manitoba refused to pay for abortions performed outside of hospitals, while New Brunswick and Nova Scotia sought to prohibit private abortion clinics altogether. By contrast, in Ontario the Liberal government of Premier David Peterson followed the earlier lead of Quebec and announced that it would both allow clinics and pay for clinic abortions. The other extreme was represented by Prince Edward Island, where hospital boards had not allowed doctors to perform abortions since 1982. Following the *Morgentaler* decision, the chairman of the province's largest hospital, the Queen Elizabeth in Charlottetown, announced that it would continue to deny doctors permission to perform abortions. Thus, by the first anniversary of the Supreme Court's *Morgentaler* decision, there was less uniformity in access to abortion services across Canada than before.[3]

Far from marking the final triumph of their cause, as pro-choice activists first thought, the *Morgentaler* decision had sparked a new round of trench warfare at the provincial level. Pro-choice groups typically responded to the new provincial policies by challenging them in court, often with success. Pro-life activists took to the streets. Angry with the Mulroney government's paralysis and frustrated by the courts, they began to manifest a new militancy.

In Februrary, 1989, 150 pro-life activists took a page out of the Morgentaler book of civil disobedience. They used a sit-in demonstration to shut down the Everywoman's Health Clinic in Vancouver. When over 100 protesters refused to obey a court injunction to end the blockade, the police arrested thirteen demonstrators. When the protesters still refused to promise to stay away from the clinic, they were charged with contempt of court.[4] At trial they invoked the defence of necessity and requested a trial by jury. To their dismay, Judge Josiah Wood refused both requests.[5] While there were valid technical reasons for both rulings, to Canadian pro-lifers it appeared that Canadian judges were using one set of rules for Morgentaler and another set for them. At the peak of the Vancouver sit-in protests, the Supreme Court of Canada delivered its decision dismissing the *Borowski* appeal.

The following month, the Vancouver pro-life demonstrators upped the ante by adopting the tactics being used by the militant Operation Rescue in the United States. They chained themselves to the clinic's doors, again shutting it down until police could cut through the chains and carry them off. The embittered Joe Borowski captured the new mood of many Canadian pro-lifers:

> Enough is enough; we are going to fill the jails with our bodies. We are going to do what the negroes did in the United States. They filled up the jails. They clogged the justice system. We consider abortion far worse than apartheid and racial discrimination.[6]

Another consequence of the policy vacuum was the appearance of a new kind of legal action: the "abortion injunction" case. While the players changed, the plot was always the same: a relationship goes sour and the father goes to court seeking an injunction to stop his former partner from aborting "their child." There had been such cases in Alberta[7] and Manitoba,[8] but no judge was willing to issue an injunction. Ending as quickly as they began, these cases had attracted only fleeting public attention. This changed on July 4, 1989, when an Ontario Supreme Court judge in Toronto granted Gregory Murphy a temporary injunction preventing his ex-girlfriend, Barbara Dodd, from having an abortion. Murphy basically advanced the same legal arguments as Borowski: that to allow Dodd's abortion would violate the section 7 and section 15 rights of their unborn child. While the injunction was overturned a week later, the fact that it had been issued at all, plus the fact that it occurred in Canada's media capital, made it headline news across the country for the next week. Pro-life and pro-choice forces rallied, marched, and shouted until July 11, when Dodd received her abortion – for free – at the Morgentaler Clinic on Harbord Street. Rather than fade away, the Dodd-Murphy saga reignited a week later when Barbara Dodd, wearing a pro-life T-shirt, called a press conference to announce that she regretted her choice of abortion and had

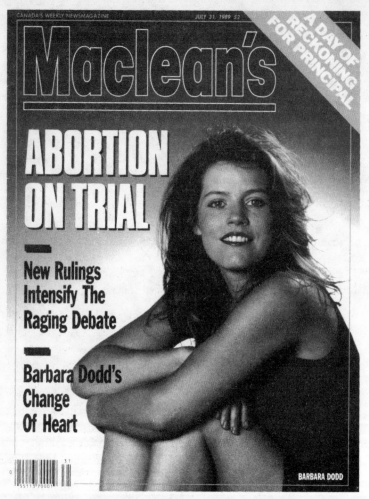

CANADA'S WEEKLY NEWSMAGAZINE   JULY 31, 1989 $2

Maclean's

A DAY OF RECKONING FOR PRINCIPAL

ABORTION ON TRIAL

New Rulings Intensify The Raging Debate

Barbara Dodd's Change Of Heart

BARBARA DODD

Cover of July 31, 1989, issue of *Maclean's*. (*Courtesy* Maclean's: Canada's Weekly Newsmagazine © *Maclean Hunter Ltd.*)

acted under pressure of her family and pro-choice activists. The next week she appeared on the cover of *Maclean's*.[9]

As if this were not enough for one week, on July 5 the U.S. Supreme Court released its decision in the *Webster* case, upholding a Missouri law prohibiting public hospitals and other publicly funded facilities from performing or facilitating abortions.[10] *Webster* was widely interpreted as the first step toward overturning *Roe v. Wade* by a Supreme Court increasingly dominated by judges appointed by conservative Republican President Ronald Reagan. Four of the five judges voting to uphold the Missouri law were Reagan appointees. Pro-life Americans applauded the decision while pro-choice groups condemned it and warned that abortion rights were being threatened by "the Reagan Court." While legally irrelevant in Canada, the *Webster* decision stirred a pot already simmering over the Dodd-Murphy injunction.

On July 7, reports from Quebec brought the news that Jean-Guy Tremblay had persuaded a Quebec Superior Court judge to issue a preliminary injunction against his pregnant ex-girlfriend, Chantal Daigle, who was midway through the second trimester. Pro-choice leaders once again protested what they denounced as unwarranted judicial interference in the private decisions of Canadian women. However, when the injunction against Barbara Dodd was set aside in Toronto several days later, they were confident that the Daigle affair would come to a similar, quick end.

To their dismay, the opposite occurred. On July 17, Judge Viens of the Quebec Superior Court upheld the injunction, ruling that "a conceived child that is not yet born is a human being" protected under Article 1 of the Quebec Charter of Human Rights.[11] Daigle immediately appealed this decision to the Quebec Court of Appeal, which, because of the urgency of the matter, heard it on July 20.[12] Pro-choice advocates were stunned again when, on July 26, a divided Court of Appeal upheld the injunction. With her pregnancy now in its twentieth week, Daigle filed a hasty appeal to the Supreme Court of Canada. For only the second time in the Court's history, Chief Justice Dickson recalled the justices from their summer vacation to hear the application for leave to appeal on August 1. The appeal was granted and a hearing date was set for August 8. Never before in the Court's history has a case moved from trial to the highest court in the land with such speed.

But what a difference a month made. While the *Daigle* case had begun as a purely private dispute, it was now a *cause célèbre* for both sides of the abortion battle. Predictably, organizations from both camps requested intervener status for the August 8 Supreme Court hearing. Less predictably, given the critical lack of time to prepare or hear such arguments, the Supreme Court granted all requests. It then sought to contain the time problem by allowing each group only ten minutes of oral argument – barely enough time for most lawyers to clear their throats.

A lineup of opposing groups and scrums of lawyers made the courtroom appear like a rugby tournament on the morning of August 8. Appearing on Daigle's behalf were the Canadian Abortion Rights Action League (CARAL), the Women's Legal Education and Action Fund (LEAF) and the Canadian Civil Liberties Association (CCLA). On the other side were the Campaign Life Coalition, Canadian Physicians for Life, L'association des médecins du Québec pour le respect de la vie, and REAL Women of Canada – all supporting Tremblay and the Quebec Court of Appeal ruling. Somewhat pathetically, the federal government intervened to defend its "right to legislate at the federal level" with respect to abortion, despite the fact that its failure to legislate for the past eighteen months was a principal cause of the whole affair.[13] Outside the Supreme Court building were hundreds of pro-choice and anti-abortion demonstrators waving placards, chanting slogans and hurling the occasional insult at one another.

After suffering setbacks in both the *Morgentaler* and *Borowski* cases, the pro-life movement was ecstatic about *Daigle*. Not one but two courts had now accepted what the pro-life movement had been arguing for years: that the fetus is simply an unborn person, a human being, and is therefore entitled to the same protection of life as all other persons. The facts of the *Daigle* case also favoured the pro-life position. Daigle's pregnancy was voluntary. There were no extenuating circumstances such as rape or incest. She had stopped taking her birth control pills in February, and in the first four months of her pregnancy she had made no attempts to terminate it. The pregnancy represented no health threats, either to her or her baby. Finally, she was already in the twentieth week (twenty-second by the time of the Supreme Court hearing) of her pregnancy. An abortion at this stage would destroy much more than the fingernail-sized zygote sucked out with a vacuum aspirator. There was only one reason for this abortion: Chantal Daigle no longer wanted to bear her child. This was a classic case of a "lifestyle abortion": the hardest to justify morally and the least accepted in the court of public opinion. Pro-life leaders hoped it would encounter similar difficulties in a court of law.

The advanced state of Daigle's pregnancy and her vague reasons for wanting an abortion made this an unfavourable "test case" for the pro-choice groups. Intervening in the *Daigle* case violated LEAF's litigation strategy of seeking incremental change in favourable fact circumstances. As Wayne MacKay, a constitutional expert from Dalhousie University, observed: "I am not sure they want this to be their big case on the rights of the fetus."[14] While LEAF could hardly stand on the sidelines in such a case, its leaders must have been nervous about their involvement. From a tactical point of view, taking the *Daigle* case to the Supreme Court was like going for the home run instead of the sacrifice bunt. Past experience indicated that the Supreme Court was not very likely to serve up home runs on the issue of abortion.

The legal issues in the *Daigle* case turned primarily on the Quebec Charter of Human Rights and Freedoms, but they had clear implications for the Canadian Charter. Unlike section 7 of the Canadian Charter, section 1 of the Quebec Charter speaks of the "right to life" of every "être humain" or "human being" rather than "persons." Section 2 declares that "Every human being whose life is in peril has a right to assistance."[15] A majority of the Quebec Court of Appeal judges was willing to use the broader connotation of "human being" (compared to "person") to find legal protection for Chantal Daigle's unborn child.

Justice LeBel found the concept of "human being" to constitute a prima facie case for the fetus: "it is difficult to deny that the fetus, especially once it reaches this stage of development, becomes part of humankind . . . even if it has not yet reached the stage of life outside the body of the mother."[16] LeBel reinforced his finding by referring to the Quebec Civil Code's provision of various kinds of legal protection for the unborn. Section 18 of the Code declared that "every human being possesses juridical personality. . . . [and] has the full enjoyment of civil rights, except as otherwise expressly provided by law." Subsequent sections of the Code authorized the appointment of "curators" for "children conceived but not yet born" and allowed them to be designated as lawful inheritors in wills.[17]

Justice Nichols found that the Quebec Civil Code by itself recognized the right to life of the unborn: "It would be paradoxical," he wrote, "if the legislator had wanted to protect the patrimonial rights of an unborn child but at the same time had remained indifferent to his right to life."[18] The third and final judge for the majority considered that the fetus had a "natural right" to be carried to term. Wrote Justice Bernier:

The child conceived but not yet born, regardless of the term that is given to his civil status, constitutes a reality which must be taken into consideration. It is not an inanimate object, nor anyone's property, but a living human entity, distinct from that of the mother that carries it, which two human beings have given existence to . . . and which . . . is entitled to life and to the protection of those who conceived it.[19]

Justices Chouinard and Tourigny rejected the majority's interpretation of both the Quebec Charter and the Civil Code. There was no clear evidence that the term "human being" was intended to include the fetus. As for the rights of the "child conceived but not yet born" in the Civil Code, the dissenters noted that these rights could only be exercised by "the child who is born and viable." While not denying the existence of any rights for the fetus, the dissenting judges found that they were too vague and ill-defined to overrule "the fundamental right of the appellant to decide her health and security in complete freedom."[20]

On the morning of August 8, 1989, the Supreme Court convened to review the Quebec Court of Appeal's decision. Of immediate concern was whether the Court would uphold or overturn the injunction that had prevented Chantal Daigle from having an abortion. But behind the injunction question was a legal issue with practical consequences reaching far beyond the Daigle-Tremblay dispute: Is the fetus a "human being" and thus protected by the Quebec Charter of Rights? As the partisans from both sides demonstrated on the front steps of the Supreme Court building, all nine Supreme Court justices, counsel for the two litigants, and the nine interveners began to sort out the conflicting answers given by the Quebec Court of Appeal. The justices listened passively all morning as opposing counsel presented their arguments. After breaking for lunch, the Court was set to resume when Daigle's lawyer, Daniel Bedard, approached the bench. He had just learned, he told the justices, that his client had received an abortion and so ended her twenty-two-week pregnancy.

The justices appeared shaken, and it was not clear what would happen next. Daigle's case suddenly seemed as moot as Borowski's. With Daigle's pregnancy terminated, the injunction no longer had any practical effect. One option was for the Court simply to dismiss the case as moot. Daigle was potentially subject to either civil or criminal contempt charges for disobeying the injunction, but this was a matter for the Quebec Court of Appeal to decide. Chief Justice Dickson asked the

Cover of January, 1990, issue of *Chatelaine*. (*Courtesy* Chatelaine *magazine*
© *Maclean Hunter Ltd.*)

lawyers for Daigle and Tremblay if they wished to continue. Tremblay's lawyer opposed continuing, but not Bedard. The issues behind
the injunction remained, he declared, and so posed the threat of similar
injunctions against other women. The Court recessed briefly, then
announced it would finish hearing the case. Less than two hours later,

the Chief Justice announced that the Court had unanimously voted to overturn the injunction and would issue its reasons at a later date.[21]

The next day front-page headlines blared the news of the decision across Canada: "Court lifts injunction after Daigle abortion . . . Pro-choice advocates support decision."[22] Canada's thirty-two-day abortion mini-drama had come to a climactic end. The victory for the pro-choice side seemed as complete as the defeat of the high hopes of the pro-life movement. Chantal Daigle had become a national celebrity. Five months later, *Chatelaine* magazine named her "newsmaker of the year."[23] In the continuing policy vacuum created by the Mulroney government's inaction, the Supreme Court increasingly appeared to be the institution in charge of Canadian abortion policy.

Three months later, the Supreme Court released its written reasons for the Daigle decision in the form of a unanimous, unsigned "Judgment of the Court." The decision focused primarily on the issue of whether the fetus had a right to life under Quebec law and whether, as a corollary, the father had a right to protect it from an abortion. The Court answered both questions with an emphatic "no."[24]

The key to this "difficult and controversial question," wrote the Court, was "whether a fetus was intended by the National Assembly of Quebec to be a person under s.1."[25] "In our view," the judges continued,

the Quebec Charter . . . does not display any clear intention on the part of its framers to consider the status of a fetus . . . this lack of an intention to deal with a fetus's status is . . . a strong reason for not finding fetal rights under the Charter. . . . If the legislature had wished to grant fetuses the right to life, then it seems unlikely that it would have left the protection of this right to such happenstance.[26]

The attempts by Tremblay's lawyer and pro-life interveners to establish the "humanity" of the fetus through scientific evidence and ethical arguments were rejected as inappropriate. "The task of properly classifying a fetus in law and in science are different pursuits," the Court declared. The Court must restrict its reasons for decisions to purely legal reasons. "Decisions based upon broad social, political, moral and economic choices," the Court concluded, "are more appropriately left to the legislature."[27]

Tremblay's lawyer had also argued that proof that the fetus was protected by the Quebec Charter could be found in the "plain meaning" of its words. The adjective "human" denotes membership in the human race and the gerund "being" signifies "existing." Surely the fetus is a "human being" in the clear sense of these words. "This argument is not persuasive," wrote the Court.

> The meaning of the term "human being" is a highly controversial issue ... and it cannot be settled by linguistic fiat. A purely linguistic argument suffers from the same flaw as a purely scientific argument: it attempts to settle a legal debate by non-legal means.[28]

The claim that the fetus is also protected by the Civil Code was dispatched for similar reasons. Again the Court stressed the absence of any clear intention of the framers to this effect. As for the rights of the "child conceived but not yet born" explicitly found in the Civil Code, the Court took the same position as the dissenting judges in the Quebec Court of Appeal: that these rights can only be exercised by "the child who is born and viable."[29]

Tremblay's lawyer had also tried to use section 7 of the Canadian Charter of Rights to establish a right to life for the fetus – the same argument that Joe Borowski had made. Again the Court ducked the question, this time by invoking a 1986 precedent, *Dolphin Delivery,*[30] which held that the Charter does not apply to civil disputes between private parties. The issue in *Dolphin* was whether an employer's use of a common-law-based injunction prohibiting secondary picketing by the striking union violated the union's right to freedom of expression. *Dolphin Delivery* stands for the rule that for the Charter to apply, there must be some form of "state action." Tremblay could not point to any law or other form of government action that violated section 7. It was therefore "unnecessary" to decide the section 7 claim on behalf of the fetus, wrote the Court, and "unnecessary constitutional pronouncements should be avoided."[31]

At this point, the Supreme Court had decided all that was necessary to dispose of the *Daigle* appeal.[32] Rather than conclude, however, the Court launched into a new examination of the rights of the fetus under common law, as opposed to the civil law that is unique to Quebec. Why would the Court undertake to answer legal issues that were not pertinent to the case at hand? The Court did not try to conceal its policy-making purpose. "It is useful," they wrote, "to do so ... to avoid the repetition of the appellant's experience in the common law provinces."[33]

The Court's historical survey of abortion legislation found that while "the fetus has always been protected to some extent in our law ... abortion has not generally been considered equivalent to murder."

From this somewhat ambivalent record they concluded "that it could be argued that . . . a fetus has not been viewed as having the rights of a person in the full sense."[34] Their survey of the case law of Canada and several other common-law jurisdictions found that in similar and relevant cases, judges had usually – although not always – reached the conclusion that "a fetus is treated as a person [in law] only where it is necessary to do so in order to protect its interests after it is born."[35] This brief but emphatic excursion into the common law made it clear that the Court did not want to see any more *Daigle*-esque cases, and that it was not willing to wait for legislative action to clear up the legal ambiguity nourishing the abortion-injunction cases.

Unlike the *Morgentaler* and *Borowski* decisions, the release of *Daigle* was a political non-event. The climax of the *Daigle* drama had been on August 8, when the Court invalidated the injunction that Daigle had already defied. When the Supreme Court released the reasons for its decision three months later, there was little public interest. This political obscurity notwithstanding, the *Daigle* decision says a great deal about the politics of the Charter.

From one perspective the *Daigle* decision could be understood as a continuation of the judicial self-restraint evident in the *Morgentaler* and *Borowski* cases, in which the Court once again refused to become entangled in the abortion conflict. By invoking the "state action" doctrine of *Dolphin Delivery,* the Court dodged the issue of fetal rights under section 7 of the Charter, thereby leaving Ottawa a free hand in fashioning a new abortion law. True, the Court had ruled that the fetus was not protected by the Quebec Charter, but the Quebec Charter was only a statute. If the Quebec Assembly thought that the Supreme Court had misunderstood its "intended meaning" of "human being," then it could easily amend the act. In sum, the Court had quickly and narrowly dispatched the Tremblay-Daigle conflict without encroaching on the larger legislative question of a national abortion policy.

Yet on closer reading, there were undercurrents of judicial activism in *Daigle,* undercurrents that flowed in a pro-choice direction. To begin with, the Court could be charged with violating its own maxim against unnecessary judicial pronouncements, and not once but twice. When the justices learned that Chantal Daigle had received her abortion, why did they persist in ruling on the legal issues involved rather than declaring the case moot, which it clearly was? Similarly, why did the Court expand the scope of its ruling to include the common law when this was not necessary for a Quebec appeal?

The Court, of course, had its reasons: "in order to resolve the important legal issue raised so that the situation of women in the position in which Ms. Daigle found herself could be clarified."[36] They might have added, "and not repeated." This aspect of the justices' decision was clearly motivated by their sympathy with Daigle and, by extension, with other women who might find themselves in a similar situation.

Those who shared this sympathy applauded the Court's decision. But what about those who thought that it was wrong to abort a perfectly healthy twenty-two-week-old unborn child simply because the mother had changed her mind about her relationship with the father? From this perspective, it was bad enough that Daigle had aborted her unborn child. To bend the Court's own rules to extend this option to others was hardly seen as defensible. Did this mean that a person's approval or disapproval of the results of the Court's decision coloured one's approval of the means used to reach it? Perhaps. But this did not change the fact that for many this aspect of the *Daigle* decision encouraged the suspicion that the Supreme Court was being less than neutral on the abortion issue.

In fact, there were competing reasons – legal reasons – why the Court should have declared the case moot and avoided deciding the issue of fetal rights. At a time when other Charter cases were taking from three to five years from trial to final decision by the Supreme Court, *Daigle* traversed this entire path in exactly one month. Of course there were special reasons for this. But why, after being advised of her abortion, did the Court persist in proceeding on such short notice and with such little input? Lawyers had only one day after leave was granted to file affidavits and then only one week to prepare their cases. Interveners (except for the federal government) were given only ten minutes of oral argument. As Peter Russell observed before the Court had granted leave:

> It is very difficult to accommodate her [Daigle's] timetable and still do justice to the issues. . . . You do not want to produce it [a constitutional ruling on abortion] in a hothouse, emergency atmosphere. This opinion will be with us for centuries.[37]

Once Daigle's pregnancy was terminated, so was the "emergency." Why did the Court deem it necessary to continue?

The suspicion of critics was reinforced by a second aspect of the *Daigle* decision: its very clear and very negative implications for a *Borowski*-like Charter challenge to any future federal abortion law. Technically speaking, *Daigle* had no direct impact on section 7 Charter claims on behalf of the fetus. The Court avoided addressing Charter issues because of the lack of any "state action." The focus of the Court's analysis of fetal rights was the Quebec Charter, not the Canadian Charter. Yet anyone familiar with *Borowski* could recognize fatal similarities between the two. The concept "human being" (the term used in the Quebec Charter) was inherently broader than "person" (the term used in the Canadian Charter), and thus more capable of a judicial construction that included the fetus or unborn child. If pro-life advocates could not persuade the Court that the fetus was a human being, especially when the particular fetus in question was twenty-two weeks old, then it was unlikely they could ever persuade the Court that the fetus, in the abstract, was a "person."

A future pro-life claim under section 7 of the Charter would also have to contend with the method of interpretation used in *Daigle.* In *Borowski,* Morris Shumiatcher had urged the Court to adopt a "purposive" approach to Charter interpretation, then bombarded the judges with scientific and medical evidence to show that the "persons" branch of the "living tree" now included the unborn. In *Daigle,* the Court ignored the "purposive" approach in favour of strict fidelity to the intent of the framers as they construed it. It also curtly rejected the use of scientific evidence as an illegitimate attempt "to settle a legal debate by non-legal means." Without a wholesale change of heart (or personnel) on the Canadian Supreme Court, it was hard to imagine any future pro-life Charter challenge surviving this obiter. Intentionally or otherwise, the Supreme Court seemed to have used the facts of *Daigle* to decide the issues of *Borowski.*

Joe Borowski had spent ten years and nearly half a million dollars to bring the issue of the rights of the unborn before the Supreme Court. He was told to try again if and when a new abortion law was enacted. Chantal Daigle had spent thirty days and had won.

At his initial trial in 1983, Borowski's lawyer, Morris Shumiatcher, had assembled a panel of nine expert witnesses in genetics, embryology, and neonatal medicine who testified as to "the individuality, separateness and the uniqueness" of the human qualities and characteristics of the unborn. This testimonial evidence was brought to the Supreme

Court, repeated by Shumiatcher, and challenged by pro-choice interveners. In *Daigle,* interveners had one day to file their factums, one week to prepare their oral arguments, and ten minutes each to present them. Although the Court stressed that mootness *per se* was no longer an absolute barrier to continuing, it applied the traditional concept of mootness to discontinue Borowski's case. Once Daigle had proceeded with her abortion, her case was equally moot. Why, under these circumstances, sceptics wondered, had the Court persisted in deciding the issue of fetal rights? Why had it treated *Borowksi* and *Daigle* so differently?

The Court's sharply contrasting approaches to Charter interpretation in the *Daigle* and *Morgentaler* cases also raised questions about judicial bias. Why did the Court adopt a narrow and legalistic approach to determine fetal rights, but a broad, purposive approach to decide abortion rights? In *Morgentaler,* Chief Justice Dickson began by declaring:

> The goal of Charter interpretation is to secure for all people "the full benefit of the Charter's protection". To attain that goal, this Court has held consistently that the proper technique for the interpretation of Charter provisions is to pursue a "purposive" analysis of the right guaranteed. A right recognized in the Charter is to be understood . . . in the light of the interests it was meant to protect.[38]

To discover the "interests [the Charter section] was meant to protect" the judges must of course identify the "underlying philosophy" that in turn allows the Court to add "implied" meaning. In practice, the invocation of a purposive interpretation almost always serves as a prelude to a widening of the scope of the right in question. Justice Wilson's "discovery" of an implied right to abortion and Chief Justice Dickson's very broad definition of security of the person both typified the results of a purposive approach.

By contrast, in the *Daigle* judgment there was no mention of a purposive approach. Instead, the Court was consumed by fidelity to the framers' intent. The Court was probably correct in *Daigle* when it reasoned that "If the legislature had wished to grant fetuses the right to life, then it seems unlikely that it would have left the protection of this right to such happenstance." But this was precisely Justice McIntyre's point in his *Morgentaler* dissent: "the Charter is entirely silent on the point of abortion," and the legislative history made it clear that this omission was intentional. Why were the three plurality opinions in *Morgentaler* completely silent on the "intent of the framers"?

Similar contrasts were evident in the Court's assessment of the relevance of non-legal reasons in the two cases. In *Daigle*, the Court adopted a very narrow view of relevant information: "Decisions based upon broad social, political, moral and economic choices are more appropriately left to the legislature."[39] This position was difficult to square with the Court's behaviour in *Morgentaler*, where the majority opinions relied extensively on the "social facts" presented in the Badgley and Powell reports, research that had been commissioned by legislatures to serve legislative decision-making.

The Court's exclusion of "scientific" evidence in *Daigle* was hard to reconcile with the judicial discussions of fetal development, trimesters, and viability in *Morgentaler*. Indeed, after her emphasis on viability as the permissible point for state intervention to protect the fetus, one might have expected Justice Wilson to attach some significance to the advanced state of Chantal Daigle's pregnancy, with the "baby" on the threshold of viability. This was an important consideration in the majority judgments in the Quebec Court of Appeal.

In *Daigle*, the Court eschewed any "philosophical and theological debates about whether the fetus is a person."[40] Yet in *Morgentaler* Justice Wilson quoted freely from John Stuart Mill's theory of liberty ("pursuing our own good in our own way . . . so long as we do not attempt to deprive others of theirs")[41] to support her interpretation of the right to liberty in section 7. Such recourse to philosophy was not unusual in the Court's earlier Charter jurisprudence. The Court's frequent "purposive approach" to Charter interpretation often drove the judges "beyond text" and into the realm of political and legal theory. Their early Charter decisions were liberally sprinkled with excerpts from political and legal theorists such as Mill, Alexis de Tocqueville, Ronald Dworkin, John Rawls, H.L.A. Hart, and others. As one critic of the *Daigle* decision observed, "If metaphysical arguments are or may be 'relevant,' why were they not considered? And if scientific arguments are not 'determinative,' they must by implication at least be relevant. Why were these ignored?"[42]

Questions such as these challenged the view that *Daigle*, like *Borowski*, was another example of the Supreme Court's deference to legislative handling of abortion policy. At the most explicit and obvious level, this view of judicial self-restraint was accurate. But at a more subtle level, there was contradictory evidence. The *Daigle* majority used the methods of the *Morgentaler* minority. Why had the Court exercised the techniques of judicial self-restraint when ruling on the rights of the unborn, but the tools of judicial activism when dealing with the rights of the mother?

CHAPTER 23

Parliament Tries Again

The Supreme Court's three abortion decisions still left Parliament with a relatively free hand to craft a new abortion law. While the Court acquitted Morgentaler, told Borowski to go home, and affirmed the legality of Daigle's decision to abort, it had avoided broad, sweeping pronouncements on either a woman's right to abortion or, to a lesser extent, the fetus's right to life. The Canadian Court did not repeat the attempt by the American Supreme Court to construct a new national abortion policy in one bold stroke of the judicial pen. The ball was still in Parliament's court. In the wake of *Daigle,* the Mulroney government finally decided to act.

The abortion-injunction cases had embarrassed the Tory government. Prime Minister Mulroney, viewing them as a consequence of the post-*Morgentaler* policy vacuum, saw them as posing an issue of leadership.[1] Within a month of the *Daigle* decision, Mulroney formed a caucus committee composed of both pro-life and pro-choice MPs and ordered them to reach a consensus. They reported back several weeks later with a compromise measure, which the government introduced in the House of Commons on November 3, 1989, as Bill C-43.

Bill C-43 would have made it an indictable offence to "induce an abortion" unless "induced by or under the direction of a medical practitioner who is of the opinion that if the abortion were not induced, the health or life of the female person would be likely to be threatened." The bill went on to define "health" as including "physical, mental and psychological health." "Medical practitioner" was left to provincial definition and was thus not limited to doctors. "Opinion" was defined as "an opinion formed using generally accepted standards of the medical profession." The maximum penalty for violating these restrictions was set at two years.

The imprint of the *Morgentaler* decision on Bill C-43 was clear. The government was proposing procedural but not substantive changes. It had ignored Wilson's solo position on a woman's liberty to decide abortion for herself and instead had closely followed the reasoning of the Dickson-Lamer opinion. Bill C-43 would retain abortion in the Criminal Code but throw out the old TAC mechanism, making abortion legally available on the opinion of a single doctor of the pregnant woman's choice. "Health" was left undefined in the old abortion law and thus subject to wide variations in interpretation – the target of Dickson's criticism. Bill C-43 made explicit that health was to be given the broader meaning of mental and psychological as well as physical health. Finally, Bill C-43 did not restrict abortions to accredited hospitals, a requirement that had restricted access and caused delays under the old law.

Bill C-43 was, as the government repeated constantly, a compromise measure. It said abortion was wrong in principle but available in practice. It still treated abortion as a crime but created a broader and more efficient exemption procedure than the old abortion law. As one legal expert put it: "It [was] anti-choice but it [was] not pro-life."[2] It was, in fact, the kind of compromise solution that is found in most Western European nations. In a comparative study of abortion laws in twenty Western democracies, Professor Mary Ann Glendon concluded that when the "legislative process is allowed to operate" in this controversial policy field, the result is likely to be a muddy, middle-ground compromise "that is apt to be distasteful to pro-life and pro-choice activists alike" but acceptable to the majority.[3]

In Canada, however, the legislative process did not operate in the manner observed by Glendon in most European regimes. Instead, the pro-life and pro-abortion extremes, which had dominated the earlier stage of courtroom politics, continued to play a leading role in the legislative arena. Certainly neither extreme of the abortion conflict was prepared to accept the compromises of Bill C-43. The front-page headlines in the *Globe and Mail* announced the bill's frosty reception: "Abortion bill draws hail of criticism; Lack of accessibility, protection for fetus cited."[4]

Caught in the crossfire of opposing criticisms, Bill C-43 was ultimately defeated. Although it was approved by a "free vote" in the House of Commons, 140–131, on May 22, 1990, both pro-life and pro-abortion MPs voted against it. This alliance of extremes against the middle failed largely because the "free vote" did not apply to the cabinet, which maintained its solidarity and voted *en masse* in favour of the bill. A similar critical mass supporting the legislation did not exist in the Senate, however, and there the "curious alliance of pro- and anti-abortion forces" prevailed, amassing exactly enough votes against the legislation to balance those in favour (forty-three votes were cast on each side). Since a tie is considered a defeat under Senate rules, the legislation died. The government announced that it would make no further attempts to enact new abortion legislation.[5] In effect, the preferences of the pro-abortion activists, temporarily implemented by the Supreme Court in Morgentaler, had become established public policy: no law at all.

The failure in Canada of the kind of compromise common in Europe was no doubt attributable in part to the climate of polarized intransigence promoted by the black-and-white, rights-based quality of Charter litigation. From the day it was announced, Bill C-43 was attacked as a violation of the Charter. Liberal justice critic Robert Kaplan protested that Bill C-43 could not "meet the tests of the Constitution and the Charter" and urged the government to refer it to Courts before debate. NDP justice critic Dawn Black rose to declare that "there is a serious problem of access in this country, a problem the government has chosen to intensify."[6] Allan Hutchinson, a Charter expert from Toronto, wrote that Bill C-43 "provides an opening for the pro-choice supporters to air [this] whole issue of accessibility. The government has a constitutional obligation under the Charter to ensure that any legislative benefits are equally available."[7] Feminist Charter experts suggested that Bill C-43 also violated a woman's liberty under section 7 and was a form of "sex discrimination" prohibited by section 15.[8]

Not surprisingly, pro-life activists claimed that the bill violated the section 7 right to life of the unborn child, the issue the Court had declared moot in its *Borowski* decision. While the enactment of a law would solve the mootness problem, pro-life leaders were less sanguine about the prospect of judicial vindication of their claim. "We have wasted our time and thousands and thousands of dollars on Supreme Court cases," declared Stephen Jalsevic, a director of Campaign Life Coalition. "The pro-abortion people seem to have far more influence on lawyers and courts and judges. I think [litigation] will be the last thing on our agenda."[9] Nevertheless, despite this preference for the legislative arena, pro-lifers were no more apt than their pro-abortion counterparts to relent on principle in favour of compromise. Their tendency intransigently to stand on principle had many sources, but it was encouraged and strengthened by the polarizing nature of the politics of rights.

CHAPTER 24

The Politics of Rights

The abortion trilogy illustrates how much and how fast the Charter of Rights has changed Canadian politics. Less than twenty-five years ago, the federal government enacted major reforms to the abortion law. During this long and controversial process, there was never once a suggestion to use a court challenge to try to influence the process of abortion law reform. Interest-group use of litigation was perceived as an illegitimate attempt to do an "end run" around "responsible government." From start to finish, the 1969 reform was entirely a government-parliamentary matter.

Within six years, this had begun to change. Encouraged by the American Supreme Court's 1973 abortion decision, *Roe v. Wade,*[1] Henry Morgentaler set out on a one-man crusade of civil disobedience to challenge Canada's abortion law. The Supreme Court of Canada thought so little of his *Roe*-inspired "right to privacy" argument that they rejected it *during* oral argument, told the Crown that it need not even reply, and subsequently sent Henry Morgentaler to prison. Eleven years later, the same man was back in the same court challenging the same law, only this time his arguments were based on the Charter of Rights and this time he won. The Supreme Court declared Canada's abortion law unconstitutional. What had been unthinkable in the sixties, and impossible in the seventies, became a reality in the eighties.

Morgentaler's ultimate victory was remarkable not just because it changed the abortion law, but because it cut against the grain of the Canadian legal tradition. In 1975, the year that the Supreme Court sent Morgentaler to prison, Kenneth McNaught, one of Canada's foremost historians, wrote that in Canada attempts to use the courts as an instrument for political change had rarely succeeded and were generally regarded as illegitimate, not least because they smacked of Americanism.[2] From the rebellion of 1837 to the hanging of Louis Riel to the FLQ crisis of 1970, McNaught traced a common strand of Canadian commitment to the beliefs that "order must underlie liberty" and "resort to violence, no matter how just the cause, must be decisively condemned."[3] This belief in "ordered liberty" was still vital on the eve of the adoption of the Charter, as was evident in Justice Hugessen's 1974 sentencing of Morgentaler in Montreal. In sentencing him to eighteen months in prison, Hugessen declared that Morgentaler's "massive and public flouting of the law . . . set at risk the entire fabric upon which our society is founded" and represented the actions not of a "democrat" but an "anarchist."[4]

Only a decade later, the continued accuracy of this analysis became doubtful, suggesting still deeper changes in the Canadian polity. Government funding of interest groups and test cases contradicted the view that the use of the courts to pursue social change was illegitimate, while Morgentaler showed that it was even possible to succeed. Nor does civil disobedience evoke the automatic disapproval it once did. It was perhaps predictable that Morgentaler's example would be followed by pro-life activists. But public flouting of the law by large corporations, as in the Sunday closing controversies in Ontario and Alberta, was something novel. As for the tradition of not tolerating the political use of illegal violence, government responses to the Oka and Kanewake confrontations of 1990 suggested this, too, was changing. Collectively, these changes represented a waning of British influence and a waxing of American ideas and practices. There is a growing amount of evidence, both empirical[5] and anecdotal,[6] to support such a thesis.

The Canadian abortion cases cannot be explained by the Charter alone. The wording of the Charter was purposely silent on the topic of abortion and the right to privacy. The abortion trilogy can only be properly understood in the context of developments beyond the courtroom and the Charter. Like the acquittal of Dorothea Palmer in the 1937 contraception trial, Morgentaler's victory was as much an effect of social change as it was a cause. It reflected the emergence of feminism as a major force in Canadian politics.

Judges, of course, deny this, at least when they have their robes on. They like to compare their exercise of judicial review to a carpenter's use of a square: hard, precise, and impersonal. Both the majority and dissenting judgments in *Morgentaler* wrote that their task was simply "to measure the content of s. 251 against the Charter." This was also how Justice Estey explained the Court's decision to the public: we measured the abortion law by the Charter, "like a tailor measures a sleeve. It didn't fit, so we threw it back to Parliament."[7] In cases like the abortion trilogy, this type of talk cannot be taken seriously by non-lawyers, and in fact is not even taken seriously by lawyers when they are *entre nous*.

In practice a constitution functions more like a sponge than a carpenter's square, absorbing the never-ending shifts in political opinion and social values from one generation to the next. The medium of adaptation is judges, especially Supreme Court judges. The growth of feminist influence in Canadian political, educational, and legal elites was a necessary pre-condition for the *Morgentaler* decision. The Charter provided Morgentaler a new lever, but its successful use was contingent on a more receptive legal and political environment.

There was almost no feminist input into the 1969 abortion law reform. In 1975 there was a feminist presence but little influence. By 1986, when Morgentaler returned to the Supreme Court, this situation had changed dramatically. In 1982 the first woman justice, Bertha Wilson, was appointed to the Supreme Court of Canada. Wilson went on to write the feminist perspective on abortion into her concurring opinion in the *Morgentaler* decision. In 1987 a second woman, Claire L'Heureux-Dubé, was appointed to the Court. During this same twenty-year period, the number of women in Canadian law schools went from less than 10 per cent to almost half.

Stung by their lack of success under the 1960 Bill of Rights, feminists worked to influence the drafting of the 1982 Charter of Rights and then mobilized public support for its adoption. Aware that constitutional rights are neither self-interpreting nor self-actualizing, feminists put in place the various institutional means that would be necessary to actualize the potential of their Charter blueprint for sexual equality. The National Action Committee on the Status of Women helped to organize LEAF to conduct strategic litigation of women's rights under the Charter. Feminists were also active in the creation of the Court Challenges Program (CCP) in 1985, a $9 million fund to pay for equality (and language) rights litigation. LEAF in turn became the single largest recipient of CCP funding, including funding for its interventions in the *Borowski* and *Daigle* cases. (The feminist orientation of the CCP was confirmed by its rejection of funding requests from REAL Women in both these cases.)

These changes within the legal world reflected parallel changes in the larger political landscape. Feminists converted their legal defeats of the seventies into political victories. They persuaded Parliament to amend the Indian Act to end the disabilities that previously attached to Indian women.[8] Parliament was also persuaded to amend the Unemployment Insurance Act to cover all pregnancy-related unemployment.[9] While political elites still resisted many feminist policy proposals, they had become careful not to offend feminist sensibilities, for fear of bad public relations and political backlash.

Nor were the emergence of feminism and the abortion issue limited to Canada or even North America. Both emerged as new factors in the politics in most Western industrial democracies during the same period. Between 1965 and 1984, seventeen of twenty European and North American nations liberalized their abortion laws.[10] The social conditions that gave rise to both the movement and the issue – industrialization and the mechanization of physical labour, urbanization, the displacement of the industrial and farm sectors by the service sector of the economy, and the commercial availability of the birth control pill – were common to all seventeen societies. In other words, Canada would have had an abortion reform movement (and opposition) without either Henry Morgentaler or the Charter of Rights. What the latter two did was to give abortion politics in Canada a peculiarly legalistic character, unlike any other democracy except the United States.[11]

The emergence of feminism as a force in Canadian politics has been part of a larger reorientation of political conflict in Canada and other Western democracies. Feminism is only one of a cluster of new political issues that cut across the old class-based lines of political cleavage. These new "social issues," as they are sometimes called, also include environmental protection, state promotion of cultural pluralism and equal status for minorities, educational policy, disarmament and peace issues, and a more permissive sexual morality, including abortion.[12]

These issues have been collectively described as the politics of "post-materialism" because they do not track along the same lines of class conflict (or labour-management) that characterized politics in the industrial (or "materialist") democracies from the mid-nineteenth to the mid-twentieth centuries. The politics of post-materialism is concerned not so much with the redistribution of wealth between capital and labour as with the social issues. The post-materialist agenda tends to divide old allies and bring old adversaries together. The abortion issue, for example, has driven pro-lifers like Borowski and Shumiatcher out of the NDP. Similarly, the environmental movement has united old adversaries such as unions and management in the west coast timber, lumber, and pulp industries.

These new concerns are most prevalent outside the working classes. Seymour Martin Lipset has observed that in post-war Western democracies, the most dynamic agent of social change has not been Marx's industrial proletariat but a new "oppositionist intelligentsia," drawn from and supported by the well-educated, more affluent strata of society. [13]

> The reform elements concerned with postmaterialist or social issues largely derive their strength not from the workers and the less privileged, the social base of the Left in industrial society, but from segments of the well educated and affluent, students, academics, journalists, professionals and civil servants. [14]

In Canada, the Charter has served as a lightning rod for many groups of the post-materialist or New Left. [15] The connection of the Charter and post-materialism was evident in the conflict over the 1987 Meech Lake Accord. The Accord was originally conceived by the Mulroney government and the other nine provincial governments as a means to "bring Quebec back into the constitutional family." This was to be achieved by an omnibus constitutional amendment that would have recognized Quebec's status as a "distinct society" and its right to "protect and promote" this distinctiveness. In the end, the Accord was defeated by an *ad hoc* coalition of groups who said the Meech Lake Accord betrayed both the Charter and the groups it protected. Deborah Coyne, a leader of the Meech opposition, described her organization, the Canadian Coalition on the Constitution, as follows:

> The Charter's appeal to our non-territorial identities – shared characteristics such as gender, ethnicity and disability – is finding concrete expression in an emerging new power structure in society. . . .

This power structure involves new networks and coalitions among women, the disabled, aboriginal groups, social reform activists, church groups, environmentalists, ethnocultural organizations, just to name a few. All these new groups have mobilized a broad range of interests that draw their inspiration from the Charter and the Constitution. . . .[16]

Given the outcome of Meech Lake, the power of this coalition of "Charter Canadians," as Alan Cairns has described them, cannot be doubted.[17] Together with some improbable allies, the Charter Canadians achieved what was unimaginable only a decade earlier: the defeat of a constitutional amendment that enjoyed the support of all eleven first ministers and of the leaders of both opposition parties. While this coalition was initially spontaneous, it is now as entrenched in Canada's unwritten constitution as the Charter is in the formal Constitution. Indeed, each is the reflection of the other.

The Meech Lake affair may be seen as two different constitutions battling for control of the Canadian state.[18] One is the old constitution, with its roots in Confederation. The other dates only from 1982. The old constitution is the constitution of governments, federalism, and French-English dualism. Since this constitution belongs to the governments, its guardians believe it may be appropriately changed by the governments – by first ministers' conferences. Under it, constitutional politics is mainly a process of bargaining among political elites. Implicitly, this old constitution has always recognized the special status of Quebec. Meech Lake merely made this explicit through the "distinct society" clause.

The new constitution is the constitution of the Charter. It is concerned with individuals and their rights and freedoms. It is also concerned with group rights, but not in the old sense of only the French and English. The new constitution is multicultural and asserts the equal status of ethnic Canadians and aboriginals with the two founding peoples. Since this new constitution belongs to "the people," it should not be amended without their participation and consent. Charter Canadians objected to Meech Lake not only because of its content, but also because they were excluded from the closed and private process that produced it.

The Charter is, of course, uniquely Canadian, but the various social movements that have rallied around it are not. These social movements would certainly be present in Canada without the Charter. They would not, however, have gone so far so fast. The Charter has conferred the status and the institutional means to influence public policy more effectively. Because of the symbiotic relation these groups have with the Charter and the legalized form of politics it supports, I have elsewhere described these groups as the "Court Party."[19]

The opposite, however, is not true. Without a Court Party, the Charter and the Supreme Court would not have attained their new prominence. Post-materialism provided the political *zeitgeist* that breathed life and energy into the Charter by providing the army of true believers who lifted it out of the inert pages of the statute books and made it a vital force, and the courts powerful new actors, in Canada's political process. Some have described this as the "Charter Revolution." From the perspective of post-materialism, however, the Charter has been not so much the cause as the means by which the Court Party has pursued this revolution.

The abortion trilogy illustrates as well as any three cases could a new dimension in Canadian politics – the "politics of rights." The adoption of the Charter did not (with several important exceptions) create new rights so much as it created a new way of making decisions about rights in which courts have played a more central and authoritative role.[20] The Charter has created a new forum: courts; a new set of decision-makers: judges; and a new resource: not votes or money but simply the "right argument." Interest groups who "lose" in the traditional arenas of electoral, legislative, and administrative politics can now turn to the courts for a second kick at the can. This is the politics of rights, "the [new] forms of political activity made possible by the presence of [constitutional] rights."[21]

Interest-group litigation has been encouraged by both the Court and the government since 1982. The government's Court Challenges Program has funded hundreds of language and section 15 equality cases since its creation in 1985. Since one of the criteria for funding is the likelihood that the case will have "consequences for a number of people," interest groups seeking to make strategic use of Charter litigation have been the primary beneficiaries of the program. It has been estimated that over 80 per cent of the litigation grants go to interest groups.[22]

The Supreme Court itself has encouraged interest group use of Charter litigation through a variety of procedural rulings and decisions. Its 1981 decision in *Borowski* broadening the rules of standing made it easier for interest groups to get their feet in the door of the local courthouse. The Court's liberal interpretations of "mootness" culminating in the second *Borowski* decision made it easier for litigants (except for Borowski) to stay in the courts even after their disputes ceased to exist. Finally, the Supreme Court's "open door" policy for interveners has made it easy for groups who were not involved in the earlier stages of a Charter case to participate in the final appeal.

Nothing, however, has encouraged Charter litigation more than the Court's willing embrace of the noninterpretivist approach to assigning meaning to Charter rights. The effective sundering of constitutional law from constitutional text has maximized the discretion of judges, thereby giving almost all interest groups at least the hope of winning a test case on the back of a plausible interpretation of a Charter right, regardless of its original or intended meaning. Individuals and interest groups representing every ideological stripe – from the National Citizens' Coalition to the Canadian Union of Public Employees, from the Canadian Jewish Congress to anti-Semite Jim Keegstra – have flocked to the courts to claim the protection and assistance of the Charter. In the Supreme Court's first 100 Charter decisions, at least sixty-three interest groups were present as litigants or interveners in seventeen cases.[23]

The *Morgentaler* and *Borowski* cases are particularly telling examples of how the judicially induced malleability of the Charter's meaning can elicit constitutional challenges based on diametrically opposed interpretations of the same Charter section. How could section 7 of the Charter protect both a right to life and a right to abortion? The answer, of course, was that it protected neither, at least not explicitly. Both Morgentaler and Borowski claimed that these rights were "implied" by the broad contours of "life, liberty, and security of the person . . . [and] the principles of fundamental justice." When freed from the constraints of fidelity to original understanding, judges can and do create new rights that were not intended, or even were purposely excluded, as in the case of abortion.

Many Charter experts, following the lead of Justice Lamer's opinion in the *B.C. Motor Vehicle Reference,* have minimized the significance of judicial fidelity to the original or intended meaning of constitutional language by characterizing it as an American idiosyncrasy.[24] This "Canadian school" likes to subsume all constitutional law – the Charter, as well as federalism – under the benign shade of Lord Sankey's "living tree." Like most appeals to nationalism, this argument generates more heat than light. The issues underlying the interpretivist/noninterpretivist debate involve constitutional logic, not nationality. The debate is not one-sided, and it is a mistake not to take it seriously.

It is one thing to adopt the interpretivist version of the "living tree" imagery, thereby allowing judges to adapt the constitution to new factual situations. It is quite another to give judges a free hand to create new constitutional rules while working with the same old facts. The first adds new meaning, but the second changes the original meaning. The former is necessary to preserve constitutionalism over time. The latter challenges the very logic of a "written constitution." What is the point of "carving in [constitutional] stone," so to speak, the "binding" rules of a nation's politics, if judges are immediately free to amend the meaning intended by those rules. If flexibility and adaptability to social change are the most important virtues of a constitution, why did Canada ever abandon the "unwritten constitution" inherited from Great Britain, the ultimate in "living tree" constitutionalism.

Even if one accepts the legitimacy of non-interpretivist rewriting of the constitution, it would still seem more appropriate in the case of an old constitutional provision than a very recent one. After all, the standard justification of non-interpretivism is that living generations should not be bound by the constitutional decisions of dead ones. This argument is not without problems,[25] but to the extent that it is valid, it surely applies more strongly to such documents as the Constitution Act, 1867 than to the 1982 Charter. At the time the Court heard the Morgentaler appeal, the Charter was less than five years old and the appeal turned on Charter provisions where the intent of the framers was as clear as such things ever get.

In any case, the Supreme Court has been inconsistent on the issue of original intent. When it has suited their purposes – in cases like *Quebec Protestant School Board Association,*[26] *Alberta Labour Reference,*[27] and of course *Daigle* – the judges have been quick to hide behind the intent of the framers. This was not surprising. Indeed, it is how judicial review is supposed to work in theory. Judicial fidelity to original intent can enhance the authority of the Court's decision by making it clear, especially to the losing side, that the Court's decision is not based on the policy preferences of the judges but on the constitution itself. With its decision in the *B.C. Motor Vehicle Reference,* however, the Supreme Court denied itself this important support. Once the Court said in both word and deed that the framers' intent should receive only "minimal weight" in interpreting the meaning of a Charter right, future appeals to it tend to be viewed as opportunistic attempts to justify the desired result. Rather than evoking public acceptance of the Court's decisions, these sporadic appeals tend to inspire cynicism about the judges and ultimately about the entire Charter enterprise.

The *Morgentaler* and the *Borowski* cases illustrated the "politics of rights" writ large. Neither man represented the lonely individual who, wronged by the system, humbly came before the Supreme Court asking for redress. For both, the use of the courts was a calculated political choice. It was a choice based on repeated rejections by political parties and public opinion polls. Both were represented by some of Canada's best and most expensive legal talent. Their legal expenses – over a quarter of a million dollars each – were mostly picked up by the pro-choice and pro-life movements whose causes they championed.

The abortion trilogy also reveals different ways to use the Charter to influence public policy. The first is to challenge directly the validity of an existing law, the path chosen by both Morgentaler and Borowski. The debate over Bill C-43 reveals a second: to invoke the principles of the Charter (and the not-so-veiled threat of future litigation) to shape public policy *during* the legislative process.[28] When the first tactic succeeds in invalidating a policy, the second tactic may suffice to prevent its reintroduction in some amended form. The claim that a bill violates the Charter can be used to stigmatize the bill and mobilize opinion (within cabinet, caucus, or the public at large) against it. The more credible the claim, the less likely the government is to proceed with the bill.

This perspective also discloses the closer relationship between the courthouse and the legislative assembly under the Charter. Interest-group use of Charter litigation may be understood as legal battles in a larger political war. The objective of the litigants is not to enforce the law of the Charter but to use the Charter to change the law of the government. The Supreme Court's final rulings provided the winners with new resources with which to return to the larger political struggle. Legal defeat does not necessarily mean political defeat: consider Morgentaler's ultimate victory in Quebec in the seventies. Nor does legal victory ensure political victory: consider the apparent success of the pro-life movement in the United States to limit if not reverse *Roe v. Wade* in the *Webster* case. With these caveats in mind, however, success in the judicial arena is always preferable. In the Canadian abortion cases of the 1980s, the success of the pro-choice parties has helped them achieve their policy objectives for the foreseeable future.

This is the new Canadian version of the "politics of rights." The various rights enumerated in the Charter become "political resources of unknown value in the hands of those who want to alter the course of public policy."[29] Judicial pronouncements notwithstanding, the Charter is not so much the cause as the means through which such change is sought. Individuals and interest groups can recast their policy goals in the rhetoric of rights and then take them to the courts to be "enforced." Whether they succeed depends largely on how the judges exercise their considerable discretion to interpret the Charter.

Lawyers are trained to think about winning cases in terms of the "right argument." Cases like the abortion trilogy suggest that often it is more a question of the "right judge." The Court's unreserved (and inconsistent) embrace of noninterpretivism has maximized the judges' discretion to the point that they appear to be able to reach almost any result they want. This was certainly the appearance given by the four different judgments delivered in the Court's *Morgentaler* decision. Only one justice out of seven declared a constitutional right to abortion. The other four members of the majority coalition found only procedural violations of the Charter, and they were further divided on the seriousness of these violations. The two dissenters said there was no constitutional violation.

This division of the Court was not caused by technical disagreements over a narrow point of law. Rather, it reflected a growing division on the Court between two different theories of Charter review, two different conceptions of the proper role of the judge. During its first two years of Charter cases (1984-85), the Supreme Court was unanimous in 87 per cent (thirteen out of fifteen) of its decisions. In 1986, this figure dropped to 55 per cent and has remained at about 64 per cent ever since. During the same timeframe, unanimity in non-Charter decisions remained constant at above 80 per cent.[30] The fractured *Morgentaler* decision accurately reflected the growing division of the Court.

One wing of the Court, exemplified by Justice Wilson, adopted an activist, noninterpretivist approach to applying the Charter. As evidenced by her opinion in *Morgentaler,* Justice Wilson was inclined to read in new and even unintended meaning to the broadly worded principles of the Charter, and she was not reluctant to strike down parliamentary enactments that failed to meet her vision of the Charter. The other wing of the Court was best exemplified by Justice McIntyre's judicial self-restraint and interpretivist approach to applying the Charter. The Charter, McIntyre wrote, was not "an empty vessel to be filled with whatever meaning we might wish."[31] The McIntyre approach attempted to minimize judicial discretion by limiting Charter rights to their "original meaning," as disclosed (when possible) by the intent of the framers, and as a result was usually more deferential to Parliament's policy decisions.

These two different approaches to interpreting the Charter led to very different results. A study of the Supreme Court's first 100 Charter decisions revealed that the judges had very different "voting records" on Charter cases. Predictably, Justice Wilson had the highest percentage of votes supporting individuals' Charter claims, 53 per cent, while Justice McIntyre had one of the lowest, 23 per cent. The Court average was 35 per cent.[32]

The contrast between McIntyre and Wilson was still more stark when the number and "directionality" of their dissenting and concurring opinions were taken into account. The decision to write a concurring or dissenting opinion indicates a judge's dissatisfaction or disagreement with the majority opinion. Repeated use of concurring and dissenting opinions indicates that a judge is outside the mainstream of the court. Significantly, Justices Wilson and McIntyre wrote the most dissenting opinions, yet never dissented together.[33] Not only did they depart from the majority most frequently, but they did so in opposite directions. In each of her thirteen dissents, Wilson supported the individual's Charter claim. McIntyre supported the crown in ten of his eleven dissents. Twenty-eight of Wilson's thirty-one concurring and dissenting opinions supported a broader interpretation of the Charter than the majority. (*Morgentaler* was one of these.) In all sixteen of his dissenting and concurring opinions, McIntyre supported a narrower interpretation of the Charter.[34]

These statistics confirm what most Charter experts already knew: the meaning of the Charter, and thus the "existence" of a right, can vary from one judge to another. In many Charter cases, the policy preferences (conscious or otherwise) of a judge combined with his or her judicial philosophy are more likely to determine the outcome than the text of the Charter. Different judges "find" different rights. To put this point in context, if the justices of the Supreme Court had been as fond of fetuses as they were of bilingualism, Joe Borowski would probably be on the lecture circuit and Henry Morgentaler out of business.

A version of this previously heretical view was actually voiced by Justice Estey, *after* he retired from the Court, in an interview with the *Globe and Mail.*

> Justice Estey said it worries him that Canadians still do not realize how decisions vary according to the personality of each judge. As the misconception is gradually corrected, he said, people may lose respect and faith in the institution. . . . People think a court is a court is a court. But it is elastic. It is always sliding.[35]

In fact, it is less likely that people will lose respect for the court than that they will simply want to know more about a judicial nominee before he or she is appointed. As the political implications of this fact are recognized by affected political actors and interest groups, there will be growing pressure to appoint the "right kind of judge" to Canadian appeal courts.

To most Canadians, the political controversies sparked by the recent nominations of Robert Bork (1987) and Clarence Thomas (1991) to the United States Supreme Court were politically repugnant.[36] They were perceived as transparent attempts to control the meaning of American constitutional law by controlling the appointment of Supreme Court judges. Such attempts at "court-packing" appear to strike at the foundations of judicial independence and thus the "rule of law" tradition. For better or for worse, however, the Canadian Supreme Court's relatively activist and noninterpretivist approach to the Charter is likely to encourage a growing politicization of the judicial appointment process in Canada.

"Where power rests, there influence will be brought to bear."[37] This was written in the 1950s by a leading American political scientist to explain American lobbyists' concentration on administrative agencies. In the 1980s, this analysis provided an equally compelling explanation for the new attention being paid to judicial appointments to the American Supreme Court. There is no *a priori* reason to assume that this axiom does not apply equally to Canadian democracy, and events in the wake of *Morgentaler* revealed a new attitude toward judicial appointments. Angela Costigan, counsel for Choose Life Canada, a national pro-life lobby group, criticized the decision as "the expression of personal opinion by the judges," and indicated that in the future her group would try to influence the appointment of judges who shared its position. Norma Scarborough, president of the Canadian Abortion Rights League, responded by declaring that while her group had never tried to influence judicial appointments in the past, it would, if necessary, in the future. "We are going to protect our position as much as possible," she declared.[38]

When Justice William Estey announced his intention to resign from the Supreme Court two months after the *Morgentaler* decision, the search for his replacement immediately attracted the attention of pro-life and pro-choice groups. The *Globe and Mail* reported that "activists in the abortion debate and representatives of ethnic communities are lobbying hard. . . . Many members of the ruling PC Party's right-wing . . . are putting pressure on PM Mulroney to appoint a conservative judge." Member of Parliament James Jepson, one of the most outspoken pro-life Tory backbenchers, explained the importance of the new Supreme Court appointment: "We now have a chance to put men and women on the bench with a more conservative point of view." While emphasizing that he had never lobbied for a judicial appointment before, Jepson continued:

> But this one seems to have caught the people's attention. Unfortunately, with the Charter that Trudeau left us, we legislators do not have final power. It rests with the courts. . . . You have seen the battling in the United States for the [most recent] Supreme Court nominee. Well, it doesn't take a rocket scientist to see we have the same situation here now.[39]

In the end, the pro-life lobbying had no apparent effect on the government's appointment of Toronto lawyer John Sopinka to fill Estey's seat on the Court. But Jepson's comments represented a sharp break with past Canadian practice and were not an isolated incident. The year before, when the Mulroney government appointed former Manitoba Premier Sterling Lyon, an outspoken critic of the Charter, to the Manitoba Court of Appeal, Charter groups protested and called for some form of public scrutiny of nominees prior to appointment.[40] Demands for public screening of judicial candidates are not likely to disappear as political elites become more sophisticated in their understanding of the connection between the "right argument" and the "right judge."

These developments are consistent with the judicial appointment practices of other democracies with written constitutions and judicial review. Attention to the politics and judicial philosophies of would-be Supreme Court judges is also consistent with democratic norms of legitimacy. Most Canadians are no longer willing to accept the spectacle of an unelected Senate blocking government policy. (Even the

pro-choice *Globe and Mail* criticized the Senate's defeat of Bill C-43.)
The more the Supreme Court exercises its new power under the Charter, the more Canadians are going to want to know something about the backgrounds of their future constitutional rulers *before* they take office. To take just one example, when Bertha Wilson was appointed to the Supreme Court in 1982, no one noticed that five years earlier she had chaired a policy committee of the United Church that strongly endorsed liberal reform of the abortion law. It seems unlikely that this type of information would go unnoticed any longer. For better or for worse, the relationship between courts and politics is a two-way street. The more that judges influence the political process, the more political actors will seek to influence the selection of judges.

While the empowerment of judges under the Charter has inevitably drawn more attention to the judicial appointment process, the presence of the section 33 "legislative override" or "notwithstanding" clause may mitigate the more excessive forms of court-packing witnessed in recent American politics. The legislative override is unique to the Canadian constitution and provides an alternative means to deal with what a government views as an unacceptable or mistaken judicial interpretation of the Charter. Rather than using the blunt instrument of judicial appointment – which can leave its ideological imprint on the Court for years and even decades – section 33 allows a legislature to remove surgically, as it were, the effect of an unacceptable Charter decision without permanently "disfiguring" the composition of the Court. It seems unlikely, for example, that the more extreme examples of court-packing in American politics – President Roosevelt's in the 1930s and President Reagan's in the 1980s – would have been considered necessary if something like the section 33 legislative override had been available.

Many Canadian commentators consider this the vice, not the virtue, of section 33 – that it will make it *too* easy for governments to override Charter decisions. For evidence, these critics point to the best-known and most controversial use of section 33 to date: the Quebec government's decision to reinstate its "French-only" public signs law following the Supreme Court's ruling that this policy violated the Charter right to freedom of expression.[41] In the uproar that followed Quebec's use of the legislative override, even Prime Minister Mulroney declared that the Charter was "not worth the paper it was written on" so long as section 33 remained intact, and vowed to work for its removal.

These kinds of blanket condemnations of section 33 are premised

on a view of constitutional rights and judicial review that is more myth-
ical than real. The section 33 critics tend to think of constitutional
rights as judicially enforceable moral rules and draw a sharp distinction between the realm of rights and the realm of politics. Politics is
characterized as the realm of self-interest, driven by will and ruled by
compromise. Rights are portrayed as the realm of justice, governed by
reason and discerned by impartial judges. The beauty of the Charter,
according to this view, is that it lifts questions of rights out of the grimy
give and take of party politics and into a sphere where independent
judges, exercising reason, not will, can define and defend rights against
the excesses of majority-rule democracy.

The politics of rights, as illustrated by the abortion trilogy, serves as
an antidote to this "myth of rights." While the dichotomy of rights and
interest certainly animates the enterprise of constitutional rights, in
practice it is impossible to keep them distinct. As the abortion trilogy
illustrates, both individual and collective self-interest are usually
present in Charter litigation; nor are reason and consideration of principle absent from the deliberations of Parliament. The extensive development of interest-group litigation under the Charter, encouraged in
part by the Court's own decisions, ensures that political interests will
find their way into the courtroom. When judges determine what is or is
not a "reasonable limitation" on a Charter right by sifting and weighing
social facts, the distinction between judging and legislating is also
blurred. As Chief Justice Antonio Lamer observed on the tenth anni-
versary of the Charter, determining what constitutes "reasonable limitation" on a right is "to make what is essentially what used to be a political call."[42] At the same time, the existence of Charter precedents, combined with the threat of future litigation, ensures that legislators take
into account the same appeals to moral principles and fairness that are
heard in court.

In sum, the differences between courts and legislatures, while
important, are not as absolute as the critics of section 33 tend to claim.
Both must fashion law from an impure compound of interest and right.
Both must exercise practical judgment. Neither is infallible. From this
perspective, just as judicial review serves as a check on legislative
decision-making, so section 33 provides a check on judicial decision-
making. It is in this sense that Peter Russell has described and defended
section 33 as providing a form of "legislative review of judicial
review."[43]

The value of this contribution to institutional "checks and balances" is not just that it negatively blocks the "mistakes" of the other branch. It can also stimulate a creative and productive dialogue between the two different branches of government, each with its respective strengths and weaknesses. It would be just as perverse to require elected governments to acquiesce passively in every judicial pronouncement as it would be to encourage judges to approve meekly every legislative act. The latter would defeat the very purpose of judicial review, while the former would undermine any meaningful form of democratic self-government.[44]

Mutual persuasion, not coercion, is the medium of exchange appropriate to the challenge of giving concrete meaning to constitutional rights. Everyone recognizes the government's obligation in constitutional litigation to try to persuade the Court of the rightness and reasonableness of its legislation. Less obvious but no less real is the obligation of the Court to persuade the government of the rightness and reasonableness of its judgments. Indeed, the obligation to persuade is ultimately more incumbent on the Court than the government. Courts can coerce individuals, but, "possessing neither the purse nor the sword," they cannot coerce governments.

In the end, no constitutional court can hold out forever against sustained popular opposition. American history is littered with the metaphorical corpses of Supreme Court majorities who tried to block sustained political majorities.[45] Recent developments in France confirm that this is not an American idiosyncrasy.[46] Democracies do not tolerate for long courts that get too far ahead or too far behind public opinion. This does not mean that a constitutional court cannot lead or brake public opinion, but its success depends on its ability to persuade.

In Canada, section 33 institutionalizes and thereby formalizes this relationship between democracy and judicial review. In so doing, it creates the framework for a constitutional dialogue, not just between courts and governments, but also between political parties. The legislative override cannot be decreed by an order-in-council. Section 33 requires legislation, and legislation requires three readings and parliamentary debate. This ensures ample opportunity for opponents to criticize the government both inside and outside the legislative chambers. Moreover, any use of section 33 expires five years from the date it is proclaimed – the maximum time permitted between elections in Canada. This means that before a legislative override can be re-enacted, general elections must be held, thereby providing the opportunity for opposition parties to mobilize public opinion and to force the government to defend publicly its use of the override power.

Government by argument and persuasion is very much what parliamentary democracy is all about. A parliament is, after all, a place where people *parler* – or talk. In a liberal democracy – that is, in a society committed not just to conducting its affairs by majority rule, but also to respecting individuals and minorities – such talk will include talk about rights. In the most global sense, this "rights talk" is what the adoption of the Charter of Rights has brought to Canada.[47]

As today's university students (most of whom came of age politically *after* 1982) must be constantly reminded, the Charter did not bring rights to Canada. Canada was very much a free and democratic society prior to 1982. Its many imperfections notwithstanding, the Canadian record on human rights and civil liberties prior to 1982 would easily rank in the top ten in the world, and arguably ahead of the United States, which already had a constitutional bill of rights. What Canada did not have, however, was "rights talk." British constitutionalism and the belief in "ordered liberty" cast their long shadows over both the thought and speech of Canadian politics. "Peace, order and good government" were the trump cards of Canadian political rhetoric. Our ancestors enjoyed rights – or liberties, as they preferred to call them – but they did not talk a great deal about them. A decade after the adoption of the Charter, rights talk is all about us. Via the media, rights talk has spilled out of the courtrooms and into the surrounding social environment, permeating political discourse and behaviour.

The advent of rights talk to Canadian politics holds out both promise and peril. For most Canadians the positive contribution of rights talk is more obvious. It is an antidote to positivism, the idea that might makes right. It leavens democratic discourse by pointing to standards of justice that transcend "the will of the people." The appeal to rights can be used to challenge coercive assertions of self-interest and power. It reminds both governments and citizens that there is more to self-government than self-interest. Rights talk provides a rhetorical sword and a legal shield to groups and individuals who find themselves the target of majoritarian malice or government oppression.

Rights talk, however, also has its down side. This has recently been explored by Mary Ann Glendon, drawing on American political experience. The assertion of rights is often grounded in immediate self-interest, fuelled by the inarticulate but powerful sense that "I have a right to do what I want."[48] This kind of moral relativism is the very opposite of the traditional view of rights as standards of right and wrong that exist independently of individual or collective opinion. Motivated by selfishness and moral relativism, rights talk can contribute to a "hyper-individualism" that erodes the social and political fabric.[49]

Rights talk tends to carry the adversarial character of the courtroom into society at large, threatening to create natural adversaries out of those who were previously considered natural friends: parents and children, husbands and wives, teachers and students.[50] Since rights talk can express only self-interest, any inequality in these relationships is automatically presumed to prejudice the interest of the dependent party. The possibility of a mutually beneficial common interest or altruistic behaviour is denied.[51] In this respect, Glendon argues that rights talk represents only half of the political equation. Rights talk, she suggests, provides an incomplete political vocabulary, because it cannot express the equally important concepts of personal, civic, and collective responsibilities.[52]

Glendon reports that rights talk has also negatively influenced public debate and behaviour in contemporary American politics. She argues that rights talk has tended to inflate political claims with a moral absolutism, encouraging unrealistic expectations and making mutual understanding and political compromise more difficult.[53] Rights talk "promotes mere assertion over reason-giving" and can become "the language of no compromise," writes Glendon. "The winner takes all and the loser has to get out of town. The conversation is over."[54]

Glendon argues that abortion policy and politics in America illustrate the negative aspects of judicialized politics and rights talk.[55] While almost all of the European countries she studied had liberalized their abortion laws, most still provided some form of protection for the fetus. Typically, the abortion law was part of a broader family policy that included birth control, alternatives to abortion, and economic support for low-income or single-parent families. While an abortion could be rather easily obtained in these countries, the legislative framework sent out a message that it was not to be considered just another form of birth control and that there was public support for alternatives. Contrary to the "accepted wisdom" in the United States, compromise on abortion was "not only possible but typical."[56] How had the European democracies been able to achieve what appeared impossible in the

United States? Through the consensus-building made possible in the legislative process, concluded Glendon. In the U.S., by contrast, the Supreme Court's *Roe v. Wade* decision had "shut down the legislative process of bargaining, education, and persuasion on the abortion issue."[57]

How much of Glendon's analysis applies to abortion politics in Canada? It is important to remember that *Morgentaler,* unlike *Roe v. Wade,* did not shut the door on legislative regulation of abortion. Thus the central criticisms made of *Roe* are not applicable to *Morgentaler* and the Supreme Court of Canada. Still, the fate of Bill C-43 suggests that the polarizing effects of rights talk is at work in the Canadian body politic. As noted in the preceding chapter, the Mulroney government's attempt to fashion a new abortion policy represented a compromise. It said that abortion was still wrong in principle but available in practice. It was neither pro-choice nor pro-life. It also clearly followed the constitutional requirements articulated by four of the five judges in the *Morgentaler* majority. Notwithstanding these characteristics, it was defeated on the combined strength of the pro-choice and pro-life factions in the Senate, neither of whom would accept such a compromise.

While this outcome was not dictated by the Supreme Court's decision in *Morgentaler,* it was facilitated by it. After the decision, the rights talk inspired by the Charter encouraged moralistic confrontation and discouraged compromise. In the end, the pro-choice and pro-life extremes united to defeat a compromise abortion policy that had the support of the political middle. Canada thus joined, indeed surpassed, the United States as the only Western democracy not to provide at least symbolic support for the unborn child, while still respecting a woman's freedom to choose. Ironically, Canada's new "non-policy" goes even further than Dr. Henry Morgentaler thinks appropriate. Morgentaler believes there is no justification to abort a healthy and viable fetus in a non-threatening pregnancy after the twenty-fourth week of a pregnancy.[58] If rights talk has carried public policy even further than the chief protagonist for the pro-choice side thinks appropriate, this is surely evidence that it has not served Canadians well in this instance.

While the abortion trilogy represents only a thin slice of the Charter pie, it is a rich and revealing one. We must be careful about making conclusive judgments on the Charter based on the study of a single set of cases, but we can learn a great deal about the politics of rights. Whether one thinks that the Supreme Court made the right or wrong choices in these cases is less important than the realization that the judges were indeed making choices and not simply "applying the law of the Charter." To understand this is to begin to understand the Charter. A country can take its constitution out of politics, but it cannot take the politics out of the constitution. For this very reason, constitutional law is much too important to be left solely in the hands of lawyers and judges.

Postscript

In the early hours of Monday morning, May 18, 1992, a bomb ripped through the Morgentaler Clinic in Toronto. The force of the explosion punched a gaping hole through the brick exterior, crumpled interior walls, and spewed debris out onto Harbord Street. When the smoke cleared, the building was a total loss. There were no arrests, and, two months after the blast, no suspects had been identified.

Morgentaler and pro-choice activists were shaken and outraged. Harbord Street was much more than just another abortion clinic. It was a symbol of their struggle and eventual triumph. To see it blown to bits was viewed as a personal assault. Morgentaler bitterly denounced the attack and blamed pro-life extremists, possibly from the United States. Pro-life leaders denied any complicity in the attack. They also condemned the bombing, but not in terms strong enough to satisfy Morgentaler. Rev. Ken Campbell, president of Choose Life Canada, said that he did not condone the bombing, but added that his group had warned the government that "this would be the consequence of the failure to stop violence against humanity at facilities like this." "When we have state-sponsored violence," he added, "when as many human lives are terminated daily at this facility as in the explosion at the Nova Scotia mine,[1] then violence begets violence."[2] This hardly satisfied Henry Morgentaler, and two weeks later he angrily replied that the responsibility for the bombing must be placed on the "intolerance" of "fundamentalist religious groups."[3]

Beyond the fingerpointing, however, there arose a new and, for many, a more troubling question: Did the clinic bombing represent a further Americanization of Canadian society? While such attacks are no longer rare in the States (over 100 bombings and fires in the past ten years), this was a first for Canada. As CARAL president Kit Holmwood exclaimed, "This happening in Canada? I don't believe it."[4] The bombing stirred memories of the 1989 massacre of fourteen female students by gunman Marc Lepine at the Ecole Polytechnique in Montreal. Again, this kind of enigmatic violence was supposed to occur in the United States, not in Canada. What was happening? Canadians' sense of distinctiveness once again seemed vulnerable.

It was ironic that these re-awakened fears of Americanization occurred in the context of the Morgentaler Clinic and the Supreme Court's Charter ruling that allowed it to operate. The Charter itself has been a strongly Americanizing force in Canadian law and politics, and no case better exemplifies this trend than *Morgentaler* – an action whose architect actually conceived it as a Canadian version of *Roe v. Wade*. Indeed, at times Canadians seem more American than the Americans about "their rights." Concepts such as "responsible government" and "citizen" have all but disappeared from our political vocabulary. Canadians' new infatuation with rights was reflected in Prime Minister Mulroney's impromptu observation that the Charter was "not worth the paper it is written on" so long as the section 33 legislative override was available.[5] Interest group litigation was viewed as an illegitimate American idiosyncrasy only a decade ago. Today it is not only accepted but encouraged by public funding.

These visible symptoms of Americanization attest to still deeper changes in the Canadian political psyche. Until as recently as the 1970s, there was precious little official toleration of lawlessness as a form of political protest. In 1970 Prime Minister Trudeau used massive military intervention to snuff out the FLQ crisis and received overwhelming public support for doing so. Several years later two different appeal courts, confronted with Henry Morgentaler's civil disobedience, sent him to jail. As Kenneth McNaught observed at the time, these responses were consistent with the traditional Canadian view that "resort to violence, no matter how just the cause, must be decisively condemned."[6]

The aftermath of the May 18, 1992, bombing of the Morgentaler Clinic in Toronto. (*Courtesy Canapress Photo Service*)

How distant these images and this maxim seem from Canada today. The tactics that landed Henry Morgentaler in jail in the 1970s made him a celebrity in the 1980s. Perhaps it was inevitable that pro-life activists would adopt Morgentaler's own tactics of civil disobedience to obstruct access to abortion clinics. But the practice of civil disobedience has not been confined to the battlefield of abortion. Canadians have been treated to the spectacle of wealthy Toronto furrier Paul Magdar publicly flouting Ontario's secular Sunday-closing law, not in the name of moral principle but simply to make more money. Of course, the financial appeal of Sunday shopping was not limited to furriers, and soon Loblaws, Eaton's, and other corporate giants were also opening for business on Sunday, the law notwithstanding. This practice of "corporate civil disobedience," where pillars of the establishment publicly flout the rules of the establishment, would have been unthinkable in the Canada of the seventies. What began as an isolated incident of civil disobedience at the outset of the eighties had become a growing fashion by the close of the decade.

The rising incidence of civil disobedience had been accompanied by a parallel increase in acts of uncivil disobedience: the violent confrontations by native activists at Oka and Kanawake in Quebec during the summer of 1990; the use of guns by the native "Lone Fighters" to block the Oldman River Dam in Alberta during the summer of 1991; the mini-race riot in Toronto in May, 1992. Rather than unconditionally condemn such use of illegal violence (the instinctive response of the "old Canada"), some leading arbiters of public opinion implicitly defended the perpetrators of violence by blaming the incidents on Canadian racism. The bombing of the Morgentaler Clinic came hard on the heels of the racial violence in Toronto in May, 1992, claiming its place as the latest incident of uncivil disobedience.

Some might protest with reason that approval of civil disobedience does not mean acceptance of uncivil disobedience, such as at Oka or in the Morgentaler bombing. But can a society embrace one without inviting the other? Does lowering the threshold for one necessarily lower the threshold for the other? And, indeed, where is the line drawn between civil and uncivil disobedience? Such pro-life advocates as Joe Borowski would claim, for example, that the more than 5,000 abortions Morgentaler performed prior to his initial arrest were violent, uncivil acts of disobedience. He was not, after all, simply refusing to pay taxes or engaging in a hunger strike.

Others might object that the recent incidents of uncivil disobedience – Oka, Oldman River Dam, the Toronto riot, the abortion clinic bombing – are not equivalent, but this is simply because they sympathize with the perpetrators of the violence in some incidents but not in others. While it is only human to play favourites, it is naive to think that a society can pick and choose which groups use uncivil disobedience. If we are going to develop the habit of forgiving (by way of explaining) lawlessness in the name of causes we support, we had better be prepared for lawlessness in the name of causes we oppose as well.

There is also more than a little irony in Henry Morgentaler's condemnation of moral zealotry and call for "reasoned, democratic discourse" on abortion policy. His own behaviour – in which he broke the law not once to trigger a test case, but thousands of times – did not show much "respect for opponents even while disagreeing with them."[7] More importantly, this impatience with the politics of consensus is actually encouraged by the Charter.

Judicial review of constitutional rights represents a legalized substitute for the "right to revolution," the right to refuse to obey unjust laws. It thus shares a common root with civil disobedience. Most versions of modern liberal political theory hold that a citizen is not obliged to obey an unjust law, i.e., one that violates his or her rights. While this "right of revolution" makes perfect sense in theory, in practice armed insurrection is too dangerous to exercise, both for the aggrieved individual and for society. Constitutionally entrenching rights that are enforceable via judicial review provides a more practical alternative: if a law violates your rights, you can go to the courts and ask that the law be declared invalid. Judicial review sublimates and thereby domesticates the theoretical "right of revolution."

While this solution appears neat in theory, it can become dangerous in practice if the moral threshold that triggers rights claims – and the rejection of government based on the consent of the governed – becomes too low. This was the view of leading American constitutional scholar Alexander Bickel at the end of the sixties. When asked if the problem with American politics was lack of morality, he responded that the problem was just the opposite; that there was too much morality in American politics.[8] Democracy, or government by consensus, Bickel warned, "cannot sustain the continuous assault of moral imperatives." Moral oversensitivity is as threatening as moral obtuseness.[9]

Bickel's criticism clearly applies to the persons who bombed the

Morgentaler Clinic and anyone who condones it. But the warning also applies to individuals and groups who would wrap themselves and their political objectives in the Charter and "demand their rights." When groups claim their cause is the "moral equivalent of war," democracy and the rule of law are in for trouble. The "moral majority" is usually singled out as the culprit of this kind of self-righteous intolerance. But what about the "moral minority"? Does the fact that moral views are strongly held by a minority (rather than a majority) give them any more right to impose their preferred policies on the rest of society in the name of "rights"?

Moral zealotry is not a monopoly of majorities or minorities, of the right or the left. In whatever form, it is the enemy of liberal democracy. Liberal democracy was born in the eighteenth century largely to combat moral zealotry of a religious nature. Religious zealots still exist, but the ideological carnage of the twentieth century suggests that we have far more to fear from zealots devoted to secular causes.

The Charter hardly threatens us with such calamities. But it does harbour a tendency toward moral stridency, toward government by edict and coercion rather than by conversation and persuasion. This tendency must be recognized and resisted. The Charter is not a moral *deus ex machina* that can be periodically invoked to rescue Canadian society from itself. This view is an impoverished and ultimately dangerous understanding of political justice. The Charter and the appeal to rights must be placed in the context of Canada's traditional and richer understanding of political society: "The moral consensus of a free state is not something mysteriously prior to or above politics; it is the civilizing activity of politics itself."[10]

Notes

Preface

1. Anthony Lewis, *Gideon's Trumpet* (New York: Vintage Books, 1966).
2. Carl Baar, "Using Process Theory to Explain Judicial Decision-Making," *Canadian Journal of Law and Society* (1986), 64-65.
3. Alphonse de Valk, *Morality and Law in Canadian Politics: The Abortion Controversy* (Montreal: Palm Publishers, 1974).
4. Eleanor Wright Pelrine, *Morgentaler: The Doctor Who Couldn't Turn Away,* 2nd ed. (Halifax: Goodread Biographies, 1983).
5. Anne Collins, *The Big Evasion: Abortion, the Issue That Won't Go Away* (Toronto: Lester & Orpen Dennys, 1985).
6. Rainer Knopff and F.L. Morton, *Charter Politics* (Toronto: Nelson Canada, 1992).

Chapter 1

1. Unlike Canada, in the United States ordinary criminal law falls under state jurisdiction. There are thus fifty different criminal codes in the U.S. compared to the single, Federal Criminal Code for all of Canada. At the time of the *Roe v. Wade* decision, four states – Alaska, Hawaii, Washington, and New York – had already amended their abortion laws to allow therapeutic abortions for mental health and/or social reasons.
2. Anne Collins, *The Big Evasion: Abortion, the Issue That Won't Go Away*

(Toronto: Lester & Orpen Dennys, 1985), 12. Collins also uses this quotation in the title of one of her chapters, "The Progress of Unreasonable Men."

Chapter 2

1. *R. v. Bourne,* [1939] 1 K.B. 687.
2. See Lawrence H. Tribe, *Abortion: The Clash of Absolutes* (New York: W.W. Norton and Co., 1990), 28-29.
3. *Ibid.*
4. Alphonse de Valk, *Morality and Law in Canadian Politics: The Abortion Controversy* (Montreal: Palm Publishers, 1974), 1.
5. *Ibid.,* 1-5.
6. *Ibid.,* 9-18.
7. *Ibid.,* 22-23.
8. *Ibid.,* 35-42.
9. *Ibid.,* 43-48.
10. *Ibid.,* 48.
11. *Ibid.,* 72-80.
12. *Calgary Herald,* December 20, 1967, 2.
13. de Valk, *Law and Morality,* 57.
14. *Ibid.,* 105-08.
15. *Ibid.,* 110.
16. *Ibid.,* 111-13.
17. *Ibid.,* 115-18.
18. *Ibid.,* 119-26.
19. *Ibid.,* 121.
20. *Ibid.,* 81.
21. *Ibid.,* 108.
22. *Ibid.,* 126.
23. Larry D. Collins, "The Politics of Abortion: Trends in Canadian Fertility Policy," *Atlantis* (Spring, 1982), 3.
24. *Ibid.,* 5.

Chapter 3

1. See Robert M. Campbell and Leslie A. Pal, eds., *The Real Worlds of Canadian Politics: Cases in Process and Policy* (Peterborough, Ont.: Broadview Press, 1991), 12.
2. *Ibid.*
3. Eleanor Wright Pelrine, *Morgentaler: The Doctor Who Couldn't Turn Away,* 2nd ed. (Halifax: Goodread Biographies, 1983), 25.

4. *Ibid.,* ch. 1.
5. *Ibid.,* 14.
6. Interview with the author, November 14, 1991.
7. Pelrine, *Morgentaler,* 25.
8. *Ibid.*
9. *Ibid.,* 28.
10. Interview with the author, November 14, 1991.
11. "Free-standing" means an abortion clinic outside and independent of a normal hospital. Morgentaler and other pro-choice advocates argued that such free-standing clinics would be much cheaper and more accessible than the then current policy of only permitting abortions in certified hospitals.
12. Pelrine, *Morgentaler,* 34.
13. *Ibid.,* 80.
14. *Ibid.,* 83.
15. Henry Morgentaler, letter to the author, November 8, 1991.
16. "Report on 5641 outpatient abortions by vacuum suction curettage," *Canadian Medical Association Journal,* 109 (December, 1973), 1202-05. When Morgentaler was arrested the following month, the *CMA Journal* apparently decided to delay publishing the article until after the trial.

Chapter 4

1. See Ted Allen, "Meet Joe Borowski," *Winnipeg Tribune,* December 6, 1969, 3.
2. Pat Annesley, "The Outsider Moves In," *Maclean's* (December, 1970), 42.
3. T. Allen, "Meet Joe Borowski."
4. *Ibid.*
5. *Ibid.*
6. *Ibid.*
7. Anne Collins, *The Big Evasion: Abortion, the Issue That Won't Go Away* (Toronto: Lester & Orpen Dennys, 1985), 5.
8. *Ibid.*
9. Annesley, "The Outsider Moves In," 42.
10. Allen, "Meet Joe Borowski," 3
11. Interview with author, August 6, 1991.
12. Annesley, "The Outsider Moves In," 42.
13. T. Allen, "Meet Joe Borowski."
14. Annesley, "The Outsider Moves In," 39.

Chapter 5

1. These cases are discussed by Kenneth McNaught, "Political Trials and the Canadian Political Tradition," in M.L. Friedland, *Courts and Trials: A Multi-Disciplinary Approach* (Toronto: University of Toronto Press, 1975), 137-61.

2. See William Kaplan, *State and Salvation: The Jehovah's Witnesses and Their Fight for Civil Rights* (Toronto: University of Toronto Press, 1989).

3. McNaught, "Political Trials," 138.

4. *R. v. Palmer,* [1937] 2 D.L.R. 609 (Ont. Mag. Ct.).

5. See Angus McLaren and Arlene Tigar McLaren, *The Bedroom and the State: The Changing Practices and Politics of Contraception and Abortion in Canada, 1880-1980* (Toronto: McClelland and Stewart, 1986), 116-19.

6. *Ibid.,* 103-16. Recent attempts to portray Kaufman as a philanthropist are made somewhat suspect by Kaufman's own views of his project. Kaufman viewed birth control primarily as a means to reduce the tax burden of the upper classes by reducing the "over-population" of the lower classes. Kaufman believed that too many children in the lower classes constituted "an unbearable relief burden" and even "a menace to society." Before launching the PIB, Kaufman had encouraged and paid for the voluntary sterilization of the workers in his factory in Kitchener. His disillusion with the diaphragm programs run by the birth control clinics was based on his conclusion that "the lower types" were "too shiftless to cooperate properly." Like many of the early birth control activists, Kaufman was also a eugenicist; that is, he believed that government should discourage reproduction among the "lower elements" of society. McLaren and McLaren (pp. 111-12) report that "poor married couples with several children [were] his targeted clientele." Meanwhile, Kaufman thought the birth rate among the upper classes was already too low. His rather uncharitable view of the working classes was reflected in his response to data suggesting that his contraceptives were not as effective as he claimed. Contraceptive failure, Kaufman observed, was due more to "calibre of the parents" than the methods. Nor would it be easy to categorize Kaufman as a feminist. See note 7, below.

7. Kaufman clearly viewed the case as "his" and not Dorothea Palmer's. Indeed, he viewed Palmer as a potential liability because she was "not a desirable character" or "the sort of person he wanted to represent the PIB publicly." In order not to jeopardize the success of "his" case, Kaufman told Wegenast not to call Palmer as witness (thereby avoiding cross-examination) and ordered her not to speak to the press. At the end of trial but

before the verdict was known, Kaufman declared the trial a "success" regardless of the outcome – regardless, that is, of whether Palmer went to jail or not. After the verdict of not guilty was delivered, Kaufman promptly fired Palmer. See McLaren and McLaren, *The Bedroom and the State,* 116-19.

8. *Ibid.,* 118.

9. *Ibid.*

10. [1937] 2 D.L.R. 609, 616.

11. *Ibid.,* 619.

12. Eleanor Wright Pelrine, *Morgentaler: The Doctor Who Couldn't Turn Away,* 2nd ed. (Halifax: Goodread Biographies, 1983), 95.

13. Letter to author from Claude-Armand Sheppard, September 4, 1991.

14. Kaplan, *State and Salvation,* 235.

15. Pelrine, *Morgentaler,* 106-07, 110-11.

16. (1884) 14 Q.B.D. 273.

17. For a book-length account of this famous case, see A.W. Brian Simpson, *Cannibalism and the Common Law; The Story of the Tragic Last Voyage of the Mignonette and the Strange Legal Proceedings to Which It Gave Rise* (Chicago: University of Chicago Press, 1984).

18. [1939] 1 K.B. 687.

19. Pelrine, *Morgentaler,* 102.

20. Section 45. Every one is protected from criminal responsibility for performing a surgical operation upon any person for the benefit of that person if

    a. the operation is performed with reasonable care and skill, and

    b. it is reasonable to perform the operation, having regard to the state of health of the person at the time the operation is performed and to all the circumstances of the case.

21. Pelrine, *Morgentaler,* 115.

22. *Ibid.,* 118.

23. *Globe and Mail,* November 15, 1973.

24. *Ibid.*

Chapter 6

1. Eleanor Wright Pelrine, *Morgentaler: The Doctor Who Couldn't Turn Away,* 2nd ed. (Halifax: Goodread Biographies, 1983), 122.

2. Under American practice the state can appeal a jury acquittal through a "Bill of Exceptions." The appeal is limited to questions of law. The purpose of a Bill of Exceptions is to determine if the trial judge made an error in law, and if so, to prevent it from becoming a precedent. A successful

appeal, however, does not overturn the original acquittal of the accused. Under the American constitution, the accused cannot be retried because of the right against "double jeopardy" – being tried twice for the same crime.

3. Pelrine, *Morgentaler,* 123.
4. Criminal Code, Section 613 (b)(i).
5. Pelrine, *Morgentaler,* 124.
6. The other exception was when an appeal court was not unanimous in upholding a jury acquittal.
7. Pelrine, *Morgentaler,* 124.
8. Reprinted in Pelrine, *Morgentaler,* 131-32.
9. *Ibid.,* 136-37.
10. *Ibid.,* 139.

Chapter 7

1. Pat Annesley, "The Outsider moves in," *Maclean's,* December, 1970, 42.
2. Ted Allen, "Meet Joe Borowski," *Winnipeg Tribune,* December 6, 1969, 3.
3. Annesley, "The Outsider moves in," 42.
4. *Ibid.,* 40.
5. *Ibid.,* 38.
6. *Ibid.,* 40.
7. Anne Collins, *The Big Evasion: Abortion, the Issue That Won't Go Away* (Toronto: Lester & Orpen Dennys, 1985), 3.
8. *Ibid.*
9. *Ibid.,* 10.
10. "Borowski claims right to set moral standards," *Winnipeg Free Press,* May 14, 1971; "Joe sees Moral toboggan slide," *Winnipeg Tribune,* May 14, 1971, as quoted in Collins, *The Big Evasion,* 10.
11. "Text of Borowski Memo," *Winnipeg Tribune,* September 4, 1971, as quoted in Collins, *The Big Evasion,* 10.
12. *Ibid.,* 11.
13. Interview with author, August 6, 1991.
14. Collins, *The Big Evasion,* 4.
15. Interview with author, October 8, 1991.

Chapter 8

1. By the late sixties, a conservative reaction to the Warren Court's activism on behalf of liberal values had set in. Conservatives in the U.S. Senate blocked President Johnson's attempt to appoint a successor to the retiring Chief Justice Warren. Richard Nixon successfully campaigned for the presidency in 1968 on the promise to appoint "strict constructionists" to

the Supreme Court. Conservative "court-curbing" efforts escalated with the election of Ronald Reagan in 1980. See F.L. Morton, "Judicial Review and Conservatism in the United States and Canada," in Barry Cooper, Allan Kornberg, and William Mishler, *The Resurgence of Conservatism in the Anglo-American Democracies* (Durham, N.C.: Duke University Press, 1988), 163-84.

2. R.I. Cheffins, "The Supreme Court of Canada: The Quiet Court in an Unquiet Country," *Osgoode Hall Law Journal,* 4 (1966), 259-360.

3. The only the other instance was the intervention of the Lord's Day Alliance in the 1962 "Sunday Closing" case of *Robertson and Rosetanni v. the Queen,* [1963] 1 S.C.R. 651. The Alliance evidently feared that the Crown would not defend the Lord's Day Act with sufficient vigour.

4. Bora Laskin, "The Institutional Character of the Judge," *Israel Law Review,* 7 (1972), 329.

5. Sheppard and Flam presented a total of seventeen different arguments to the Supreme Court. Sheppard argued the seven that involved interpretation of the Criminal Code, common law, and procedural issues. Flam presented the arguments based on federalism and the seven Bill of Rights claims.

6. Greenspan has subsequently written that he would not make this argument again because he has changed his position on the abortion issue. For an interesting discussion of how a lawyer's morals influence what kinds of cases and arguments he makes, see Edward L. Greenspan and George Jonas, *Greenspan: The Case for the Defence* (Toronto: Collins Paperbacks, 1987), 292-95.

7. Greenspan's recollection of the incident was that de Grandpré was alleged to have said that if "he were given the rope, he would hang Morgentaler himself." (Greenspan and Jonas, *The Case for the Defence,* 295.) Sheppard has indicated that he never attributed this remark, or heard it attributed, to de Grandpré. (Letter to the author, February 10, 1992.)

8. Greenspan and Jonas, *The Case for the Defence,* 295.

9. Letter to the author, February 10, 1992.

10. Greenspan and Jonas, *The Case for the Defence,* 295.

11. Letter to the author, February 10, 1992.

12. Eleanor Wright Pelrine, *Morgentaler: The Doctor Who Couldn't Turn Away,* 2nd ed. (Halifax: Goodread Biographies, 1983), 142.

13. *Ibid.,* 144-45.

14. *Ibid.,* 146-47.

15. See Peter Russell, "The Anti-Inflation Case: The Anatomy of a Constitutional Decision," *Canadian Public Administration* (1977), 632.

Chapter 9

1. Eleanor Wright Pelrine, *Morgentaler: The Doctor Who Couldn't Turn Away,* 2nd ed. (Halifax: Goodread Biographies, 1983), 147-52.
2. *Morgentaler v. the Queen* (1975) 20 C.C.C. (2d) 452, 491.
3. *Ibid.,* 479, 469.
4. *Ibid.,* 461.
5. Pelrine, *Morgentaler,* 152.
6. *Ibid.*
7. *Ibid.,* 188.
8. *Ibid.,* 187.
9. *House of Commons Debates,* July 3, 1975, 7232.
10. Bill C-71, Omnibus Bill to Amend the Criminal Code.
11. Larry D. Collins, "The Politics of Abortion: Trends in Canadian Fertility Policy," *Atlantis* (Spring, 1982), 12.
12. *Ibid.,* 13.
13. Pelrine, *Morgentaler,* 187, 208. Also Bernard M. Dickens, "The *Morgentaler* Case: Criminal Process and Abortion Law," *Osgoode Hall Law Journal,* 14, 2 (1976), 246-47.
14. Pelrine, *Morgentaler,* 190. Anne Collins, *The Big Evasion: Abortion, the Issue That Won't Go Away* (Toronto: Lester & Orpen Dennys, 1985),143.
15. Pelrine, *Morgentaler,* 200.
16. *Ibid.*
17. Letter to the author from Claude Armand Sheppard, September 4, 1991.
18. Pelrine, *Morgentaler,* 213.
19. Letter to the author from Claude-Armand Sheppard, September 4, 1991.
20. The following year, the Manitoba Court of Appeal ruled that while an Attorney-General had the discretion not to prosecute a particular case based on its peculiar fact situation, there was no legal power to grant "a blanket dispensation [from enforcement] in favour of a particular group or race." *R. v. Catagas* (1977) 38 C.C.C. (2d) 296 (Man. C.A.). To allow provincial attorneys-general to enforce the Criminal Code selectively would undermine the federal government's power in this area. Also see *Controlling Criminal Prosecutions: The Attorney General and the Crown Prosecutor* (Law Reform Commission of Canada: Working Paper No. 62, 1990), 16-17.

Chapter 10

1. Anne Collins, *The Big Evasion: Abortion, the Issue That Won't Go Away* (Toronto: Lester & Orpen Dennys, 1985), 67.

2. "In camera: An Interview with Morris Shumiatcher," *Canadian Lawyer* (June, 1979), 33.

3. See Morris Shumiatcher, *Man of Law: A Model* (Saskatoon: Western Producer Prairie Books, 1979), 9.

4. *Ibid.*

5. *Ibid.,* 34.

6. *Ibid.,* 36.

7. Interview with author, August 10, 1991.

8. *Ibid.*

9. See Chapter 3, above.

10. "Borowski guilty of assault," *Globe and Mail,* April 20, 1979, 11.

11. "Refuses to pay his income tax, loses his new auto to sheriff," *Globe and Mail,* November 18, 1978, 11.

12. The Federal Court has both a trial and an appeal division. It is a "purely federal" court inasmuch as Ottawa creates and maintains it and also appoints its judges. Unlike the Supreme Court of Canada, however, the Federal Court is "itinerant": its members travel around the country to hear and try cases, rather than requiring litigants to come to Ottawa.

13. Peter Russell, *The Judiciary in Canada: The Third Branch of Government* (Toronto: McGraw-Hill Ryerson, 1987), 311.

14. *Ibid.,* 319-23.

15. In 1982 the Supreme Court of Canada ruled that this jurisdiction is shared. See *Jabour v. Law Society of British Columbia et al.,* [1982] 2 S.C.R. 307. The *Jabour* case was argued the same day as the Borowski appeal, May 27, 1981. Since the jurisdictional question was identical in both cases, it was not discussed in the *Borowski* case.

16. *Borowski v. Minister of Justice of Canada and Minister of Finance of Canada,* [1980] 5 W.W.R. 283.

17. *Borowski v. Minister of Justice of Canada and Minister of Finance of Canada,* [1980] 3 W.W.R. 1.

18. Alexis de Tocqueville, *Democracy in America,* ed. J.P. Mayer, trans. George Lawrence (Garden City, N.Y.: Anchor, 1969), 103.

19. 412 U.S. 669 (1973).

20. The concept of the oracular court is developed in Chapter 7, "The Oracular Courtroom," in Rainer Knopff and F.L. Morton, *Charter Politics* (Toronto: Nelson Canada, 1992).

21. [1924] S.C.R. 331.

22. *Thorson v. A.-G. Canada,* [1975] 1 S.C.R. 138, 162-63.

23. *Ibid.,* 101.

330

24. [1976] 2 S.C.R. 265.
25. *Ibid.*, 271.
26. *Ibid.*
27. *Minister of Justice of Canada and Minister of Finance of Canada v. Borowski et al.*, [1982] 1 W.W.R. 97, 100.
28. *Ibid.*
29. *Ibid.*, 103-06.
30. *Ibid.*, 107.
31. *Ibid.*, 115.
32. *Ibid.*, 116.
33. *Ibid.*
34. *Ibid.*
35. *Ibid.*, 117.
36. Collins, *The Big Evasion,* 49-50.
37. *Minister of Justice of Canada and Minister of Finance of Canada v. Borowski et al.*, [1982] 1 W.W.R. 97
38. Collins, *The Big Evasion,* 49.
39. Interview with the author, October 8, 1991.

Chapter 11

1. Ironically, a decade later, the Charter now appears to pose the single greatest obstacle to keeping Quebec in the Canadian confederation. Quebec's push for the Meech Lake Accord (1987-1990), and the "distinct society" clause in particular, was intended to blunt the impact of the Charter on Quebec's language, education, and culture policies instituted in Bill 101. In the wake of the defeat of the Meech Lake Accord, Quebec made it clear that the operation of the Charter in its present form was unacceptable.
2. Roy Romanow, John Whyte, and Howard Leeson, *Canada Notwithstanding: The Making of The Constitution, 1976-1982* (Toronto: Carswell-Methuen, 1984), 61.
3. *Ibid.*
4. The existing amending procedure still required the British Parliament to amend the British North America Act, 1867 to give effect to constitutional changes agreed to by the eleven Canadian governments. This procedure would have to be used one last time to bring a new amending formula into effect, but then subsequent amendments would be a purely "made in Canada" affair, thus the term "patriation" of the Constitution.
5. Romanow *et al., Canada Notwithstanding,* 216.
6. *Ibid.*, 217.

7. *Ibid.*, 96.

8. Quoted in David Milne, *The Canadian Constitution: From Patriation to Meech Lake* (Toronto: James Lorimer, 1989), 85.

9. Richard Gwyn, *The Northern Magus: Pierre Trudeau and the Canadians* (Toronto: McClelland and Stewart, 1980), 53.

10. *Canadian Journal of Economics and Political Science,* 24 (1958), 297.

11. *Ibid.*, 248.

12. *Minutes of Proceedings and Evidence* of the Special Joint Committee of the Senate and the House of Commons on the Constitution of Canada, First Session of the Thirty-Second Parliament, 1980-81, November 6, 1980 to February 13, 1981, 9:124.

13. "CCLA News Notes on the Constitution," February, 1981.

14. *Globe and Mail,* January 13, 1981.

15. *Minutes of Proceedings and Evidence* of the Special Joint Committee, 9:61.

16. The *Persons Case* is discussed at greater length in Chapter 13.

17. *Minutes of Proceedings and Evidence* of the Special Joint Committee, 22:54.

18. *Ibid.*, 24:99.

19. *Ibid.*, 22:24.

20. *Ibid.*, 29:36.

21. *Ibid.*, 33:58.

22. *Ibid.*, 34:116. Unlike the pro-choice groups, Campaign Life also objected to the Charter in principle, because it would effect "a shift in power from Parliament, which is subject to public opinion, to the Supreme Court of Canada, which is not" (34:117). Both sides thus anticipated that a Charter – or more specifically, the constitutional sub-culture that would shape Charter interpretation – would be more receptive to the pro-choice position. This anticipation proved prophetic.

23. The government did replace "everyone" by "every individual" in section 15, but this was intended to prevent corporations (i.e., artificial persons) from using the equality rights to challenge government economic regulations, especially restrictions on foreign ownership and investment. See Peter Hogg, *Canada Act 1982 Annotated* (Toronto: Carswell, 1982), 14-15.

24. *Minutes of Proceedings and Evidence* of the Special Joint Committee, 43:46.

25. *Ibid.*, 43:50.

26. Romanow *et al., Canada Notwithstanding,* 245-46.

27. *Ibid.*

28. *Minutes of Proceedings and Evidence* of the Special Joint Committee, 46:30.

29. *Ibid.*, 46:32.

30. *Ibid.*, 46:43.

31. *Ibid.*

32. *Ibid.*, 46:45.

33. Romanow *et al.*, *Canada Notwithstanding*, 257.

34. Anne Collins, *The Big Evasion: Abortion, the Issue That Won't Go Away* (Toronto: Lester & Orpen Dennys, 1985), 49-50.

35. *Ibid.*

36. *Re Constitution of Canada* (1981), 125 D.L.R. (3d) 1.

37. Michael Mandel. *The Charter of Rights and the Legalization of Politics in Canada* (Toronto: Wall and Thompson, 1989), 24-34.

38. Hogg, *Canada Act 1982 Annotated*, 314, as quoted in Mandel, *The Legalization of Politics in Canada*, 28.

39. R.S. Kay, "Courts as Constitution-Makers in Canada and the United States," *Supreme Court Law Review*, 4 (1982), 33, as quoted in Mandel, *The Legalization of Politics in Canada*, 28.

40. Mandel, *The Legalization of Politics in Canada*, 26.

41. *Ibid.*

42. *Ibid.*, 29.

43. *Ibid.*, 30.

44. *Ibid.*, 32.

45. Peter H. Russell, "The Effect of a Charter of Rights on the Policy-Making Role of the Canadian Courts," *Canadian Public Administration*, 25 (1982), 1-33.

46. Collins, *The Big Evasion*, 41.

47. [1981] 12 *Can. Parl. Deb.*, H.C., 13300.

48. Joannne McGarry, "Charter won't change abortion situation," *Western Catholic Reporter*, March 30, 1981.

Chapter 12

1. Luana Parker, "Interview with Dr. Henry Morgentaler," *Maclean's*, October 4, 1976, 4-12.

2. Letter to the author, November 8, 1991.

3. Eleanor Wright Pelrine, *Morgentaler: The Doctor Who Couldn't Turn Away*, 2nd ed. (Halifax: Goodread Biographies, 1983), 214-15.

4. Anne Collins, *The Big Evasion: Abortion, the Issue That Won't Go Away* (Toronto: Lester & Orpen Dennys, 1985), 24, 30.

5. Committee on the Operation of the Abortion Law, *Report* (Ottawa, 1977), 17.
6. Larry D. Collins, "The Politics of Abortion: Trends in Canadian Fertility Policy," *Atlantis* (Spring, 1982), 13.
7. *Ibid.,* 14-15.
8. Collins, *The Big Evasion,* 33.
9. Badgley Committee, *Report,* 135.
10. *Ibid.,* 55.
11. Pelrine, *Morgentaler,* 219.
12. Letter to the author, November 8, 1991.
13. *Ibid.*
14. *Ibid.*
15. There was, of course, no guarantee that the necessary funds would actually be raised, and Dr. Morgentaler reports that in the end he was still saddled with a $100,000 debt that he paid out of his own pocket. Letter to the author, November 8, 1991.

Chapter 13

1. Anne Collins, *The Big Evasion: Abortion, the Issue That Won't Go Away* (Toronto: Lester & Orpen Dennys, 1985), 50.
2. *Ibid.*
3. *Ibid.*
4. *Ibid.,* 51-52.
5. Howard Burshtein, "Charter opens new horizons," *National* (Canadian Bar Association), February 2, 1984, 7.
6. *Ibid.*
7. *Transcript of Evidence and Proceedings,* 106-07. Official Court Reporters, Regina, Saskatchewan, May 9-13, 16-18, 20, 25-27, 1983. This transcript was subsequently published in book form by Alliance Against Abortion: *Trial for Life,* vols. I and II (Winnipeg, 1984). All subsequent quotations from the trial transcript are taken from these two volumes and are cited as *Transcript* with a page number.
8. *Ibid.,* 114.
9. *Ibid.*
10. *Ibid.,* 124.
11. Like Manning in the *Morgentaler* case, Shumiatcher claimed that several sections of the Charter were violated by section 251. In addition to section 7, he claimed the abortion law violated section 12 of the Charter, the right against cruel and unusual punishment; section 14, the right to be represented, in this case, before the TAC; and section 15, the right to the equal

protection of the law without discrimination because of age. These additional Charter claims were contingent on and hence subsidiary to the section 7 claim, since they would all stand or fall on the issue of whether the unborn child was deemed to be a "person."

12. *Transcript,* 128.

13. *Ibid.*

14. *Henrietta Muir Edwards v. Attorney-General of Canada,* [1930] A.C. 124 (P.C.).

15. *Ibid.*

16. Morris C. Shumiatcher, "I Set Before You Life and Death: Abortion – Borowski and the Constitution," *University of Western Ontario Law Review,* 24 (1987), 25.

17. *Transcript,* 137.

18. *Ibid.,* 622.

19. *Ibid.,* 158.

20. *Ibid.,* 214.

21. *Ibid.,* 211.

22. *Ibid.,* 205.

23. *Ibid.,* 85-86.

24. *Ibid.,* 246.

25. *Ibid.*

26. *Ibid.,* 250.

27. *Ibid.,* 260.

28. *Ibid.,* 275.

29. *Ibid.,* 288.

30. *Ibid.,* 287.

31. *Ibid.,* 330, 334.

32. *Ibid.,* 337.

33. *Ibid.,* 390.

34. *Ibid.,* 400-01.

35. *Ibid.,* 405. Sherman Elias and George J. Annas, "Perspectives on Fetal Surgery," *American Journal of Obstetrics and Gynecology,* April 1, 1983.

36. *Ibid.,* 414. John Fletcher, "Maternal Bonding in Early Ultrasound Examinations," *New England Journal of Medicine,* 17 (Feb. 1983).

37. *Ibid.,* 422-23.

38. Interview with author, October 8, 1991.

39. *Transcript,* 601-02.

40. Pat McNenly, "Surprise move in Regina abortion trial," *Toronto Star,* May 21, 1983.

41. Collins, *The Big Evasion,* 70.

42. *Transcript,* 635.
43. *Ibid.,* 617-18.
44. *Ibid.,* 628.
45. *Ibid.*
46. *Ibid.,* 614, 618.
47. *Brown v. Board of Education,* 347 U.S. 483 (1954). For litigation strategy, see Richard Kluger, *Simple Justice* (New York: Vintage Books, 1977).
48. *Transcript,* 718-20.
49. *Ibid.,* 747.
50. *Ibid.,* 736.
51. *Ibid.,* 737.
52. *Ibid.,* 785
53. *Ibid.,* 789.
54. Hedonism and selfishness are standard pro-life critiques of the pro-choice position, but recently there are echos of these critiques among feminist writers as well. See Collins, *The Big Evasion,* 189-91.
55. *Ibid.,* 70.

Chapter 14

1. Anne Collins, *The Big Evasion: Abortion, the Issue That Won't Go Away* (Toronto: Lester & Orpen Dennys, 1985), 57-59.
2. Interview with the author, September 11, 1991.
3. *Ibid.*
4. *Globe and Mail,* May 6, 1983, 10.
5. *Globe and Mail,* May 7, 1983, 15.
6. *R. v. Catagas* (1977) 38 C.C.C. (2d) 296 (Man. C.A.).
7. Collins, *The Big Evasion,* 63.
8. *Globe and Mail,* February 3, 1983, C7.
9. Interview with the author, February 3, 1992. In fact, after the preliminary inquiry Penner did stay charges against five of those who had been charged along with Morgentaler.
10. Collins, *The Big Evasion,* 64.
11. *Ibid.,* 63.
12. *Globe and Mail,* May 8, 1983, 8.
13. Collins, *The Big Evasion,* 59.
14. *Ibid.*
15. *Ibid.,* 71.
16. *Ibid.,* 59.
17. *Ibid.,* 72.
18. This is precisely what eventually happened. After the Supreme Court of

Canada struck down section 251 in January, 1988, Manitoba dropped the charges; the seized equipment was returned and the clinic reopened. However, Morgentaler remained personally bitter toward Penner about his treatment in Manitoba. He described Penner's refusal to control the police or the prosecutors as "a slap in the face of the NDP tradition." After it was all over, Morgentaler mused that "the odd thing was that the NDP government of Manitoba prosecuted me and my associates with much more vigour than did the conservative, Tory government of Ontario." Letter to the author, November 7, 1991.

19. *Globe and Mail,* June 8, 1983, 5.

20. Collins, *The Big Evasion,* 73. The extent of Morgentaler's initial involvement in the Toronto clinic has become somewhat of a controversy. Collins (see pp. 73, 78, 79) writes that in the beginning Norma Scarborough and a handful of other Toronto women took the initiative. They met with Morgentaler at least once but only for advice. Morgentaler sees it differently, claiming that "I was in on the planning of the Toronto clinic from the start and both of these groups knew that and otherwise they would not have gotten involved." Letter to the author, November 8, 1991.

21. Letter to the author, November 8, 1991.

22. Collins, *The Big Evasion,* 79-80.

23. *Rights, Freedoms and the Courts: A Practical Analysis of the Constitution Act, 1982* (Toronto: Edmond/Montgomery, 1975).

24. Morris Manning, interview with the author, October 10, 1991.

25. Collins, *The Big Evasion,* 121.

26. *Globe and Mail,* July 4, 1985, M1, M6.

27. Collins, *The Big Evasion,* 82.

28. *Globe and Mail,* June 16, 1983, 1.

29. Collins, *The Big Evasion,* 83.

30. *Globe and Mail,* July 6, 1983, 1.

Chapter 15

1. *Globe and Mail,* July 7, 1983, 3.

2. Anne Collins, *The Big Evasion: Abortion, the Issue That Won't Go Away* (Toronto: Lester & Orpen Dennys, 1985), 84-85.

3. *Ibid.*

4. *Ibid.,* 93.

5. *Ibid.,* 87. Morgentaler disputes the accuracy of Collins's account, stating that "throughout this period I had maintained an excellent relationship with the leadership of CEAC and OCAC and it was clear to all of

them that the clinic could not have been started and the objective not attained without me." The dissension, he added, was "mostly sour grapes from a few people who were strident and difficult within the group and who eventually left." (Letter to the author, November 8, 1991.) These views are not mutually exclusive. As Norma Scarborough has recalled, it was a volatile coalition filled with high-energy people with diverse political views. "Conflicts were inevitable." (Interview with the author, March 4, 1992.)

6. [1984] 1 W.W.R. 15.
7. *Ibid.*
8. Morris C. Shumiatcher, "I Set Before You Life and Death: Abortion – Borowski and the Constitution," *University of Western Ontario Law Review,* 24 (1987), 1, 22.
9. *Ibid.,* 23.
10. *Globe and Mail,* November 10, 1983, 24.
11. Oral argument began on November 21, 1983, and did not finish until April 5, 1984. Justice Parker did not hand down his ruling until July 20. It was another three months (October 15) before the actual jury trial began.
12. This part of the hearing is described in some detail by Collins, *The Big Evasion,* 95-117.
13. See Donald Horowitz, *The Courts and Social Policy* (Washington, D.C.: The Brookings Institute, 1977), 45-49.
14. Laskin specifically requested the various parties and interveners in the 1976 *Anti-Inflation Reference* to present empirical evidence as to the extent of the "economic emergency" and the effectiveness of wage and price controls in combatting inflation. See Peter H. Russell, "The Anti-Inflation Case: The Anatomy of a Constitutional Case," *Canadian Public Administration* (1977), 632.
15. Collins, *The Big Evasion,* 131.
16. *Ibid.,* 119.
17. *Ibid.,* 121.
18. Manning's Charter arguments, other than the section 7 "liberty" argument, included the following. They are discussed in more detail below in the section on the Supreme Court's decision in the second Morgentaler case. (1) Section 251 violates a woman's freedom of religion and conscience, contrary to section 2(a) of the Charter. (2) The lack of a right of appeal from the decision of a TAC violates the procedural rights set out in section 7. (3) The concept of "health" used in section 251 is so undefined and unclear as to violate the "void for vagueness" principle incorporated in section 7 of the Charter. (4) Section 251 constitutes cruel and unusual punishment,

contrary to section 12. (5) The uneven application of the abortion law across Canada violates the equal benefit of the law provision of section 15.

    Manning also presented four non-Charter arguments: (1) that section 251 violates the federal division of powers because it is not really criminal law but law in relation to health policy, and thus falls under provincial jurisdiction; (2) that section 251 is an unconstitutional delegation of legislative power to the Minister of Health; (3) that section 251 confers on TACs a quasi-judicial power in violation of section 96 of the Constitution Act; (4) that the prosecution of the defendants in Ontario constituted an abuse of process by the Crown, since the Crown was not enforcing the same law in Quebec and one of the defendants had already been acquitted of similar charges three times.

19. Morris Manning, interview with author, October 10, 1991.
20. Collins, *The Big Evasion*, 125.
21. The legislative intent behind section 7 is discussed in Chapter 11.
22. Collins, *The Big Evasion*, 125.
23. *Ibid.*, 126.
24. *Griswold v. Connecticut*, 381 U.S. 479 (1965).
25. *Eisenstadt v. Baird*, 405 U.S. 438, 453 (1972).
26. *Ibid.*, 453.
27. *Lochner v. New York*, 198 U.S. 45 (1905).
28. *Roe v. Wade*, 410 U.S. 113 (1973).
29. The connection between judicial activism and politicization of the appointment process is discussed at greater length in F.L. Morton, "The Politics of Rights: What Canadians Should Know About the American Bill of Rights," *Windsor Review of Legal and Social Issues*, 1 (1989), 61-96.
30. Collins, *The Big Evasion*, 176.

Chapter 16

1. Bill Walker, "Selection of jury slowed down again at Morgentaler trial," *Toronto Star*, October 17, 1984.
2. Anne Collins, *The Big Evasion: Abortion, the Issue That Won't Go Away* (Toronto: Lester & Orpen Dennys, 1985), 250.
3. *Globe and Mail*, October 19, 1984.
4. John Terry, "Abortion Verdict Sparks Debate on Value of Jury Researchers," *Canadian Lawyer* (1985), 28-29.
5. Morgentaler has denied the accuracy of this figure but did not volunteer the true amount. Nor was it rebutted at trial.
6. *Globe and Mail*, November 1, 1984.

7. *Toronto Star,* November 9, 1984, A1.
8. "Morgentaler's lawyer defends jury selection," *Toronto Star,* December 15, 1984.
9. This account is taken from Valerie P. Hans and Neil Vidmar, *Judging the Jury* (New York: Plenum Press, 1986), 81.
10. Amitai Etzione, "Science: Threatening the Jury Trial," *Washington Post,* May 20, 1974.
11. Hans and Vidmar, *Judging the Jury,* 90.
12. *Ibid.,* 92.
13. Mike Crawford, "Are selection experts stacking juries?" *The National* (February, 1985), 30-31.
14. Hans and Vidmar, *Judging the Jury,* 90.
15. In the *Morgentaler* case, Marks and Fargo charged only for their expenses.
16. Crawford, "Are selection experts stacking juries?"
17. Harry Kalven, Jr., and Hans Zeisel, *The American Jury* (Boston: Little, Brown and Co., 1966), 493-98.
18. *Ibid.*
19. Terry, "Abortion Verdict Sparks Debate."

Chapter 17

1. "Abortion acquittal," *Globe and Mail,* November 9, 1985.
2. *Globe and Mail,* April 12, 1984, A1.
3. Affidavit of Dr. Janet Ajzenstat, filed with Supreme Court of Ontario (Court of Appeal), April 4, 1985.
4. *Ibid.*
5. Letter to the author, June 17, 1985.
6. *Perka et al. v. The Queen,* [1984] 2 S.C.R. 243.
7. Justice Wilson wrote a concurring opinion in which she argued the "justification" version of the defence of necessity should be retained. She illustrated this argument with the example of a doctor who performed an otherwise illegal abortion in order to fulfil "his legal obligation to treat the mother," citing Laskin's dissenting judgment in the Court's 1976 *Morgentaler* decision. This concurring judgment suggests that Wilson certainly had the Morgentaler trial in mind while deciding *Perka.* If accepted by a majority, Wilson's reasoning would have preserved the availability of a broader version of the defence of necessity for Morgentaler to use at his Toronto jury trial. This behaviour takes on special interest in light of Wilson's subsequent strong pro-choice judgment in the Court's 1988 *Morgentaler* decision. A legal realist would be quick to spot a common denominator to these unrelated decisions.

8. The following account is drawn from Winifrede Prestwich, "No License to break the law," *The Interim,* June, 1985, 10-11.

9. *Regina v. Morgentaler, Smoling and Scott,* [1985] 52 O.R. (2d) 353.

10. The framing of section 7 is discussed in Chapter 11.

11. *Regina v. Morgentaler, Smoling and Scott,* [1985] 52 O.R. (2d) 353, 380.

12. *Ibid.,* 428.

13. *Ibid.,* 431.

14. See F.L. Morton, Peter H. Russell, and Michael J. Withey, "The Supreme Court's First One Hundred Charter of Rights Decisions: A Statistical Analysis," *Osgoode Hall Law Review* (1992).

15. [1985] 2 S.C.R. 486.

16. *Ibid.*

17. Morris C. Shumiatcher, "I Set Before You Life and Death," *University of Western Ontario Law Review,* 4 (1987), 24.

18. See Rainer Knopff and F.L. Morton, *Charter Politics* (Toronto: Nelson Canada, 1992), 108-10.

Chapter 18

1. Note the important qualification of this statement in Chapter 24, where I suggest that the Charter was as much an effect as a cause of social change.

2. *Hunter v. Southam Inc.,* [1984] 2 S.C.R. 145, 155.

3. *R. v. Therens,* [1985] 1 S.C.R. 613.

4. *Singh et al. v. Minister of Employment and Immigration Board,* [1985] 1 S.C.R. 177.

5. *Law Society of Upper Canada v. Skapinker,* [1984] 1 S.C.R. 357.

6. *Hunter v. Southam Inc.,* [1984] 2 S.C.R. 145. The Chief Justice was quoting American constitutional scholar Paul Freund.

7. *The Queen v. Big M Drug Mart,* [1985] 2 S.C.R. 295.

8. *Reference re British Columbia Motor Vehicle Act,* [1985] 2 S.C.R. 486.

9. There were only five Bill of Rights cases in which an individual won the case against the government. In only one case – *Drybones v. The Queen,* [1970] S.C.R. 282 – was a statute declared invalid. (This was a provision of the Indian Act that made it a crime for an Indian to be intoxicated while off a reserve. The four other cases are *Brownridge v. the Queen,* [1972] S.C.R. 195 (right to counsel before taking breath test); *Lowry and Lepper v. The Queen,* [1974] S.C.R. 195 (right to hearing before sentencing); *A.-G. Ontario v. Reale,* [1975] 2 S.C.R. 624 (right to an interpreter during judge's charge to the jury); *R. Shelley,* [1981] 2 S.C.R. 196 (reverse onus clause too broad).

10. Of the six, four were federal and two were provincial. The federal statutes

included The Lord's Day Act, The Anti-Combines Act, the Narcotics Control Act, and the Immigration Act. The provincial statutes were Quebec's Bill 101 (Charter of the French Language) and the British Columbia Motor Vehicle Act.

11. 18 D.L.R. (4th) 321.
12. See G. Pyrcz, "Pressure Groups," in T.C. Pocklington, ed., *Liberal Democracy in Canada and the United States* (Toronto: Holt, Rinehart and Winston, 1985), 341-74.
13. Paul A. Pross, "Pressure Groups: Adaptive Instruments of Political Communication," in Pross, ed., *Pressure Group Behaviour in Canadian Politics* (Toronto: McGraw-Hill Ryerson, 1975), 18.
14. *Operation Dismantle v. the Queen,* [1985] 1 S.C.R. 441.
15. *National Citizens' Coalition Inc. v. A.-G. Canada,* [1985] W.W.R. 436.
16. *A.-G. Quebec v. Quebec Association of Protestant School Boards,* [1984] 2 S.C.R. 66.
17. "Ministers Announce Extension of Court Challenge Program," Government of Canada official news release, September 25, 1985, 2.
18. Kenneth McNaught, "Political Trials and the Canadian Political Tradition," in M.L. Friedland, ed., *Courts and Trials: A Multi-Disciplinary Approach* (Toronto: University of Toronto Press, 1975), 137-61.
19. See Ian Brodie, "Interest Groups and the Charter of Rights and Freedoms: Interveners at the Supreme Court of Canada" (M.A. thesis, University of Calgary, 1992), Chapter 1.
20. Morris Manning, interview with the author, April 13, 1992.
21. *Société des Acadiens v. Association of Parents,* [1986] 1 S.C.R. 549.
22. Manning also presented three non-Charter constitutional issues: Did the abortion law exceed Parliament's federal jurisdiction over criminal law? Did the abortion law effect an unconstitutional delegation of the federal criminal law power to the provinces? Did the TACs exercise a judicial rather than an administrative function, thereby usurping the section 96 powers of the regular courts?
23. Manning's twenty citations of American legal periodicals outnumbered his references to both Canadian (eighteen) and British (four) articles.
24. Appellant's Factum, *Morgentaler et al. v. The Queen, Supreme Court of Canada,* 14.
25. This and the other quotations in this paragraph, unless otherwise indicated, are from the author's own notes of oral argument before the Supreme Court, October 8, 1986.
26. Kirk Makin, "Court is skeptical on 'right' to ignore law on abortion," *Globe and Mail,* October 9, 1986, A1.

27. The account of this reception is drawn from Peter Calamai, "Morgentaler abortion trial working on several levels," *Calgary Herald,* October 12, 1986. At the time, Calamai was the Supreme Court reporter for Southam News.

Chapter 19

1. *Re: Objection to a Resolution to Amend the Constitution (Quebec Veto Reference),* [1982] 2 S.C.R. 793.
2. *Attorney-General of Quebec v. Quebec Association of Protestant School Boards,* [1984] 2 S.C.R. 66.
3. *Reference re Manitoba Language Rights,* [1985] 2 S.C.R. 347.
4. See Rainer Knopff and F.L. Morton, *Charter Politics* (Toronto: Nelson Canada, 1992), Chapter 6.
5. For a fuller explanation, see *ibid.,* 5, 116-17, 132.
6. *Morgentaler v. The Queen,* [1988] 1 S.C.R. 30.
7. *Ibid.,* 171.
8. *Ibid.,* 173-74.
9. *Ibid.,* 181.
10. *Ibid.,* 182-83.
11. *Ibid.*
12. *Ibid.,* 183.
13. *Ibid.,* 133. To make the same point differently, if section 251 punished only the doctor who performed the abortion and not the woman/patient, this would be an open-and-shut case of criminal conspiracy, with no need or reason to explore the issue of a woman's right to an abortion.
14. *Ibid.,* 137-38.
15. *Ibid.,* 138-39.
16. *Ibid.,* 141.
17. *Ibid.,* 143.
18. *Ibid.,* 143-46.
19. *Ibid.,* 149.
20. *Ibid.,* 151.
21. *Ibid.,* 152-54.
22. *Ibid.,* 157-58.
23. *Ibid.,* 53.
24. *Report on Therapeutic Abortion Services in Ontario* (Toronto: Ministry of Health, 1987).
25. *Morgentaler v. The Queen,* [1988] 1 S.C.R. 30, 69.
26. *Ibid.,* 70.
27. *Ibid.,* 56.

28. *Ibid.,* 110.
29. *Ibid.,* 121-22.
30. *Ibid.,* 113.
31. Anne Collins, *The Big Evasion: Abortion, the Issue That Won't Go Away* (Toronto: Lester & Orpen Dennys, 1985), 194.
32. *Ibid.*
33. Letter from Laura McArthur, President, Right to Life Association of Toronto and Area, to the Canadian Judicial Council, February 2, 1989.
34. *Ibid.* Emphasis in original.
35. Charles Evan Hughes, *Addresses* (New York: Harpers, 1916), 185.
36. Letter from Jeannie Thomas, Executive Secretary, Canadian Judicial Council, to Laura McArthur, President, Right to Life Association of Toronto and Area, February 21, 1989.
37. *Ibid.*
38. [1985] 1 S.C.R. 177.

Chapter 20

1. The text of the government's motion was as follows:

"That, in the opinion of this House, the Supreme Court of Canada having declared that the provisions of the *Criminal Code* relating to abortion are inconsistent with the provisions of the *Canadian Charter of Rights and Freedoms* and are therefore of no force or effect, the government should prepare and introduce legislation, consistent with the Constitution of Canada including the *Charter of Rights and Freedoms,* which reflects the fundamental value and inherent dignity of each human being and the inherent worth of human life, and which achieves a balance between the right of a woman to liberty and security of her person and the responsibility of society to protect the unborn; and

"Such legislation should prohibit the performance of an abortion, subject to the following exceptions:

"When, during the earlier stages of pregnancy: a qualified medical practitioner is of the opinion that the continuation of the pregnancy of a woman would, or would be likely to, threaten her physical or mental well-being; when the woman in consultation with a qualified medical practitioner decides to terminate her pregnancy; and when the termination is performed by a qualified medical practitioner; and

"When, during the subsequent stages of pregnancy: the termination of the pregnancy satisfies further conditions, including a condition that after a certain point in time, the termination would only be permitted where, in the opinion of two qualified medical practitioners, the continuation of the pregnancy would, or would be likely to, endanger the woman's life or seriously endanger her health."

2. This information and much of what follows came from Mary Eberts's "Great Cases" lecture at the Faculty of Law of the University of Calgary on December 7, 1988, and a subsequent interview with the author. Eberts's lecture provided an account of the behind-the-scenes manoeuvring and thinking of LEAF leading up to its intervention in the October, 1988, *Borowski* hearing. Hereafter cited as Eberts lecture.

3. The Court's closed-door policy on interveners provoked sharp public criticism from various Charter-oriented groups who saw the policy as jeopardizing their ability to use the Charter. Beginning in 1987, the Supreme Court did an about-face and has subsequently allowed almost all requests for intervener status. See Ian Brodie, "Interest Groups and the Charter of Rights and Freedoms: Interveners at the Supreme Court of Canada" (M.A. thesis, University of Calgary, 1992).

4. Eberts lecture.

5. *Ibid.*

6. Letter from Morris Manning to Edward Sojonky, May 18, 1988.

7. *Ibid.*

8. Affidavit of Constance Gwendolyn Landolt, May 5, 1988, "Notice of Motion in the Supreme Court of Canada between Joseph Borowski, appellant, and the Attorney General for Canada, respondent," 4.

9. See Danielle Crittenden, "REAL Women Don't Eat Crow," *Saturday Night,* May, 1988, 27-35.

10. *Ibid.*

11. *Ibid.,* 32.

12. *Ibid.,* 33-35.

13. Eberts lecture.

14. *Ibid.*

15. *Ibid.*

16. *Senate Debates,* June 28, 1988, 3730.

17. *Toronto Star*: "Ottawa trying to shelve appeal on fetus rights," July 13, 1988; "Abortion issue leaves Tories in deadlock," July 14, 1988; "Pro-life Tories angered by move to shelve ruling on fetus rights," July 15, 1988.

18. "Ottawa trying to shelve appeal on fetus rights," *Toronto Star,* July 13, 1988.

19. "Pro-life Tories angered by move to shelve ruling on fetus rights," *Toronto Star,* July 15, 1988.

20. *Ibid.*

21. "Supreme Court rejects bid to delay abortion hearing," *Toronto Star,* July 20, 1988.
22. Eberts lecture.

Chapter 21

1. *Transcript of Appeal Proceedings on October 3, 1988,* Supreme Court of Canada, vol. I, 25.
2. *Ibid.,* 10.
3. *Ibid.,* 17.
4. *Ibid.*
5. *Ibid.,* 21.
6. *Ibid.,* 20-21.
7. *Ibid.,* 94.
8. *Ibid.*
9. *Ibid.,* 18.
10. *Ibid.,* 31.
11. *Ibid.*
12. *Ibid.,* 34, 35.
13. *Ibid.,* 86-87.
14. *Ibid.,* 43.
15. *Ibid.,* 44.
16. *Ibid.,* 54.
17. *Ibid.*
18. *Ibid.,* 101.
19. Dr. Harley Smyth, *Factum of the Appellant,* 6.
20. *Ibid.,* 36.
21. *Ibid.,* 37.
22. David Vienneau, "Pro-life activist brings remains of two fetuses to Supreme Court," *Toronto Star,* October 5, 1988, 3.
23. Linda MacCharles, "Anti-abortionist uses fetuses to dramatize case at court," *Ottawa Citizen,* October 5, 1988.
24. *Borowski v. Canada (Attorney-General),* [1989]) 1 S.C.R. 342.

Chapter 22

1. *Globe and Mail,* November 23, 1988.
2. "B.C. Spending $20 million to discourage abortion," *Globe and Mail,* April 6, 1988, A1-A2.
3. The source of this information is Christine Rideout, "The Effect of the Charter on Canadian Public Policy and the Public Policy Process" (Senior Honours thesis, Political Science, University of Calgary, 1989-90).

4. *Globe and Mail,* February 24, 1989.

5. "Judge denies trial by jury for anti-abortion protesters," *Globe and Mail,* February 28, 1988, A1-A2; "B.C. Judge unmoved by heat of anti-abortion arguments," *Globe and Mail,* March 1, 1989, A1-A2.

6. *Toronto Star,* March 10, 1989.

7. *Mock v. Brandanburg* (1988), 61 A.L.R. (2d) 235.

8. *Diamond v. Hirsch,* unreported decision of Manitoba Court of Queen's Bench, rendered July 6, 1989.

9. *Maclean's,* July 31, 1989.

10. *Webster v. Reproductive Health Services,* 109 S.Ct. 3040 (1989).

11. *Tremblay v. Daigle,* [1989] R.J.Q. 1980 (Que. S.C.).

12. *Daigle v. Tremblay* (1989), 59 D.L.R. (4th) 609 (Que. C.A.).

13. The Attorney-General of Quebec also focused on the federalism issue raised by the injunction: Does the issuance of an injunction that is based on provincial laws prohibiting an abortion, which is a matter of federal criminal jurisdiction, violate the federal division of powers? In the end, the Supreme Court did not address this issue.

14. Quoted in Robert D. Nadeau, "The Anatomy of Evasion: A Critique of Daigle," in Ian Gentles, ed., *A Time to Choose Life: Women, Abortion and Human Rights* (Toronto: Stoddart, 1990), 188.

15. The preamble and sections 1 and 2 of the Quebec Charter read as follows:
    Whereas every human being possesses intrinsic rights and freedoms designed to ensure his protection and development;
    Whereas all human beings are equal in worth and dignity, and are entitled to equal protection of the law;
    1. Every human being has a right to life, and to personal security, inviolability and freedoms. . . .
    2. Every human being whose life is in peril has a right to assistance. Every person must come to the aid of anyone whose life is in peril, either personally or calling for aid, by giving him the necessary and immediate physical assistance. . . .

16. *Daigle* (Que. C.A.), 632.

17. Articles 338, 345, 608, 771, 838, 945, and 2543 of the Civil Code.

18. *Daigle* (Que. C.A.), 617.

19. *Ibid.,* 613.

20. *Ibid.,* 620.

21. *Tremblay v. Daigle,* [1989] 2 S.C.R. 530, 538.

22. "Court lifts injunction after Daigle abortion . . . Pro-choice advocates support decision," *Globe and Mail,* August 9, 1989, A1.

23. *Chatelaine,* January, 1990.

24. Since the Court answered this first question in the negative, it did not need to address the other two issues: Is an injunction the proper remedy in this case? Does the injunction encroach upon federal criminal law jurisdiction?

25. *Daigle* (S.C.C.), 553.

26. *Ibid.*, 555.

27. *Ibid.*, 553.

28. *Ibid.*, 553-54.

29. *Ibid.*, 560.

30. *R.W.D.S.U. v. Dolphin Delivery,* [1986] 2 S.C.R. 573.

31. *Daigle* (S.C.C.), 571.

32. The corollary issue of "father's rights" depended heavily on the existence of a prior finding of the "right to life" of the fetus. Once the latter was denied by the Court, the "father's rights" argument was quickly and easily dispatched.

33. *Daigle* (S.C.C.), 565.

34. *Ibid.*, 567.

35. *Ibid.*, 563. Several abortion-injunction cases very similar to Daigle had been decided against the father/husband. The Court's version of the *Montreal Tramways* case was considered the controlling precedent in the area of tort law. The outcomes of cases under provincial child welfare legislation – cases in which childrens' aid societies sought court orders to intervene to protect unborn children from the effects of the drug or alcohol abuse of their mothers – were evenly divided between "mother's rights" and "fetal rights." See *Montreal Tramways v. Léveillé,* [1933] S.C.R. 456.

36. *Daigle* (S.C.C.), 571.

37. Quoted in Nadeau, "The Anatomy of Evasion," 188.

38. *Morgentaler* (1988), 51-52.

39. Daigle (S.C.C.), 553.

40. *Ibid.*, 552.

41. *Morgentaler* (1988), 166-67.

42. Nadeau, "The Anatomy of Evasion," 191.

Chapter 23

1. Graham Fraser, "Mulroney sought compromise from Tory caucus on new bill," *Globe and Mail,* November 4, 1989, A8.

2. Professor Bernard Dickens, quoted in Kirk Makin, "New law could face years of court challenges, Ottawa warned," *Globe and Mail,* November 4, 1989, A8.

348

3. Mary Ann Glendon, *Abortion and Divorce in Western Law* (Cambridge, Mass.: Harvard University Press, 1987), 40.

4. "Abortion bill draws hail of criticism; Lack of accessibility, protection for fetus cited," *Globe and Mail,* November 4, 1989, A1.

5. Robert M. Campbell and Leslie A. Pal, eds., *The Real Worlds of Canadian Politics: Cases in Process and Policy,* (Peterborough, Ont.: Broadview Press, 1991), 45-46.

6. "Ministers in abortion debate appeal for calm, compromise," *Globe and Mail,* November 8, 1989, A5.

7. Cf. Allan Hutchinson, "Challenging the abortion law," *Globe and Mail,* November 13, 1989, A7.

8. Sheilah L. Martin, "The New Abortion Legislation," *Constitutional Forum,* 1, 2 (Winter, 1990), 5-7.

9. Quoted in Makin, "New law could face years of court challenges."

Chapter 24

1. 410 U.S. 113 (1973).

2. Kenneth McNaught, "Political Trials and the Canadian Political Tradition," in M.L. Friedland, ed., *Courts and Trials: A Multidisciplinary Approach* (Toronto: University of Toronto Press, 1975), 138.

3. *Ibid.,* 146, 154.

4. See Chapter 6.

5. See Paul Sniderman, Joseph F. Fletcher, Peter H. Russell, and Philip Tetlock, "Liberty, Authority and Community: Civil Liberties and Canadian Political Culture," paper presented at the annual meeting of the Canadian Political Science Association, Windsor, Ontario, June 9, 1988; Neil Nevitte and Roger Gibbins, *New Elites in Old States: Ideologies in the Anglo-American Democracies* (Toronto: Oxford University Press, 1990); Neil Nevitte, "New Politics, the Charter and Political Participation," in Herman Bakvis, ed., *Representation, Integration and Political Parties in Canada* (Toronto: Dundurn Press, 1992).

6. Peter Hogg, author of one of the most authoritative textbooks on Canadian constitutional law, recently (1991) recounted that when he arrived in Canada from New Zealand in the late 1960s, the dean of his new law school asked him to teach the course on constitutional law because no one else wanted to. Today, he continued, that same law school is besieged with applicants to teach constitutional law, almost all of whom want to teach only the Charter of Rights, and most of them would be content to teach only section 15 (the equality rights section)! My own Ph.D. thesis at the University of Toronto began as a comparative study of the treatment of

sexual equality issues by the supreme courts of the United States and Canada. When I submitted my first full draft in 1979, my thesis supervisors told me that I would have to drop the Canadian dimension of the thesis because there were not enough materials to support a comparative analysis.

7. *Globe and Mail,* April 27, 1988, A5. As Michael Mandel has pointed out, this view hardly "squares" with another of Estey's comments in the same interview. See note 35, below. Michael Mandel, *The Charter of Rights and the Legalization of Politics in Canada* (Toronto: Wall and Thompson, 1989), 41.

8. Former section 12(1)(b) of the Indian Act stripped Indian women who married non-Indians of their official Indian status. No similar disability applied to Indian men who married non-Indian women. In 1972 the Supreme Court rejected a sex discrimination challenge to this section in *A.-G. Canada v. Lavell and Bedard,* [1974] S.C.R. 1349.

9. In the 1976 case of *Bliss v. A.-G. Canada,* [1979] 1 S.C.R. 183, the Supreme Court had upheld the denial of regular UI benefits to a woman who could not qualify for the more restricted maternity leave benefits. See Leslie A. Pal and F.L. Morton, "Bliss v. Attorney-General of Canada: From Legal Defeat to Political Victory," *Osgoode Hall Law Journal,* 24, 1 (1986), 141-60.

10. Mary Ann Glendon, *Abortion and Divorce in Western Law* (Cambridge, Mass.: Harvard University Press, 1987), 11.

11. This is the central thesis of Glendon's study, *Abortion and Divorce.* Glendon argues that the judicial, as opposed to the legislative, development of abortion (and divorce) policy in the United States has been harmful. Glendon completed her study before the 1988 *Morgentaler* decision, but much of what she attributes to the United States now seems to apply to Canada. The West German Constitutional Court also rendered an important abortion ruling, but Glendon argues (pp. 25-33) that it did not close off legislative bargaining and compromise the way *Roe v. Wade* did.

12. Seymour Martin Lipset, *Consensus and Conflict* (Oxford: Transaction Books, 1985), 196. Lipset and others attribute this political realignment to deeper structural changes within the political economy of most Western industrial democracies: historically unprecedented levels of material affluence, education, communication, mobility, and the displacement of the manufacturing and agricultural sectors of the economy by the new service sector. Structural change produces value change. Economic growth, public order, national security, and traditional morality decline in importance. They are replaced by concerns for individual freedom, social

equality, and quality of life – peace, environmentalism, and so forth. Structural change also results in new sources of wealth and power.

13. *Ibid.,* 187.

14. *Ibid.,* 196.

15. In Canada and the United States it technically should be called the "new New Left" to recognize the original "New Left" of the radical student movement of the sixties.

16. Deborah Coyne, "How to Escape the Meech Lake Morass and Other Misadventures." Notes for remarks to the annual meeting of the Council of Canadians, Ottawa, October 14, 1989, 3.

17. See Alan Cairns, "The Limited Constitutional Vision of Meech Lake," in K.E. Swinton and C.J. Rogerson, eds., *Competing Constitutional Visions: The Meech Lake Accord* (Toronto: Carswell, 1988), 247-62.

18. This is a central theme in Cairns, "The Limited Constitutional Vision of Meech Lake."

19. See F.L. Morton and Rainer Knopff, "The Supreme Court as the Vanguard of the Intelligentsia: The Charter Movement as Post-Materialist Politics," in Janet Ajzenstat, ed., *Two Hundred Years of Canadian Constitutionalism* (Canadian Study of Parliament Group, forthcoming).

20. This is a paraphrase of Peter Russell's insight, "The Effect of a Charter of Rights on the Policy-Making Role of Canadian Courts," *Canadian Public Administration,* 25 (1982), 1-33.

21. Stuart Scheingold, *The Politics of Rights: Lawyers, Public Policy, and Political Change* (New Haven: Yale University Press, 1974), 83.

22. Ian Brodie, "Interest Groups and the Charter of Rights and Freedoms: Interveners at the Supreme Court of Canada" (M.A. thesis, University of Calgary, 1992).

23. *Ibid.* These numbers underestimate the level of interest group activity, because they do not count cases like *Morgentaler* and *Borowski* as interest group litigators, since they appear to be suits brought by private individuals. Brodie elaborates how the concept of "non-government" or "private" intervener must be qualified since many of the "private" groups who intervene are largely publicly funded. Brodie found that over half of these interest groups received funding from the Secretary of State. Many received Court Challenges grants as well.

24. Lamer: "We would do . . . our own Constitution a disservice to simply allow the American debate to define the issue for us, all the while ignoring the truly fundamental structural differences between the two constitutions." *Reference re B.C. Motor Vehicle Act,* [1985] 2 S.C.R. 486. Lamer

was actually referring to the "substantive/procedural" distinction in section 7, but this issue was inextricably meshed with reference to the historical record of the framers' intent. The result seems to have been to extend Lamer's strictures against "Americanizing" the Charter to the interpretivist theory of judicial review.

25. See Rainer Knopff and F.L. Morton, *Charter Politics* (Toronto: Nelson Canada, 1992), 123.

26. *Attorney-General of Quebec v. Quebec Association of Protestant School Boards,* [1984] 2 S.C.R. 66. "This set of constitutional provisions was not enacted by the legislator in a vacuum. . . . the legislator knew, and clearly had in mind, the regimes governing Anglophone and Francophone linguistic minorities in various provinces of Canada . . . and their intention was to remedy the perceived defects of these regimes by uniform corrective measures, namely those contained in s. 23 of the Charter."

27. *Reference re Public Service Employees Relations Act, Labor Relations Act, and Police Officers Collective Bargaining Act of Alberta,* [1987] 1 S.C.R. 313.

28. Mary Eberts, "The Use of Litigation Under the Canadian Charter of Rights and Freedoms as a Strategy for Achieving Change," in Neil Nevitte and Allan Kornberg, eds., *Minorities and the Canadian State* (Oakville, Ont.: Mosaic Press, 1985), 53.

29. Scheingold, *The Politics of Rights,* 6-7.

30. See F.L. Morton, Peter H. Russell, and Michael J. Withey, "The Supreme Court's First One Hundred Charter of Rights Decisions: A Statistical Analysis," *Osgoode Hall Law Review* (1992), Table 11.

31. *Reference re Alberta Public Service Employee Relations Act,* [1987] 1 S.C.R. 424.

32. Morton, Russell, and Withey, "The First One Hundred Charter Decisions," Table 13.

33. *Ibid.,* Table 12.

34. *Ibid.,* Tables 14 and 15.

35. *Globe and Mail,* April 27, 1988, A5.

36. Judge Robert Bork was nominated for the U.S. Supreme Court by President Ronald Reagan. Bork was an outspoken critic of the judicial activism characteristic of the liberal Warren Court. His appointment would have created a majority of five conservative judges, a group that might well have overturned a number of liberal precedents, including the 1973 *Roe v. Wade* abortion decision. Liberals in the Senate organized to defeat the Bork nomination. Thomas, a conservative black judge nominated by

352

President George Bush, was confirmed, but only after widely publicized and televised Senate hearings that focused on accusations of sexual harassment.

37. V.O. Key, *Politics, Parties, and Pressure Groups* (New York: Thomas Y. Crowell, 1958), 154.

38. "Public to demand say in court appointments?" *Lawyer's Weekly,* February 12, 1988, 1.

39. "Reduced role for politicians urged in naming of judges," *Globe and Mail,* May 16, 1988, A1.

40. "Lawyers approved Lyon's post in advance," *Globe and Mail,* January 8, 1987, A5; "Check bias of judges before appointment, Ontario lawyers urge," *Globe and Mail,* January 30, 1987, A14.

41. *A.-G. Quebec v. Ford et al.,* [1988] 2 S.C.R. 712; *Devine et al. v. A.-G. Quebec,* [1988] 2 S.C.R. 790.

42. "How the Charter changes justice," *Globe and Mail,* April 17, 1992, A17. For a full analysis of the legislative character of section 1 analysis, see Knopff and Morton, *Charter Politics,* 37-49, 152-61.

43. Peter H. Russell, "The Effect of a Charter of Rights on the Policy-Making Role of the Canadian Courts," *Canadian Public Administration,* 25 (1982), 32.

44. For a more elaborate view of section 33 as part of a system of checks and balances, see Knopff and Morton, *Charter Politics,* Chapter 8, esp. 228-31.

45. Lincoln and the Republicans overthrew the pro-slavery, pro-South court of Justice Taney. Roosevelt and the New Deal Democrats eventually exterminated the pro-business, laissez-faire Court of the 1920s and 1930s. The Reagan-Bush Republicans appear on the verge of sweeping away the Warren Court of the 1960s and its legacy of liberalism.

46. The French Constitutional Council, all of whose members had been appointed during the previous Gaullist governments, tried unsuccessfully to block the domestic programs of the newly elected socialist government of François Mitterand after 1981. See F.L. Morton, "Judicial Review in France: A Comparative Analysis," *American Journal of Comparative Law,* 36 (1987).

47. Mary Ann Glendon, *Rights Talk: The Impoverishment of Political Discourse* (New York: The Free Press, 1991).

48. *Ibid.,* 8-9.

49. *Ibid.,* x.

50. This description of "adversarialism" is taken from Clifford Orwin's

review of George Grant, *English-Speaking Justice*, in *University of Toronto Law Journal*, 30, 1 (1980), 114.

51. *Ibid.*

52. Glendon, *Rights Talk*, x.

53. *Ibid.*, x-xi, 14.

54. *Ibid.*, 14, 9.

55. Glendon, *Abortion and Divorce*, Chapter 1.

56. *Ibid.*, 40.

57. *Ibid.*, 2.

58. Interview with the author, November 14, 1991. Dr. Morgentaler stated that he has never disputed the scientific facts about fetal development, only their interpretation. His position is that it is irrational to ascribe the legal status of human person to a fetus prior to evidence of brain-wave activity (usually about five and a half months) and viability outside the womb (usually about twenty-four weeks). After this point, he believes that abortion is justified only if there is damage to the fetus or a danger to the mother.

Postscript

1. Two weeks earlier, twenty-six miners were killed in an underground explosion at the Westray coal mine in Pictou County, Nova Scotia.

2. *Globe and Mail*, "Blast destroys abortion clinic," May 19, 1992, A1, A5.

3. *Globe and Mail*, "Placing the blame for anti-abortion violence," June 12, 1992, A17.

4. *Globe and Mail*, "Blast destroys abortion clinic," May 19, 1992, A1, A5.

5. *House of Commons Debates*. 6 April 1989, 153.

6. Kenneth McNaught, "Political trials and the Canadian political tradition," in M.L. Friedland, ed., *Courts and Trials: A Multi-Disciplinary Approach* (Toronto: University of Toronto Press, 1975), 146.

7. *Globe and Mail*, "Placing the blame for anti-abortion violence," June 12, 1992, A17.

8. Alexander M. Bickel, *The Morality of Consent* (New Haven: Yale University Press, 1975), 119.

10. Bernard Crick, *In Defence of Politics* (Baltimore: Penguin Books, 1964), 24.

Appendix 1: Time Line of Principal Events and Decisions

	Morgentaler	Borowski
	1922 Born in Lodz, Poland	**1932** Born near Wishart, Saskatchewan, fourth of ten children
pre-1960	**1939-45** Parents and sister killed in Nazi concentration camps **1951** Immigrates to Montreal and becomes doctor **1957** Begins four years of psychoanalysis	**1946-1958** Works mining, logging, and fishing camps in northern Canada **1958** Moves to Thompson, Man., to work in INCO mines
1960		**1962** Becomes active in union movement (USW)
	1964 Elected President of Montreal Humanist Fellowship	**1965** Sleeps on steps of Manitoba legislature to protest INCO's control of Thompson
1965		**1966** Protests MLA pay raise with second sleep-in on steps of Manitoba legislature

Canadian Politics	Supreme Court of Canada	Comparative
1937 Dorothea Palmer acquitted of distributing birth control materials	**1949** Abolition of Appeals to the JCPC	**1938** *R. v. Bourne* (U.K.) Court rules abortion legal when performed to preserve a woman's physical or mental health.
	1957 *Roncarelli v. Duplessis*	**1957** Wolfenden Report
1959 *Chatelaine* calls for reform of abortion law		
1960 Canadian Bill of Rights		
1963 CMA and CBA debate abortion reform	**1963** *Robertson and Rosetanni v. the Queen*: upholds Lord's Day Act	
1966 CMA and CBA endorse abortion reform		

356

Morgentaler	Borowski
1967 Advocates decriminalization of abortion before parliamentary committee	
1968 Performs first abortion	**1968** Goes to jail three times to protest new sales tax
1969 Closes family practice to specialize in contraception and abortions	**1969** Elected NDP MLA from Thompson; appointed to Schreyer cabinet: Minister of Transportation and Public Works
1970 Police raid clinic; first arrest and charges	
	1971 Resigns from cabinet to protest public funding of abortions
	1972 Refuses to pay income taxes to protest public funding of abortions
1973 March: announces that he has performed 5,000 illegal abortions May: performs abortion on television Aug.: second police raid; arrested, new charges Nov.: acquitted by jury	**1973** Sentenced to five days in jail for refusing to pay income taxes

1970

Canadian Politics	Supreme Court of Canada	Comparative
1967 Justice Minister Trudeau introduces abortion reform bill		**1967** U.K. Parliament adopts abortion reform
1968 Trudeau elected Prime Minister		
1969 New abortion law approved by Parliament; s. 251 of Criminal Code amended	**1969** *Drybones v The Queen*: first instance of statute declared invalid under Can. Bill of Rights	
1970 October FLQ Crisis; War Measures Act		
		1971 New York adopts liberal abortion law
1972 Trudeau re-elected	**1972** *Lavell and Bedard v. A.-G. Canada*: Court rules that Can. Bill of Rights requires only equality in the application and administration of laws, not equal laws	
	1973 Bora Laskin appointed new Chief Justice	**1973** U.S. Supreme Court *Roe v. Wade* decision strikes down abortion laws in 46 states

Morgentaler	Borowski
1974 April: Quebec Court of Appeal reverses jury acquittal and directs verdict of guilty	
1975 March: SCC rejects appeal; goes to prison June: acquitted by jury for second time	**1975** Sentenced to 20 days in jail for refusing to pay income taxes
1976 Jan.: A.-G. Basford orders retrial of first conviction; released from prison Sept.: third jury acquittal Dec.: PQ government announces that it will no longer enforce abortion law in Quebec	
	1978 Hires Morris Shumiatcher as lawyer; files statement of claim challenging validity of abortion law
	1979 Sentenced to 3 months in jail for refusing to pay income taxes
	1980 May: begins 80-day fast to protest absence of rights for unborn in Charter of Rights Dec.: wins decision on standing in Supreme Court

1975

1980

Canadian Politics	Supreme Court of Canada	Comparative
	1974 Oct.: Morgentaler appeal	**1974** France adopts more lenient abortion law
1975 Parliament receives "Petition of One Million" to protect rights of unborn; Badgley Committee appointed		
1976 July: "Morgentaler Amendment" to s. 613 of Criminal Code Nov.: Parti Québécois wins, forms new government	**1976** *Anti-Inflation Reference*	**1976** West Germany adopts more lenient abortion law
1977 Badgley Report		
		1978 Italy adopts more lenient abortion law
1979 Conservatives win; Joe Clark becomes PM		
1980 Feb.: Trudeau and Liberals return to power May: Sovereignty-association defeated in Quebec referendum Oct.: Trudeau announces unilateral patriation		**1980** Reagan elected U.S. president; Republican platform pledges to appoint judges who "respect the sanctity of life"

Morgentaler	Borowski

1982
Announces plans to open
abortion clinics in Toronto
and Winnipeg

1983
June: Winnipeg clinic raided
by police
July: Toronto clinic raided
by police
Nov.:Toronto trial opens;
Manning launches pre-trial
motion

1983
May: Trial for Life in Regina
Oct.: J. Matheson
dismisses Borowski's
Charter claim

1984
Oct.-Nov: jury trial in
Toronto results in acquittal
Dec.: police raid Toronto
clinic, lay new charges

1985

1985
Ontario Court of Appeal
overturns jury acquittal,
upholds validity of s. 251

1985
Appeal heard by
Saskatchewan Court of
Appeal

1986
Second abortion clinic
opened in Toronto

Canadian Politics	Supreme Court of Canada	Comparative
1981 Joint House-Senate Committee on the Constitution completes hearings	**1981** *Patriation Reference*	
1982 Charter of Rights adopted as part of Constitution Act, 1982	**1982** Bertha Wilson, first woman appointed to Supreme Court	
1983 40,000 pro-lifers stage largest ever abortion-related rally at Queen's Park		**1983** Ireland votes 2:1 in national referendum to prohibit abortions
1984 Feb.: Trudeau resigns as PM Sept.: Conservatives elected; Brian Mulroney new Prime Minister	**1984** April: Brian Dickson becomes new Chief Justice; first Charter decisions strike down Lord's Day Act and education section of Bill 101	
	1985 *Reference re B.C. Motor Vehicle Act*: embraces non-interpretivism	
1986 Liberals win Ontario elections, Peterson becomes Premier; PEI abolishes all TACs, becomes first "pro-life province"	**1986** Hears *Morgentaler* appeal	**1986** U.S. President Reagan appoints William Rehnquist, dissenter in *Roe v. Wade*, Chief Justice of Supreme Court

Morgentaler	Borowski
	1987 Saskatchewan Court of Appeal rejects appeal
1988 Jan: Supreme Court of Canada declares abortion law invalid, acquits Morgentaler, Scott, and Smoling	**1988** July: Supreme Court of Canada refuses government request to postpone Borowski appeal Oct.: Supreme Court of Canada hears appeal
1989 Opens abortion clinic in Nova Scotia and is charged with violating provincial law banning abortions outside of approved hospitals	**1989** Supreme Court of Canada rules case is moot and rejects appeal

1990

Canadian Politics	Supreme Court of Canada	Comparative
1987 Meech Lake Accord announced	**1987** Claire L'Heureux-Dubé becomes second woman appointed to Court	**1987** U.S. Senate rejects nomination of Judge Bork to Supreme Court
1988 July: Mulroney abortion resolutions defeated in House of Commons Nov.: Mulroney re-elected		**1988** Supreme Court appointments become an issue in U.S. presidential election; Bush and Republicans win
1989 July: Dodd and Daigle abortion injunction cases Nov.: federal government introduces Bill C-43 to amend abortion law	**1989** Aug.: rules in favour of Chantal Daigle; no right to life for fetus in Quebec Charter	**1989** U.S. Supreme Court decides *Webster v. Reproductive Services*, sharply restricting *Roe v. Wade* precedent
1990 May: Bill C-43 approved by House of Commons (140-131) in free vote June: Meech Lake Accord expires unratified		
1991 Bill C-43 rejected by Senate (43-43) in free vote		

INDEX